HISTORY OF TOURISM
IN THE BAHAMAS

HISTORY OF TOURISM
IN THE BAHAMAS

A Global Perspective

Angela B. Cleare

Library of Congress Control Number: 2006908620
ISBN: Hardcover   978-1-4257-3670-5
                  Softcover   978-1-4257-3669-9

This book was printed in the United States of America.

To order additional copies of this book, contact:
Xlibris Corporation
1-888-795-4274
www.Xlibris.com
Orders@Xlibris.com
31394

CONTENTS

LIST OF TABLES—CHAPTERS 1-12

FOREWORD

I am privileged to have been requested by Ms. Angela B. Cleare to write a brief Foreword to her Book on the History of Tourism in The Bahamas. Quite apart from tracing the history of the evolution of tourism to become the premier economy of The Bahamas she has accomplished a tour de force of literary performance. It has not always been so with the economy of The Bahamas.

We have been populated entirely by strangers to these Islands, foreigners who were uprooted both white and black from their natural social and economic environment. We were prepared for over 300 years to engage freely in what were illegal activities on a massive scale. We were Pirates for well over 50 years in the 17th and 18th Centuries. Today piracy may seem a romantic interlude, but it was after all an illegal activity. For as long as 200 years late into the 19th Century Wrecking had been the favourite activity of Bahamian seamen, sometimes legitimate but more often illegal. It spawned a boat building tradition in which free black men and white men excelled; sometimes providing the most public revenue. Blockade running, another illegal activity, generated unprecedented income for The Bahamas during the American Civil War.

Many Bahamian modern day fortunes had their beginning in profits earned from illegal bootlegging in the 1920's when The Bahamas was launched on her fourth and most prosperous era of illegal activity.

After the bootleg era honest tourism gave The Bahamas a major industry not tinged with criminality.

This History is appropriately identified and was no doubt intended by the Author to contribute to the teaching and research capacity of Teachers in The Bahamas and the Caribbean. This objective has been achieved, plus the social and economic respectability of an industry free from crime.

Ms. Cleare traces the History of Tourism with precision and a litany of tourism figures and the comparisons of economic figures which were of financial benefit to all segments of The Bahamas. Eighty-five years ago the concept of promotional funds being provided by the Government had not yet been considered. But by 1950 the provision of advertising funds for The Bahamas as a tourist destination for a 12 months' season was fully launched.

Fifty-five years ago tourist visitors were near 50,000. In 2004 these figures stood well over 5 Million.

Ms. Cleare has chronicled with details the effect on the Bahamian Community of the income from tourism which over the years has become the major industry of The Bahamas, and has from being viewed with scepticism by the greater Caribbean been embraced with regional enthusiasm.

Indeed it produced an innovative approach to the development of the Bahamian Archipelago with the promotion of the policy of creating tourism anchor properties in all the inhabited Islands of The Bahamas, as the catalyst for the future economic prosperity of the Nation.

A unique feature of the History of Tourism is Ms. Cleare's list of those whom she calls Tourism Giants and Stalwarts of the Twentieth Century, who contributed to the place which the industry holds in the economy, its social life and its politics.

Ms. Cleare has made a major contribution to the History of The Bahamas, for which we all should thank her.

Hon. Paul L. Adderley.

PREFACE

Tourism has been the vehicle which enabled The Bahamas to make the transition from a simple economy based on fishing, privateering and a failing sponge industry, to a sophisticated modern economy thriving on the production of services. Tourism, accounting for as much as 70% of national income, 50% of total employment and 40% of government revenue, has now become the bedrock of the economy.

The Bahamas is blessed in many ways. These islands are advantageously positioned near the North American continent with the Atlantic Ocean on one side and the Caribbean Sea on the other. But the greatest blessing of all is the beautiful and rich natural environment that makes The Bahamas one of the best places in the world to live and play. Our geography and climate have been conducive to the development of an enviable service economy with tourism as its centrepiece.

The natural advantages of the 700 islands of The Bahamas, which continue to serve as key ingredients for this success, are the moderate climate, countless miles of beautiful beaches, crystal clear sea, and indeed the largest oceanic archipelagic nation in the tropical Atlantic Ocean, teeming with spectacular marine life. Of equal importance is the acceptance by the Bahamian people that tourism thrives in an environment where the host nation is friendly and hospitable. Other less known natural attributes are the extensive ocean hole and limestone cave system, the world's second largest breeding colonies of West Indian flamingos, numbering 60,000, found on the island of Inagua, over 300 species of birds, and two-thirds of the world's rock iguanas.

The nation is fortunate to have been headed by a series of political, technical, and professional leaders, assisted by contracted agencies and consultants, along with pioneers in the private sector, who have effectively steered the course of this industry. They realized that these natural attributes provided a basis for development, and that they could be used in the skillful marketing of the tourism product. Steps were therefore taken to ensure the availability of efficient transportation and communication facilities, to develop an on-shore tourist plant, and to inspire the local population to respond to the challenges of the developing tourism sector. The result of their effort has been to transform The Bahamas into one of the most successful tourist destinations in the world.

This publication discusses the accomplishments of those visionaries and reviews the history of Bahamian tourism from the arrival of the first recorded tourist in 1492 up to the year 2005. Each chapter begins with a synopsis of the prevailing global trends impacting Bahamas tourism, and presents marketing and product development programmes implemented under the respective regimes, culminating with the results of such initiatives as measured through tourism statistics. The regional position of The Bahamas within the Caribbean, comparative trends and statistics, are also presented. Since modern communications, transportation, and infrastructure, including airports and harbours, are prerequisites for a thriving tourism industry, the evolution of such a system is also briefly reviewed. The penultimate chapter discusses the socio-economic impact of tourism on the local community, including some of the negative impacts suffered in The Bahamas as a result of the concentration on tourism as the main industry. The last chapter reviews tourism trends and challenges that the country faces in the upcoming decades. At the end of this publication, biographies of some of the tourism stalwarts who have been influential in the development of Bahamas tourism are presented.

This book builds on papers produced by the writer in 1971 as a requirement for a Diploma in Management at the University of the West Indies, and in 1981 as a thesis for the MBA with the University of Miami. The material was combined with extensive research throughout the travel industry and the Department of Archives, interviews with tourism pioneers, along with the 30 plus years' experience of the writer at the Ministry of Tourism.

In researching the pre-1960's material at the Department of Archives, certain publications were of invaluable assistance. These included the early editions of the Nassau Magazine, the Bahamas Handbook and Businessman's Annual, articles in the Nassau Guardian and Tribune, along with local historical works written by Dr. Gail Saunders, Paul Albury, Randol Fawkes, Michael Craton, Ansil Saunders and Peter Barratt. Profound thanks to Dr. Gail Saunders, Ms. Elaine Toote, and the staff in the Research Section of the Department of Archives for the countless photocopies. Dotty Zinzow of Bahamas Magazine provided me with several back copies of that magazine.

Dupuch Publications was extremely helpful. Six years ago, when I discussed this idea with Mrs. Sylvia Perfetti Dupuch, she offered encouragement, and immediately supplied relevant articles from the Bahamas Handbook. Following her death, Mr. Etienne Dupuch Jr. and Etienne Dupuch III also made available back copies of the Bahamas Handbook, which provided much historical information. Janice Saunders of Majestic Tours along with Linda Turtle provided very old editions of Nassau Magazine dating as far back as 1942 and offered much additional insight into the tourism picture during the early years. Paul Aranha contributed the data on the history of aviation and aircraft.

Heartfelt thanks are extended to Mrs. Jeanette Bethel who was kind enough to read and edit the entire document and who put forward so many recommendations for improving the flow of the document. I am indebted to Monique Moss Hepburn for taking on the tedious job of checking the various drafts for typographical errors and inconsistencies and for her thorough approach to the task, and to William Dean who also vetted the document. Derek Smith made available his entire photographic library for this purpose and supplied numerous photographs.

Special gratitude is extended to the Honourable Paul Adderley, one of the foremost historians and literary critics, for graciously consenting to review the book and write the Foreword; also to Dr. Gail Saunders for checking the historical information in the publication and to Etienne Dupuch III, Robert "Sandy" Sands, June Maura, Joanne Maura, and Eric Wilmott for their input. Appreciation is also extended to those who provided photographs, data and interviews or offered support or assistance, as shown in the Acknowledgements. Special thanks are extended to Bishop Michael Eldon, Joan Albury, Glenn Bannister, Dr. Sandra Dean Patterson, Langton and Eva Hilton, Debbie Knowles Cartwright, Lois Symonette and Melanie Farrington for their encouragement and who urged me to continue the project after my laptop, vital data and photographs were destroyed in the Ministry of Tourism/Straw Market fire of 2001.

This book is dedicated to my daughter, Tara Cleare, who is also my best friend and critic, and to those trailblazers spotlighted in this book—with special tribute to my mentor, the late Sir Lynden Pindling, who sought me out in London, England, shortly after he took over the Government and asked me to join Tourism, and with whom I had the distinct pleasure of working during his two terms as Minister of Tourism.

It is hoped that this publication will be a source of inspiration to young persons interested in joining this exciting and dynamic industry, a source of pride to those who have gone before, as well as a useful tool for school projects and research.

Angela Wells Cleare
December, 2006
Nassau, Bahamas

ACKNOWLEDGEMENTS

Editor: Dr. Jeanette Bethel—former Permanent Secretary, Ministry of Tourism

Proofreader: Monique Moss Hepburn—Director, Hotel Licensing, Ministry of Tourism

Assistant Proofreader: William Dean

Foreword: Hon. Paul Adderley

Review of Book: Robert Sands, David Johnson, Dr. Gail Saunders, Ms. June Maura, Eric Wilmott

Extensive Interviews: Etienne Dupuch, Jr., the late Mrs. Sylvia Perfetti Dupuch, Sir Clifford Darling, Donald Delaney, William Saunders (Majestic Tours), Harcourt Bastian, Duke Errol Strachan, Peanuts Taylor, Sir Clement Maynard, Bishop Michael Eldon, Paul Aranha, Robert Sands, Duke Errol Strachan.

Extensive Historical Data and Documents: Dr. Gail Saunders, Ms. Elaine Toote and the staff in the Research Section of Department of Archives, June Maura and Joanne Maura (researching data on the Dundas Centre, Bahamas Airways, etc.).

Book Cover: Ambrose Fernander

Other Historical Data:

Entertainment—Duke Errol Strachan (for sharing the history of the local entertainment industry and his album of clippings about local entertainers), John Chipman, Ray Munnings, Berkeley "Peanuts" Taylor, Sabu
Airlines and Aircraft—Paul Aranha (for contributing data on the early history of the airline industry and of Bahamas Airways, along with photos of the first aircraft used in the industry); David Johnson
Time Share—Diana Lightbourne and Chris Adderley

General—RH Curry, Yvette Bethel (Royal Bank), Inga Bowleg (John Bull), Julian Brown (Bimini), Eva Hilton (information on Joseph Spence, a former co-worker), Bahamas National Trust (material on the environment), Rene Mack (Weber Shandwick), Linda Turtle and Janice Saunders (for the Bahamas Magazine—Feb/March 1942, Winter 1951-52, Fall 1952, Midseason 1953); Sandra Dean Patterson (the impact of tourism on alcoholism); Jackie Gibson and Hilton Johnson (Eleuthera), and Urban Bostwick (Los Cayos)

Tourism Research and Statistics: Dr. Gail Saunders, Department of Archives (Development Board statistics and other historical data); Georgina Delancy, Research Department, Ministry of Tourism

Extensive Photographs: Derek Smith of Bahamas Information Services, who shared his entire library

Other Photographs: Ministry of Tourism and Bahamas Information Services, Bahamas News Bureau and the Counsellors Ltd. photographers (Roland Rose, Wendell Cleare, Howard Glass), Chris Symonette, Ronald G. Lightbourne (photos of Lucerne Hotel and the Rozelda), Etienne Dupuch Jr. and Etienne Dupuch III (various photographs including Bay Street fire of 1942); Mrs. Joan Albury, Counsellors Ltd.; Grace Hart-Caron, James Catalyn, John Deleveaux, Kay Evans, Melanie Farrington, Mary Carroll, Athama Bowe, Richard Malcolm, Lloyd Delaney (slides of the 1958 Strike), Berkeley Williamson, Yvonne Shaw, Beverly Wallace Whitfield, Paul Aranha, Don Delahey, Marquetta Collie of Bahamas Hotel Corporation, Athama Bowe, Julia Burnside, Basil Smith, Edwin Lightbourne, Craig Woods, Yvonne Woods, Jackie Gibson and Hilton Johnson (Eleuthera), Vernice Walkine, Hon. Brent Symonette (Smithsonian photos), Clementine Butler (NTAA winners), Clarence Rolle; Vincent Vanderpool Wallace (photo of 1991 Straw Market fire); Frank Comito and staff of Bahamas Hotel Association and Stanley Toogood.

Biographies: Stalwarts listed in the publication as well as other individuals who provided data on the Stalwarts—H.G. Christie, Ltd., Duke Hanna, Ding Cambridge, Ray Munnings, Inga Bowleg, Robert Sands, Chris Justellien, Wendell Jones, Eric Wilmot.

Computer: Melanie Farrington (for the loan of a laptop after the Bay Street fire)

General Support and Encouragement: Tara Cleare, Lois Symonette, Langton and Eva Hilton, Glen Wells and family, Glenn Bannister, Sandra Dean Patterson, Lois East, Melanie Farrington, Monique Moss Hepburn, Lillis Swann, Andrea Coakley, Joan Albury, Bonnie Rolle, Bishop Michael Eldon, Kayla Burrows, Colin Higgs and Patricia Rodgers (current and former Permanent Secretary of Tourism respectively), Sheila Cox, Rowena Rolle, Yvonne Woods, Diana Lightbourne, Baltron Bethel, Renee Mayers, Vincent Vanderpool Wallace and Vernice Walkine (former and present Director General of Tourism respectively) and the Honourable Obie Wilchcombe, Minister of Tourism.

1

TOURISM: A GLOBAL PERSPECTIVE

Tourism Definition

Tourism involves the temporary, short-term movement of people outside of places where they normally live. In its official definition, the World Tourism Organization (UNWTO) describes tourism as "activities of a person travelling to a place outside his or her usual environment for less than a specified period of time and whose main purpose of travel is other than the exercise of an activity remunerated from within the place visited". The term "usual environment" excludes trips within the place of residence and routine trips; "less than a specified period of time" is intended to exclude long-term migration, and usually refers to trips shorter than a year; and the phrase "exercise of an activity remunerated from within the place visited" is intended to exclude migration to take up a work assignment.[1]

A distinction is also made between types of visitors, based on their length of stay. A **Stopover Visitor** is one who stays at least one night, but not more than one year, in the country visited. A **Day Visitor** or **Excursionist** is a visitor who stays in the country visited for less than 24 hours, without overnight stay.

International Tourism refers to travel from one country to another. **Domestic Tourism** refers to travel within a particular country. In this publication, attention will be focused on International Tourism.

Historical Factors Influencing Travel

Although large-scale tourist travel is a new phenomenon, people have travelled for various reasons from earliest times. Prehistoric travel was often based on search for food or livelihood. Upper-class Egyptians and Greeks, travelling for religious reasons, are said to be among the first culturally motivated tourists. The Romans, inspired by interest in exotic foods, entertainment and their openness to new cultures, saw value in travel for its own sake.

During the medieval period (from 5th to 15th centuries A.D.), travel came almost to a standstill. Travel, derived from Middle English word *travail*, (meaning to toil, or make a toilsome journey) was indeed burdensome, unpredictably dangerous, and demanding during this time. The breakup of the Roman Empire put a halt to many of the advances the Romans had introduced. Roads were not maintained and became unsafe. Thieves waited to prey on those who dared to travel.

War and religion have induced the movement of hundreds of thousands of people. The Crusades undertaken by European Christians during the 11th, 12th and 13th centuries, brought large numbers of Europeans to the Middle East.

With the Renaissance, the intellectual and artistic movement beginning in the 14th century, when a few prestigious universities were established, travel for education was introduced, largely by the British, and this trend became especially popular beginning in the 16th century. The young British aristocrat, as well as members of the rising middle class, visited the Continent to round out their education. By 1670, an extended tour of Europe, known as the *Grand Tour*, became an integral part of an aristocrat's education. In the 18th century, English inns gained the reputation of being the finest in the world. Voyagers passed along information to each other about the best places to stay and eat. One of the earliest guidebooks was "The Pilgrim's Guide", dating back to the 13th century.

Travel for health also became important in the 17th century, prompting visits to health spas, springs and boiling holes believed to possess healing properties. Soon hotels and entertainment built up around these attractions. Around 1750, the English spas lost their favoured position when sea water became popular for medicinal purposes. By 1963, three-quarters of the holidays taken within Britain were spent by the sea.[2]

In the United States, the first building specially built as a hotel was the 73-room *City Hotel*, which opened in New York in 1794. Considered a very large property, it also had meeting rooms and became the social centre of the city. New York's first skyscraper was the six-storey *Adelphi Hotel*, constructed in 1877. When the 170-room *Tremont House* became the first Five-Star Hotel in 1829, its private single and double rooms with water pitchers, bowls and free soap were considered an incredible innovation. The Tremont had the first bellboy, as well as the position of annunciator, the forerunner to room telephone. Their staff were highly trained, and French cuisine was offered[3]. A boom in hotel construction followed, with intense competition among cities and hoteliers to build the biggest and best hotels.

Popular reasons for holiday travel changed from century to century, or decade to decade, based on economic, psychological and/or sociological needs. Arlin Epperson[4], a travel consultant proposed a "push/pull" model in classifying motivations for travel. He lists *push* factors as the intangible desires that generate from within the person, such as the need to escape, self-discovery, rest/relaxation, prestige, challenge, and adventure. *Pull* factors are external travel stimulators, such as scenic beauty; historical areas; cultural and sporting events. For example, a relaxing week on a Caribbean beach or a scuba diving adventure in The Bahamas are inspired by a push factor, while a trip to Disney World, the Lourdes in Paris, or the Olympics would attract those motivated by a pull factor.

There are many motivations for travel, some of which are listed below:

1. Sightseeing (To see particular sights or get to know the world)
2. Events (To attend or participate in special events)
3. Weather or Health (To escape harsh temperatures)
4. Sports (for example, diving, golf, yachting, sailing)
5. Adventure (such as mountain climbing, scuba diving, hunting)
6. Honeymoon or Romance
7. Shopping
8. Gambling
9. Ecotourism (including bird watching, kayaking)
10. Cultural, Heritage, or Ethnic (To learn about the cultures of other countries or to visit places one's ancestors or family came from)
11. Education (To complete a course of study or seminar)
12. Religion (To attend a retreat, mission, congress or religious experience)
13. To visit family, friends or relatives.

With few exceptions, until the 19th and 20th centuries, economic and social realities reserved leisure travel as an activity for the wealthy, and the pre-industrial travel experience was expensive, time consuming, and uncomfortable.

Today, reasons for travel are often broadly grouped under *holiday/leisure travel* (for recreation, visits to relatives and friends, health, culture, sport, religion, vacation, or study, paid for by the individual); or *business travel* (for professional meetings, conventions, or other travel paid for by the traveller's employer).

Statistical Analysis of International Tourism

World tourism has traditionally been measured in International Tourist Arrivals and International Tourist Receipts. The tourism sector has recorded sustained growth over the past half century, despite currency crises of the 1960's, the oil crisis of the 1970's, recessions of the 1980's and '90's, 1991 Gulf War, terrorist attacks in the United States of September 11, 2001, Bali bombing in October 2002, and the 2003 War in Iraq.

Table 1-1 shows the growth rate of tourism over the past 50 years. During the period 1950-70, world tourism arrivals grew at an annual rate in excess of 9%. Since 1970, global travel has been growing at an average annual rate of 4%. In 2005 the number of international tourists travelling in the world reached 800 million, an increase of 5.5% over the previous year. Receipts from international tourism (excluding international fare receipts) rose by an estimated 3.4 in 2005 to reach $692 billion. Detailed statistics of International Tourist Arrivals and Receipts are shown in Appendix 1A.

While the uncertainties caused by war have had a negative impact on tourism by fuelling fear and delaying investment plans, tourism as an industry has demonstrated great resiliency and, to date, the sector has not suffered from a prolonged recession.

Table 1-1
International Tourist Arrivals—Average Growth Rate (1950-2000)

1950-60	10.61%	1980-85	2.73%
1960-70	9.11%	1985-90	6.93%
1970-80	5.60%	1990-95	3.77%
1980-90	4.81%	1995-2000	4.86%
1990-2000	4.3%	2000-05	3.34%

Source: World Tourism Organization, Madrid, Spain

Leading Generators of International Tourism

According to the World Tourism Organization, in 1999 there were 24 nations whose residents spent a billion or more US dollars in the countries they visited. Thirteen of these countries were in Europe, two in North America, two in Latin America and seven in other parts of the world. Six countries—Germany, the United States, Japan, the United Kingdom, France and Italy—generate approximately 50% of the world's total of tourism earnings. The leading generators of international tourism in Europe, the Americas, East Asia and the Pacific are listed in Appendix 1B. These are the countries which are targeted in the marketing plans of most host destinations. Since 1997, China has become the fastest growing tourist-generating market in the world, but with travel confined only to approved destinations.

Top Host Tourist Destinations

Table 1-2 lists the top 15 tourism host destinations in the world, based on earnings from tourism. The countries which have consistently been in the top ten most popular tourist destinations are the United States, France, Italy, Spain, United Kingdom, Austria, and Germany. International tourism receipts (excluding international transport) increased by 7% in 1994-95 and 1995-96 but the growth rate has dramatically declined since that time. Total receipts from tourism (excluding transport) totalled $475.8 billion in 2000. The ten leading destinations account for 54% of the world volume of tourism flows. The predominant host tourism destinations of the world, by region, based on earnings from tourism, along with their market share, are shown in Appendix 1B.

What is significant is that the expansion of tourism has been characterized by an ongoing geographical spread. Every year additional countries recognize the importance of tourism and are marketing their destinations to attract international tourists. In 1950, only 15 countries received nearly 100% of the 25 million international arrivals. In 1999, there were more than 70 countries and territories that played host to more than 1 million international tourist arrivals. By 1999, the top 15 tourist-receiving countries saw their share decrease to less than two-thirds and some traditionally top destinations, such as Belgium and the Netherlands, have been replaced by newcomers from Asia, Central/Eastern Europe (such as Russian Federation and Australia). However, the United States, France, Spain, Italy and the United Kingdom have retained their popularity and remain the top five tourism earners in the world.

In the past two decades, international tourism grew faster in developing countries both for arrivals and receipts, reflecting a wider redistribution of tourism revenue in favour of the emerging tourism destinations in the third world.

Table 1-2
World's Top 15 Tourism Earners
1985 vs. 1999

Rank		Country	Intl Tourism Receipts (US$ billion)		Market Share % Of World Total	
1985	1999		1985	1999	1985	1999
1	1	United States	17.9	74.4	15.4	16.4
4	3	France	7.9	31.7	6.8	7.0
2	4	Italy	8.7	28.4	7.5	6.2
3	2	Spain	8.1	32.9	7.0	7.2
5	5	United Kingdom	7.1	21.0	6.1	4.6
6	8	Austria	5.1	11.1	4.4	2.4
7	6	Germany	4.7	16.8	4.1	3.7
11	15	Hong Kong	1.8	7.2	1.5	1.6
	7	China		14.1		3.1
14		Singapore	1.6	7.5	1.4	2.03
8	14	Switzerland	3.1	7.4	2.7	1.6
9	9	Canada	3.1	10.0	2.7	2.2
	10	Greece		8.8		1.9
	11	Russian Fed.		7.8		1.7
	13	Australia		7.5		1.7
12		Belgium	1.6		1.4	
13		Netherlands	1.6		1.4	
15		Thailand	1.2	6.6	1.0	1.78
10	12	Mexico	2.9	7.8	2.5	1.7
World Total			**116.1**	**455**	**100**	**100**

Sources: "Tourism in 1992: Highlights", World Tourism Organization, Madrid, Spain, Jan. 1993
"Tourism in 1999: Highlights", World Tourism Organization, Madrid, Spain, Jan. 2000

Caribbean Tourism

Tourism in the Caribbean is fundamental to the economy of the region. According to the World Travel & Tourism Council, nearly 3.1 million jobs (13.4%) in the region are in the Travel & Tourism sector. The increase in tourist arrivals and receipts in selected Caribbean countries over the past decade is shown in Tables 1-3 and 1-4. A small group of countries, in particular, Dominican Republic, The Bahamas, Jamaica, and Barbados (and, more recently, Cuba) experience most of the arrival activity and receipts, accounting for 50% of visitor expenditures in the region. The Dominican Republic alone attracted over 14% of the total number of arrivals to the region in 2000, the equivalent of 15 smaller countries (see Appendices 1C and 1D for further statistics on Stopover Arrivals and Earnings to other Caribbean destinations).

Table 1-3
Tourist Arrivals (Stopovers) in Selected Caribbean Countries ('000)
1991-2000

Country	1991	1992	1994	1996	1998	2000	Change (%) '91-00	Market Share 2000
Antigua & Barbuda	204.7	217.9	262.9	228.2	234.3	236.7	15.6	1.1
Dominica	46.3	47.0	56.5	63.3	65.5	68.9	48.8	0.3
Grenada	85.0	87.6	109.0	108.2	115.8	128.9	51.6	0.6
Montserrat	19.2	17.3	21.3	8.7	7.5	10.3	-46.4	0
St. Kitts & Nevis	83.9	88.3	94.2	84.2	93.2	68.5	-18.4	0.3
St Lucia	159.0	177.5	218.6	235.7	252.2	269.9	69.7	1.3
St. Vincent & Grenadines	51.6	53.1	55.0	57.9	67.2	72.9	41.3	0.4
The Bahamas	1,427.0	1,399.0	1516.0	1633.1	1527.7	1596.2	11.9	7.7
Barbados	394.2	385.5	425.6	447.1	512.4	544.7	38.2	2.6
Jamaica	1,007.0	1057.9	1098.0	1162.4	1225.3	1322.7	31.4	6.4
Cuba	424.0	460.6	617.3	1004.3	1415.8	1774.0	318.4	8.6
Dominican Republic	1,416.8	1523.8	1766.9	1925.6	2309.1	2972.6	109.8	14.4
Caribbean	**11,928.2**	**12,204.1**	**16,461.9**	**17,036.3**	**19,112.9**	**20,672.8**	**73.3**	**100**

Source: Caribbean Tourism Organization

Table 1-4
Tourism Receipts in selected Caribbean Countries (Millions) 1991-2000

Country	1991	1992	1994	1996	1998	2000	Change (%) '91-00
Antigua & Barbuda	314.0	329.0	394.0	257.9	255.6	290.1	-7.6
Dominica	28.1	30.3	30.6	36.6	38.2	47.2	68.0
Grenada	41.7	42.3	59.3	59.5	61.1	70.2	68.3
Montserrat	11.9	13.7	18.5	9.7	8.0	9.0	-24.4
St. Kitts & Nevis	67.5	67.2	76.9	66.8	75.7	58.2	-13.8
St Lucia	173.4	207.9	224.1	268.5	291.3	276.7	59.6
St. Vincent & Grenadines	53.0	52.7	50.5	63.7	74.0	75.3	42.1
The Bahamas	1,192.7	1,243.5	1,332.6	1,450.0	1,354.1	1,814.0	52.1
Barbados	459.7	462.5	597.6	632.9	703.0	718.5	56.3
Jamaica	764.0	858.0	973.0	1,092.2	1,197.1	1,333.0	74.5
Cuba	387.4	567.0	850.0	1,185.0	1,571.0	1,847.6	376.9
Dominican Republic	877.5	1,054.8	1,147.5	1,765.5	2,153.1	2,860.2	225.9
Caribbean	**9,203.3**	**9,934.2**	**11,712.9**	**15,060.9**	**17,288.1**	**19,899.1**	**116.2**

Source: Caribbean Tourism Organization

The cruise industry also played an important role in the growth of the region in the 1980's and 1990's. Cruise passenger arrivals increased from 7.7 million in 1990 to 13.9 million in 2000, an annual growth of 5.9%. Five countries controlled 52% of the market share. The Bahamas alone captured 15% of the total number of cruise passengers in 1999.

Tourism Impact—Advantages and Disadvantages

As indicated, globally there has been tremendous growth in tourism over the past 50 years. This has been the direct result of huge sums invested in the marketing of the industry by government and by private sector agencies, which have recognized the tremendous economic benefits to be derived from tourism. The **advantages** of tourism to local communities are many.

Economic Factors

International tourism represents an *invisible export* of goods and services, in the sense that it is not produced, packaged, shipped or received like tangible goods. Foreign tourists, within the country visited, buy certain services (such as hotel, transportation, entertainment). They must consume food and beverages and often reserve a part of their money for purchases. The tourism industry creates opportunities for selling other goods and services. Exports, exempt from the risks of international trade, are created with no transportation costs to the exporter.

One of the greatest benefits of tourism is *job creation*. Tourism, a people industry, is labour-intensive and less automated than other industries. Tourism drives jobs across the entire economy, with a high proportion of them for women and young people. A further advantage is that many of the jobs created are in the less skilled occupations, which usually have the highest rates of unemployment.

The World Tourism Organization reports that tourism is the world's largest creator of jobs in most countries, providing employment in the year 2000 for over 250 million people, or one in 16 workers worldwide. It was also revealed that travel/tourism was a major creator of opportunities for minority employment, small business creation, and global economic and political linkages.

By creating jobs, tourism is an important *generator of national income*. In its broadest sense, tourism encompasses all expenditures for goods and services by travellers. It includes purchases of ground transportation, accommodations, meals, sightseeing tours, entertainment, souvenirs, travel agency services; it also uses services of other industries such as credit cards, advertising, data processing, insurance, information services, and publications. Tourism has a high multiplier effect with linkages to many other sectors; it creates indirect jobs in agriculture, husbandry, fisheries, construction, laundries, beauty salons, et cetera. General infrastructure and superstructure are needed as a basis for the expansion of tourism. Tourist demand causes the creation of transport, communication facilities, water supply, electricity, roads, bridges, airports, harbours and marinas. Leisure travellers encourage craft and community-based entrepreneurship. The overall positive impact of tourism can be so large that it has a dramatic effect in raising standards of living and stimulating local economies.

The *investment* potential of the tourism industry is also significant. Visitors often return to make an investment in the economic development of a country, the beauty of which they have sampled. On the negative side, while the tourism industry might serve as an instrument for attracting investors, this has sometimes worked to the detriment of developing countries. There have been cases where investors, equipped with expert advisors, have negotiated with unskilled Government officials of developing territories and have succeeded in obtaining agreements that are extremely favourable to the investor, but of little benefit to the host countries.

Tourism also helps to balance *public finances* and to provide funding for national programmes such as education, health and infrastructure. Governments derive direct revenue from tourism through departure taxes, hotel taxes, sales taxes, casino taxes as well as indirect revenue resulting from tourist spending.

One major **disadvantage** of tourism is that the industry is a highly sensitive and vulnerable one, influenced by many unforeseeable and uncontrollable factors, such as wars, social unrest and environmental incidents. Similarly, recessions, political or social disturbances within the major tourism generating countries could adversely affect the ability of those residents to travel abroad, thus crippling the tourism industry of dependent host countries. Therefore, a country which relies on tourism as its major income earner incurs some risk. But historic evidence suggests that such shifts are temporary.

Years ago, it was generally assumed that travel is not a vital need and that during a recession this budget item would be the first to be sacrificed. While this is true in some instances, the trend is changing. With increased industrialization and pressures on today's modern citizens, travel, for many, is considered a necessity. A study conducted by the Boston Globe asked members of the public to rate several items as necessities, conveniences or luxuries. The results of the survey revealed that travel was rated high in the necessity and convenience categories and quite low in the luxury category. Items (such as a dishwasher) that make life easier for more days of the year were given lower priority than travel. The conclusion is that humans do not consider travel as a luxury but have a need to "get away from it all" through travel and will sacrifice other purchases to be able to relax in a different setting, if only for a few days.[5]

Social Factors

While tourism, for many countries, has been the panacea for badly sagging national economies, it should not be considered from an economic aspect only. Travel afforded by tourism is becoming a powerful instrument in education. Travellers have the opportunity of discovering historic traditions and cultures of nations, exchanging ideas with people of different backgrounds, thus widening horizons. Tourism stimulates creativity and innovation, encourages residents to celebrate and showcase their culture and natural beauty. International tourism, bringing, as it does, people of different nationalities, traditions and beliefs face to face, can help to foster better understanding and eliminate prejudices, thus contributing to world peace.

In spite of the clear economic benefits of tourism, there can be social costs involved. Tourism can raise the cost of living, contribute to misplaced values, introduce negative behaviour such as prostitution and use of narcotics, attract undesirables and contribute to loss of cultural identity.

Because high wages are offered in the tourism industry, many young people sacrifice long-term education benefits for immediate, attractive offers in tourism. Thus, tourism tends to place constraints on education.

The behaviour patterns and spending habits of the tourist can influence the behaviour of local inhabitants. There is often a disconnect in the minds of the locals between their desire to emulate the more affluent lifestyles enjoyed by the tourists on holiday and the more limited ability of the local economy to provide for the basic needs of an expanding population. Such unrealistic expectations can impact economic progress if demands for enhanced wages in the tourist sector result in making some economies less cost-competitive in the global arena.

The history of slavery in the British Commonwealth Caribbean has contributed to one of the possible social disadvantages of the tourist industry. Before slaves were emancipated in 1838, the black man's exclusive role in these territories was to serve the white man. Local people were portrayed as "happy smiling natives", who were content with their lot and were neither willing nor capable of improving it. The growth of the tourism industry initially continued the tradition of upper class affluence, and the Caribbean islands were promoted as havens for relaxation with all comforts provided by happy natives. The influx of white overseas visitors, displaying substantially higher lifestyles, coupled with the image of tourism as a servile industry, has, in some parts of the Caribbean, created great dissatisfaction and an inability to attract an educated and skilled workforce.

Environmental Factors

For a long time, tourism was considered to be an industry without significant cultural and ecological impacts on the environment. However, many studies conducted on a global scale within the past two decades have shown that, in its various forms, tourism has been responsible for the loss of species and habitats, and degradation of the environment. The establishment of tourist activities in sensitive areas and the introduction of harmful substances to ecosystems have contributed to the problem.

On the positive side, it is precisely tourism that is contributing to the conservation of biodiversity in many destinations. What has come to be called Ecotourism is now an important instrument of preservation. Biological resources are being protected because their touristic value has been discovered.[6] On a global level, many tourism establishments are leading the way in proving how good practices, in areas such as energy efficiency, water conservation, and waste management, can reduce long-term costs, while helping to change attitudes and behaviour. Tourism, because of its widespread influence, can therefore serve as a major change agent for positive environmental action, and, with effective planning and enlightened management, can become a model of sustainability.

*   *   *

It is against this background that The Bahamas tourism story unfolds.

2

THE FIRST VISITORS AND HOSTS: FROM COLUMBUS TO THE LOYALISTS

The First Tourist—Christopher Columbus

In 1492, Christopher Columbus stumbled on one of the Bahama Islands en route to the New World. He was warmly greeted by the gentle inhabitants of The Bahamas, first at Guanahani (now San Salvador), then at Rum Cay, Long Island, Long Cay, Fortune Island, Crooked Island and Ragged Island. The Lucayan Indian "natives" presented Columbus and his delegation, whom they described as "visitors from heaven", with presents of green parrots, darts, and cotton.[1]

Although Columbus' behaviour during his 15-day stay was not the type one would expect of a visitor, Christopher Columbus can be classified as the first recorded tourist to the Bahama Islands. The arrival of this visitor proved disastrous to the gentle hosts, and ended in the Spanish colonization and eradication, by 1520, of the entire host population (estimated at 20,000)[2]. The landfall of Christopher Columbus did, however, open up the West, and begin an era which facilitated global travel.

First visitor, Christopher Columbus, greeted by gentle Arawak Indians at San Salvador, Bahamas

Without a host population, tourism has no benefits; hence the ad hoc visits by the Spanish, including Ponce De Leon and English seamen like Sir John Hawkins and Sir Francis Drake in the 16th and 17th centuries can hardly fall into the category of tourism.

The First Settlers

The first English settlers of The Bahamas were the Eleutheran Adventurers, a group of English dissidents seeking religious freedom, who arrived on Eleuthera from Bermuda in 1648. Even though these Adventurers drew up a constitution, no effective government existed.

In 1670, The Bahamas was granted to six Lord Proprietors of the Carolinas by Charles II of England. The period which followed was one of lawlessness and plunder. The most important "visitors" to The Bahamas during this era were notorious pirates.

Plundering Visitors—The Pirates

In his book "Pirates: Rascals of the Spanish Main",[3] A.B.C. Whipple paints a colourful and fascinating picture of New Providence in the 18th century during the piracy era. Because of the influence of the pirates, the island had gained worldwide notoriety. A contemporary saying was that when pirates dreamed they had died and gone to heaven, they dreamed of New Providence. The island had everything which a pirate desired. The harbour provided two ways in and out, so that no ship could trap a pirate inside the bay. The hills provided a sweeping view of the horizon where lookouts could watch for a potential victim ship. Back of the white sand and pink coral beach lay the tangled jungle where no pursuer could ever find his fleeing quarry. Commented Whipple: "a better pirate headquarters could not have been built by order."[4] It was the perfect attack base—only a few hours' sail to the Caribbean, the Straits of Florida, the Windward Passage and Providence Channels. A pirate could run to Little Bahama Bank, slip in between one of the thousands of low, sandy cays, and pounce upon the passing merchantmen as they sailed up the Florida coast. As Whipple further commented, "Nassau of that time was a sprawling, brawling tent city that would have put the worst cow town of the US Wild West to shame".[5]

"From 1697, these pirates began increasingly to use the port of Nassau. They represented the only prosperity to be seen in those days and, as long as they behaved themselves tolerably well in port, the people of New Providence were not averse to their presence. It was reported that even the Governors found pirate money irresistible, but usually made an outward show of trying to suppress the rogues."[6] Edward Teach, known as *Blackbeard*, was the most colourful of the pirates, along with the notorious females—Ann Bonney and Mary Read. The pirates' main purpose for visiting The Bahamas was to get quick and unlawful cash and valuables, at any cost.

There never was a more transient population. A few traders bought loot and sent it to the North American colonies to dispose of it. There seemed to be a tavern keeper for nearly every dozen pirates, and theirs were virtually the only substantial buildings.

After a long period of unstable rule, the Government of The Bahamas was finally vested in the Crown and on 6th February, 1718, Captain Woodes Rogers, an ex-privateer, became the first Royal Governor. When Woodes Rogers, with his small fleet of three ships arrived, the island sheltered some 3,000 pirates and more than 200 pirate ships.[7]

It was during Rogers' second term as Governor from 1729 to 1732 that a General Assembly met for the first time, and a serious attempt was made to introduce law and order and to restore commerce. As Michael Craton commented, Rogers "guided The Bahamas through stormy seas and into the comparatively calm waters of Crown control."[8] After Woodes Rogers' death in 1732, a period of illegal trade in shipwrecking began.

Earliest Tourism Record

During the governorship of John Tinker (1740-1758), Peter Henry Bruce, a military engineer, was sent from England to repair the forts of Nassau. One of the earliest records of Bahamas tourism, as we know it today, can be found in the journal of Peter Henry Bruce. He described the products of the islands in great detail, listing many kinds of trees, fruits, wild animals and 57 species of fish. He was the first writer to mention conch as a native delicacy. In the early 1740's, Bruce listed the population of The Bahamas as follows:

Heads of Families	310
Women and Children	689
Negro Male Slaves	426
Black Women and Children	538
Independent Company	100
Harbour Island and Islathera (Eleuthera)	240
	2,303[9]

Henry Bruce also made reference to the Colony's tourism potential, when he wrote:

The Bahama Islands enjoy the most serene and the most temperate air in all America, the heat of the sun being greatly allayed by refreshing breezes from the east; and the earth and air are cooled by constant dews which fall in the night. They are free from the sultry heat and little affected by frost, snow, hail, or the northwest winds, which prove so fatal both to men and plants in our other colonies. It is therefore no wonder the sick and afflicted inhabitants of those climates fly hither for relief, being sure to find a cure here.[10]

Thus, as early as the 18th century, The Bahamas, specifically Nassau, was recognized as an ideal destination for health tourism. However, the Colony was far from ready to cater to the tourism market because of inadequate communication, transportation and accommodations. The small number of visitors stayed in private Bahamian homes.

The Loyalists

The beginning of modern times was heralded with the arrival of the Loyalists. Before their arrival, the inhabitants of The Bahamas were poor. They were principally occupied in a sea-faring life—fishing, wrecking, and turtling—as well as woodcutting. There was little agriculture, except for easily grown products such as guinea corn, peas, potatoes, pumpkin and bananas.[11]

In the 1780's, many Americans who were still loyal to the British Crown began to migrate to The Bahamas from New York, Florida, South Carolina, Virginia, and Georgia. In less than five years the population of The Bahamas trebled, and the proportion of slaves increased from half to three-quarters of the whole. Loyalists had owned plantations in the southern colonies and their arrival meant an expansion of the plantation system in The Bahamas. They were accustomed to a high standard of living, and their injection of capital and ideas produced a new entrepreneurial spirit, which later benefitted the tourism industry. The first batch of Loyalists arrived in June 1783, and the exodus from America to The Bahamas continued until March 1785.[12]

In the late 18th century, while the slave population outnumbered whites throughout the British West Indies, whites and blacks were approximately even in The Bahamas and Bermuda, as shown in Table 2-1.

Table 2-1
Population—British West Indies—1791

	Whites	Blacks
Jamaica	30,000	250,000
Barbados	16,167	62,115
Grenada	1,000	23,926
St. Vincent	1,450	11,853
Dominica	1,236	14,967
Antigua	2,590	37,808
Montserrat	1,300	10,000
Nevis	1,000	8,420
St. Christophers	1,900	20,435
Virgin Islands	1,200	9,000
Bahamas	2,000	2,241
Bermuda	3,462	4,919
Total	5,462	4,916

Source: *Sources of West Indian History*, F.R. Augier and Shirley C. Gordon, Longman Caribbean Lid, Trinidad and Jamaica, 1962, p.22

The dramatic increase in the population of The Bahamas with the arrival of the loyalists is depicted in Table 2-2.

Table 2-2
Bahamian Population by Island—1783 vs. 1786

	1783			1786		
	Whites	Negroes	Totals	Whites	Negros	Totals
New Providence	755	1,739	2,494	1,572	4.019	5,591
Eleuthera	476	310	786	486	315	801
Harbour Is.	360	144	504	365	149	514
Exuma	17	15	32	66	638	704
Long Island	33	78	111	41	99	140
Cat Is.	6	9	15	59	305	364
Turks Is.	75	41	116	75	41	116
Abaco				282	384	666
Andros				2	59	61
Total	**1,722**	**2,336**	**4,058**	**2,948**	**6,009**	**8,957**

Source: Bahamas Department of Statistics

The islands of New Providence, Eleuthera, Harbour Island, and Abaco, with established host populations, led the way in tourism development in the next century. The slaves who came with the Loyalists were joined by thousands of liberated Africans who were captured by the British navy, freed, and put ashore in The Bahamas. Most Bahamians were of African descent with a minority being descended from the early English settlers and Loyalists.

Many Bahamians went into farming, trades or established businesses, which eventually provided support for a vibrant 20th century tourism industry. As demand for accommodations increased, local residents converted homes into boarding houses.

During this era, cotton flourished. In 1773 and 1774, Bahamian exports to Britain had amounted to a little more than £5,000. In 1786 and 1787, exports were valued at close to £59,000. [13] At long last, Bahamians thought that the age of illegal trade, like wrecking and privateering, had come to an end, and that the formula for a peaceful and sound economy had been found. But that was not to be, for the cotton crops were attacked by the chenille and red bug. The damage done by these pests, coupled with limited nutrients in the shallow soil, led to the demise of the cotton industry by 1800. Many of the plantations were abandoned. The sea became a stronger attraction to the Bahamian settlers than the land.

*   *   *

After the failure of the cotton industry, it became increasingly evident that some other industry was necessary to sustain the people of The Bahamas.

3

EARLY EFFORTS TO ENCOURAGE TOURISM:
THE MID 19TH CENTURY

External Developments Impacting Bahamian Tourism

Steam Power

On the global scene, until the mid 19th century, most travel was undertaken for business and vocational reasons, by road, within the boundaries of individual countries. Hence, the volume of travel was relatively small and confined to a fraction of the population. Technological advances, spawned by the Industrial Revolution, provided the impetus for tourism development.

A key positive factor was the introduction of steam power. Before the advent of the steam engine most of the world's transportation was powered by the muscles of men and animals and by forces of nature, such as wind. Transportation was by horseback or animal-drawn coaches, boats propelled by oars and sailboats. While the first steam locomotive was built in 1804, it was not until 1819 that the first steam-powered vessel crossed the Atlantic. By 1830, the first steam-drawn passenger train began operations in the United States, just four years after the first railroad company opened in the United States. In 1835, construction began on the first railroad in Canada, and, by 1855, railroads in the United States and Canada were linked by the Niagara Suspension Bridge.

Steam powered vessels made transportation more reliable, no longer dependent on the forces of nature. As the century progressed, improvements in steam boilers, and the introduction of high-powered engines, made locomotives and ships more efficient. The use of iron, and then steel, coupled with the more powerful engines, resulted in the construction of larger, more luxurious passenger ships than ever before. Transportation became more comfortable and less costly. Oceangoing English steamships of iron were in service by the late 1830's and were making transatlantic voyages by the 1850's. The United States, which concentrated for a few years on the beautiful sail-driven clipper ships, lagged behind in the building of the iron steam ships; the first iron ships for transatlantic service were built in the United States in 1872. Later in the 1870's, steel, which was lighter and stronger, replaced iron for shipbuilding.[1]

The new and faster modes of transportation, coupled with the wealth generated by the Industrial Revolution, created the markets necessary for the expansion of the accommodations sector and supplementary tourism products and services, making tourism more easily accessible to a large segment of 19th century society. Holidays gradually began to represent an important reason for a journey.

Although the first hotels date to the 18th century, their growth on any scale occurred only in the 19th century when railways and steamships created sufficiently large markets to fill the larger accommodations.

The Emergence of Travel Brokers

The burgeoning professional and merchant classes of industrial cities had the money and means of transportation to become consumers in the new travel marketplace. By the mid 19th century, the demands of an expanding and increasingly complex global market created a need for brokers to facilitate travel activities. One of the pioneers in the travel trade was an Englishman, Thomas Cook, who became the forefather of today's tour operators when he began organizing, retailing and operating inclusive tours in 1845. In the 1860's, Cook's Tours brought travellers across the Atlantic to the United States and Canada. In 1867, Thomas Cook invented the first hotel coupon. By 1879, the American market had produced its own travel arrangers and American Express invented the traveller's cheque in 1891.[2] These developments added to the convenience and financial security of travellers.

The American Civil War

Lincoln had become President of the United States in 1860, without the electoral votes of a single southern state. On 12th April, 1861, the Confederate States opened fire on the Federal forts in Charleston harbour, South Carolina, and four years of bloody civil war began in America. President Lincoln declared a blockade of the southern ports in the first week of the war, but the Federal navy was unprepared to enforce a blockade. The Confederacy depended on exporting its cotton in order to survive and needed to obtain munitions to continue the war. They, therefore, had to evade President Lincoln's blockade of the southern ports. As the war progressed, shipbuilders, ship-owners and adventurers were drawn by the vast profits of blockade-running. To be fast enough to dodge the blockade, the ships had to be built like greyhounds. Unable to carry large cargoes, it was essential that they find a neutral port within two or three days' steaming. This is where The Bahamas entered the picture. The busiest ports during the blockade were Charleston and Wilmington, North Carolina, only 560 and 640 miles, respectively, from the safety of the Abaco Cays in The Bahamas.

Blockade-running and its Impact on The Bahamas

In January 1862, following the American blockade, the British Government instructed Governor Charles Bayley to safeguard the neutrality of The Bahamas, "preventing as far as possible the use of Her Majesty's harbours, ports and coasts and the waters within Her Majesty's territorial jurisdiction in aid of the warlike purposes of either belligerent."[3] Belligerent ships were to be denied entry except in cases of extreme distress. The Governor's instructions were translated to mean that warships alone were denied the use of the islands and that all blockade-running merchant ships should be safe when they entered Bahamian waters. The adventurers ignored the danger of this trade in an attempt to reap the vast profits. Governor Bayley, in an address to the Assembly, actually rejoiced in the prosperity that resulted from the commerce with the South.

Bay Street 1861—Looking Eastward toward Rawson Square.

Bay Street in the 1860's

The import and export figures for Nassau between 1860 and 1865, shown in Table 3-1, give insight into the impact on the Colony of blockade-running. In 1860, the imports for Nassau were valued at £234,029 and by 1864 had reached the incredible peak of £5,346,112. Likewise, exports soared in value from £157,350 in 1860 to £4,672,398. In January and February 1864 alone, 20 ships ran the blockade to Nassau with 14,182 bales of cotton worth £2,750,000.[4]

Table 3-1
Impact of the American Civil War on the Economy of The Bahamas
Imports, Exports and Ship Arrivals and Departures for Nassau: 1860-65

Year	Imports	Exports	Ships Arriving		Ships Departing	
	£	£	Sail	Steam	Sail	Steam
1860	234,029	157,350				
1861	274,584	195,584	2	2	1	3
1862	1,250,322	1,007,755	74	32	109	46
1863	4,295,316	3,308,567	27	113	48	173
1864	5,346,112	4,672,398	6	105	2	165
1865			0	35	0	41

Source: History of The Bahamas, Michael Craton, p. 228

The unexpected and sudden flood of money transformed Nassau. The main street, Bay Street, was widened at a cost of £13,130 and provided with kerbstones and lights for the first time. Warehouses were constructed on the north side of the street, and a plan was developed for a completely new dock. Other new buildings sprang up nearly overnight. The public debt of £47,786 was wiped out and officers' salaries were increased by 25%[5]. The value of land, especially on the waterfront, appreciated by 300 or 400%. One of the earliest extant photographs shows Nassau harbour crowded with more than 20 tall-stacked steamers at one time. Before the war, there were rarely a dozen ships visiting within a year.

J.H. Stark, in his book *History and Guide to The Bahamas*, commented that:

> "*everyone was mad with excitement during these years of the war. The shops were packed to the ceilings and the streets were crowded with bales, boxes and barrels. Fortunes were made in a few weeks or months. Money was spent and scattered in a most extravagant and lavish manner. The town swarmed with Southern refugees, captains and crews of blockade-runners. Every available space in or out of doors was occupied. Men lay on verandahs, walls, decks and floors. Money was plentiful. Wages were doubled, liquor flowed freely and the common labourer had his champagne and rich food.[6]*"

Local Efforts to Develop Tourism as an Alternative Industry

By the beginning of the 19th century, the impact of the Loyalists and their slaves became more pervasive. With their power and influence generated from success in agricultural and commercial pursuits, they contributed to the growth of New Providence. Indeed they influenced the whole tone of Bahamian life.[7] With grants of land from the Crown, they introduced innovative architecture. The general appearance of the town was improved, with stricter laws enacted and enforced. An informal Police Force was begun, using Justices of the Peace, volunteer patrols and night guards. The Loyalists infiltrated the political process and impacted government thinking. An energetic people, they were determined to dominate their new environment and remake their fortunes. With the influx of professionals, such as doctors, lawyers, accountants and merchants, the commercial life was boosted. They opened up avenues of cultural enrichment, including a lending library, guest houses and the first newspaper; however, racial barriers were clearly established.[8] They, thus, set the environment for an embryonic tourism industry.

The ***Bahama Gazette,*** first published on 7th August, 1784 by John Wells, a Loyalist from Charleston who migrated to Nassau, was the original Bahamian newspaper, and this was followed in 1804 by the *Royal Gazette and Bahamian Advertiser*. However, these newspapers were devoted mainly to American and English contributions, advertising and other foreign works; Bahamian news was sparse[9]. The *Argus*, an anti-Government and anti-emancipation paper, was published for a few years beginning in 1831.[10]

The longest surviving newspaper in the country, the ***Nassau Guardian****,* first appeared on 23rd November, 1844. Its founder and first editor was Edwin Charles Moseley, who came to The Bahamas from England in 1837 at the request of Governor Sir William Colebrook as an apprentice to the editor of the *Argus*. While the Guardian in its early years was often attacked for lack of support of the masses or for libel, it has always played a pivotal role as a communications paper for the local tourism industry. In early issues of the ***Nassau Guardian and Colonial Advertiser***, advertisements were published listing private residents who were offering their homes as guest accommodations:

> *Victoria House*
> *West Hill Street*
> *By Nathaniel French*
> *Where Gentlemen and Ladies can be accommodated*
> *with Board and Lodging by the day, week or month.*
> *This house is located on one of the pleasantest and most healthy*
> *situations of the town, and its accommodations are adapted as well*
> *for families or for single persons*
> *Nassau, 29th November, 1844*

The name Victoria House was later changed to French's Hotel. Five years later, in 1849, Nathaniel French was offering transportation, meals and drinks along with upgraded accommodations at "French's Hotel", as indicated in a second advertisement for this boarding house in the ***Nassau Guardian****:*

FRENCH'S HOTEL
WEST HILL STREET
Near Government House

The undersigned respectfully informs the Public that he is now prepared to accommodate a number of boarders.

From his long experience in the business and the superior location of the house, he can offer to strangers and invalids accommodations unsurpassed in The Bahamas.

A carriage is kept which will be hired to boarders at reduced rates.

Breakfasts, luncheons, Dinner, or supper provided for any number on a short notice being given. Best Porter, Ale, Wine

N. French
Nassau, 28th November, 1849[11]

Today, French's Hotel is **Graycliff**, one of Nassau's charming and historic inns, recognized among the finest restaurants and wine cellars in the Caribbean. The beautiful mansion was reportedly built in the 1720's by a famous privateer, Captain John Howard Graysmith, who commanded the notorious schooner Graywolf. He is said to have earned his fortune pillaging treasure ships and attacking the enemy along the Spanish Main.

Graycliff, formerly Victoria House and French's

The **Nassau Guardian** periodically displayed advertisements of other persons interested in entering the hotel business:

HOTEL

Mrs. Thorne respectfully informs her friends and the public that she has taken those commodious premises in George Street, two doors south of Christ Church, where she intends carrying out a Hotel and Boarding House.

Mrs. T. trusts that her long experiences in the above line combined with strict attention to the comforts of her boarders will ensure for her a share of the public patronage.

Dinners, Suppers, Breakfasts, and Luncheons provided
on the **shortest notices and most reasonable terms.**
Nassau, 8ᵗʰ March, 1851

The ***Nassau Guardian*** took on the task of keeping the nation, and the tourism industry informed. The Guardian's editor, calling for expanded tourism, wrote that the trade and prosperity of The Bahamas could only be realized by establishing steam connections with the outside world and providing adequate facilities for attracting visitors in search of health tourism. He called for the construction of a hotel which would accommodate at least 500 invalids annually. Some of the leading Bay Street merchants opposed the idea.

Early Tourism Encouragement Acts and First Hotels

Recognizing market developments, efforts were made by the Bahamas Government to encourage the tourism trade through incentives for transatlantic service providers. Acts were passed by the colonial legislature in 1851 offering, for a term of five years, an annual fee of £1,000 to any person or company that would contract to "ply a good, substantial and efficient steam vessel (wood or iron) between the port of Nassau and New York."[12] The act was advertised in both Britain and America, but the subsidy was not considered attractive, and there were few takers. The first ship to attempt the voyage was the S.S. Jewess, which sailed from New York into disaster. It arrived at Nassau on 20ᵗʰ May, 1851, burned to the waterline.

It was not until the annual fee was raised to £3,000 in 1859 that a Canadian, Samuel Cunard, famous for his transatlantic fleet, agreed to take up the challenge. His contract called for monthly mail and passenger service from New York to Nassau and Havana, Cuba, calling again at Nassau on the return voyage. In November 1859, the old paddle-wheeler, S.S. Corsica, made the first of her hundreds of voyages, being replaced shortly after by the Karnak. The journey took three to five days, depending on the weather, and cost US$50 from New York to Nassau and $95 for the return trip.[13]

The First Major Hotel—The Royal Victoria

Encouraged by their success in attracting transatlantic cruise service, the Bahamas legislature passed an act "for securing the creation of an hotel on the island of New Providence". On 11ᵗʰ May, 1859, Governor Charles J. Bayley ordered the public advertisement of tenders for a proper hotel site. The tender of Timothy Darling, a Canadian businessman, who doubled as American Consul, was accepted—US$2,500 for premises located on high ground overlooking the harbour. This was a reasonable figure in those days of underdeveloped land values. Mr. Darling was paid in Treasury debentures bearing 5% interest. When efforts to raise the necessary capital for construction were unsuccessful, the Legislature assumed all responsibility and floated a loan of US$6,000—a sum which was grossly insufficient, since it had been decided that this hotel would be as elaborate and luxurious as possible. Ultimately, the cost came to £25,000 (approximately US$130,000), a big outlay in those days. Three of the four floors of the hotel were surrounded by wide piazzas, and among its advertised attractions were three promenades of 1,000 feet. In addition to the dining room, there was a restaurant on the ground floor. Over the porte-cochere was the "Gentlemen's Parlour", and on the eastern end was the "Ladies Parlour". At the end of a long bridge stretching to East Hill Street were a few "large fresh water bathrooms"[14]. Also, prospective visitors were told that "the sea bathing is very fine".

Named the Royal Victoria Hotel, after England's illustrious queen in the 30th year of her reign, the hotel (commonly called the Royal Vic) was described as "the largest and most commodious ever built in the tropics . . . a building which has few rivals in our country out of the big cities"[15]. The hotel was first leased by the Government to Mr. John S. Howell, of New York, and later it was managed by Mr. G.O. Johnson under a Board of Commissioners. The Board included the Governor, the Bishop, Mr. E.C. Moseley, Mr. H.E. Kemp, Mr. G.D. Harris and Mr. R.E. Rigby.

Royal Victoria Hotel, The Bahamas' first hotel, in the 1860's

The courtyard of the Royal Victoria Hotel

This hotel was designed to accommodate winter visitors from the snowbound northern states, but in light of the events about to enfold, had it relied solely upon these, it would very quickly have become bankrupt. By the time this hotel was completed in August 1861, Civil War was raging in the United States. The dream of a tourist market to fill the hotel seemed remote. As Nassau became the staging base for the running of supplies to the Confederacy in the Civil War, this new hotel became the headquarters of the colourful blockade-runners of the South. This hotel was strategically located to handle the influx and became a beehive of activity and the scene of nightly parties.

A special feature of the Royal Victoria was its world-famous tropical gardens, with over 200 species of exotic plants, and trees; their focal point was a huge silk cotton tree. As Villard described it: "To wander through the pebbly bypaths of this opulent outdoor green house was an unforgettable experience: from the flaming bougainvillea to the night-blooming Cereus, from Malaya's fish tail palm to the Spanish bayonet, from the South Sea Islands' bread fruit tree to the sapodilla of Yucatan, not to mention scores of other priceless botanical specimens, the display was marvelous to behold. Overhead, a lattice-work of interweaving Royal and coconut palms kept off the burning sun"[16].

The court in front of the entrance of the hotel was a favourite spot, as vendors of fruit, baskets, flowers, shell-work, sponges, and marine curios held their morning bazaar there and the boatmen came to arrange sailing and fishing expeditions. Donkey races provided much amusement for guests in the afternoons.

After changing hands several times, and on the condition that they "keep a first-class hotel", a 20-year lease on the Royal Vic was granted in 1871 to two Americans, one of whom was Lewis Cleveland, brother of Grover Cleveland, future President of the United States. Cleveland had pledged that "the subscriber will spare neither pains nor expense in his efforts to give entire satisfaction to those who, either from necessity or fancy, may choose to spend a winter in the tropics."[17] Tragically, Lewis Cleveland died the next year on his way to Nassau via cruise ship to take over the management of that hotel when the Atlantic Steamship Company's liner *Missouri* on the way from New York to Nassau caught fire off the island of Abaco. Also losing their lives during this tragedy were 84 of the 96 passengers.

From 1879 to 1898, Mr. J.M. Morton and his son, S.S. Morton of New York, leased and managed the Royal Victoria. During the Morton regime, the hotel was reportedly well managed. Among the numerous festive events hosted by the hotel was George Washington's Birthday Ball in February of each year.

Henry Flagler

In 1898, Henry M. Flagler, a wealthy oil magnate, hotel developer and pioneer developer of Florida's East Coast Railway, which would form a permanent land link to the vast northeastern tourism market, appeared on the Nassau scene. He saw great investment potential in the nearby islands of The Bahamas. The Bahamas legislature passed a new important "Hotel and Steamship Act" in 1898. Governor William

Haynes Smith negotiated a 10-year contract with Flagler, who agreed to provide a regular steamship service with the Florida coast and to purchase the Royal Victoria Hotel for £10,000, as well as the site of old Fort Nassau to build a hotel. Construction began on the new hotel in 1899, which was named the Hotel Colonial.[18] Henry Flagler modernized the Royal Vic, bringing it up to the standard of his other properties such as the Royal Poinciana and The Breakers in Palm Beach and the Royal Palm in Miami, Florida.

He renovated both the interior and exterior of the hotel and installed electricity, thus beginning the Royal Vic's development as a fashionable winter spot. Under Flagler, the hotel took on the aura of another Palm Beach, Florida, attracting wealthy visitors escaping

In 1899, Henry Flagler began construction of the Hotel Colonial, which opened in 1900

the harsh winters of North America and Europe. Relatively sedate, polite and dignified clientele now occupied the hotel. "It was a homelike leisurely atmosphere, in which a carriage drive was the most strenuous activity of the day".[19]

Telegraphic Communication—Cable Beach Acquires its Name

Under the governorship of Sir Ambrose Shea, telegraphic services were inaugurated. In 1891, Governor Shea and certain members of Parliament, recognizing "the serious political and economic disadvantages the Bahama Islands faced because of its isolated position" authorized negotiations with the Chairman of W.J. Henley's Telegraph Works Company of London, England. After several delays, in February 1892, the Henley Company successfully laid the cable connecting the Jupiter Inlet in Florida to New Providence. The Bahamas' end of the cable came ashore at Goodman's Bay and the area became known as Cable Beach. The 6th February, 1892 edition of the *Nassau Guardian* reported that the first person in the city to receive a cablegram through Bahamas Telegraph Cable was Mr. S. S. Morton, proprietor of the Royal Victoria Hotel. The message was from Tampa, Florida.[20]

Tourism vs. Other Industries

During the last quarter of the 19th century, The Bahamas experienced a deep depression. As Michael Craton reported, "Poverty was endemic throughout the islands from 1865 onwards. No settlement or class escaped the plight. It is even possible that the merchants suffered most, for theirs was the greatest fall and they had none of the cheerful resilience of those to whom bare subsistence was the norm. Nassau was drained of capital, energy and hope." [21]

Saltmaking had been an industry since the Eleutheran Adventurers, with the first salt production reportedly taking place on Eleuthera, near Preacher's Cave, and later on Exuma[22]. Before refrigeration, salt was a precious substance, essential for the preservation of meat and fish. By 1859 the "Heneagua" Salt Pond Company was formed to develop the salt industry in a big way[23]. Extensive pans were created and the industry flourished until after the American Civil War when North American competition and protective tariffs resulted in declining profits and the death of the industry.

Other products used for trade were Bahamian woods, such as mastic, madeira, mahogany and cedar, shipped to England and North America for use in building houses and ships as well as furniture making. It was believed that some of the English ships which fought at Trafalgar were partly constructed of Bahamian timber. Also prized were lesser known hardwoods like ebony, machinella and dogwood, in demand for the manufacture of small cabinets and curios, as well as logwood and braziletto exported for use in the dyeing of cloth and wild cinnamon bark shipped to Curacao for distilling of cinnamon waters.[24]

Turtle, turtle shell, fruits in season, straw work and shell-work were produced and exported in varying amounts. Some of the handicraft and products were displayed at world exhibitions. Conch shell had experienced a brief period of importance when it was exported to France and Italy for the making of brooches, until new fashions came on the scene. The value of exports of conch shell had risen from £790 in 1855 to £2,400 in 1856 and £6,351 in 1857. There is also record of canning of fruits by J. S. Johnson factory as far back as 1876.

The Bahamas became the first commercial producers of pineapples. The first cargo of Bahamian pineapples, considered superior to those produced

Tortoise Shell pins, Earrings and bracelets in Tropical fish from $1.40 up, also a complete line of Tortoise shell souvenirs starting at .64c at Johnson Bros., Bay Street (East of Post Office).

Turtle shell products were among the popular exports in the 19th century (Source: Bahamas Magazine)

in other countries, was exported to the United States in 1842 and the first canning factory was opened in 1857.[25] The best year for Bahamian pineapples was recorded in 1892 when 700,000 dozen were exported for a value of nearly £60,000. Because of the prominence of the pineapple as an industry, the first local postal stamp in 1859 incorporated a photograph of a pineapple prominently in its design along with a conch shell and in fact the original engraving submitted from Nassau implied that a portrait of the fruit should replace the traditional head of Queen Victoria. Also, large-scale production of sisal began in 1887 with 400 tons exported annually by 1899 and 1,000 tons valued at £37,574 produced by 1902. The sponge industry also flourished. The large fleet of small boats formerly used for rum-running now became carriers of a legal freight of sponges. The new cash flowed into the hands of a small and powerful clique, which became known as the Bay Street Merchants[26] until sponge beds were destroyed by a fungoid in 1938.

Despite these few successes, with the lack of minerals, industrial raw materials, productive soil, water, and cheap power, it became clear that The Bahamas could not turn to increased farming or industrialization to solve its economic needs.

With the short-lived success of other industries, Governor William Robinson (who served from 1874-80) suggested that The Bahamas make an effort to divert some of the 100,000 tourists who were travelling annually to Florida. His vision was not realized until the next century. In fact, very few people shared his view that tourism was capable of much growth. The best tourism year in the pre-20th century tourism was 1873, when Nassau welcomed 500 visitors.[27] The major impediment to tourism development was the absence of reliable transportation. The coal-burning wooden hull steam vessels which sailed out of New York were plagued with misfortune; five were lost before 1895.

First Royal Visitor to the "City of Nassau"

In 1861, Nassau welcomed its first royal visitor, Prince Alfred, son of Queen Victoria, who arrived on 3rd December aboard the H.M.S. St. George, in which he was serving as midshipman. Earlier that year, Queen Victoria had bestowed an important honour upon the town of Nassau when she issued "Letters of Patent" constituting historic Christ Church Cathedral, and ordained that "the whole town of Nassau henceforth be called The *City of Nassau*".[28]

Slavery Abolished

Although the Loyalist period resulted in a large influx of slaves with their masters, because of the failure of the plantation system, these slaves hardly suffered the rigours of the field hands in the West Indies. While there was limited demand for slaves for small farms, slaves worked more as domestic servants, or were put to work producing salt, as construction labourers, or were sent to sea on wrecking and privateering vessels.

In the rest of the region, slaves were looked upon as valuable booty, and, when brought to Nassau, were either sold to trading vessels from abroad or to local residents[29]. Vendue House, now an important historic landmark and tourist attraction, *Pompey Museum*, was the site where slaves, animals and produce were traded. The slave trade ceased in 1807 when the last arrivals were recorded. There was yet another group of Negroes, those brought to The Bahamas from slave ships captured at sea. The total number of these "free Negroes", also known as Liberated Africans, who landed between 1808 and 1860 was estimated at 6,000. Governor Sir James Carmichael Smith conceived the idea

Vendue House on Bay Street where slaves and cattle were auctioned (now Pompey Museum)

of using ungranted Crown land for settling these blacks, who were technically free, but incapable of looking after themselves in a strange land. On New Providence, the villages of Adelaide, Carmichael and Headquarters (now Grant's Town) were established for this purpose.[30]

The Abolition Act was passed in 1834. With the final emancipation of slavery in 1838, the destiny of The Bahamas now lay in the hands of free men—former masters, slaves, Eleutheran Adventurers, Loyalists, free blacks and other "belongers".

Hospitable Nature of Bahamians and Attitude to Work

It has been suggested by many that the hospitable nature of black Bahamians, as compared to blacks in other parts of the region, is directly related to the treatment of slaves. Writers have suggested that in large West Indian plantations, there were paid overseers with long whips who meted out severe punishment to slaves. In The Bahamas, by contrast, without a large plantation system, the slaves suffered less cruel treatment. Even where plantations did exist, each plantation slave family had its own plot of land to grow vegetables and fruit for home use. Deprivation was rare and starvation unknown.

Dr. Gail Saunders, in her book *Slavery in The Bahamas*, gave a much more comprehensive account of slave conditions, attitudes and work ethics in The

Bahamas. She pointed out that slaves in The Bahamas lived in organized family units, with an occurrence of a nuclear family twice as high as in other islands such as Jamaica[31]. Confirming earlier reports of diminished importance of plantation systems, she lists the varied occupations of slaves in The Bahamas in 1834: domestics, field labourers, mariners, salt labourers, drivers/overseers, nurses/midwives, trade/craftsmen, and sundry/unknown.[32] Bahamian slaves at Emancipation were generally healthy, which was attributed to temperate climate, favourable living and working conditions, reasonably good diet (an abundance of fish and conch), and the absence of endemic disease.[33]

While earlier writers suggest that punishments inflicted on slaves were generally mild, Dr. Saunders revealed that there is much evidence of extreme cruelty and brutality. For example, a slave in The Bahamas in 1784 could suffer death for burglary and rape. He would be whipped if caught selling spirituous liquor or playing dice; for striking a white person, he was subject to whipping, mutilation and even death.[34] There is evidence of isolated collective resistance in the form of slave revolts immediately prior to Emancipation. While the incidence of such revolts in The Bahamas were smaller and less frequent than those recorded in other West Indian islands, Saunders' points out that slaves showed resentment to their lot through individual and collective violence. They also engaged in passive resistance, which included refusal to work, general inefficiency, deliberate laziness, running away, and suicide.[35]

Further insight into the demeanour and culture of the working class during slavery has also been supplied by Clement Bethel, cultural composer and musical director. They entertained themselves at the end of the workday with music, dance, storytelling, games, and African cooking. Clement Bethel, in his study of Bahamian music, pointed out that the most popular form of recreation for the slaves was the ring dance. Three distinctly different types of ring dance were identified—the Fire Dance, Jumping Dance, and Ring Play—all with some type of rhythmic accompaniment such as chanting, clapping and/or drum rhythms. These forms of entertainment were used later in floor shows at local night clubs. The fusion of African and European traditions produced the Quadrille Dance performed by masters as well as slaves. Writings throughout the 19th century describe the real spirit of Bahamians, as celebrated particularly at Christmastime in the form of "rushing", now known as *Junkanoo*. The 1888 text *Land of the Pink Pearl* described various groups of Africans in The Bahamas "marching about (at Christmas) with lanterns and bands of music".[36]

James Stephen, a staunch abolitionist, while noting benefits afforded Bahamian slaves compared to their less fortunate West Indian counterparts, reflected, quite sadly, that they were nevertheless deprived of the infinitely greater benefit, "and the hope of all—Freedom". This, he said, was the crux of the matter. Good treatment of slaves was commendable, but insignificant compared to the immense evil of the system itself.

*　　*　　*

Whatever the reason for their good nature, what is certain is that the people of The Bahamas possessed natural warmth and charm—an important ingredient for the success of the tourism industry about to be exploited.

4

CREATING THE FOUNDATION FOR A BURGEONING TOURISM INDUSTRY 1900-38

External Developments Impacting Bahamas Tourism

As the 20th century unfolded, leisure travel was still the domain of a small upper class segment of global society. In the absence of infrastructure and modern modes of transportation, the travel experience was expensive, time-consuming, adventuresome and, generally, exclusive of women and children.

With technological advances, in particular the automobile and aeroplane, and modernization of the lodging and cruise ship industry, travel became more accessible and attractive to a larger number of people.

The **automobile** revolutionized domestic travel. The large scale production of cars was pioneered by the Olds Motor Vehicle Company, which had established a factory in Detroit in 1899, and the Ford Motor Company. In 1901, the Olds Motor Company produced 425 cars, and, by 1912, the Ford Motor Company, considered to be the founder of modern automobile mass production, built 75,000 identical *Model T* automobiles. Other car manufacturers adopted Ford's methods of mass-produced, standardized automobiles, resulting in large numbers of cars available at lower costs. By 1904, the first automobile was imported into The Bahamas. The increase in road travel prompted improvement of roads and growth in roadside businesses, such as drive-in theatres, restaurants, shops and motels all over the world.

Aviation History and the Birth of the "Big Four" US Airlines

Of particular importance to offshore destinations like The Bahamas was the birth of the aviation industry, which accelerated growth of overseas holiday and business travel. On 17th December, 1903, after the Wright brothers launched the aviation age by flying the first power-controlled flights, research began all over the world to improve that original, primitive airplane. By 1909, Louis Blériot of France became the first person to fly a plane across the English Channel. World War I brought many improvements to aviation, as governments took a serious interest in aviation development programmes. At the beginning of the war, most planes flew at about

60 m.p.h. but, at war's end, fighter planes could travel more than twice as fast, as engines five times as powerful were in operation.

With the surplus of planes after World War I, thousands of military planes were converted to civilian use, and formed small new airlines. The first regular international airline service was started by Henry and Maurice Farman, who used old Farman bombers to make weekly flights between Paris and Brussels. By 1917, there were 17 regularly operating airlines in Europe, Africa, Australia, and South America. Some airlines from that era still operating included: Royal Dutch Airlines (KLM), SABENA World Airlines, Lufthansa, and Qantas. In the 1920's, American aviation was slow. The few small airlines often failed after only a few months of service. Air travel was viewed generally as a dangerous sport, not a safe means of transportation. [1] Later in the 1920's, governments started to form national airlines by combining a few private airlines. One such case was Imperial Airways, formed by the British government. An incentive for development of a domestic airline industry in the United States was offered, starting in 1917, when the US Post Office was granted $100,000 to start an experimental airmail service. The US Army filled the gap until the new airlines could come online. At this time, carrying passengers was unprofitable, and the only sustained passenger airline in the United States before the new mail airlines came into being in 1926 was Aeromaritime Airways, which became the USA's first holiday passenger airline. Aeromaritime had begun flying people from Miami, Florida to Havana, Cuba and to **Nassau**, often so that the passengers could avoid the Prohibition. Eventually, these routes were used by holidaymakers, with the airline concentrating on Nassau, Bahamas. The 185-mile trip was US$85 dollars by Aeromaritime's flyingboats—more than three times the cost of the journey by ship.[2]

Meanwhile, an amphibian airline, **Chalk's Flying Service**, the world's oldest scheduled airline, was founded in 1919 by Arthur B. "Pappy" Chalk, an automobile mechanic in Paducah, Kentucky. Mr. Chalk had been introduced in 1911 to the noted aviation pioneer and seaplane pilot, Tony Janus, who subsequently gave Mr. Chalk flying lessons in exchange for repairs on his aircraft. Mr. Chalk later took up residence in Miami in 1917. Following military service in the Air Corps during World War I, Mr. Chalk began airline operations. During Prohibition, rum-running became a lucrative

1919 Chalk's Flying Service (Courtesy: Paul Aranha)

business for this airline. It introduced scheduled service to **Bimini, Bahamas** in 1919. As business grew, his company built a terminal in 1926 on a newly created landfill named Watson Island, adjacent to what later became the Port of Miami. Mr. Chalk also used the versatility of the seaplanes to assist in search and rescue efforts after the devastating Hurricane of 1926.[3]

The first major legislative step toward the creation of a private US airline industry was the 1925 Contract Air Mail Act, commonly referred to as the Kelly Act, after its chief sponsor, Rep. Clyde Kelly of Pennsylvania. Winners of the initial five contracts were National Air Transport, Varney Air Lines, Western Air Express, Colonial Air Transport, and Robertson Aircraft Corporation.[4] In 1926, airlines in the US carried 6,000 passengers. Ten different aircraft types were initially in use by 12 original mail carriers and these were the Stout 2AT, Swallow biplane, D.H. 4, Douglas M-2, Curtiss mail plane, Pitcairn, Fokker Universal, Ryan M-1, Stinson and Waco.

The Third Amendment of the Air Mail Act 1925 (called the Watres Act), passed in April 1930, resulted in mergers of smaller airlines to form larger, more stable airlines. During the mid to late 1920's, mergers and buyouts left the US airline industry with the **'big four' domestic airlines: Transcontinental & Western Air—TWA** (from a forced merger by Transcontinental Air Transport and Western Air Express—later renamed Trans World Airlines), **United Air Lines** (originally a joint venture of Boeing Airplane Company and Pratt & Witney which merged with Varney and National Air), **Eastern Airlines** (formerly Eastern Air Transport and Pitcairn Aviation), and **American Airlines,** formerly American Airways (formed out of a merger between Standard Air Lines, Southern Air Transport, Robertson Aircraft Corporation, Universal Aviation, Colonial Western).

Juan Trippe, one of the original partners in Colonial Air Transport, would later pioneer international air travel with **Pan American Airways "Pan Am"**—a carrier he founded in 1927 to transport mail between Key West, Florida, and Havana, Cuba. Pan Am grew to become America's largest international airline opening up routes across the Pacific and dominating Latin America.[5]

By 1930, the airline industry had shown tremendous growth, with 43 airlines operating a fleet of 500 aircraft domestically in the USA, and carrying 400,000 passengers.

Among those carriers was **Delta**, one of the world's oldest airlines, which began as Delta Air Services in 1928, was sold and renamed Delta Air Corporation in 1930, and took its current name in 1945.[6] Delta, like Pan Am, was later to play a significant role in Bahamas tourism.

For airlines to attract passengers away from railroads, they needed larger, faster and safer airplanes. Accidents, such as the one in 1931 that killed seven men, including Knute Rockne, a Notre Dame football coach, discouraged travel by air.[7] Aircraft manufacturers responded to the safety challenge. There were so many improvements to aircraft in the 1930's that many suggest it was the most innovative period in aviation history. Engines and cockpit instruments were improved, reducing weight and making bigger, faster and safer planes possible.

Meanwhile, in Canada, Trans-Canada Airlines, the national airline of Canada, which was subsequently renamed *Air Canada*, began operations on 1st September, 1937. In December 1948, Air Canada, operated its first flight to The Bahamas.

Cruise Ship Reform following the *Titanic* disaster

Advancement in the design and capacity of **oceanic liners** also took place during this period. One of the largest, fastest and most luxurious ocean liners was the *RMS Titanic*, designed by the Irish shipbuilder, William Pirrie, and built in Belfast in 1912. It spanned 883 feet from stern to bow, and its hull was divided into 16 compartments that were presumed to be watertight. Because four of these compartments could be flooded without causing a critical loss of buoyancy, the Titanic was considered unsinkable. On 10th March, 1912, the Titanic departed Southampton, England, on its maiden voyage across the Atlantic Ocean, carrying some 2,200 passengers and crew. The travel industry recorded one of its worst maritime disasters in history when, at 2:20 a.m. on 15th April, 1912, the Titanic sank into the North Atlantic Ocean about 400 miles south of Newfoundland, Canada. The massive ship (46,000 gross tons) had struck an iceberg two and one-half hours before. About 1,513 of the passengers died. Subsequent investigations found that the ship had been steaming too fast in dangerous waters, lifeboat space had been provided for only about half of the passengers and crew, and the *Californian,* close to the scene, had not come to the rescue because its radio operator was off duty and asleep. These findings led to many reforms in the cruise and maritime industry, such as lifeboat space for every person on a ship, lifeboat drills, the maintenance of a full-time radio watch while at sea, and an international ice patrol.

The Hotel Sector before the Great Depression

The United States **lodging industry** developed rapidly and increased in sophistication to keep pace with travel demand, which was confined primarily to domestic travel until the 1930's. In 1900, the typical first-class hotel in the United States offered steam heat, electric call bells, baths and closets on all floors, billiard room, barbershops and liveries. In 1908, the Hotel Statler chain began in Buffalo, with private baths in guestrooms, telephones and built-in radios, serving as the model for hotel construction for the next 40 years. In 1910, when the number of hotels in the USA had reached 10,000, with a total of one million rooms, the American Hotel Protective Association was founded in Chicago; the name was changed to the American Hotel Association of the United States and Canada in 1917. The first Hilton hotel was established in 1919 and Western Hotels, with 17 hotels in the Pacific Northwest, established the first US hotel management company in 1929.

The first roadside "motel" opened in California for $2.50 per night in the 1920's; and the first collegiate programme in hotel and restaurant management was initiated at Cornell University by the American Hotel Association in 1922. By 1933, hotel construction came to a halt with the Great Depression and the lodging industry recorded the lowest average occupancy rate (51%) on record. Many hotels, finding it impossible to survive, went into receivership.[8]

Evolution of Travel Agencies, Tour Operators and the World Tourism Organization

The establishment of travel agencies and tour operators was a direct response to expanding needs of the consumer in making travel plans. In the 1800's and early 1900's, the porters in motels acted as travel agents of their day. If a businessman wanted a railroad ticket, he would be directed to the porter who would go to the railroad station, purchase the ticket, or make the reservation. The railroad paid the porter a commission, and a delivery service charge was also added.

In 1909, American Express, already prominent for shipping, freight and banking services, entered the travel market, initially as an agent for rail and steamship travel and later as a tour operator. Others followed. An interesting story is printed in the brochure of *Ask Mr. Foster,* a prominent US travel agent:

> *Yes, there was a Mr. Foster in the 1880's. Ward G. Foster operated a gift shop in St. Augustine, Florida, near the fashionable Ponce de Leon Hotel. His business was gifts, but his hobby was travel—studying maps, railway timetables and hotel circulars. Since he was so well versed on travel, he was often called upon to assist tourists. It became standard practice for the hotel staff to tell their guests, "Go across the street and ask Mr. Foster; he probably knows". Dispensing information to visitors became more demanding than the gift business so he opened a new office and over the door hung the sign, "Ask Mr. Foster".*

Likewise, in the United Kingdom, Thomas Cook, born in 1808, had been coordinating transport for hundreds of passengers for many years in his role as a Baptist Missionary before officially becoming one of the first full-time travel agents in 1845.

As tourism and travel grew in importance, there was an international need for standardization of terms, training, and dissemination of information and statistics. A global tourism organization—the *International Union of Official Travel Organizations* (IUOTO)—came into existence in 1925 to serve as the coordinating body on all aspects of tourism and later as advisor to the United Nations on tourism. IUOTO assisted in standardizing tourism statistical terms so that global measurement was possible. It also served as a data bank on tourism matters and provided technical assistance and information to countries and organizations. In 1975, IUOTO was reconstituted as an inter-governmental organization called the *World Tourism Organization (UNWTO)*.

US Prohibition (1920-33)—A period of Prosperity in The Bahamas

World War I ended in November 1918 and, in December 1919, the US Congress passed the Volstead Act, making it a crime to manufacture, import or sell intoxicating liquors anywhere in the United States. This law created a period of "Prohibition", which had a positive effect on Bahamas tourism for 12 years, until Franklin D. Roosevelt, after a landslide victory in the US polls in 1932, repealed the ban on alcohol.[9]

US Prohibition turned out to be a blessing for Bahamas tourism. Between 1921 and 1933, the flourishing "rum-running" era was reminiscent of the blockade-runners of earlier years. Since the importation and re-export of liquor, which was banned in the United States, was legal in The Bahamas, the Colony became a haven for rumrunners and wealthy Americans. Enormous fortunes were made by white Bahamian merchants. The Bahamian Treasury overflowed with revenue derived from duties imposed on goods.

Nassau's harbour was packed with boats which took part in the illegal trade. West End, Grand Bahama and the island of Bimini were also important bases for the rum-running industry. **Chalk's Flying Service** played an important role in amphibious transportation between Florida and the Colony during the tourism boom.

The Royal Victoria Hotel, which was being managed by Mrs. Frank Munson since 1910, was the centre of the flourishing business during the bootlegging period. Journalist, Henry S. Villard, captured the romance of the hotel at that time: "I first saw the fabulous structure one flamingo-pink evening back in the Roaring Twenties . . . For me, as for most tourists, it was love at first sight. There she was, mellow and gracious in the gathering twilight, majestic, lofty palms, and a tremendous silk cotton tree making purple shadows in the tropical shrubbery, with the lyrical, calypso-style music of Blind Blake and his minstrels floating on the soft, seductive air: 'Mama don't want no peas no rice . . . all she wants is brandy handy all the time' . . . Victorian she was, and royal too; but with her yellow paint and white trim, her pillars and arches and long verandahs, she exuded something else besides—a combination of old world atmosphere an intimate warm, beguiling charm. What expressed this in particular was her friendly, columned, high-ceilinged lobby with its fine sweeping staircase; hotels, like their distinguished clients, can have personality and character too. To come upon the inviting open-air terrace at the edge of the lush garden, under winking stars and waving palms, was like entering a land of mystery and magic: it had no counterpart that I knew. Gleaming white tables and chairs and green striped umbrellas beckoned, while from the wide-flung doors of the bar the sound of cocktail shakers was like castanets."[10]

Royal Vic hosted some of the most memorable social gatherings in the Colony's history. The two sons of the Right Honourable Joseph Chamberlain—Austen and Neville—were entertained at a ball there when they visited in the early 1890's to

select a large acreage on the Family Islands for their father's sisal plantation which
Mr. Neville Chamberlain, who ultimately became Britain's Prime Minister, managed
on Andros for seven years. Dinners in honour of the late Viscount Burnham,
Sir Winston Churchill and other members of Parliament have been among the
memorable functions held there.[11]

Additional hotel rooms were needed to house the large number of liquor buyers
during the Bootlegging era.

Early Hotel Construction in The Bahamas

To stimulate the construction of other new hotels, the **Manufactories and Hotels
Encouragement Act** was passed in 1913. This act made it possible for hotels to receive
exemptions from import duties on materials and furniture for "building, erection,
alteration or repair of hotels". To qualify, hotel owners with sufficient capacity to
accommodate 50 guests were required to register their hotel with the Treasury, keep a
Stock Book, make a declaration that the articles were to be used solely for the purposes
stated, and enter into a bond with two sureties in double the amount of any customs
duties which would ordinarily apply on importation of such items.

To meet the increased demand for hotel rooms, construction began on Nassau's
second large hotel, the **Hotel Colonial**, which opened its doors at the turn of the
century in 1900. With 400 opulent suites designed for upscale tourists who could
afford to spend winters in exotic destinations, Henry Flagler had realized his vision of
a hotel which would be the ultimate in luxury. Flagler had built other luxury hotels
along the Eastern seaboard and had launched a steamship service linking Miami
and Nassau, and also built The Bahamas' first golf course on the grounds of Fort
Charlotte. Because of the absence of reliable transportation and wartime restrictions,
this hotel never flourished, although there was a brief period of prosperity during
the 1915 season. It was saved from bankruptcy when it was destroyed by fire on 31st
March, 1921.

Meanwhile, **Bimini**,
the Bahamian island
closest to Miami, enjoyed
a brief period of tourism
prosperity. Thomas
J. Peters, a successful
Floridian tomato grower
and real estate agent,
having noted the potential
of Bimini as a liquor base
and tourist destination,
persuaded friends from
the Miami Anglers' Club

Hotel Colonial destroyed by fire in March 1921

and other wealthy Americans to become shareholders in the development of a large luxurious hotel, the ***Bimini Bay Rod and Gun Club***. They leased land in Alice Town, North Bimini, and built the three-storey 100-room private club. No expenses were spared in developing a complete resort with beautiful ballroom, casino, restaurants, tennis courts, ice-making plant, water filtering facility, et cetera.

BIMINI BAY ROD AND GUN CLUB, FORTY-FIVE MILES EAST OF MIAMI. EXECUTIVE OFFICE, MIAMI, FLA.

Bimini Bay Rod and Gun Club, North Bimini (Courtesy: Paul Aranha)

Bimini Bay Rod and Gun Club (Courtesy: Julian Brown)

An article in the *Miami Daily Metropolis* suggested possible motives of these investors:

> One of the chief objects of the plan is to make it convenient for people at local hotels to get to a bar without transferring their winter residences to Cuba. The local hotel and apartment house contingent rather fear that Havana is going to make a much stronger competitor for Florida resorts now that the United States is dry, and they want to head off the impending rush to the 'pearl of the Antilles' by enhancing the attractiveness of the British isle nearest offshore.

A lavish grand opening took place on 11th December, 1920. Among the invited dignitaries from Nassau and Florida were the Colonial Secretary and Governor of the Colony and the mayors of Miami, West Palm Beach and Palm Beach, Florida. Estimates to build the Club ranged from $80,000-$125,000 ($1.5-$2.4 million in today's dollars).[12]

Despite the luxurious building, and the money invested, there were various problems which needed to be addressed to make the Bimini hotel venture successful: First, the size of the boats which could enter the protected harbour was restricted, because there was a need to deepen the channel from 9 to 16 feet. Secondly, there was an abundance of mosquitoes and sand flies. The most difficult issue related to access to the resort. To fill the 100 rooms, travel to Bimini would need to be inexpensive, comfortable, and reliable. Several ships were bought and run by the Club while others were operated by independent companies. However, in 1920, the combined capacity of the two most advertised ships was only 50 passengers. Also, during inclement weather travel by sea was uncomfortable. Van Campen Heilner, an Associate Editor of *Field and Stream* magazine, who lived on Bimini for a period during the 1920's, wrote in his book *Salt Water Fishing*: "Those that came to the Rod and Gun Club were so seasick after several hours of crossing the Gulf Stream that they immediately went to bed to recuperate and when they got up it was time to go home".

Seaplanes became an alternate means of transportation. When Thomas J. Peters made one of the first commercial flights to Bimini on 3rd December, 1919, the *Miami Herald* noted that this was "the first time that the local customs and immigration officers had been asked to officiate in the clearing of a flying machine from a foreign port". Chalk's airline also began scheduled seaplane flights to Bimini from Miami in 1919. The Bimini Bay Rod and Gun Club, which employed about 50 persons during the peak season, was ahead of its time. Its brief period of success can be attributed to rum-running during Prohibition. It converted to a regular hotel around 1923, catering to all types of visitors and not just the wealthy. Because it never realized a profit, the hotel closed in September 1925 and was destroyed in the 1926 and 1929 hurricanes.[13]

The Rozelda Hotel, Nassau's first apartment hotel, built by Roland Symonette in 1920 which later became the Carlton House (Courtesy: Ronald Lightbourn)

Carlton House in the 1940's. (Source: Nassau Magazine)

New Colonial Hotel re-built by Government in 1923

Back in Nassau, the *Rozelda* Hotel, the first apartment hotel, was built by Roland Symonette in 1920. The Rozelda later became the Carlton House. The government purchased from Flagler the Hotel Colonial which had been destroyed by fire. They floated a 3% loan for £430,000, and contracted with the Munson Steamship Line to build the *New Colonial Hotel* which opened in 1923, and became an instant success. Munson Steamship Line also provided cruise ship service to the Florida coast and had taken over the vital New York/Nassau service in 1917 from the Ward Line, which had plied the route for 47 years since 1879.

To satisfy the need for additional first-class accommodation, a group of Bahamians acquired the property called Waterloo Estate and formed the Waterloo Hotel Company, the shareholders of which raised £50,000 for a hotel. An act was passed in 1924 authorizing the raising of a loan of an additional £150,000 for a third "grand hotel" to be located at the eastern end of the city. After the signing of a contract with the Fred T. Ley Co., of New York, construction of the hotel began in the Spring of 1925. The work was delayed because of hurricane damage in the summer of 1926, but the hotel opened on 21st December, 1926. On New Year's Eve, 1926, the official opening of the *Montagu Hotel* took place during a gala ball. The invitation list read like the "Who's Who" of America and The Bahamas.[14]

The 200-room Montagu Hotel opens on December 31, 1926

The 200-room Montagu Hotel was six storeys high with two projecting five-storey wings. Instead of a ballroom inside the hotel, a dancing pavilion, known as the Jungle Club, was conceived by Mr. George Murphy, and built near the lake. A number of bungalows were also built on the lake for those guests wishing peace and tranquillity. When the beach immediately opposite was improved, the property was then called the *Fort Montagu Beach Hotel.*

Jungle Club ad. (Source: Bahamas Magazine 1953)

More than a quarter of a century was to pass before another major hotel would be constructed in Nassau. However, smaller hotels and guest houses opened during this era. Valeria Moseley Moss recalled that the A. Baker & Sons built the **Windsor Hotel**, the first hotel in the centre of Bay Street, in the 1930's, but the hotel did not officially open until around 1940.[15] The 30-room **Lucerne Hotel**, which opened in 1913,

Lucerne Hotel, built by R.M. Lightbourn (Courtesy: Ronald Lightbourn)

owned by Roger M. Lightbourn, was on Frederick Street (at the present location of Norfolk House). The 20-room **Allan Hotel** was across the street from the Lucerne, and featured dancing and excellent native and international cuisine prepared by a French chef. Another hotel listed in guide books during the 1920's was **Hotel Nassau**. According to the Tribune Handbook, this small hotel, built at the beginning of the century, was immediately east of the New Hotel Colonial.[16]

In the 1920's, **Graycliff** re-opened to the public, under the ownership of Polly Leach, rumoured to be a close companion of Al Capone.[17] **Polly Leach's Garden** became Nassau's most sophisticated gathering spot for local elites and visiting millionaires. In 1937, Graycliff once again became a private home, when it was purchased by Canadians, Mr. and Mrs. J. Walton Killam, who refurbished the mansion and added the Olympic-sized swimming pool. As a private home, Graycliff has hosted nobles and notables including Sir Winston Churchill, the Duke and Duchess of Windsor, Princess Alice and the Earl of Athlone, and the Duke and Duchess of Kent.

Tribune Handbook 1924

The Hotel Allan

It later opened to the public and the third Earl of Staffordshire, Lord Dudley and Lady Dudley, lifelong friends of the Duke of Windsor, bought the exclusive small hotel and restaurant. Visitors to Graycliff during the Dudley ownership included Lord Beaverbrook and Lord Mountbatten.

Over the decades, Graycliff has continued to attract the elite. The television show "Lifestyles of the Rich and Famous" placed Graycliff among the top restaurants of the world.

Graycliff has always attracted the rich and the famous. Pictured—from left Paoli Gazaroli; his father—Enriquo; entertainer Stevie Wonder, and Anthony Laing, waiter (now maitre d at Graycliff)

In 1938, a small hotel, the **Parliament**, opened on Parliament Street between Bay and Shirley Streets.

Establishment of the Bahamas Development Board

STERLING EXCHANGE

ROOM WITH PRIVATE
BATH AND ALL MEALS
only 40 Shillings a day

STEAMER FARES
New York to Nassau and
return, lowest rates

TELEPHONE (RADIO)
to U.S.A. and Canada

NASSAU-MIAMI BY AIR
round trip $35. Time, two
hours one way

A SEASIDE COURSE OF DISTINCTION

BEST WINTER CLIMATE
BATHING . . . . . . GOLF
TENNIS . . . . . FISHING
POLO . . . . . YACHTING

For information, address: The
Development Board, Nassau,
Bahamas, All Tourist Agents;
Nassau, Bahamas, Information
Bureau, 67 West 44th Street,
New York, N.Y., Murray Hill 2-1159; Munson Steamship Lines,
New York and Miami; Pan-American Airways, New York and
Miami; Nassau-Jacksonville Steamship Lines, Jacksonville; Cana-
dian National Steamships, Montreal and Boston, Mass.

DEVELOPMENT BOARD, Nassau, Bahamas

SENTRY ON FORT CHARLOTTE

COTTAGES—
PRIVATE BOARD

The Development Board is
pleased to give you service
in selecting the type and
kind of winter home you
wish, by the sea or set in
old-world tropical gardens

Development Board advertisement in the 1940's

The Development Board Act of 1914 established the **Development Board** to promote tourism, negotiate with carriers, and coordinate matters related to tourism. The first chairman was the Honourable F.C. Wells Durrant, who held office until 1917. Members of this first Board included G.H. Gamblin, J.H. Brown, W.H. Lightbourn, W.C.B. Johnson, W.P. Adderley and L.G. Brice. These gentlemen and other pioneers made a valiant effort to jumpstart the industry. However, in the absence of consistent scheduled air or sea transportation, and with the onset of war, their task was a difficult one. The Development Board operated on a budget of £3,000 per annum, which was used for advertising, public relations, subsidies for carriers, and information services[18].

M.H. Davenport of the Atlas Advertising Company of New York was retained to place newspaper and magazine advertising in the United States and Canada. Some of the magazines selected were *Metropolitan, Independent Outlook, Colliers, Vanity Fair, Country Life, Literary Digest, Travel, Cosmopolitan, Harpers, Spur* and *Town and Country.* Advertisements were placed in 15 American cities and six Canadian cities, with the lion's share on the Eastern seaboard—New York, Philadelphia, and Boston.

The Board involved the community in one of its campaigns by launching a public relations competition for the best-written tourist articles on Nassau as a tourism resort. The competition for the stories was keenly contested with 27 entries. The top five stories were published overseas and the next 12 were published locally.[19]

There were no overseas tourist offices at that time and no consistent programme of sales promotions. The only annual overseas event in which the Board participated was the Canadian National Exhibition in Toronto, at which The Bahamas secured a booth to display native products and literature.

The Board rented the second floor of the Masonic building in Nassau to establish an Information Bureau for tourists and stocked it with maps and literature. In its 1916 report, the Board boasted that it had sent out 4,369 letters in response to enquiries and commented that "it would be a distinct advantage to have a reliable handbook on The Bahamas, in concise form, which could be sent to enquirers and circulated to agencies".[20]

Visitors hosted during the December 1915 to April 1916 season totalled 2,680, which was an impressive number, bearing in mind the limited accommodations and transportation as well as the wartime restrictions. The Annual Report stated that the Hotel Colonial in 1915 was at one time feeding 700 guests daily and that 1,200 visitors were hosted at that hotel during the season and 282 at the Royal Victoria. The smaller hotels also did fairly well. Development Board members noted the desirability of attracting more reasonably priced cottage accommodations.

While the Board successfully negotiated for the establishment of steamship service between Jacksonville and Nassau in 1916, this service was short-lived. To attract sporting visitors, the Board made preparations for a Fast Cruiser Motor Boat Race from Miami to Nassau to be arranged during the 1917-18 season in conjunction with the Miami Regatta, with handsome cups as prizes. However, due to unsettled diplomatic relations between the United States and Germany caused by war, all of the steamship lines on The Bahamas route cancelled their scheduled visits to Nassau. The trickle of tourists was insufficient to fill the two large hotels, which had a combined total of 700 rooms, causing both the Royal Victoria and the Hotel Colonial to close. Concerted efforts by the Board to attract new carriers failed. The Development Board cancelled its advertising campaign and plans for the regatta, and the tourism industry collapsed.[21]

The number of visitors during the 1917-18 season was a mere 125, and the 1919-20 season was equally dismal. With little local control over the hotel product, Government initiated talks about the possibility of buying the Royal Victoria Hotel.[22]

Modernization of Nassau

At the beginning of the 20th century, Nassau, according to James H. Stark, was a very quiet and orderly city. "Strangers", he noted, "are much impressed by the absence of scenes of violence, drunken brawls, profane and abusive language in public places". Life in Nassau was slow moving but pleasant. "The people are frank, lively and generous, and hospitality is carried to an extreme unknown in England, and there are few persons, we believe, who have ever visited these islands who have not separated from

At the beginning of the 20th century, land travel was still by donkey drays and horse-drawn carriages

many of the inhabitants with regret".[23] However, the Colony was devoid of modern utilities, communications and ground transportation facilities. Men known as lamplighters made their living lighting the oil lamps on Bay Street in the evenings. The only mode of inter-island travel was by mailboat, and land travel was by donkey drays and horse-drawn carriages.[24]

Another glimpse of life in Nassau in the early 1900's is recorded by Valeria Moseley Moss in *Reminiscing*. She recalled that during the "teen years" and early 1920's, Bay Street was a vastly different place. No cars, vans or trucks in a frantic hurry, honking horns and keeping stray pedestrians on the jump, she noted. Just horse-drawn surreys with visitors on a sightseeing trip and drays with ventilated sides carting sponges, and those without sides taking large wooden packing cases from the docks to business houses. Bay Street, unpaved, was made of cracked rock, pulverized and crushed into smoothness with heavy rollers. Children, she recalled, walked along sidewalks, without being jostled. Shop owners often stood at their front doors, catching a breath of fresh air. There was no pollution then.[25]

Leon Hartman Dupuch, the father of Sir Etienne Dupuch, launched The Tribune in November, 1903

In addition to accommodations, the Colony recorded slow, but steady, modernization of communication, transportation, infrastructure, business houses, and entertainment facilities during the first 20 years of the century.

On 21st November, 1903, the second longest surviving newspaper came on the scene when the *Tribune* was launched by Leon Hartman Dupuch, the father of Sir

Etienne Dupuch. The Tribune editor was particularly vocal on injustices related to racial discrimination and in raising the consciousness of the community to local issues, including tourism related matters. While many newspapers began publication over the decades, the only two dailies still in operation are the *Nassau Guardian* and *Tribune.*

The year 1904 marked the advent of **motor vehicles** to the Colony. There was great excitement when Mr. Henry Mostyn, the American Vice Consul, imported the first motor car into Nassau in late February of that year. The 1902 Oldsmobile had a four-horse power engine and travelled at a speed of up to 20 m.p.h.[26] This was followed by an influx of imported vehicles, prompting the Legislature to pass the Motor Car Act of 1909, which established fees for vehicle registration, plates and driver's licences, as well as penalties for road offences.

In 1906, the Bahamas House of Assembly passed a Bill for the establishment of a **telephone system**. The station was officially opened on 5th October, 1906 with an exchange to accommodate 150 subscribers. Public telephones were installed in the marketplace in 1908. Stallholders and subscribers had free usage but the general public paid 1¢ for the first three minutes.[27]

Infrastructure was further improved when, on 14th June, 1908, **electric lights** were turned on for the first time on the main streets of New Providence and some private homes until 1 a.m.[28]

The rising prominence of The Bahamas as a modern city was also marked by the advent of foreign **financial centres**. In November 1908, the first foreign commercial bank, *the Royal Bank of Canada*, was established in The Bahamas. The only other bank operating in the Colony at that time was the Bank of Nassau, which had been formed in 1884. When the Bank of Nassau ran into difficulties in 1917, the Royal took over its assets, and remained the only commercial bank in the country until 1947.

The first manager of the Royal Bank was Mr. George Gamblin, a prominent Bahamian who later became a member of the Executive Council, President of the Legislative Council, Leader of the Government in the House of Assembly, and a member of the Development Board.

Royal Bank advertisement

Mr. Gamblin was knighted in 1929 in recognition of his public service to the Colony.

The historic and handsome structure on Bay Street which houses the main branch of Royal Bank was erected in 1919. The one-storey Spanish-style edifice with flat roof supported by pillars, and a marble interior, was built by Purdy & Henderson, and designed by G. Davenport. It employed a style of architecture similar to that of Vendue House.[29] Alfred deMarigny later referred to the structure of the Royal Bank of Canada, which was flanked on one side by the old Prince George Hotel, as giving Bay Street "an aura of stability". He noted that the bank and the nearby picturesque Sponge Market, "which filled the air with a pungent ocean smell, attracted tourists with a taste for the exotic."[30]

In 1911, two theatres (**movie houses**)—the Royal and the Imperial Theatres—opened. Silent movie dramas and live performances were held there. The following year the Cinematography Act was passed in May 1912 to regulate and control the exhibition of moving pictures.

In 1913 the first **Wireless Station** was officially opened by Sir George Haddon-Smith, who served as Governor of the Colony from 1912 to 1914.

The Bahamas became the focus of international attention in 1914 when photographer John Ernest Williamson brought his revolutionary invention, the Photosphere, from Chesapeake Bay to the Colony. He was the first man to produce undersea photographs in 1913 but wanted to move into film. His underwater camera system hung from a 30-foot barge, had a 4-foot wide flexible metal tube which extended 30 feet below the surface, and a 3½ ton glass-sided chamber to view the depths of the ocean. Williamson could go down the tube, set up his camera and film sea life below. His first effort was shooting young Bahamian boys diving for coins. Then he moved to the undersea world, which he described as "creeping, crawling creatures of the deep bumbling silently among the coral". Williamson made the first underwater feature movie "Twenty Thousand Leagues under the Sea" (starring Jayne Gale) in 1912-13, filmed at Clifton, which was later remade by Disney. The movie demonstrated how the photosphere functioned and the manner in which Bahama Islanders depended on the life in the sea, climaxing with scenes of Williamson's fight with a shark, which he killed with a knife while remaining within the camera's range[31]. According to Paul Aranha and Sylvia Munroe, Williamson's daughter, his 3½ ton glass-sided chamber can still be seen in a yard on Lightbourn Lane (off East Bay Street, behind Brown's Boat Basin). The movie has since been colourized.

Historic Nassau grew and prospered, with wealthy Americans, Canadians and titled English building exclusive homes during the Prohibition years. This prosperity further accelerated infrastructure improvements, as new roads were built, utilities further improved, and entrepreneurship flourished.

Stores in the Bay Street area catering to tourists and residents during this era were the **General Hardware**, owned by Arthur Sweeting, **The Park Store** on Bay and Parliament, owned by the Mather family, **Pipe of Peace** owned by Eric and Cyril

Solomon, **Bahamas Ironmongery** owned by Frank Duncombe, P.M. Lightbourne's **New Colonial Pharmacy** on the southwest corner of Bay and Frederick Street, **City Pharmacy** which claimed its prime location on Bay Street until the late 1980's. The oldest store still remaining in its original location on Bay Street is **A. Baker and Sons**, founded by Mr. Anthony Baker Saadi of Lebanon, who arrived in The Bahamas in 1890 and died in 1937. The Old English Tobacco shop, **John Bull**, which Sir Asa Pritchard opened in 1929, was located east of Rawson Square. **Black's Candy Kitchen** in the Market-George Street block was owned by Harry and Florrie Black.[32]

This period also recorded some of the worst natural disasters the Colony had ever experienced. In 1926 and 1928, **hurricanes** destroyed boats, crops, trees, infrastructure, and many buildings, but this was just the beginning. The greatest devastation was recorded by the killer hurricane of 1929, which affected nearly every household and business throughout the country, and resulted in several deaths. Described as the worst hurricane ever, it left many structures, including tourist accommodations, seriously damaged. These hurricanes crippled the local boat-building industry at Abaco and Harbour Island and it has never regained the momentum of former days. Birdlife also suffered. Robert Burnside, who was in charge of public gardens and the horticultural department of Public Works, was reportedly sent to Jamaica to obtain pairs of suitable wild birds to re-populate bird life on New Providence. [33] Since Prohibition travel was still a major factor, efforts were made to restore infrastructure as quickly as possible to resume trade.

While the stock market crash in 1929 created worldwide depression, The Bahamas, still enjoying the fruit of Prohibition, fared better than most countries in the region. Nassau's picturesque harbour was crowded with private yachts, with powerful names in industry and high finance at the helm such as William R. Vanderbilt, Vincent Astor, J.P. Morgan and E.F. Hutton.

Cruise service was inaugurated with the Canadian National Steamship Line from Halifax. Trans-Atlantic service from Britain made its debut with the Pacific Steam Navigation's liners sailing from Liverpool. Liquor money continued to flow, and in 1929 the government deepened Nassau Harbour and built modern **Prince George Wharf**, named after H.R.H. Prince George, who visited Nassau in 1928. He would later become King George VI, when, in December 1936, his brother abdicated the throne to marry "the woman he loved", twice-divorced American-born Wallis Simpson.

Pan American Introduces scheduled Air Service

With the increased demand for air travel, Pan American World Airways, founded in 1927, began serious negotiations about initiating regular service to Nassau. Planes over Nassau were rare in those days. The Nassau Magazine Mid-season 1960 edition recorded an interesting article on Pan American's first 30 years of service to Nassau. The publication reported that, on 1st October, 1928, a Pan American World Airways team, comprising John Hambleton, Vice President of the airline, company attorney, James E. Young and Capt. Edward Musick, senior pilot from Pan American World Airways boarded a flight from Miami to Nassau for a meeting about the service. As the plane circled over the downtown area, tremendous excitement swept over the island. By the time the plane anchored in the water off the Eastern Parade, and a small boat came out from shore, most of Nassau, including reporters, had reached the scene. They learned that Pan American, soon to celebrate its first birthday, having already launched successful scheduled flights between Florida and Havana, was looking at the feasibility of establishing service between Miami and Nassau. It was Sidney Farrington, CBE, MLC, who had helped the young United States airline earn the right to link Nassau by air with the rest of the world. The Sikorsky-38 amphibian aircraft was capable of making the 187-mile journey between Miami and Nassau in two to four hours depending on the weather.

Seaplane (Courtesy: Paul Aranha)

The talks were successful and on 2nd January, 1929, Pan American flew into Nassau for the first time on schedule, with Captain Musick at the controls again, with all eight passenger seats filled. The first year of scheduled flights produced only 200 paying passengers, but cargo holds and empty seats were filled with mail, greatly improving the efficiency of mail communication.[34]

Pan Am seaplanes landed in the harbour and later tied up at a floating dock that extended from the old Pan American building (which for many years was the office of the Royal Bahamas Police Traffic Division) in front of Lover's Lane. As advances in technology occurred, Pan American upgraded its fleet. First there was the S-38 flying boat, then the Commodore, with 20 seats in its long,

An early Sikorsky sea plane—the type which pioneered the Miami–Nassau service of Pan American World Airways.

Sikorsky seaplane (Courtesy: Paul Aranha)

slender fuselage. Also an amphibian, the Commodore followed the S-38 pattern by landing in Nassau Harbour and taxiing to the shore along the Eastern Parade. Later a Pan American terminal office was built on East Bay Street near Bahamas Air Sea Rescue Association (BASRA) headquarters and the Eastern Parade.

The Post-1930 Era

Captain the Honourable Sir Bede Clifford, who served as Governor of the Colony from 1932 to 1934, was a strong proponent of tourism. In his maiden Parliamentary Speech from the Throne, he outlined projects to receive priority during his busy, almost five-year tour of duty. These included: a radio-telephone service to the US mainland; joint ownership linking Government, transportation, tourism and hotel operations; advertising and promotion of tourism, and widening and deepening of Nassau Harbour.[35]

Governor Clifford's dream for improved radio-telephone services with the United States was realized with the official opening of the first radiotelegraphy circuit between the United States and The Bahamas on 16th December, 1932. The system, which was installed by the American Telephone and Telegraph Company, established communication between a battery of telephones installed in the main lobby of the New Colonial Hotel and New York. The first call by Governor Clifford attracted widespread local and international press. The Chief of the Columbia Broadcasting System arranged for their star announcer, Ted Husing, broadcaster for Columbia Broadcast Company (CBS), to groom Sir Bede in giving the first link-up address with nearly 100 US radio stations.

It was announced at that time that receiving apparatuses and booths, to be used by hotel guests and locals residing in the immediate area, were under construction at both the New Hotel Colonial and the Fort Montagu Hotel. [35] The *Nassau Guardian* described this new development as "another big asset to attract winter visitors".[36]

On 25th January, 1933, The Bahamas recorded another first in radio broadcasting. In conjunction with Ted Husing, the first network broadcast was transmitted from the

Pan Am advertisement in the 1950's

new Hotel Colonial. On this occasion, in addition to the usual speeches by dignitaries, local artists provided musical entertainment. The Joseph String Group performed such Bahamian classics as "Mama Don't Want no Peas no Rice no Coconut Oil", "1891", and "Bahama Mama", while the Cambridge Orchestra performed such hits as "Delia" and "John B Sail". Also included in the programme were the Bahamas Police Force Band, and the Grant's Town Sextet which performed "Heaven is Shining". The broadcast received rave reviews from Canadians, some of whom described it as a magnificent achievement, the finest piece of publicity for a tourist resort in many months, if not years.[37]

Ushering in the era of electronic communication for the masses, broadcast radio began in The Bahamas on 11th May, 1937. Colonial Secretary, J.H. Jarrett, who was also chairman of the Development Board at the time, pointed out that The Bahamas was perhaps the first British West Indian Colony to establish a Government Broadcast station. As war was about to break, this tool proved invaluable in communicating with residents throughout the far-flung islands of The Bahamas.[38]

The Dundas Civic Centre

During the period up to 1930, the few large hotels, as well as boarding houses and winter residents, because of the paucity of trained labour, were forced to import staff to perform most of their professional and domestic services. This need began to be addressed with the establishment, in May 1930, of the Nassau Improvement Society by Lady Dundas, the wife of the Colonial Secretary, the Honourable Charles Dundas, who later became the Governor. The original aim of this Society, as listed in their early Constitution, was to "promote the interests and wellbeing of the masses residing in The Bahamas, to give them better ideals of home life, hygiene, sanitation, and to teach the dignity of labour intelligently performed."[39]

By 1931, a derelict old building, formerly the Woodcock School, and one acre of land were acquired for formalized training. The lease of the premises was acquired from the Diocesan Council of the Anglican Church by the Nassau Improvement Association. On 13th June, 1931, the official opening ceremony for the Dundas Civic Centre, in the centre of Grant's Town, was performed by His Excellency the Honourable Charles Dundas. During the summer of 1931, instruction was offered in sewing, dressmaking, hygiene and gardening under the big cotton tree, by members of the Association and volunteers, and Mrs. Dundas personally conducted classes in domestic science within the dingy school building. In September 1931, the Centre acquired the services of an English instructor, donations of crockery, glassware and cutlery, aluminium cookware, bathroom equipment, and running water, and the Centre became fully operational with 61 students. The aim of the programme became twofold: first to "turn idle young men and girls into self-respecting wage earners and thereby supply new homes, hotels, and boarding houses with trained recruits in or near Nassau" and, secondly, "to enhance the attractions of wintering in the island of New Providence by making life easier for the holiday maker."[40] Over the next few years additional furniture and equipment for a full kitchen and bedroom were donated by winter residents to turn the school building into a model home, thus enabling the students to learn professional domestic skills.

In February 1932, the class of 1931 had an opportunity to show off their skills when the first demonstration of table waiting, bedmaking, et cetera, was given to invited guests at the Dundas Civic Centre and met with an enthusiastic reception. Two months later, after a garden party at Government House was served by uniformed students from the Dundas Centre, the public interest was aroused. The Government later provided a subsidy to pay the salary and living expenses for a qualified instructor from overseas. The Centre began to flourish and each student paid a small contribution of six pence per week, merely a fraction of the cost of the training.[41]

Special interest was generated when Mr. George Murphy, then the Manager of the Montagu Beach Hotel, indicated to the Nassau Improvement Society that if the Centre could turn out quality young waiters, he would hire them the following year. Thus, in winter of 1933, 80 of the students of the Dundas Civic Centre were employed by the Fort Montagu Hotel, marking the first time that professional domestic local labour was employed in the hotel industry. Although the centre could only accommodate up to 100 students, the demand was so great that several hundred were admitted, and those without the capacity and attributes were weeded out. Between 1933 and 1938, over 500 waiters, cooks and butlers were supplied to hotels, boarding houses, and private homes. Because none of the students had secondary education, the only qualification for entry into the 8-month programme as a waiter or butler was an ability to read and understand a hotel menu, so that they could intelligently answer questions of guests related to the menu.[42]

By 1938, Governor Dundas could boast that all of the staff of Government House, with the exception of one supervisor, were Bahamian. He called for support for the expansion of the Dundas Civic Centre in terms of both instructors and physical buildings, to be able to meet the growing demand for trained domestic help, to achieve the policy of supplying 75% of the domestic labour within local accommodations. An Expansion Fund was established, and the first benefactors were Governor Dundas, the Chief Justice and Lady Tute, Lady Oakes, Sir Harold Christie and Sir Francis Peek. The funds were used to acquire new expanded premises on Mackey Street in 1939, thus enabling the centre to meet the growing needs of both New Providence and the Family Islands. The Dundas Civic Centre remained operational until the 1960's. In spite of the excellent role performed by the Centre in the training of Bahamians for the tourism industry, there was not as much official support for the aims of the Centre.[43]

The first land flight in Cable Beach

Capt. Paul Aranha, a local pilot and entrepreneur, speaking on the topic Aviation in The Bahamas at a meeting of the Bahamas Historical Society, noted that 9th November, 1934 was an important day in aviation history in The Bahamas when an airport landing took place on a road in Cable Beach, involving two aviators, Dr. Albert E. "Bert", Forsyth, a Bahamian medical doctor practising in New Jersey, and Charles Alfred "Chief" Anderson. Forsyth was a descendant of Loyalists, who had been born in Nassau in 1897 but his father, Horatio Forsyth, had moved, with his family, to Jamaica where Bert had grown up. Anderson, who earned his Private Pilots Licence in 1929, had qualified for an Air Transport Rating in 1932, making him the first black pilot to be officially recognized as achieving that level of aeronautical skill. That same year, Anderson and Forsyth had flown across the United States—from the East Coast to the West Coast and back.[44]

The two experienced pilots were on an island hopping trip to New Providence, Cuba, Haiti, the Dominican Republic, and all the way to British Guiana, on the "Spirit of Booker T. Washington", a single-engine two-seat Lambert Monocoupe aircraft, on its **Pan-American Goodwill Flight.** The flight was scheduled to land on a road in Cable Beach.

Not only was there no airport on the island, but, having been held up in Miami for repairs to the plane's engine, the sun had already set before they reached the island and there were no aids-to-navigation to help the pilots find Cable Beach, nor did they have air-to-ground communications to ask for help. The pilots did not relish the thought of landing on a small road in the dark of night. It was Etienne Dupuch who found a solution to the problem. He asked the waiting car owners to park their vehicles in such a way as to illuminate the darkening road. Even with this make-shift lighting, the landing was not straightforward, because the excited crowd kept running onto the road, but the touchdown, once it happened, entered the history books—an important, but often overlooked, page in the annals of Bahamians-in-aviation.[45]

Dr. Forsyth was inducted into the New Jersey Aviation Hall of Fame in 1985, the year before he died at age 89. Anderson who passed away in 1996, also at the age of 89, and held numerous aviation awards, is best remembered as the Chief Flight Instructor and mentor of the famed "Tuskegee Airmen" of World War II. His 40-minute flight with First Lady Eleanor Roosevelt during her Tuskegee visit in 1941 was the catalyst that led to the training of the first African American military pilots, the "Tuskegee Experiment".[46]

Bahamian-born Bert Forsyth was inducted into the New Jersey Aviation Hall of Fame in 1985. He died the following year at the age of 89.

Albert E. Forsyth

Foreign and Local Investment to support the Tourism Industry

In the In the 1930's, the government leased land next to the golf course in the Cable Beach area to George Murphy, Manager of the Royal Bank of Canada. Murphy built the *Hobby Horse Hall* racecourse, providing a popular outlet for residents and tourists. Another major development in the attractions for visitors was the opening of Nassau's first casino. Sir Bede Clifford, persuaded the Crown to allow a gaming industry, on grounds that only visitors would be allowed to gamble. As a result, the *Bahamian Club* opened in 1920 on West Bay Street opposite the Esplanade. The club, owned and operated by Mr. C.F. Reid of New York, was open during the winter season, was popular for visitors and men of means.

Harold G. Christie achieved notable success in promoting property investment, which had a direct impact on the tourism industry. When there was a boom in land sales in Florida in the 1930's, Christie used his charm to secure introductions to the rich and famous and was successful in luring many of them to The Bahamas to invest in winter homes, businesses and tourism establishments. According to his personal assistant, Reginald Walker, "he could look at a piece of real estate and immediately visualize what it could become if sufficient capital were invested in it. He believed wholeheartedly in the concept that the best export trade a country can develop p is selling land which could not be turned to agricultural use. The purchaser can't take it away with him—it's always there—and whatever he spends on it directly benefits the country."[47]

One of the most important investors of the era was Canadian **Harold (Harry) Oakes**, discoverer of the Lake Shore Mines, Canada. In late 1934, when Harold Christie learned that Oakes had arrived in Palm Beach, Florida, he immediately put a plan in place to lure this multi-millionaire to Nassau. He arranged a meeting with him in Florida, and brought him and his wife to Nassau at his expense. Oakes' interest grew as Christie explained his vision of placing Nassau on the map as a tourist centre and described the goals of a new airport, hotel refurbishment, golf course enlargement, and development of new water sources.[48] Having been attracted by the absence of taxes and the charms of Nassau, Oakes agreed to wind up his affairs in Palm Beach. He asked Christie to arrange for his residency papers and later his Bahamian citizenship.

In the winter of 1936-37, Mr. & Mrs. Harold Oakes came to Nassau with their lawyer, Walter Foskett, as house guests of Harold Christie. He acquired "Westbourne" in the Cable Beach area as his elaborate home. He made his permanent return to Nassau as a baronet after having spent six months in London, England, where he was knighted in 1939 on the birthday of King George VI.[49] Sir Harry purchased land throughout Nassau and invested heavily in the tourism industry.

In 1939, when the Government decided to build three 3,000 feet runways on crown land "bordering on the Blue Hills Road and between that and Harold Road",

Harry Oakes generously agreed to clear and scarify the land with his machinery.[50] In December 1939, Oakes purchased the airport, which was later named the "Oakes Field Airport" and developed it. The agreement between Government and Harry Oakes stipulated that the Government could take the property back if the ground was used for any purpose other than an airfield. On 14th December, 1939, history was made when the first land plane from Miami landed on the new airfield.[51] It was Harold Christie who made the flight possible and who, in an interview after arriving on the inaugural flight, announced his intention to acquire 25 planes for the route.[52]

Harry Oakes continued to invest in the tourism industry. He developed the first golf course and the Bahamas Country Club and purchased the British Colonial Hotel, becoming a powerful force in the country until his mysterious murder on 8th July, 1943.

Big Game Fishing

According to Ashley Saunders, the big game fishing industry started on the Bahamian island of Bimini in 1920, when several great catches were recorded in the Gulf Stream by American sportsmen fishing out of the Bimini Bay Rod and Gun Club, utilizing Bahamian fishing guides.[53]

Bimini gained international recognition for this sport in the 1930's after wealthy American sportsfishing enthusiast, Louis R. Wasey, and fishing guide, Tommy Gifford, arrived on that island. Prior to 1930, there were no hotel facilities and docks nor were basic amenities for sports fishermen available—no ice, fresh water, electricity, weight-scale and no fresh bait. In February 1933, Kip Farrington made history when he landed the first blue marlin ever taken in the waters off Bimini. Two weeks later, another American, Betty More, hooked and fought a 502-pound blue marlin for more than four hours. The fish was finally landed by Mr. Wasey two hours later. News of the big catch established Bimini as the world's big game fishing hotspot, attracting fishing greats from all over the world. The native Biminites at that time were primarily interested in fishing around the reefs with hand line for scale fish for food or trade. They were not interested in big game fish, nor did they have the gear and techniques of big game fishing. In 1933, Wasey assigned Tommy Gifford to train the locals as big game fishing guides.

To cater to the large number of visiting sports fishermen, both Bahamians and foreigners invested in the hotel industry. Mamie Newbold, whose family had migrated from Spanish Wells, Bahamas, during the shipwrecking period and who had pioneered the restaurant business in the 1920's, built a two-storey wooden hotel, *Sea Crest* in 1933, becoming the first Bahamian-owned hotel on Bimini. Also in 1933, Mrs. Helen Duncombe, wife of Mr. H. F. Duncombe, the island's Commissioner, formerly of Kent, England, built the *Compleat Angler*, which was constructed with weathered, but beautiful, timber from an old liquor barge resembling an old-fashioned

English Inn. The charming hotel, with a capacity for 23 guests, housed the famous, the wealthy and the adventurous, including Nobel Prize winning author, Ernest Hemingway. In 1936, Nassauvian Neville Stuart, who migrated to Bimini in 1932, built the *Bimini Big Game Fishing Club*. In 1948, Harcourt Brown, from Bimini, built *Brown's Hotel and Restaurant* on the waterfront.[54]

Ernest Hemingway in Bimini (Courtesy: Jane Day)

Some of the world's top anglers and personalities who visited Bimini regularly, beside Ernest Hemingway, included Julio Sanchez, Helen Lerner and George Albert Lyon.

Entertainment in Nassau

A popular rendezvous in Nassau for tourists and yachtsmen was *Dirty Dick's* tavern, located at 250 and 252 Bay Street. It was founded in 1930 by the late Mr. Bruce Kilroy Thompson who had many years earlier established wine and spirit firms. Dirty Dick's took its name from a tavern of the same name established in 1745 at Bishopsgate, London, England. The story is told that the eccentric personage after whom the tavern was named was

DIRTY DICK'S at 250 and 252 Bay Street, Nassau, was founded in the 1920's

Dirty Dick's (Source: Bahamas Magazine)

Nathaniel Bentley, who, over 200 years earlier, was one of the best-known characters in the city of London. Bentley reportedly experienced an unhappy love affair; his intended bride died suddenly on the day set for their wedding. Soon after, he adopted the habits of dress and personal appearance which gained him the famous nickname that was transferred to his wineship and later adopted by the proprietors of the Nassau tavern. Dirty Dick's in Nassau boasted much of the atmosphere of bars in typical English inns, and became the most popular tavern in the region.[55]

Professional Musicians

Among the bands providing a taste of authentic Bahamian culture were Paul Meeres and Bert Cambridge.

Cambridge Orchestra—first band of professional musicians (Courtesy: Ding Cambridge)

Making its debut in 1923 was the *Cambridge Orchestra,* said to be the first band of professional musicians in The Bahamas. The ensemble, though small, competed with bands imported from the USA to perform at the Royal Victoria and British Colonial Hotels for the winter season. Because local bands were often bypassed in favour of foreign bands, the leader of the Cambridge Orchestra discussed the matter with Governor Bede Clifford, who ordered that all hotels requiring permission to bring a foreign band must employ also a native group. This served as an incentive for bands and other entertainers to study music and play professionally, demanding the respect that the art deserved. Members of the Orchestra included Bert Cambridge, pianist (leader); Harold Curry, violinist; John "Sir Coke" Coakley, saxophonist; Oliver Mason, trumpetist; Mannaaseh "Massa" Strachan, bass; Arthur Pinder, trombonist and Harold "Baby Face" Deveaux, drummer.[56]

The 1930's signalled the beginning of the most significant chapter in Bahamian entertainment, with the rise to popularity of Paul Meeres, who built the first over-the-hill theatre and became the role model and protégé of future local entertainers. As a talented dancer and entertainer, his name dominated the Paris theatrical circles for years. He returned to Nassau at the height of his career in the 1930's to share his success with his people. He built a fabulous theatre and 50-room hotel, Chez Paul Meeres, in the heart of Market Street. Paul Meeres was a pioneer who became the role model for many upcoming local performers. Among the entertainers whom he mentored and trained were Berkeley "Peanuts" Taylor and John "Chippie" Chipman.[57]

Paul Meeres built the first major nightclub, Chez Paul Meeres, in the heart of Market Street (Courtesy: Duke Errol)

Both the Cambridge Orchestra and John Chipman are spotlighted in greater detail at the end of this book.

Repeal of Prohibition

In 1932, Franklin D. Roosevelt had campaigned against the US ban on alcohol, and after his landslide election, the 19th amendment was repealed. By 1933, Prohibition, which had created a tourism boom for The Bahamas, was over.

The Royal Victoria Hotel, on the crest of affluence, was abruptly empty of guests. This magnificent edifice, which had enjoyed unparalleled success, became a white elephant. Other accommodations and merchants suffered the same fate. Many Britons and Americans who had doubled or tripled their income headed home. The Stock market crash of 1929 had an adverse effect on most of the Bahama Islands, although the effect on Bimini was not as great due to its proximity to the US mainland.

Other Industries

With the decline in tourism in Nassau and many of the Family Islands, some attention was placed on development of other industries and alternative employment. The sisal industry was declining in importance. Tomatoes, first introduced in 1875 and exported to the United States, became unprofitable when the American Government imposed an import duty to protect Florida growers. Sponge beds were severely damaged during the 1926 and 1929 hurricanes. Bahamian author and teacher, Ashley Saunders, records that the development of The Bahamas crawfishing industry started at Bimini in 1920 when Elisha Weech began buying crawfish for $1 a dozen, took them to Florida and resold them for a small profit. Prior to this time, crawfish was regarded as having little economic value other than an occasional article of food and as bait for scale fish.[58]

The salt industry provided the greatest economic benefits following the collapse of the tourism industry. In 1936, the Erickson Brothers, New Englanders, came to Matthew Town, Inagua, Bahamas, revived the salt industry, providing full employment and the need to bring in Turks Islanders to help with the yearly harvest.[59] Great expansion of the salt works took place during the 1960's after control was acquired by the Morton Salt Company.

Vision for Tourism as a legitimate industry

Governor Sir Bede Clifford, along with Harold Christie, believed that the Colony's economic future lay in its attraction as a holiday resort. As Prohibition had ended in the US, Sir Bede decreed that "if we can't take the liquor to the Americans, we must bring the Americans to the liquor".[60] When he was being urged to introduce income tax, he responded that "the best way to attract money is: No Taxes!"[61] It was during Sir Bede's tenure as Governor that some of the most famous visitors were hosted, including Winston Churchill, Franklin Delano Roosevelt and the Duke and Duchess of Kent (who honeymooned at Government House).

Sir Bede was equally concerned about upgrading the tourist product. A talented writer, he wrote a booklet on Bahamian fortifications, which was published by the Development Board. He was also largely responsible for the improvement to the forts, introduction of picturesque uniforms on sentries posted at Fort Charlotte, and upgrading of Bay Street. *Clifford Park*, named in his honour, the major site for national celebrations on New Providence, is a fitting tribute to Sir Bede's many accomplishments during his tenure as Governor of The Bahamas.

Like Governor Clifford, Harold Christie (later Sir Harold) was a strong proponent of tourism. After the repeal of Prohibition had left the country in deep depression, Christie is said to have invited the white merchants, *The Bay Street Boys,* to his office to reveal his plan for developing a stable economic base for the island. He explained to the merchants that The Bahamas had a great opportunity to exploit its natural assets to the world. He urged them to adopt a long-range plan for the tourism. Prospective visitors would be divided into three categories: 1) those who came for the day; 2) the working people who came for a holiday; and 3) the main target group—the wealthy of the East Coast, who could provide long-term and consistent benefits by buying vacation homes, returning year after year and bringing guests who in turn would join them as part-time residents.[62]

Harold Christie travelled all over the world on promotional trips. He achieved much success in luring wealthy businessmen and investors to Nassau.

By 1937, the best tourism season during this period, visitor arrivals nearly doubled, exceeding the 20,000 population of New Providence for the first time in Bahamian history.

Tourism Performance

Table 4-1
TOURIST ARRIVALS FOR SELECTED BIENNIA
1929-1939

	ARRIVALS BY SHIP				BY AIR	TOTAL
	Landed*	Excursionists*	Transients*	Total Arrivals by ship	Arrivals by Seaplane	Arrivals By Ship and Seaplane
Jan. 1929-Dec. 1930	**	12,505	4,434**	**16,939**	363	**17,302**
Jan. 1930-Dec.1931	**	14,185	3,761**	**17,946**	831	**18,777**
Jan. 1936-Dec. 1937	8,332	21,484	13,948	**43,764**	2,968	**46,732**
Jan.1938-Dec. 1939	9,901	30,099	14,629	**54,629**	3,774	**58,603**

*   Landed: Persons who remain for several days, weeks or months, including winter residents
     Excursionists: Persons on steamers remaining in port for 1 day
     Transients: Persons who cruise on steamers which run on regular schedule to Nassau
** Transient Figures for 1929-31 represent both Transient and Landed Visitors, arriving on ships from:
     N.Y. Canada—1,796 (1929-30) 2,045   Miami 2,638 (1929-30) 1,716
     (1930-31)   (1930-31)

Source: Annual Reports of the Development Board

Anticipation

The Honourable Charles Dundas had arrived in The Bahamas in November 1937 and there was nothing to suggest that he would not hold the post of Governor for the usual period of five years. But back in England, since the start of the war, the British Government had been faced with the difficult problem of what to do with the Duke of Windsor, who had abdicated the British throne for "the woman he loved". In December 1936 he had adopted France as his new home. After rumours began to surface that the Germans were trying to persuade him to collaborate with them, the British Government wanted him out of Europe, preferably far removed from the area of conflict. He consented to be sent to The Bahamas as Governor.

*   *   *

News that the Duke of Windsor, who had been head of a mighty empire, was to become Governor of a small Colony of less than 100,000 people was almost unbelievable to the Bahamian people, and indeed the world. The next decade was to be one of the most exciting in the history of tourism in The Bahamas.

5

WORLD WAR II AND ITS AFTERMATH
1939-49

The Global Environment

World War II, the most widespread and destructive war in history, which lasted from 1939 to 1945 involving all the great powers and most of the smaller nations of the world, had a dramatic effect on global tourism. Leisure travel during the war years came to a standstill. However, World War II brought rapid advancement in airplanes. The power of piston engines in airplanes doubled and the average speed of fighter planes increased from 300 to 450 m.p.h. The most outstanding aviation development of the war period was the jet engine. The first jet-powered airplane, the German Heinkel He-178, made a flight in 1939 but a practical jet fighter plane, the Lockheed P-80, was not developed until 1944. The first jet airliner was Britain's Comet, which began operating in 1949. By the 1950's, jets were used in great numbers.

During this period, the average room rate in United States' hotels dropped from US$5.60 in the 1930's to $3.21 in the 1940's. Confidence in the resurgence of the lodging industry was exhibited by many of the larger hotels and chains during the post war years. Westin introduced the first guest credit card in 1946, which is also the year that *Best Western* was founded, and the first casino hotel, the *Flamingo*, opened in Las Vegas. In 1947, Westin established *Hoteltype*, the first hotel reservation system, and New York City's *Roosevelt Hotel* installed television sets in all guest rooms. Hilton became the first international hotel chain with the opening of the *Caribe Hilton* in San Juan, Puerto Rico in 1949.[1] By the late 1940's, the economic, social and technological developments had begun to make individual and group travel possible for all.

The Evolution of Airports and Aircraft in The Bahamas

Paul Aranha, speaking at a meeting of the Bahamas Historical Society, gave a comprehensive history of the evolution of the airline industry in The Bahamas and named some of the individuals who played roles in the development of the airline industry. He referred to Harry Oakes and Harold G. Christie as the founding fathers of

Bahamian commercial aviation.[2] Harold Christie started *Bahamas Airways* in 1939, thus making a tremendous contribution to the development of the Family Islands.

BAL (Courtesy Paul Aranha)

Bahamas Airways Ltd's - Douglas DOLPHIN - 1936

At Oakes Field - Sidney Farrington, Sir Harry Oakes, Walter Foskett, unidentified individual, H. G.Christie (later Sir Harold), Aubrey Bethel.

1936 Douglas Dolphin (Courtesy Paul Aranha)

Oakes Field was one of two important military installations during World War II—and Nassau's first international airport. British South American Airways (BSAA) and British Overseas Airways Corporation (BOAC), which became British Airways, made regular flights to the Oakes Field airport. Their four-engined Lockheed *Constellation* and Boeing *Stratocruiser* airliners took about 24 hours to cross the Atlantic, making several stops on the way. On the 'southern' route, the aircraft landed at Lisbon, the Azores and Bermuda.[3]

World War II changed aviation in The Bahamas. Many Bahamians who volunteered for service with allied air forces pursued careers in civil aviation on their return. When the Japanese attack on Pearl Harbour brought the United States of America into the war, Oakes Field became an important military aerodrome and brought about the construction of a second, bigger, military airfield.[4]

Aranha explained that at key points around the Atlantic, the allies established a new pattern of air force Operational Training Units (OTUs), whose purpose was to train RAF aircrews, but these OTUs also played an important role in the convoy—and escort-systems as well as in oceanic-reconnaissance and submarine-chasing. Run by the Royal Air Force, Oakes Field was expanded into an OTU, where several hundred allied crews were trained.[5]

The second air base, Windsor Field, named in honour of the Duke of Windsor, accommodated RAF Transport Command, ferrying men and planes from the factories in the United States to the war zones in Africa and Europe. Windsor Field was shared with the United States military, which had built both bases. After WW II ended, Windsor Field was closed and abandoned and Oakes Field was, again, the centre of aviation.

Having survived the war years, Bahamas Airways grew and prospered and the Nassau Flying Club, provided an avenue where Bahamians could learn to fly. People, Aranha pointed out, are the foundation of a sound aviation industry, noting that "good people and second-rate planes are far more effective than good planes and second-rate people", for aviation is like a team-sport. Pilots depend on all of the other areas of airline expertise—from engineers and mechanics, reservations and counter personnel, and countless others.[6]

Aranha cited expatriates who led the way and stayed on to acquire Bahamian status such as Colyn Rees, an RAF Ferry Command pilot who was very active in the Nassau Flying Club, Bobby Hall & Lambert Albury, active instructors in the 1950's and 1960's. The President of the NFC, at one time, was Ezra Forsyth, who had worked for Pan Am as a radio operator, and his son, Joseph "Bouncer" Forsyth, became Chief Flying Instructor. The late Jack Graham came to The Bahamas with the Royal Air Force, doubled as a ground and fight engineer with BAL, putting in many hours airborne in the PBY Catalina. Sid Larkin was another who stayed and worked as an engineering manager at BAL, remaining a leading member of the Masonic Lodge long after the demise of the airline.[7]

Aranha also paid tribute to dedicated Aviation 'Agents' in Family Island stations served by airlines. In Abaco, Neville Key and Beverly Curry handled Green Turtle Cay, while Yvonne Albury was in charge at Marsh Harbour. John Marshall was the Agent at George Town, Exuma; Alice Waugh at West End, Grand Bahama; Ivy Simms at Long Island. When Freeport built an airport, Hugh Reiss, an American, was the Agent. In terms of Bahamians, Fred Higgs was a key figure at Nassau International Airport as were Gary Wallace and Ettie Isaacs. Henry Pyfrom was one of the first post-war Bahamian pilots and his wife, Janet, was Chief Stewardess.

In its early days, Bahamas Airways Limited depended on seaplanes and amphibians until government built more airports in the Family Islands and, gradually, these water birds gave way to land planes. After the 1931-vintage, twin-engined Douglas Dolphin—of which only a few seem to have been built—the fledgling airline operated a single-engine Loening, which became the Douglas Duck. The Model 16 Commodore—14 of which were built in 1929 by the Consolidated Aircraft Corporation—was the civilian version of the military XPY-1. Capable of carrying up to 33 passengers, the Commodores were the luxury airliner of their day and were sold to the New York, Rio and Buenos Aires Airline (which merged with Pan Am). The last of those Commodores was still flying 20 years later, carrying passengers for Bahamas Airways Limited.[8]

The mainstay of BAL's amphibious fleets were the Grumman G-21 Goose and the Grumman G-44 Widgeon. A smaller follow-up to the Goose, designed for executive transport, the Widgeon, entered service in 1940 but, after the war, Grumman refined the Widgeon for commercial use by altering the hull profile for improved handling on water and increasing the seating capacity of this G-44A to six. The Consolidated PBY Catalina, which has been described as the greatest of all flying boats, was one of the most versatile aircraft ever built and in a class by itself. The Catalina played a shorter, but vital role, in the development of scheduled routes. It was, in fact, developed as a flying-boat from the already mentioned Commodore but soon was converted into an amphibian.

Goose VP BAM at Green Turtle Cay, Abaco—(Courtesy: Paul Aranha)

Leonard Thompson—BAL's Goose aircraft (Courtesy: Paul Aranha)

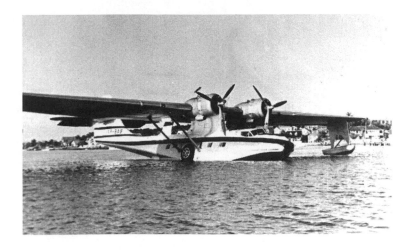

VP-BAB afloat (Courtesy: Paul Aranha)

VP-BAB PBY (Courtesy: Paul Aranha)

During WW II, the PBY was extensively used by the military in all theatres of the war, including being based in George Town, Exuma for anti-submarine patrol. Some 4,000 were built, but BAL operated only one of these and that aircraft became a favourite of the people in Abaco, where it gave door-to-door service between Nassau and Hope Town, Man O'War Cay and Green Turtle Cay, Abaco, accommodating 12 passengers. More recently, Sir Harold Christie had one based at Nassau International Airport. [9]

As seaplanes are expensive to operate, especially in salt water, Bahamas Airways introduced a variety of land planes, as more and more airports were built, and, steadily, cut back on the number of Family Island settlements that could be reached directly. Turbine engines and turbo-prop planes were still a thing of the future when BAL introduced the DH-114 Heron, a 17-passenger feeder-liner. This postwar, British-built landplane, of which some 160 left the production-line, had four 250-hp engines and a speed of about 140 mph. BAL operated two of them, VP-BAN and VP-BAO. The Handley-Page HP-81 HERMES, a 1948, civilian version of the 4-engined *Hastings* bomber, was one of the first new British airliners to enter post-war service with BOAC and eventually flew for BAL. Its standard passenger-carrying ability was 40, but it could carry up to 63. VP-BCA and VP-BCB were two twin-engined, 6-passenger Aero Commanders that BAL operated on charter and to perform daily patrols of The Bahamas archipelago for the Royal Bahamas Police Force. The aircraft that became best-known on BAL's Family Island routes was the Douglas DC-3, a twin-engine landplane equipped with 30 passenger-seats that flew at a cruising speed of some 160 miles per hour. [10]

DC3 VP-BBT (Courtesy: Paul Aranha)

Recalling his memories of Bahamas Airways, Aranha noted that when he joined BAL in 1963, as a First Officer flying the DC-3, there were many Bahamian ground staff but few Bahamian pilots. The only Bahamian-born pilots above him on the Pilots' Seniority List were Philip Farrington, Henry Pyfrom and Al Hall. Harcourt Fernander joined later.[11]

BAL's first turbine-powered aircraft was the British-built Vickers Viscount, the world's first gas-turbine engined aircraft in airline service and the most successful post-war British airliner, with 445 being sold. This 52-passenger plane was ideally suited for BAL's short-range routes and operated, primarily, the Nassau-Miami service but later, linked Freeport to Nassau and Florida. It had large freight and luggage compartments and was fitted with Rolls-Royce Dart turbo-prop engines. In 1966, while owned by BOAC, Bahamas Airways placed an order for Hawker-Siddeley HS-748 aircraft, each powered by two Rolls Royce Dart turbo-prop engines, to replace the DC-3 on the Family Island routes and, in November, the first group

BAL's first turbine-powered aircraft VP-BCE (Courtesy Paul Aranha)

of pilots, including Henry Pyfrom and Paul Aranha, went to England for training on the type. Starting in January 1967, the 4 aircraft [VP-BCJ, VP-BCK, VP-BCL and VP-BCM] went into service as they came off the assembly-line. These 44-passenger planes flew on BAL routes until October 1970.[12]

After Bahamas Airways Limited was put into voluntary liquidation on October 9,1970, F/O Cartner and Capt. Aranha ferried this BAC One-Eleven (300) via Montreal, Goose Bay (Labrador) and Keflavik (Iceland) to Bournemouth (Hurn) airport in England.

BAC-One Eleven (Courtesy Paul Aranha)

In 1968, when BOAC sold BAL to John Swire & Sons, the owners of Hong Kong's Cathay-Pacific Airline, BAL acquired their first pure-jet aircraft, the B.A.C. One-Eleven, which went into service in November of that year. At first, BAL leased two new, 79-seat "One-Eleven Series 400", to get the jet-service started, while their own two, 99-passenger "One-Eleven Series 500" aircraft could be manufactured and put into service. Later, a second-hand "One-Eleven Series 300", with 79 passenger seats, was leased and added to the fleet. Finally, BAL ordered a third "One-Eleven Series 500", this one equipped with an extra fuel-tank to give it the range required for BAL's proposed new route to New York/JFK airport. This aircraft made its maiden test-flight at the BAC factory on 9th October, 1970—the day that the shareholders put Bahamas Airways Limited into voluntary liquidation—ending 34 fatality-free years of flying.[13]

Aranha pointed out that BAL was not the only airline that operated before the creation of Bahamasair in 1973. Bahamas Air Traders/Island Flying Service/Out Island Airways represented the second-tier domestic air service at the time. They, too, used the Widgeon, Goose, Aero Commander and DC-3 and introduced the DeHavilland Twin Otter, a STOL plane able to land on Harbour Island. Pilots at Island Flying Service included Capt. Gil Hensler and Bahamian Edward Albury, who later became Deputy General Manager at the new Bahamasair in 1973 and was pulled out of retirement in 1992 to re-structure Bahamasair's aircraft-maintenance programme.[14]

The Local Scene with the Duke of Windsor as Governor

The War Years turned out to be an eventful period for The Bahamas with far-reaching historic and social developments.

When Britain entered the War in September 1939, recruitment began in The Bahamas for a local Volunteer Defense Force. Four companies, totalling close to 500 men who came from all of The Bahamas, were on guard at vulnerable points. Nassau served as the Royal Air Force Training Base and as Western Bastion of the Southern "Air Bridge", which ferried aircraft to combat zones in Africa, Europe and the Far East.

The seasonal tourism industry remained constant during the first two years of the war, fueled by American visitors. However, when the United States entered the War in response to the Japanese attack on Pearl Harbour on 7th December, 1941, the international tourist business collapsed. The bulk of the visitors to Bahama Islands after 1941 were military—British, American and Canadian airmen. As the war progressed, enemy submarines began operating close to The Bahamas.[15] Helping in the war relief effort was The Bahamas branch of the British Red Cross, which had been established in November 1939, along with the War Materials Committee, formed in June 1940 to supply Britain with local materials or products. Under the energetic chairmanship of Sir Etienne Dupuch, editor of the Tribune, quantities of supplies, such as knitted woolen comforts for the Fighting Forces, hospital supplies, tobacco products, and accessories, were shipped to Britain each fortnight for distribution.

Fortunately some employment was provided through development projects undertaken by Sir Harry Oakes and other wealthy residents such as Swedish industrialist Axel Wenner-Gren. Around the outbreak of the war in 1939, Dr. Axel Wenner-Gren, having acquired possession of most of the land on Hog Island, had begun development. He cut a canal, just west of the old bridge, that divided the island while creating a lagoon in the centre. A portion of the lagoon passed under his residence which was later converted to the gourmet restaurant Café Martinique. Several hundred jobs were also created by activities of the War Materials Committee.

An historic day for The Bahamas was 17ᵗʰ August, 1940, when the **Duke of Windsor,** Edward the Eighth, the former King of England, arrived in Nassau to become the 55ᵗʰ Governor of the Colony. After only about three months in The Bahamas, the Duke and Duchess were universally popular. Indeed, the Duke's presence in The Bahamas was the best advertisement the Colony had ever had. Many American tourists and European friends of the royal family came to get a glimpse of His Royal Highness and his Duchess in their island kingdom. Large-scale entertainment by the Duke and Duchess was not considered appropriate. However, as

Duke and Duchess of Windsor

Governor, the Duke of Windsor and his wife presided at many of the fundraising events organized to help the war effort and hosted occasional parties.

The Duke of Windsor, as governor, showed remarkable enthusiasm and he quickly grasped the problems and needs of the Colony. With tourism dried up, the Duke and his new Government were anxious to provide employment for the people.

During his first three years as Governor, the Duke was forced to deal with three difficult events—a riot, a Bay Street fire, and a vicious murder—all of which required his personal intervention and attracted international press to the Colony.

1942 "Burma Road" Riot

In May 1942, the Duke flew to Washington, D.C., to negotiate with President Roosevelt the recruitment of Bahamian farm labour and to arrange for the further involvement of The Bahamas in the total war effort. A few days after the Duke's departure, social upheaval erupted in Nassau. It started when the United States and the United Kingdom governments decided to build two air bases in Nassau—one at Oakes Field where Sir Harry Oakes had already developed a small landing field, and the other in the Pine Barrens at the western end of the island now known as Windsor Field. Some 2000-3000 jobs were to be made available. Under the supervision of the US army Engineering Department, an American firm, Pleasantville Construction Company, began work on 20ᵗʰ May, 1942. A grievance erupted because Bahamians were paid at the local prevailing rate of four shillings a day, while the Americans were paid at a higher rate. The Americans let it be known that they considered the Bahamian rate ridiculously low and that they were certain the contractors would pay more if allowed to do so. The Bay

Street merchants objected on the grounds that an increase in the local wage would upset the economy. Under increasing local pressure, the Pleasantville Construction Company withdrew its offer of higher wages for the locals and conformed to the wishes of the Bahamas government.

On Monday morning, 1st June, 1942, hundreds of labourers, many carrying machetes, sticks or clubs, marched into town and gathered on Bay Street. When one member of the mob hurled a bottle through the glass window of a shop, the riot commenced. In a few hours, Bay Street was in shambles. In the face of mounting tension and industrial unrest, a state of emergency was declared, and the Riot Act was read. A curfew was imposed until 8th June, prohibiting any person, other than a member of the armed forces or police, from being out of doors between 8 p.m. and 6 a.m. Fifteen gunshots were fired; five of the rioters were killed, seven seriously wounded and 40 suffered minor injuries.[16]

The Duke's return to Nassau from Washington was greeted with much anticipation by the working class who had heard about the Duke's sympathy for the underprivileged of England. Arrangements were immediately made to have union leaders meet with the Duke's committee. The Duke promised to have the matter reviewed and the workers returned to work on 4th June. The Duke announced at the end of June that, with some difficulty, he had been able to get the daily wage of unskilled workers raised from four shillings to five shillings a day and, in addition, there would be a free meal on the site.[17]

Bay Street Fire

Bay Street Fire of June 28, 1942—Duke of Windsor assists in fire operations. Photo Stanley Toogood, © Dupuch Publications

Before the community could recover fully from the effects of the riot, another disaster struck. On 28th June, 1942 a fire started in a small store on Bay Street, swept on to George Street, and, before it could be brought under control, the oldest business block in the city had been destroyed. Nassauvians still relate how the Duke of Windsor, smudged with soot and soaked to the skin, personally directed volunteer groups, while struggling with the fire hoses, side by side with hundreds of fire fighters from 1:30 a.m. to 6:30 a.m. The Duchess also played a role in the disaster by forming a Red Cross party to salvage goods from the burned buildings.[18]

Murder of Sir Harry Oakes

Yet another tragic event occurred which attracted major international publicity. On 8th July, 1943, Sir Harry Oakes, then a member of the Legislative Council, was found dead in his bed, the victim of a savage murder. Horror surged throughout the Colony, for Sir Harry had been a great benefactor of The Bahamas, beautifying the island, improving facilities and relieving unemployment. The Duke of Windsor, a personal friend of Sir Harry, made a great effort to see that the investigation was a thorough one. While the son-in-law, Alfred de Marigny, was charged with the murder, he was acquitted, and the murder remains unsolved. The unsolved tragic murder dealt a blow to the image of the Colony as a tranquil, peaceful haven, and some of the events and rumours were a lasting embarrassment to the Duke and Government of the day.[19]

Nassau—the Riviera of the Western Hemisphere

As the popularity of The Bahamas grew as an exclusive beach resort area, with attributes rivaling the Riviera in the Mediterranean coast, Nassau was described as the picturesque "Riviera" of the Western Hemisphere. The Development Board used its limited resources to promote the destination.

During the early 1940's, the Development Board was headed by Sidney Farrington, CBE, who was Pan American's first representative in The Bahamas, and later by Harold G. Christie, who was made a Companion of the Most Excellent Order of the British Empire in 1949 in recognition of his services in "selling" the then Colony to investors and visitors.

The Development Board's Peace advertisement

Even though global travel was curtailed because of war, The Bahamas was still appealing as a tourism destination, attracting special events such as **film production**, which bolstered the economy.

In the summer of 1941, Paramount Pictures filmed *Bahama Passage* in and around The Bahamas. Starring Madeleine Carroll and Stirling Hayden, scenes were filmed at Harbour Island, Eleuthera and Sandy Cay, Exuma. The Prince George Hotel, in downtown Nassau, which served as Paramount's headquarters, became a hive of activity during the filming. Located on the waterfront, this hotel was particularly convenient for the movie crew who could land their boats right on the terrace as they dashed off every few days to one of the islands to film scenes for the movie. The world premiere of the movie took place at Nassau's Savoy Theatre on Bay Street on 11th December, 1941 and was attended by the Duke and Duchess of Windsor. Proceeds were donated to the Bahamas War Committee for forwarding to England.

Paramount's spectacular results with this filming provoked serious consideration for Nassau as a tropical Hollywood. The chief advantage of The Bahamas, as described by film producers, was the weather, allowing seldom-interrupted succession of bright, sunny days, coupled with the brilliant colours of the sky, sea and flowers, lending themselves to good Technicolor films.

Regulations forbidding the sale of US dollars to Bahamians kept most people at home during the war years; thus winter residents and well-to-do Bahamians organized social events to occupy their time, while raising funds for the war effort.

In February 1941, The Bahamas hosted its first movie world premiere when George Bernard Shaw's "Major Barbara" made its debut at the Savoy Theatre.

Crowds flocked to Montagu Park, Nassau's one-mile race track, for the weekly races. There were seven races per afternoon and the track opened twice a week during the high season, February and March, and once a week in April.

A yachtsman's paradise, The Bahamas naturally became a racing centre. In March 1942 the International Spring Championships of the Star Class fleets sailed off Nassau in March 1942. On 10th February, ocean yachts sailed in the big annual race from Miami to Nassau. The venue for the race was Montagu Bay.

Shopping was also a favourite pastime. With exceptionally low duties on goods entering The Bahamas, shops in downtown, Nassau, were well stocked with English doeskins in a variety of shades, tweeds, linens, china and other products at low prices. Wine and liquors, French perfumes and beauty preparations were promoted as bargain items, with prices below those in the United States and Canada.

Although tourism was concentrated in Nassau, winter residents and army officers organized regular Family Island trips and sporting expeditions.

Linkages with the tourism industry through food production were realized with the opening in 1940 of the Hatchet Bay Farm, Eleuthera, which supplied milk and poultry to Nassau hotels and stores. A range of native-made products such as coconut straw hats, coconut and sisal bags, dyed fish scales, shells made up into attractive ornaments, cameos cut from conch shells, conch pearls and other jewellery cleverly carved by hand were sold to tourists. During the decades of the 1930's, 40's and 50's Biminites were engaged in a successful sea shelling industry. These shell "pickers" would spend the day combing beaches and shallow waters of Bimini Bay for choice sea shells, which were placed in buckets or tin cans, cleaned, polished, sorted and sold to local agents who sold them in Nassau and

Bay Street in the 1940's

Bahamian life in the 1940's. Source: Bahamas Magazine

Miami.[20] Other leading industries with a linkage to the tourism industry were the weaving of rugs by hand, using native palm straw, tile making at the Nassau Tile Factory and mahogany furniture from Mosko's Bahamian factory.

An event which encouraged linkages was the annual *Bahamas Fair*, which created opportunities for craftsmen, artisans and farmers to showcase their wares. In 1940, the Bahamas Chamber of Commerce organized the first Bahamas Fair ever held in the Colony. The objective of this show of Bahamian arts, craft, and agricultural products was chiefly to assist in the development of Bahamian industries by showcasing wares of the Family Islands, thus increasing self-sufficiency. The 1941 Fair was almost twice the size of the first. Exhibitors were grouped into several categories—agricultural, handicraft, needlework, home economics, animal husbandry, shell and straw work and marine sections. There was a vast improvement in the quality of products the second year. Among the islands represented, along with New Providence, were Long Island, Abaco, Eleuthera, Exuma, Cat Island, Long Cay. Throughout their tenure, the Duke and Duchess were strong supporters of "Things Bahamian".[21]

Duchess of Windsor wears a tiara made of Bahamian shells

The Duchess of Windsor in a straw hat made by a local artisan

Bahamian hand-made products and souvenirs on display at Bahamas Fair

Transportation Costs in the 1940's

Nassau continued to be serviced from Miami by Pan American Airways (Pan Am), which provided the fastest and most frequent schedules in Nassau's history. Pan Am's airfare on its powerful DC3A's for the daily 70-minute service from Miami to Oakes Field, Nassau was $36.00 round trip, $20.00 one-way.[22]

Oakes Field Airport

According to the Bahamas Magazine, the cost of airfare on Bahamas Airways' 7-passenger Douglas seaplane was $8 (£2) one way and $12 (£3) round trip, to Harbour Island, Governor's Harbour and Hatchet Bay.[24] Along with Pan Am, Chalk's also continued to play an important role in transporting notable personalities of that era such as Errol Flynn, Judy Garland, Ernest Hemingway, Howard Hughes and Al Capone to The Bahamas.

Throughout the year, motor vessels with neat, though limited, accommodations for passengers, left Miami frequently during the week, bound for Nassau. The Miami-Nassau voyage lasted about 16 hours. The fare was $15.00 return or $9.00 one-way. The charge for automobiles when accompanied by a passenger was $15.00 one-way or $25.00 round trip. Passengers often brought their own vehicles for $25 (round trip).[25] A few of these ships proceeded to other islands after stopping at Nassau. Family Island trips became increasingly popular.

In terms of cruises, Eastern Steamship Lines' Yarmouth made 24 overnight sailings in the winter of 1941. The New York-Miami-Nassau round trip fare at that time was $85. The M/V Monarch did the Nassau-Miami run. The "floating universities" gained popularity in 1940, when groups of students came to The Bahamas on cruise ships.

Taxi rates ranged between 12 and 16 shillings ($2-$3) per car per hour, and 25% higher after midnight. The government tax was 6 shillings (or $1.20) for cruise passengers making continuous round voyage and 12 shillings (or $2.50) for round-trip stopover passengers.

Hotel Accommodations

Rates for some of the major hotels operating on New Providence in 1941 are shown in Table 5-1. Most hotels opened three months of the year but the

Prince George, the Windsor, the Parliament Hotel and the Rozelda Apartment Hotel were open year round. Private clubs catering to the elite were the Bahamas Country Club, Nassau Yacht Club, the Emerald Beach Club and the Porcupine Club. The Bahamas Country Club was one of the show places of the island, boasting an 18-hole golf course, tennis, swimming and water-skiing on a beautiful beach. **Lyford Cay**, another private development, was the hideaway for the rich and famous.

Cumberland House

Prince George Hotel (Courtesy Ronald Lightbourne)

Table 5-1
Rates at Selected Accommodations on New Providence—1941

HOTEL	LOCATION	RATE
British Colonial Hotel	Downtown harbour-front Bay Street	£2.5.0 up Sgl; £4.6.0 Dbl
Rozelda Apartment Hotel	Downtown Nassau	15/-up Sgl; £1.10.0 Dbl
Prince George Hotel	Downtown Nassau on the harbour	£1.0.0 up Sgl; £1.15.0 Dbl
The Windsor Hotel	Downtown Nassau	15/-up Sgl; £1.10.0 Dbl
Parliament Hotel	Parliament Street between Bay and Shirley	15/-up. Sgl; £1.10.0 Dbl
Cable Beach Manor	Housekeeping units on Cable Beach	£1.7.6 up for efficiency
Lofthouse and Dean Cottages	George Street near Government House.	£1.5.0 up Double
Lucerne Hotel	Frederick Street	7/6-10/-Sgl ; £1.2.6 Dbl
Hotel Charlotte	Charlotte Street, just off Bay Street	7/6-12/6 Sgl; 15/- Dbl
Cumberland House	Cumberland Street	£1.5 Sgl; £1.5.0-£3.15 Dbl

Note: The legal tender was the British Pound notes and British silver coins, although United States currency was generally accepted. The conversion rate in the 1940's was £1 = US $4
Source: Nassau Magazine, Volume IX, February-March 1942

A number of **private homes** also catered to visitors and employed a full staff year-round. One such property was *Los Cayos*, west of Buena Vista on Augusta Street, owned by Arthur Vernay, a noted conservationist, who sold his home in England and moved to The Bahamas. Mr. Vernay was instrumental in the preservation of the flamingo and worked with both Henry Nixon in Inagua and Mr. Headley Edwards who trained the flamingoes at Ardastra Gardens. In an interview at his Young Street home, Urban Bostwick, who served as Mr. Vernay's butler for 40 years, shared some of his memories and photographs of his tenure in the hospitality industry. He recalled that Mr. Vernay, who also owned a beach house on Cable Beach, had a staff of 19 to cater to maintain his two homes and cater to his numerous guests. There were four foreign staff—an English Butler (William Chandler), a French Maid, two Scottish Chefs/Cooks and 15 native staff. Mr. Bostwick noted that local staff were trained at the Dundas Civic Centre. He and Henry Wright had the good fortune to work with Mr. Chandler, who trained them well. Other local staff included Hazel Darling, an excellent cook who assisted the French chef, a maid, gardener, orchidologist, watchman, handymen and yard staff. He noted that among the many house guests hosted by Mr. Vernay was the Duke of Windsor. During World War II, when the foreign staff, were unable to travel back to Nassau to resume their duties, Mr. Vernay recruited staff from the United States. He was unhappy with their performance and promoted Mr. Urban Bostwick to head Butler and he also assumed responsibility for the entire household staff. After Mr. Vernay's death in 1960, Mr. Bostwick continued on at Los Cayos under the employ of Mrs. Vernay, who died in 1979. Mr. Bostwick was later employed as Property Manager at Ambassador Beach and Pastry Chef at the Cable Beach Hotel.[26]

Los Cayos, home of noted conservationist, Arthur Vernay

Arthur Vernay and guests

The **Family Islands**, although virtually unknown, were the playground for an elite group of wealthy visitors who returned year after year to enjoy the unspoilt tranquillity. Ernest Hemingway (1898-1961) visited Bimini for the first time in 1935 and returned many times in 1936 and 1937. In some literary circles, it is alleged that Hemingway's experiences on Bimini may have inspired him to write *The Old Man and the Sea* for which he received the Pulitzer Prize in 1953. According to Ashley Saunders, Hemingway's fishing guide on Bimini, he landed several record fish and worked on magazine articles and novels.[27]

The Duke and Duchess of Windsor made frequent trips by yacht to Cat Cay and other islands. The English journalist Pamela Murray in an article "*Nassau Nineteen Forty-One*" ended her story: "much as I have enjoyed the comforts of the British Colonial Hotel . . . it is the morning I spent on Harbour Island which will stick in my memory". She said that there was an enchantment about that island from the famous sign "Goats and Coconuts" in Dunmore Town to the sophistication of the bungalows. She continued: "If I am ever able to retire from inkslinging, it will be to Harbour Island, where the youngest children dance the rumba and where the choir boys wear scarlet cassocks".[28]

Accommodations for the "Coloured"

During this period, hotels in the Bay Street area were reserved for whites. Therefore, several professional blacks in The Bahamas built small guest houses or converted rooms within their houses as facilities for visitors of colour. Dr. Claudius R. Walker built the **Rhinehart Hotel** on Baillou Hill Road in the early 1940's. The facility included 14 guest rooms and an auditorium which could seat up to 300 people. The Rhinehart attracted all classes of blacks from abroad and within The Bahamas. This hotel became the in-spot among blacks for wedding receptions, concerts, and political events and for many black church groups and other conventions from abroad. The International Elks Convention was held there in the 1940's, attracting visitors coming from all over the United States. The building which formerly housed the Rhinehart has been designated a historic building under the Antiquities & Monuments Act.[29]

Other small hotels operating in the 1940's were the *Alpha Hotel*, on the corner of St. James Road and Shirley Street, owned by Mr. William Cash, catering to the domestic market, and **Weary Willies**, on Hay Street and Baillou Hill Road owned by Willie Neely.

Three prominent women who opened their homes to visitors of colour were Mamie Worrell, Flo Major and Pearl Cox. They offered inviting guest accommodations with a personal touch, becoming a home-away-from-home primarily for black travellers.

Flo Major, a native of Grenada, met and married Bahamian athlete Charlie Major when they were both living in New York. They married and moved to The Bahamas in the 1940's, taking up residence at the Major's homestead on Fowler Street (south of the gas station at the corner of East Bay and Fowler Streets). To meet the need for accommodations for people of colour, in light of the racist policies of the period, the Major family operated their two-storey home as a guest house. According to Sir Clement Maynard, a good friend of the family, Flo Major was a superb cook and an excellent entertainer, whose guest house catered to an upscale clientele. Among the frequent guests was trumpeter Louis Amstrong, who could often be seen sitting on the porch of the guest house, enjoying the fine hospitality. Flo Major was also who prepared full-course meals for private parties. Because both Flo and Charlie had developed many contacts during their stay in New York, and those who visited told their friends about the first-class Bahamian experience, Flo's Guest House enjoyed full occupancy most of the year. The Guest House operated well into the 1960's.[30]

Shortly after Flo Major entered the hospitality business, Mamie Worrell opened her home *Laurelhurst-by-the-Sea,* on East Bay Street, to visitors of colour. Like the Majors, Mamie Warrell catered to professional upscale Black Americans. Her guests were primarily from the southern United States. It was not unusual for groups of friends (such as The Links) to gather on the upstairs porch of Worrell's Guest House and share spirited fun as they watched a passing parade both on the main street below and the waterfront across the street. The names of visitors to Worrell's Guest House, Like Flo's Guest House, would read like a "Black Who's Who" among Black Americans and included Mr. & Mrs. W.E.B. Dubois, Black entertainers like Roy Hamilton, Sydney Poitier, and Harry Belafonte.

A full bio of Mrs. Mamie Worrell is included at the end of this book among the Stalwarts who helped to build the Bahamian tourism industry.

The Police Band becomes the centre of local entertainment

It was also during this period that the **Royal Bahamas Police Force Band** began to play a significant role in the tourism industry, Although policing in Nassau started in 1729, with one constable who worked with a magistrate, the Police Force Band was not formed until March of 1840 under the command of Inspector General John Pinder with the strength of 16 men. Some 53 years later it was reported that the Band consisted of 12 members who performed normal police duties, but were given time off to practise for official engagements. The band was allowed two four-hour periods a week to practise, and played for official engagements only but received no extra pay. In the early 1900's, the small band was well equipped, after donations of instruments by such local residents as Leon Dupuch, and gave a concert on Fridays on the Library Green, now known as the Garden of Remembrance.

In the 1940's, it was reported that the Police Band performed during the opening of the legislature along with the Volunteer Defense Force. After marching to Bay Street, the band formed a guard of honour in front of the Public Buildings, to the delight of visitors and residents.[31]

It was in the early 1950's that the Police Band experienced greatest improvements. Arrangements were made for warrant officer EduBauchaire, bandmaster of the US Air Force Band, New Mexico to visit Nassau and give the band music instruction. In 1952, with the acquisition of additional brass instruments, complete instrumentation for a military band of 18 was accomplished. By the end of that year, the band had performed for 39 public engagements. In 1956, the then Commissioner of Police, Colchester Weymss, recruited 12 specialists. Among the men recruited was Dennis Morgan, a retired officer from the Worchestershire Regiment. Morgan arrived in The Bahamas in 1958 from Jamaica and became director of the Police Band, and retained this title until 1978. During his tenure, much improvement in the band and the introduction of the pomp and ceremony took place. A change of attire was approved, with the band being allowed to wear the white pit helmet adorned with a red feather and a chain attached to the peak. Leopard skins worn by the drummers and a red belt with gold stripes replaced the leather belts. The dark blue trousers with red stripes and white bush jackets became the standard. These adjustments resulted in an impressive uniform.

On the recommendation of Mr. Morgan, the band became a permanent unit. The Beating of the Retreat was introduced and the lowering of the flag at 6:00 p.m. week days, which was accompanied by a bugler, and later developed into a grand ceremony.

Other Entertainment

Prominent night spots of the day were the *Jungle Club* in the Montagu Hotel, *Paul Meeres Cabaret Club* and *Dirty Dicks* which came on the scene in 1943. Other large hotels—British Colonial, Royal Victoria and Prince George—also boasted popular bars and entertainment for dancing. *"Blind Blake"*, spotlighted at the end of this book, was one of the popular entertainers of the time. During this period, the **Nassau Guardian** published regular reports of "John

Blind Blake at Royal Vic

Lou Adams band performs at British Colonial

Canoe" (later known as Junkanoo) parades during the Christmas season.

Post War Period

During post-war years, after work on the bases had finished, there was little employment in the Colony, forcing planeloads of Bahamians to depart for the United States for jobs as farm and factory labourers. The economy was bolstered after 1945 when English capital, escaping taxation following the Labour Party's victory at the polls, was channeled to The Bahamas for property investment. Real estate prices soared, the building industry was stimulated, and gradually tourism began to regain its post-War level.

To keep up with the competition, many of the larger hotels underwent refurbishment or management changes. In 1949, Mrs. Munson sold the Royal Victoria Hotel to Royal Little, and the management embarked on a million dollar restoration programme, including addition of a swimming pool, an outdoor bar, partial air conditioning and luxury apartments. A Blockade-Runners' Bar was elegantly decorated with scenes of Royal Vic's living past. The Fort Montagu Beach Hotel was sold by the local company to Canadian Gordon Fairley, who later sold it to George Elcock. W.E. Butlin, MBE, purchased the hotel in late 1948, and in April 1950 he leased it to Gordon Ltd., a company owned by Messrs. Sam and Harry Miller of New York.

In 1946, Donald Delahey established *Playtours*, a full-service travel agency, which was to play a leading role in tourism development in the 1950's and 1960's.

From left: Jane Meadows, Donald Delahey, who established Playtours in 1946, and Audrey Meadows

In April 1948, *R.H. Curry*, which had been established as a travel agency in 1936 by a prominent local investor, Mr. R.H. Curry (who had served as Chairman of the Bahamas Development Board in 1926-27), received its International Air Transport Association (IATA) licence to operate as a tour operator. IATA was the agency which authorized a travel agent or tour operator to sell air transportation and receive commissions from its Association members. IATA also developed the worldwide system of fare calculations, and would hold conferences at which rates or fares were set for transportation between different countries.

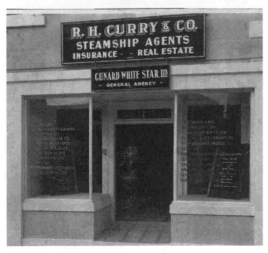

R.H. Curry, founded in 1936, received its IATA licence as a tour operator in 1948

R.H. Curry ad. (Source: Nassau Magazine, 1953)

Tourism Performance

Table 5-2
Breakdown of Visitor Arrivals—1949

Visitors—by Air and sea		Visitors—Stopovers vs. Transients	
Air	21,722	Stopovers	14,865
Sea	10,296	Transients	17,153
Total	**32,018**	**Total**	**32,018**

As can be seen from the Table 5-2, when visitors started to come to The Bahamas again in larger numbers after the war, the statistics were not very encouraging. The 32,018 who arrived in 1949 were actually 2,000 less than those of twelve years earlier.

This flat growth was in direct contrast to neighbouring Florida which was achieving notable post-war success through tourism promotion funded by a cooperative government/private sector promotion fund of several million dollars. Contributors to Florida's fund were the State Advertising Commission, resort city governments, Chambers of Commerce, transportation companies, hotels, utility companies and other business organizations. Their huge tourism investment paid handsome dividends.

After close study of Florida's tourism success, the Bahamas Development Board, along with influential members of the Bahamian community, lobbied for increased tourism promotion. There was much opposition to this suggestion, since tourism was viewed as fickle and not a serious long-term economic alternative. Politicians, with fresh reminders of the blow to tourism following World War II, argued that it was not prudent to depend on tourism since further unrest or an outbreak of disease could cripple the industry overnight. A minority group felt that tourism was the best alternative.

A delegation called on the Acting Governor of The Bahamas, Derek Evans, and urged that Mr. Stafford Sands, an able lawyer and politician, whose mental energy and ability to get things done were well-known, be appointed Chairman of the Development Board. Governor Evans agreed.

*   *   *

Following The Bahamas General Election of 1949, the many new members of the Legislature were persuaded to provide the funds for large-scale tourist promotion. The phenomenal results of this gamble are revealed in the next two chapters.

6

PIONEERING SPIRIT, PROMOTION AND YEAR-ROUND TOURISM—1950'S

External Factors Impacting Bahamian Tourism

Travel Becomes more Affordable

In the 1950's, there was rapid recovery from the tourism collapse suffered during World War II. Real incomes grew substantially; the economic environment was one of affluence and optimism. With the improvement in standards of living and a rise in per capita income, travel was no longer reserved for the elite, the rich and the famous, but was more affordable to the working class.

Technological advances—the rapid development of transportation, especially in the airline industry—along with price reduction on fares with the introduction of package tours, opened travel to the masses. The 1950's marked the beginning of the jet age, reducing travel time and improving the efficiency of thc airline sector. In 1956, Britain and France began working separately on a supersonic aircraft that would fly at twice the speed of sound. This period also heralded developments in space travel in the United States when the National Aeronautics and Space Administration (NASA) was established in October 1958, and, in 1959, seven men were chosen by NASA to become America's first astronauts.

The spread of education, through television and the media, awakened the desire for travel. There was also a new attitude evolving that travel could satisfy the thirst for a cultural and educational experience and escape from the rigours of city life. At the same time, social legislation by member states of the International Labour Organization (ILO) shortened the work week, ensured an annual paid holiday, and early retirement, thus encouraging middle-class participation in leisure travel.

Hotel Branding

In the United States, advances in the lodging industry and standardization of hotel service was achieved through hotel chains. In 1952, in Memphis, Tennessee,

Kemmons Wilson opened his first Holiday Inn. In 1954, Howard Dearing Johnson initiated the first Howard Johnson motor lodge franchise, and Ramada opened in Arizona the first in its series of inns. In 1957, J.W. Marriott opened his first hotel, the Twin Bridges Marriott Motor Hotel, in Arlington, Virginia, and Jay Pritzker bought his first hotel—The Hyatt House in Los Angeles.[1]

Chain hotels spread throughout North America and later to the Caribbean. The success of these chains could be attributed to the consumer's preference for a recognized "brand" of hotel. Holiday Inn capitalized on this convenience by successfully using the theme "No surprises" in its advertising campaign. By 1963, the concept of "no surprises" had become so popular that 100 Holiday Inns had been built. Existing hotel chains added new amenities to remain competitive. For example, Hilton was the first chain to install direct-dial telephone service in 1957 and the in-room coffee concept was developed by Atlas Hotels in the mid-1950's. In 1964, Travelodge developed wheelchair-accessible rooms, in response to the cry for handicapped-friendly travel facilities. In 1966, Intercontinental introduced business lounges, ice and vending machines in guest corridors and street entrances for hotel restaurants.[2] Also, during the 1960's hotels spread from urban and resort areas to rural, suburban and airport locations.

Meanwhile, in Europe, Gerard Blitz, a Belgian, created a new type of vacation when he established the first Club Méditerranée (Club Med) Village in Alcudia, Spain, in 1950, as an all-inclusive informal tent resort. By 1959, 20 Club Med villages had been established, catering to trailblazers interested in breaking their everyday routines in unique natural settings with the ambience and spirit created by energetic staff known as Gentils Organisateurs (G.Os), translated "friendly hosts". Club Med crossed the Atlantic in the late 1960's and opened its first Caribbean villages in Guadeloupe in 1968, Mexico in 1974 and in The Bahamas three years later—on Paradise Island in 1977 and Governor's Harbour, Eleuthera in 1978.

July 17, 1955 ushered in an innovative entertainment concept in the tourism industry with the opening of *Disneyland*, Walt Disney's $17 million theme park, built on 160 acres of former orange groves in Anaheim, California. It realized staggering profits, attracting tourists from all over the world.

Air-conditioning makes Year-Round Tourism Possible

Another world phenomenon, with significant impact on tourism, was the introduction of air-conditioning. Even though the first air conditioning machine for a printing plant was built as far back as 1902 in Brooklyn, New York, it was not until the 1920's that movie theatres, department stores and restaurants installed air conditioners. After World War II, air conditioning became popular throughout the world. Before air conditioning became widespread, the tourist season was four months long—from December to Easter—in warm-weather destinations like The Bahamas. Initially, older hotels invested in small air-conditioning units, which could cool a single room, and higher rates were demanded for these deluxe accommodations. While new, fully air-conditioned hotels had become widespread in Florida in the 1940's, it was not until 1954 that The Bahamas could boast a fully air-conditioned hotel. The humid summer could now be endured and year-round tourism was finally possible.

The Bahamas Government's New Commitment to Tourism

During this period, the Bahamas Government provided extraordinary support to the tourism industry, through large budget allocations, which enabled massive overseas promotion to be carried out, along with subsidies and the introduction of special events.

In 1950, the Bahamas Legislature made the bold move to increase the tourism budget by 66% from £94,031 to £156,150, and to continue to vote large sums annually for tourism promotion. In 1951, the number of visitors to Nassau increased to 68,502—more than double the annual level during the 1946-49 period, and the upward trend in tourism arrivals continued throughout the decade. As can be seen from Table 6-3, the vibrancy of the tourism industry impacted Government revenue, as double-digit increases were recorded nearly every year.

This unparalleled success can be attributed to the far-sighted promotional policy of the Development Board and its chairman, *Stafford L. Sands,* who was appointed in 1950, and knighted in 1963. A successful Bay Street lawyer and member of the House of Assembly since 1937, Sir Stafford began the Colony's transition from an exclusive winter resort catering to 30,000 annual visitors

Sir Stafford Sands—first Minister of Tourism

to a successful year-round tourism mecca. Other members of the Development Board in the early 1950's were H.G. Christie, C. Trevor Kelly, C.W.F. Bethell and R.H. Symonette.

New hotel development, an aggressive communications and promotional strategy, and airline expansion were important elements of Sir Stafford's strategy.

Resort Development

In 1950, the hotels, restaurants, and clubs in The Bahamas were old and limited. Because they were not air-conditioned, the intense heat forced most of them to close in the summer. The three large hotels and most of the smaller properties dated back to the 1930's. Exceptions were the posh residential clubs on Cable Beach, the Balmoral (1948) and Bahamas Country Club. Because existing properties, including guest

Balmoral Club

Balmoral Club, built in 1948

houses and bungalows, which housed long-stay visitors, were unable to meet the demand, price gouging became commonplace. A Guardian editorial in January 1952 bemoaned the widespread overpricing by those owners of houses and bungalows. The editor warned that such price gouging could ruin the industry and "kill the goose that lay the golden egg".[3]

To encourage the construction of new hotels and modernization of existing establishments to cater to the expanding tourist industry, the Bahamas Government passed the *Hotels Encouragement Act* in 1954. The Act allowed customs duty refunds on materials imported for use in the construction and furnishing of a new hotel, or for refurbishing a property. The Act also granted a ten-year exemption from real property tax and a 20-year exemption from direct taxation on hotel earnings. Hotels on New Providence with a minimum of 20 bedrooms could qualify for the exemption, and for Family Island properties the minimum number of rooms required to qualify was ten.

In 1952, hotel owners and managers formed the *Bahamas Hotel Association* (BHA) to jointly promote their properties and to help the Development Board market The Bahamas as a destination. Its first president was Reginald Nefzger, then Managing Director of the British Colonial Hotel, and the Executive Director was Lorraine Onderdonk, who served faithfully in the post for more than 20 years. The seven original member hotels of the BHA were the Royal Victoria, British Colonial, Montagu Beach, Prince George, Parliament, Carlton House and Cumberland House. The association developed a series of bargain rate packages to keep the hotels open through the offseason. In 1952, a typical summer Full American Plan (AP) package, which included ground transfers, accommodations and three meals, was priced at $75 for seven days in Nassau, excluding airfare. BHA also initiated courtesy training for hotel employees.

Reginald Nefzger becomes the first President of the Bahamas Hotel Association in 1952

Hotel European Plan (EP) rates (room only), per person, double occupancy (two persons sharing a room), ranged from $9 to $15 per person per day for a smaller hotel like Pilot House Club and Carlton House, and $12 to $22 in a larger hotel like Montagu Beach, Royal Victoria and British Colonial. The larger properties also offered a Modified American Plan (MAP) rate, which included room, breakfast and dinner, ranging from $20 to $28 per person (double occupancy), and up to $45 for a suite. A comfortable guest house could be rented at $8.00 per room and an apartment hotel room for as low as $10 per day.[4]

Nassau

In Nassau, seven new hotels were completed between the period 1953-59. In Cable Beach the *Emerald Beach Hotel*, under the operation of Texas and California hotel magnate Leo F. Corrigan, opened its doors to the vacationing public for the first time on

Emerald Beach Hotel, the first centrally air-conditioned Hotel, opens in August 1954

11th August, 1954. The luxurious $3.5 million hotel, with 300 rooms, became Nassau's largest and first fully air-conditioned hotel. It offered water sports as well as tours to other

Dolphin Hotel began operations in 1956

resort islands as a part of its entertainment programme. The hotel, with Nassau's first convention centre, boasting 8,000 square foot convention hall seating up to 600 persons, was extremely successful in attracting group business.[5]

On 15th December, 1956 the fabulous 2,500-acre *Coral Harbour Club* was officially opened in Coral Harbour. In attendance were the Governor, His Excellency the Rt. Hon. Earl of Ranfurly, and the Countess of Ranfurly and many other distinguished residents and visitors to Nassau. The following year, in 1957, the Coral Harbour Yacht Club was commissioned enabling the resort to offer charter boats, water skiing, skin diving, regattas and fishing tournaments.

The *Dolphin Hotel,* which began operations in July 1956, at the corner of West Bay and Nassau Streets, added 67 ocean-front rooms in 1957; a five-room penthouse topped the five-storey structure. Another new hotel in the Western Esplanade harbour-front area during this period was the five-storied 56-room *Mayfair,* owned by retired English businessman, Ernest Batley, and operated by the Clifford Hotels Ltd.

The *Pilot House Club*, next to Nassau Yacht Haven on East Bay Street, became the favourite resort for yachtsmen. The resort derived its name from an old house reportedly constructed in the early 1800's, which was purchased in 1950 by Robert H. Symonette. His intention was to create an informal gathering place with bedrooms, restaurant and bar for visiting yachtsmen.

The Pilot House Hotel got its name from this house constructed on the site in the late 1790's or 1800's and purchased in 1950 by Robert H. Symonette

Pilot House was designated the official headquarters for Nassau Speed Week, the Rod and Reel Division of the Bahamas Angling Club, the Out Island Squadron, the Bahamas Automobile Club, and the Bahamas Power Boat Association. Membership in the club was open to anyone in the world who had caught a World Record.[6]

In 1959 the elitist *Lyford Cay Club* came on the scene. Designed by golf architect, Dick Wilson of Delray Beach Florida, it operated exclusively on a membership basis.

The Pilot House Club on East Bay Street became the favourite resort for Yachtsmen in the 1950's-1970's (now Gold Circle)

As the decade was coming to a close, Frank Crothers, president of Robert Law (Bahamas) Ltd., commissioned architect, Charles F. McKiraham of Fort Lauderdale, Florida to build "the most beautiful hotel in The Bahamas". Thus, on 25th January, 1959, the *Nassau Beach Hotel* opened in Cable Beach. The hotel's 278 rooms located throughout three wings, formed a horseshoe so that each had an uninterrupted view of the sea. Contract Interiors

Nassau Beach hotel opens in 1959

of Boston added the finishing touches to the lobby and rooms, with imported European furnishings. Staff—bellboys, waitresses, waiters, bartenders, bus boys and maids—wore striking costumes designed by D'armigene, employing the colours of the islands. On the premises was a Howard Johnson restaurant, decorated in the motif of the most luxurious Johnson motor lodges in the United States. This new hotel was described as a "super-spectacular luxury resort." [7]

To keep pace, most of Nassau's old established hotels modernized their buildings and décor, or added new facilities, including single-unit air-conditioning to many of their rooms. For example, the Fort Montagu Beach Hotel added 30 new air-conditioned poolside rooms, featuring private balconies, large picture windows and walk-in closets. The British Colonial underwent renovations costing $1.5 million in 1957. The Royal Victoria Hotel, still the leading hotel, could now boast among its offerings a new luxurious salt-water garden swimming pool, Starlight Terrace Bar featuring Blind Blake and his Calypso band, handsome Harlequin Room for special functions, and "ample air-conditioned rooms available". [8]

A new charming guest house "*Sun And . . .*" opened in Nassau in 1957. It was owned by Pete Garner, a Squadron Leader in the Royal Air Force who had come to Nassau four years previously as Aide-de-Camp to the Governor of The Bahamas. A few smaller guest houses still received their share of the business. Among them was the *Singing Kettle Guest House,* located three minutes from the Drake Hotel, and the *Buena Vista Guest House* on Delancey Street which became popular for its sumptuous cuisine.

Bay Street in the 1950's

Shopping was a regular pastime for both stopover visitors, who stayed in hotels, and cruise ship passengers. Nassau was popular for exclusive European products, which could be purchased at competitive prices, its variety of fine liquors, wines and whiskies, and local straw products. Sightseeing tours, marine tours, as well as golfing expeditions, were also popular.

In the 1950's, horse and carriage rates were $1.40 per person per hour and 70¢ for each additional half hour. Taxi fares were just 28¢ per person for the first mile, and 14¢ for each additional mile. A city tour was $3 per person and a country tour $4. Motorbikes could be rented for US$3.00 per day. Fishing trips were $7.00 per person, and motorboats could be hired for $4.00 a day. At the Bahamas Country Club, green fees were $4.00 a day, and horseback riding at the Oakes Stables was $1.40 an hour.[9]

Grand Bahama

Billy Butlin (later knighted), who had purchased a large tract of land at West End, Grand Bahama in 1948, built the first phase of *Butlin's Vacation Village,* which opened on 15th February, 1950, with 250 rooms. The plan called for a self-contained

500-room "holiday camp", an airstrip, power plant, conference halls, dock, swimming pools and shops. The cost of a week's vacation was $99, and for a time the hotel was full.[10] In July 1950, Butlin told the *Miami News* that he expected to have the entire holiday village finished in time for the winter season. However, mainly due to the inflated cost of construction, the project was losing money and creditors had it closed down. The creditors formed Grand Bahama Properties Ltd. to administer the assets. The hotel re-opened in 1955, after extensive renovations, as an upscale fishing resort called the *Grand Bahama Club*, but did not flourish. Peter Barratt in his book *Grand Bahama: A Rich and Colourful History*, suggests that this $8 million holiday camp idea was about ten years ahead of its time.[11]

The birth of Freeport/Lucaya

Meanwhile, Wallace Groves, a Virginian financier, who had settled and invested heavily in The Bahamas during World War II, became an important investor on Grand Bahama. He had acquired and developed Little Whale Cay in the Berry Islands, and, in 1946, bought the ailing Abaco Lumber Company, which had lumbering rights in both Abaco and Grand Bahama. He set to work modernizing and mechanizing the operation, and greatly increased the output. Peter Barratt, in his book, reported that Abaco Lumber Company in Pine Ridge, Grand Bahama was, in its heyday, the largest single employer in The Bahamas with nearly 1,800 people on the payroll. In the early 1950's, Groves sold the Grand Bahama lumbering rights, in order to concentrate on a much bigger project—the creation of Freeport.[12]

Groves approached Stafford Sands, who was his lawyer, about his ambitious plan for the development of a "free port" community in the pine barrens of Grand Bahama. Sands was able to convince the Government of the feasibility of the plan, and, on 4th August, 1955, the Hawksbill Creek Agreement between the Honourable A.G.H. Gardner-Brown, Acting Governor of The Bahamas, and Wallace Groves, President of the Grand Bahama Port Authority Limited, was signed. In this original agreement, Government conveyed 50,000 acres of land, with an option for an additional 50,000 acres, to the Port Authority, and promised freedom from customs duty, excise, export and stamp taxes for 99 years. The Agreement further guaranteed exemption from real property and personal taxes for 30 years (later extended to 2015). The developers agreed to create a deep water harbour and to convert the scrubland into a lucrative industrial area, encouraging industries.

Wallace Groves presented the Government with a blueprint for the development, and between 1955 and 1960 Phase 1 was completed. This stage focused on the harbour and involved surveying, site planning, dredging, and completion of a deep-water harbour. At Freeport Harbour, all but the largest tankers, cargo ships and cruise ships could anchor offshore in 50 feet of water, with space for five ships to be fuelled at once. At least £6 million was sunk into

Freeport by Wallace Groves, along with shipbuilding tycoon D.K. Ludwig (who invested in the harbour). Peter Barratt gives a good account of the industrial development of the island and the problems encountered,[13] as well as progress achieved following the involvement as shareholders of Charles W. Hayward (a wealthy British industrialist and chairman of the Firth-Cleveland Group) and Jack Hayward (both later knighted).

In 1959, *Caravel Club*, an 8-unit guest cottage and restaurant, was constructed for the convenience of clients. This club and the *Fishing Hole Guest House* were the only accommodations in Freeport, Grand Bahama. The **Bahamas Handbook** quoted Groves as saying that many visitors had "expressed interest in vacationing here, but we just haven't room for them". Plans were about to be unveiled for two 18-hole golf courses, luxurious hotels and a casino.

The Family Islands

Before the 1950's, significant resort development existed only on Bimini and Grand Bahama, although a few small guest houses had sprung up on other islands, but during this decade the **Family Islands** tourism product expanded, as new hotel developments came on stream and airline service improved.

Eleuthera led the Family Islands in tourism growth. Arthur Vining Davis, the American entrepreneur and president of ALCOA, a leading aluminium manufacturer, purchased 35,000 acres of real estate after having been introduced to Eleuthera by Sir Harold Christie in 1939. In 1952, Davis made plans to build a 300-room hotel in Half Sound, South Eleuthera, but the government refused to approve the development. Davis sold his holding to Pan American Airlines founder Juan Trippe, who successfully transformed Eleuthera into the #1 destination in the region. He built the exclusive *Cotton Bay Club* and *Rock Sound Club*, with its 18-hole golf course designed by Robert Trent Jones. Juan Tripp introduced 2 Boeing 707 aircraft daily, from the U.S mainland—a notable achievement for a Family Island. Nearby Windermere Island became an exclusive destination for members of the British royal family such as Lord Mountbatten and Prince Charles. The Cotton Bay Club was a jewel of The Bahamas for two decades, and this triggered further development and linkages throughout the island.[14]

Among the other major Family Island resorts which made their debut in the 1950's were the *Lighthouse Club* in Fresh Creek, Andros, the exclusive resort community created by Dr. Axel Wenner-Gren, which opened in February 1954; *Peace and Plenty Inn*, in George Town Exuma, which opened in 1954 with 20 seaside double bedrooms; *French Leave*, the 75-room resort in Governor's Harbour, Eleuthera owned by Philadelphia-born Craig Kelly who, in 1956, abandoned his glamorous career as an actor in favour of the more relaxed life of a tropical island. By 1959, air service was being offered to Abaco (Marsh Harbour), Bimini, Andros Town, Eleuthera (Rock Sound and Governor's Harbour), and Exuma (George Town).

HE the Governor, Rt. Hon. Earl of Ranfurly (centre), and the Countess of Ranfurly visit Andros for the opening of the Lighthouse Club in February 1946. They are met by Alex Wenner-Gren, owner

ROCK SOUND CLUB

Rock Sound Club, owned by Arthur Vining Davis

In 1956, actor Craig Kelly purchases and operates the French Leave (which later became Club Med) in Governor's Harbour, Eleuthera

The Environment

The success of tourism is linked to a healthy environment. Visitors to The Bahamas are attracted by the unpolluted marine and terrestrial environment, including abundant fishing grounds, crystal clear waters for yachtsmen and boaters, blue holes, caves, caverns, endemic birds and wildlife. A leader in conservation legislation, Bahamas legislation protecting turtles, sponges, fish and wild birds date back to the 1700's and 1800's and the *Wild Birds Protection Act* of 1905 is recognized as the first of its kind in the Caribbean. Other environmental success stories relate to the preservation of the flamingo population and the establishment of the first land and sea park in the region.

Before World War II, there was a sizable flock of flamingos on the west side of Andros. But when Nassau became a Royal Air Force training base in the early 1940's, the flamingos, exposed to the disturbance of low flying aircraft, left their sanctuary for the salt swamps and uninhabited wilderness of Inagua. When Robert Porter Allen, Director of Research for the National Audubon Society, arrived in the Caribbean to do a full scale survey in 1950, he discovered that the Andros population had been reduced to "12 rather sad-looking birds". He also found that in the previous 35 years, 15 flamingo nesting sites in the Caribbean islands had been abandoned.[15]

After learning that Inagua harboured a large flamingo colony, Porter met with a local resident of that island, Sammy Nixon, known to be the best hunter. Porter was overjoyed when Sammy introduced him to the substantial breeding colony of 1,000 flamingos. He met with the late Arthur S. Vernay, a distinguished explorer and conservationist, and L.E. Forsyth, an authority on Bahamian wildlife. The discovery of the flamingo colony spurred this concerned group to form the *Society for the Preservation of the Flamingo*. In 1952, Sammy Nixon and his brother, Jimmy, were appointed the first flamingo wardens in Inagua. The wardens' primary duty was curbing their fellow islanders' taste for flamingo steak, and under their care, the flamingo colony thrived, becoming a unique treat for ecotourism, and helping to repopulate the rest of the Caribbean.

Robert Porter Allen, Director of Research for the National Audubon Society, conducts research on the flamingoes in Inagua (Courtesy: BNT and Sandy Sprunt)

Brothers Sammy (left) & Jimmy Nixon become the first flamingo wardens in the 1950's

Left to right: Sammy Nixon, Robert Allen and Jimmy Nixon at Camp Vernay named after Arthur Vernay, conservationist (Courtesy: BNT and Sandy Sprunt)

HRH Prince Philip (front right) at Camp Vernay in Inagua (Courtesy: BNT and Sandy Sprunt)

Bahamas National Trust escorts HRH Prince Philip through the Flamingo rookery. Left to right: Lynn Holowesko, Basil Kelly, one of the Duke's aids, Alexander "Sandy" Sprunt, Gary Larson and Glenn Bannister (front)

Meanwhile, another group of conservationists began research on Exuma as the potential site for a national park. In 1953, superintendent of the Everglades National Park in Florida, Daniel B. Beard, launched a campaign to encourage the establishment of a section of the Exuma Cays as a protected area. In February 1956, Beard received a letter from the Governor of The Bahamas confirming that the Crown had set aside approximately 22 miles of the Exuma Cays from Shroud Cay to the Little Bell Island, provided some organization would take responsibility for management, research, and the financial support of the programme.

Exuma Cays Land and Sea Park headquarters

Beard and Carleton Ray, the then Assistant Director of the New York Aquarium, headed up a survey, under the auspices of the New York Zoological Society, to explore the feasibility of establishing a park in the Exuma Cays. The report was received by the Bahamas Government in 1958 and the Exuma Cays Land and Sea Park, the first of its kind in the world, was officially established. Comprising 176 square miles of land and sea, it is more than twice the area of New Providence.

"26 bonefish in a day's outing" was the record set by Colonel Thorne at the Bang Bang Club on Pot Cay, Andros. While great strides were made in environmental protection in the 1950's Catch and Release fishing was not one of the initiatives

The following year, on 13th July, 1959, the Bahamas National Trust (BNT), a Non Governmental Organization (NGO) was established by an act of Parliament. While the BNT grew out of efforts to protect the flamingo and to manage the first land and sea park, its mandate, as stated in the Act, was the protection of all areas of natural beauty and significance for the benefit of The Bahamas. Holding "in trust" the priceless heritage of the country, the BNT—a unique collaboration of the private sector, scientific interests and the government—promotes policies that aim to reconcile economic development with scientifically based conservation principles. Later the BNT was granted a 99-year lease by the government for 287 square miles of Inagua for a nominal sum and the Inagua National Park was created. A plan was put in place to manage the Exuma Park as a replenishment area and the Inagua Park, which was to become the home of the largest breeding population of flamingos in the world. Both parks serve as models for conservation in the region.[16]

Stafford Sands' Promotional Strategy

Having convinced the private sector to invest in the hotel plant, Sands' next step was to attract visitors to fill these hotels. The tourism budget was spent nearly exclusively on communications, promotions and incentives to carriers. He used three primary promotional vehicles—newspaper and magazine advertising, a massive public relations campaign in North America and England, and an effective sales promotion campaign. He appointed Victor Chenea as General Sales Manager of the Development Board. Chenea, a retired Vice-President of Traffic and Sales for Pan American, operated from an office in Miami. [17]

Advertising

The advertising agencies contracted to handle the North American campaign were Grant Advertising of Miami, Kelly-Nason Advertising of New York, and Robinson-Hannagan Associates from 1955. United Kingdom advertising started in the late 1950's and was handled by Charles Lytle. Four-colour, one- and two-page display ads were placed in selected national consumer magazines in the United States and Canada, supplemented by high-fashion magazines in the winter. The Bahamas' fishing and marine attractions were promoted in outdoor advertising. Newspaper advertising, often in two colours, appeared in gateway cities and the most productive markets, with secondary developmental markets added to the mix as test markets. The Bahamas' advertising was so spectacular that, by 1956, it was being copied by competitive destinations.[18]

Public Relations

The second channel of the Development Board's promotional effort was publicity. The Development Board hired experienced public relations firms—Hill and Knowlton, Inc., New York and Sidney Barton, Ltd., London—to provide publicity direction, contacts and placement for the North American continent and the United Kingdom. With their contacts within media circles, they were successful in luring top journalists and newscasters to the Colony to produce stories, as well as film promotion specialists and celebrities. They also developed creative promotions offshore and within the islands, to generate additional publicity. Among the media promotions were contests in various cities in the United States and Canada. Winning contestants were extravagantly hosted in The Bahamas and photos used for further promotion throughout North America.[19]

In addition, Hill and Knowlton operated a well-trained news bureau staff in Nassau, headed by Carl B. Livingston, Director of Publicity, and a press relations branch in Miami. Their main function was editorial; story and picture captions were produced for distribution to hundreds of national magazines and newspapers in the United States, Canada and Great Britain. One of the most successful features of the News Bureau's operation was its hometown picture programme. They would take photographs of visitors of prominence from big cities, as well as persons of average importance in smaller cities, and forward the photographs to their hometown newspapers. On average, 2,000 photos per year were accepted, creating exposure in an inexpensive, but effective, way.[20]

The P.R. efforts paid off. Almost every important United States and Canadian magazine carried Bahamas material in their editorial sections. The Bahamas became a regular feature in leading magazines and newspapers—*Business Week, Esquire, Cosmopolitan, Times, Mademoiselle, Harper's Bazaar, Ladies Home Journal, House Beautiful* and fishing magazines. For example, the popular US magazine *Redbook* (with a circulation of 6 million) featured Nassau as a honeymoon paradise in a six-page article. Also, many popular magazines used scenes of Nassau as backdrops for their fashion shoots. By offering free trips and touting the benefits of a beach holiday in a vacation paradise, the agencies were also able to attract the rich and the famous from all over the world, including top movie stars.

Charles Bethel (right), manager of the Development Board, and his wife chat with Eddie Fisher

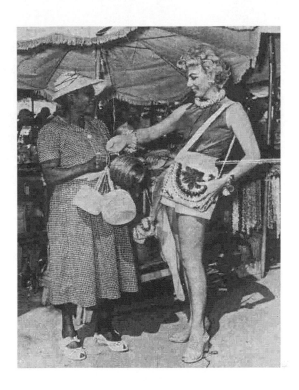

Actress Dolores Gray enjoys a day of shopping at the straw market

Tyrone Powers (left) and his family spend a day at the beach

Charles Bethel (right) of the
Development Bank meets Dag
Hammershald

Bing Cosby at Blackbeard's Tavern

Lady Oakes wedding at St. Mary's, Nassau, draws a crowd of out-of-town visitors

Sales

To implement the sales plan, Sands established branch tourist offices in six North American cities—New York, Chicago, Miami, Pittsburgh, Dallas and Toronto. In 1959, a further office was opened in Los Angeles. The information office in London was placed under the direction of a salesman for the United Kingdom. Capable men with experience in selling travel were hired to head the sales offices, under Victor Chenea's direction.

Twice each year, Sir Stafford brought advertising and public relations staff together in Nassau to sit with the Board to help map an overall promotional campaign for the next season. The meetings were conducted six to seven months in advance of the season for which promotional plans were being made.[21]

Stafford Sands, chairman of the Development Board, takes his Sales Team on a boat trip. From left: Sir Stafford, District Managers: Robert Sandquist (Dallas), Kurtz Henley (Miami), V.E. Chenea (GSM), Gordon Grant (Chicago), Al Munday (Toronto) and William Thacher (New York). Photo Roland Rose

Special Promotions and the Family Island Regatta

Sales promotions were organized on-island or through tourist offices operating within the major tourist markets. Many of these events, designed to bring excitement to the tourist product, were planned for summer and fall to address the seasonality problem and attract visitors to the islands year round.

The Development Board launched onshore dozens of events—fishing tournaments, sports car racing, Nassau-Miami Power Boat Races (from 1956), sailing regattas, cruise convoys for yachts, water skiing competitions, even "*Junkanoo in June*", to give summer visitors a taste of the parade.

In the 1950's Junkanoo in June was held during the summer months to increase visitor enjoyment while presenting a taste of the Christmas festival

Of significance was the annual Speed Week, initiated in 1954. The organizing committee included Sir Sydney Oakes, Robert Symonette, and Donald Delahey. Advisor to the committee was Captain Sherman F. "Red" Crise, a popular figure in international sports car racing. Speed Week drew annually about 100 sports car drivers from all parts of the world. The five-mile high-speed international competition, using, for the most part, the perimeter roads of the former Oakes Airfield, was under the General Competition Rules of the Royal Automobile Club. Stirling Moss was a popular champion of the Trophy event.

Race Adviser Captain Sherman "Red" Crise (right) speaks with officials before start of the race

Famed race car drivers from all over the world participate in Speed Week 1955

Lady Oakes, wife of Sir Sidney Oakes, is the only woman driver in Speed Weeks

Fishing tournaments created excitement and drew many visitors and loyal clientele who returned year after year. Such sporting events included the Bahamas Winter Fishing Tournament, Wahoo Round-Up, the Bimini White Marlin Tournament, Blue Marlin tourney and the Tuna Tournament operated by the Big Game Fishing Club, and the annual Bahamas Summer Fishing Tournament

It was during this era that the *Out Island Regatta* (name later changed to *Family Island Regatta*) was born. By the early 1950's, the traditional sailing workboats faced an uncertain future, as fishermen were slowly abandoning them in favour of motorized vessels. Howland Bottomley and Linton Rigg, American yachtsmen who arrived on Exuma in the 1950's, was attracted to the functional, locally made beautiful sailboat. Along with a small group of other American and Bahamian yachtsmen, Bottomley and Rigg conceived the idea of holding a regatta for the Bahamian working sailing craft. It would provide an opportunity for cruising yachtsmen to witness one of the last working sailing fleets in action and introduce them to the magnificent cruising waters of The Bahamas.[22]

In April 1954, nearly 70 Bahamian sloops, schooners and dinghies gathered in Elizabeth Harbour, Exuma for three days of racing. The first prize, £100, was won in 1954 by Rolly Gray, who after his success in subsequent Regattas earned the title "Grand Master of Bahamian Yachting."[23]

The Out Island Squadron, made up of interested Bahamian and American yachtsmen, was formed to organize the Regatta on an annual basis. As the event gained in popularity, boats came from farther and farther to compete: Long Island, Andros, Ragged Island, Cat Island, Acklins, and the Abacos. Each year the competition became more intense and the number of domestic and international visitors increased. As Niger Calder commented, this regatta played a tremendous role over the years in the preservation and evolution of the boatbuilding tradition in the Islands.[24]

The Tour Operators Association and the Travel Trade

Local tour operators were organized into an association in July 1957 through the initiative of Donald Delahey of *Playtours*. *The Bahamas Tour Operators and Sightseeing Association* helped in developing proper rates and tours and assisting in the marketing of the country. The original members were William Saunders (Majestic Tours), Michael Maura (Michael Maura Tours), Philip Brown (Philip Brown Tours), Howard Johnson (Howard Johnson Tours) and Gene Savage (Nassau Tours), the only non-Bahamian. The first President of the Tour Operators Association was Don Delahey, Howard Johnson was Vice President, and William Saunders, Secretary.[25]

Members of the newly formed Tour Operators Association: Standing Michael Maura Seated from left—William Saunders (Majestic), Phillip Brown (Philip Brown Tours), Howard Johnson (Howard Johnson Tours), Donald Delahey, (Playtours) and Gene Savage (Nassau Tours) *(Courtesy: Bill Saunders)*

The Sightseeing and Tour Operators Association became active in the travel trade, working closely with the Development Board. Because of the importance of travel agencies and tour wholesalers in packaging the tourist product and making it available to the travel public, much attention was devoted to educating these travel intermediaries about the hotels, attractions and benefits of booking The Bahamas. Familiarization trips and sales promotions thus became important events on the calendar.

The Bahamas actively participated in the annual conventions of the American Society of Travel Agents (ASTA), the trade association of which most travel agents in North America were members.

When it was learned that the ASTA World Congress would be held in Miami in Autumn 1952, the Development Board quickly put in place an advertising and promotional programme to target these agents. They used the front cover of *Bahamas Magazine* to entice conventioneers to visit The Bahamas before returning home. Sir Stafford Sands, Development Board Chairman, ended his open letter to ASTA agents in the magazine, with this statement: "The Development Board's slogan this past year has been 'Everybody's going to Nassau'. During the year ahead, it might well be changed to 'Almost Everybody Has Been to Nassau', and we might add, 'They're all coming back!'"

In May 1956, 179 delegates from the Midwest and Southeast chapters of ASTA met in Nassau for a 5-day conference. It was the first time in history that the group had ever met outside the United States. Many of the agents also made a side trip

to the Rock Sound Club, Eleuthera, where they were entertained by representatives of Mr. Arthur Vining Davis, owner of the Club. Sir Stafford Sands paid tribute to the travel agents and said The Bahamas' "good neighbour policy with agents in the United States and Canada had largely been responsible for the great increase in tourism"[26].

The President of ASTA, Tom Donovan, in a speech at the concluding banquet, commented that Nassau had experienced the greatest growth in the number of visitors in any area of the world of similar size. "During the next five to seven years" Mr. Donovan said, "we can expect The Bahamas to have at least 250,000 visitors each year. We of the travel business have come to realize that the Bahamas Development Board has done more in a shorter time to sell travel than any other country or area in the world".[27]

ASTA President, Tom Donovan, (right) pays tribute to Stafford Sands

Group and Incentive Travel boast Occupancy in Offseason

In the 1950's, the hotels could now boast spacious meeting rooms and other ancillary convention facilities such as display space, stenographic service, publicity and photographic coverage, communications and transportation and, most important, courteous staff. The promotional thrust for convention business was geared to two key factors—*facilities* and *fun*.

In 1951, the Colony attracted its first convention group, the Florida Hotel Association, which met in Nassau. That was the start of a trend, nurtured by the sales staff of the Ministry of Tourism through specialists in the travel trade, with groups booked reaching as high as 168 in 1959, or 8.8% of total arrivals (See Table 6-1).

Table 6-1
Group Movements to The Bahamas
1955-60

Year	Groups Booked	Persons Involved	% of Annual Tourist Total
1955	83	7,500	5.6
1956	122	10,000	6.8
1957	137	15,200	7.8
1958	100	12,400	6.9
1959	168	21,500	8.8
1960	256	31,300	10.4

Data excludes groups of less than 25 persons and groups arriving by sea using the ship as hotel[28]

Incentive group travel became popular during this period. Contests to increase sales had traditionally been used by large American companies, with attractive prizes offered such as cars and other commodities. In the late 1940's and early 1950's, prize trips to foreign resorts as a sales incentive became an even more attractive proposition for persons who met their sales quota. The sponsoring corporations spared no costs in providing their top sales performers with top-of-the-line all-expenses-paid vacation prizes. One such group, the Fedders-Quigan Corporation, became such a strong supporter that they chose The Bahamas for three of their annual sales incentive awards, following aggressive group solicitation led by Donald Delahey of Playtours. In 1954, they flew their first group of 90 winners and in fall 1957 they brought 5,000 top sales performers to Nassau over a seven-week period.[29] Then in 1960, they chose Grand Bahama when 2,400 salespersons from that company enjoyed their third sales incentive trip at the Grand Bahama Club.

Corporations had discovered that these incentive promotions paid off in increased sales of their product, while benefitting the local economy. Incentive business proved to be particularly lucrative for The Bahamas, since the overseas sponsoring companies purchased the best available packages to pamper top performers, and these visitors also brought their own spending money to buy local souvenirs, wares and special services.[30]

The Piel Group experience local entertainment (Source: Nassau Magazine)

Hog Island, a popular day trip, before its development as Paradise Island

In November 1956, another noteworthy promotional event, Piel's Beer Treasure Hunt, was launched. Termed one of the most successful promotions ever staged, it brought to Nassau 26 lucky contestants, 32 members of the American press, 12 officials of a New York brewery and its advertising agency, Young and Rubican. The hunt was held on beautiful Cabbage Beach on Hog Island (now Paradise Island). At the end of their trails they dug deep into the powdery sands to unearth an antique treasure chest, in which was a weathered scroll which was, in effect, a deed to the prize. Top prize was an island in The Bahamas, complete with a furnished vacation home, a dock, Abaco-built fishing boat and fishing gear.[31]

Groups involved as many as 6,000 persons, such as the J.I. Case Co. sales meeting in 1958. The group and incentive business helped the country to become a year-round tourist destination since many of the meetings were held during the traditionally slow periods of summer and fall. Their contribution to overall hotel occupancy, boosting revenue, "word of mouth" publicity and repeat visits, was phenomenal.

Big Films Generate Publicity and Income

The spectacular marine attributes of The Bahamas continued to attract filmmakers. In Spring 1954, underwater scenes from *Twenty Thousand Leagues Under the Sea* were filmed in the Colony. This Jules Verne epic starred Kirk Douglas, James Mason and Peter Lorre. Some 60 motion picture technicians, cameramen, divers and directors were in Nassau for the production. Howard Lightbourne, a Bahamian undersea expert, led the Disney exploration team to Goulding Cay, off Lyford Cay at the western tip of New Providence. The film won Academy Awards for Art Direction/Set Decoration and Special Effects.

While filming in The Bahamas, Kirk Douglas visits the Straw Market

In 1955, *Flames of the Island*, starring Yvonne De Carlo, was shot around the Montagu Beach Hotel and on the charter boat, *Alpha*.

Apart from the publicity these films generated for the country, the production companies spent thousands of dollars in the local community on accommodations, meals, services, extras and government taxes.

New Air Terminal and expansion of Air Service

During the1950's, air service

Kirk Douglas wears a wetsuit in preparation for an underwater scene in Bahamian waters for the remake of the film "Twenty Thousand Leagues under the Sea" in 1954

to The Bahamas soared, with huge new post-war planes bringing three times the number of people, at nearly twice the speed, and at lower fares than ever before. The short runway at the

Oakes Field airport was being taxed to the limit by the new four-engine aircraft of the era.

In January 1956, the Airports Board accepted the tender of £248,262 from Higgs and Hill for the construction of an airport terminal building at Windsor Field. The building was designed by Norman and Dawbarn, Architects and Civil Engineers of London. By 1957, the two-storey terminal was completed. The 26,075 square feet of public area more than doubled the square footage in the three terminal buildings at the Oakes Field airport. The new terminal had the additional advantage of concentrating all airport activities together and enabling future extensions.[32]

As will be noted from Appendix 3-F, *Pan American* Amphibian continued to be the primary air carrier to The Bahamas. In response to the Government's promotional thrust, Pan American began expansion of its service in 1951, when it transported 29,000 passengers on the Miami-Nassau route, that is a 50% increase over 1950. In Fall 1954, Pan Am increased its service to three planes a day from Miami to Nassau throughout the year, with extra sections added as needed. The airline was now competing with *British Overseas Airways Corporation* (BOAC) on the Miami-Nassau route. By the end of the decade, between the two airlines, there were 4-6 flights daily from Miami in the winter, taking just 55 minutes and costing only $30 round-trip. On 1st February, 1957, Pan American inaugurated Nassau-New York daily service, with DC-7 Clippers.

By 1954, BOAC was flying double deck Stratocruisers non-stop daily, from New York to Nassau in 4½ hours, for just $125 round-trip once a week. Also by 1956, *More visitors are flying to Nassau* BOAC commenced service to London, England via Bermuda. *Mackey Airlines* operated daily service from Fort Lauderdale and West Palm Beach and later expanded its route to West Palm Beach, Tampa, Montego Bay and Kingston. *Trans-Canada Airlines* was flying four engine North Star

BOAC's stratacruiser

Skyliners to Nassau 3-5 times weekly from Toronto and Montreal via Tampa, and non-stop during the winter at fares from $90-$99 round trip.[33] In 1957, *Cubana Airlines* inaugurated Havana-Nassau service, with two trips a week. Inter-island air service was handled by BOAC with scheduled flights to principal islands.

Cruise Ships bring Stopover Visitors

Cruise travel was extremely important during this era, since many of the cruise passengers were stopover visitors who stayed in The Bahamas for two days or more; however the harbour facilities in Nassau were inadequate. Ships docked at either Clifton Pier, in south-west, New Providence, or Prince George Wharf, downtown, Nassau. In the absence of dock facilities, many ships were unable to be ferried to shore during inclement weather and were often forced to bypass the port of Nassau. New Customs facilities, on a second storey at the eastern end of the 600-foot-long warehouse at Prince George Wharf were opened by His Excellency Governor Raynor Arthur on 29th July, 1957, facilitating faster, more efficient customs clearance. Controller of Customs, E.H. McKinney, thanked the Development Board for suggesting the new facilities and the Legislature for providing funds to make the new accommodations possible. Sir Stafford Sands, chairman of the Development Board, termed it a "much needed and long overdue passenger facility".[34]

The New York tourist market became more accessible when, in 1952, Home Lines began weekly, year-round service from New York aboard the 24,400-ton SS Nassau, formerly the SS Europe. Fares began at just $125 R/T per person. The SS Nassau left New York Friday evening, arriving in Nassau on the following Monday morning. She would leave Nassau each Tuesday evening, returning to New York on Friday morning. The ship delivered long-stay visitors, since passengers could return to New York by a later sailing.

Miami continued to be the main cruising port. Several cruise ships sailed weekly from Miami on 3-day cruises; the fare was $44 round trip. In 1954, following an agreement between the Bahamas Development Board and the McCormick Shipping Corp, the SS Queen of Nassau, the refurbished Yarmouth Castle, began making two sailings from Miami to Nassau each week with a layover of two days and one night in Nassau on each trip. In 1957, following the opening of the new harbour facilities, P. & O. Steamship Company in Miami announced that the cruise passenger service by SS Florida between Miami and Nassau would be doubled. Cruise passengers on SS Florida spent two nights at sea and two days and a night in Nassau.

With the help of the Yachtsman's Guide, cruising The Bahama Islands by private boat or yacht was also popular.

International air and sea carriers operating in the 1950's are shown in Appendix 3E.

Trickle Down Effect of Tourism throughout the Community

In the 1950's, the positive effect of the influx of visitors could be seen throughout the island of New Providence—beaches, hotels, taxis, straw market, Bay Street stores, restaurants, banks, Hobby Horse Hall, and local entertainment spots and nightclubs.

While diving had been a long-time popular pastime for the adventurous, in 1959 Bronson Hartley and his wife, Martica, opened up the underwater wonderland to everybody, with the invention of his diving helmet. Hartley, who built his first diving helmet when he was 11, offered diving cruises with his special diving helmet to sea gardens off Athol Island, providing an educational and exciting activity for tourists of all ages.

Hobby Horse Hall, the local race track, continued to be a popular attraction for locals and tourists. To better meet the needs of families, it opened a playground in 1952, where parents could leave their children while they enjoyed the Friday afternoon races.

The Bahama Playhouse (opposite the Olympia Hotel on West Bay Street) and many of the hotels offered concerts and plays during the winter season featuring distinguished actors and actresses from London, Broadway, and Hollywood.

Native Entertainers Thrill Locals and Visitors

The Development Board, recognizing the potential of the Royal Bahamas Police Force Band, local bands and artists to attract and entertain visitors, used them as a part of its marketing campaign. Many new entertainers came on the scene, two of whom—Legendary *Freddie Munnings, Sr.* and Folk Musician *Joseph Spence*—are highlighted at the end of this book.

Popular nightclubs during the era were the *Silver Slipper* on East Street (built in the late 1930's or early 40's); *Zanzibar* on Baillou Hill Road (built in 1945-46), *Cat & Fiddle,* Nassau Street (built in 1951 by Stanley Toogood and later run by others including Freddie Munnings). It was noted that when Ghana gained its Independence in 1957, the *Ghana Room* at the Cat N' Fiddle was opened in tribute to Ghana (closed in the late 60's), and in the 1970's it was run by Ray Munnings and known as the *Lion's Den*. The **Conch Shell** on Blue Road came on the scene in 1951[35].

Veteran entertainer Freddie Munnings

Freddie Munnings and his Orchestra

"Fireball" Freddie Taylor performs at the Cat 'N the Fiddle

"Fireball" Freddie Taylor meets Brook Benton (left), who arrives at the Airport to perform at the Cat 'N the Fiddle

Legendary entertainer, Joseph Spence

Colourful character "Sweet Richard" performs at Junkanoo

1958 Strike and Closure of the airport in Nassau

While the 1950's was a successful period for tourism, the only year in which visitor arrivals did not increase was 1958 and this was a direct result of the 1958 Strike. Clifford Darling (later knighted, who was to become a Minister in the PLP Government and the Governor General of the country) played a prominent role in labour relations and the General Strike of 1958. In an interview with the author, Sir Clifford related the events leading to the industrial action. As the main source of business for taxi drivers was airport transfers, taxi drivers would go to Oakes Field, the only airfield at that time, as early as 2 a.m. to be first in line for transferring tourists arriving on the 9 a.m. Pan Am flight from Miami, the only service operating at that time. Very often they got no jobs because the hotels would send their own limousines to collect guests and choose taxi drivers at random to handle the surplus.

As President of the Taxi Cab Union, Sir Clifford made representation to the Bahamas Hotel Association and Governor Sir Raynor Arthur. The Governor intervened and gave taxi drivers the privilege of transporting passengers from the airport for two months while negotiations took place. Lynden Pindling, who was later knighted and became the Prime Minister in an independent Bahamas, served as the legal advisor for the union, as they negotiated 20 points of disagreement. Nineteen of the 20 points were resolved. The last unresolved point, which led to the General Strike in January 1958, related to the first-come first-served system at the airport. The Union used a bulletin board at the airport to record the names of taxi drivers as they arrived, to ensure fairness in allocating jobs. When the 8-week period of transportation of visitors by the Union, as mandated by the Governor, had expired, the first-come first-served principle was no longer respected and the old system of doing business prevailed. The Taxi Union, joined by the Federation of Labour led by Randol Fawkes, along with Lynden Pindling, called a strike which lasted for 19 days and included all hotel and airline workers, longshoremen, teachers, et cetera. The airport closed, the tourism industry came to a standstill, and the entire country was affected.

According to Sir Clifford, this was a difficult period for the Union, which had to provide three meals a day for all of the striking workers. He and many others had to use their personal savings to supplement the funds of the Union to assist workers, many of whom faced severe hardship. After the strike, the first-come first-served system went into force. It was made clear, however, that a taxi driver next on line would not be eligible to take passengers if he did not adhere to the Union rules: clean, presentable vehicles, acceptable dress code and professional behaviour, et cetera. Despite the victory, workers faced many challenges, as employers were reluctant to take them back, and many had been evicted by their landlords. A fund was started to bring relief. Sir Clifford recalls that this 1958 Strike, in spite of the tremendous sacrifice, united black Bahamians from all walks of life and had a strong influence on majority rule in 1967.[36]

1958 Strike

Racial Discrimination

Up to this time, there was racial discrimination in the large hotels and in many businesses on Bay Street, including the Savoy Theatre. Blacks were not allowed to socialize in hotels. Blacks were not shown in any advertisements, other than in a service capacity. Each edition of the Bahamas Magazine contained dozens of photographs of tourism events in the country; blacks in the photographs were noticeably absent. The only non-whites allowed in hotels were workers and entertainers.

The Tribune carried a report which became the focal point of an attack on racism in the Colony. In December 1953, Hugh Springer, an eminent Barbadian barrister and Registrar of University College of the West Indies, and a number of prominent men, were enroute to London when their British Overseas Airways Corporation (BOAC) plane experienced engine trouble. Expecting a short stopover in Nassau, dinner arrangements were made for the men. However, Springer was excluded from dining at the Prince George Hotel on the grounds of his colour. He was advised to have dinner in the airport cafeteria. He called Sir Etienne Dupuch whom he had met earlier that year. Dupuch hosted him to dinner and accommodated him for the night—and printed a story on the incident.[37]

Sir Clifford Darling also recalled the first time blacks in the United States were specifically targeted in Tourism's promotional campaign. Recognizing that the Bahamas Government was spending large sums to attract tourists from all over the world, Sir Clifford along with the Chairman of the Taxi Drivers Association, Wilbert Moss, Clarence Bain, taxi driver, and a travel agent from Detroit visited the Development Board Chairman, Stafford Sands, in the mid 1950's, asking him to include blacks in ads, and to add ethnic publications such as *Ebony* to their advertising list. Sands, in a subsequent meeting, gave £700 each to Messrs. Moss and Bain to spend as they saw fit in promoting the ethnic market. They put together a photographic and slide presentation, accompanied by the best calypso music, and toured Miami, Atlanta and Tallahassee, meeting with black leaders and religious groups. Several black groups visited Nassau as a result of this promotion, including the 100-member LINKS Convention. Because blacks could not stay at the large hotels at that time, they were accommodated at the black-owned guest houses. Sir Clifford further recalled that since these small properties could not accommodate the entire group, a few of the large hotels gave special permission for these black guests to stay at their properties.[38]

A big step towards equality was made on 23rd January, 1956, when Sir Etienne Dupuch stood on the floor of the House of Assembly and proposed a resolution to ban racial discrimination in all public places in The Bahamas. He protested when the Speaker of the House took the resolution out of his hands and sent it to a committee that would allow it to die. He was threatened with arrest when he defied the Speaker. The House hastily adjourned in confusion. The next day the hotels

In January 1956, Sir Etienne
Dupuch proposed a resolution
to ban discrimination in
public places

in Nassau announced that all racial barriers had
been lifted from their establishments. One by one,
every public place opened its doors to all persons,
regardless of colour, bringing racial discrimination
to an end in the Colony.

Tourism Performance in the 1950's

The Development Board's well-planned,
targeted approach to tourism promotion was
successful in spreading The Bahamas tourism
message all over the world and resulted in booming
years for Tourism. Tables 6-2 and 6-3 highlight the
direct relationship between tourism promotion,
annual visitors and the Colony's revenue. Of the
45,371 visitors in 1950, 21,093 were Stopovers
who vacationed in The Bahamas for weeks. In
1951, the number of visitors to Nassau increased
to 68,502—more than double the annual level
during the 1946-49 period. Increases averaging
20% per annum were recorded during the decade,

with total visitors exceeding the 100,000 mark by 1954 and ¼ million milestone by
1959. The only year in which an increase was not recorded was 1958.

In the 1950's, 91% of visitors were from the United States, 5% from Canada
and 1.5% from the United Kingdom. Arrival statistics did not include yachters to
The Bahamas nor private flyers to the Family Islands. In discussing the reason for
the exclusion of yachtsmen in tourism statistics, Stafford Sands pointed out that it
was not the Board's policy to include in the statistics any visitors for which accurate
tabulation could not be made.

Table 6.2
Visitor Breakdown and Cost Per Visitor
1949-59

YEAR	VISITORS TO NASSAU/ PAR.IS.	VISITORS TO GR. BAH. & FAM. IS.	TOTAL VISITORS* AND % INCREASE		DEV. BOARD TOURISM BUDGET	COST PER VISITOR
1949	32,018	-	**32,018**		£94,031	£2.18.6
1950	45,371	-	**45,371**	41.70%	£156,150	£3. 8.8
1951	68,502	-	**68,502**	50.98%	£199,474	£2.18.2

1952	84,718	-	**84,718**	23.67%	£292,247	£3. 8.8
1953	90,485	-	**90,485**	6.81%	£311,490	£3. 8.8
1954	109,605	-	**109,605**	21.13%	£340,386	£3. 2.0
1955	132,434	-	**132,434**	20.83%	£413,326	£3. 2.4
1956	155,003	-	**155,003**	17.04%	£475,242	£3. 1.2
1957	194,618	15,095	**209,713**	35.30%	£556,813	£2.13.1
1958	177,867	18,791	**196,658**	-6.23%	£658,482	£3. 7.0
1959	244,258	20,500	**264,758**	34.63%	£730,250	£2.15.2

* Excludes yachtsmen   rate: £ = $2.80
Source: Annual Reports of the Bahamas Development Board

The expenditure by visitors was reflected in the Government revenue for the period. During the first year of active promotion in1950, Nassau's total visitors increased by more than 40% from 32,018 to 45,371, and Government revenue jumped from £1.3 million in 1949 to £6.5 million in 1959. By 1959, Government revenue jumped to £6,456.795.

Table 6-3
Government Revenue: 1950-59

Year	Total Govt Revenue	% Inc	Year	Total Govt Revenue	% Inc.
1950	£1,579,748	18.8	1955	£3,507,963	13.3
1951	£2,044,385	29.4	1956	£4,078,921	16.3
1952	£2,397,097	17.2	1957	£4,938,958	21.1
1953	£2,610,678	8.9	1958	£5,198,975	5.3
1954	£3,095,541	18.6	1959	£6,456,795	24.2

rate: £ = $2.80   *Source: Annual Reports of the Bahamas Development Board*

Without scientific measurement devices to measure expenditure, Stafford Sands estimated that the average visitor spent £71 (US$200) in The Bahamas, excluding air or ship transportation. Using this figure, the total visitor expenditure for the year 1958 would work out at $39 million, and the 1959 visitor expenditure would be estimated at $53 million. The tourism contribution to the economy is significant recognizing the low cost per visitor. For example, by dividing the 1958 Development Board budget (£658,482) by the total visitors for that year (96,658), the cost per visitor is estimated at only £3.7.0 per visitor, and in 1959, the cost for generating a single visitor was even lower—£2.15.2 (see Table 6.2).

Of even greater significance was the fact that during the last five years of this decade the largest percentage of new tourists came during the offseason and summer, a period when, in previous years, most of the hotels were forced to close because of absence of guests.

Special Recognition for Sir Stafford Sands

In Summer 1954, the Bahamas Development Board and its chairman, Stafford Sands, were singled out for special recognition for outstanding record in travel. In an unprecedented gesture, the Florida Chamber of Commerce awarded a plaque to Sir Stafford "in appreciation of cooperation in making the Florida-Bahamas area an outstanding vacation playground".[39] In recognition of his work in assisting Sir Stafford, Vic Chenea, the General Sales Manager of the Development Board, was appointed an Honorary Officer of the Most Excellent Order of the British Empire (Civil Division) in Her Majesty the Queen's Birthday Honours List in 1959 (an honour that is rarely awarded to an American).

By the late 1950's, with the improvements in transportation and construction of new resort facilities in the Family Islands, the Development Board was set to expand its promotional plans to this new "Resort Empire". In predicting 1960's growth, Stafford Sands, quoted in a ***Bahamas Handbook*** article, suggested that "in years to come Nassau would remain the flourishing tourist capital of The Bahamas, but its rate of growth will slow slightly as the golden era of tourism channels increasing amounts of direct tourist wealth into a new and almost unexplored area for resort pioneering".[40] The rate of growth did not decline, but continued to accelerate, due, in part, to external factors.

Impact of the Cuban Revolution on Bahamas Tourism

In 1959, Fidel Castro, a young revolutionary, overthrew Fulgencio Batista and made himself dictator of Cuba. This was the beginning of communism and cessation of trade to Cuba, an island which had previously dominated Caribbean tourism. From 1960, when the island closed, tourists who normally flocked to Cuba sought alternative vacation destinations. The Bahamas, primarily because of its proximity to North America and its strong promotion, received the lion's share of this business.

*   *   *

The Colony was on the crest of an unprecedented renaissance in tourism, as developers made investments in elaborate resorts and the Colony took its place as the Number 1 Caribbean resort.

7

TOURISM DEVELOPMENT IN THE 1960'S INCLUDING THE CREATION OF PARADISE ISLAND AND FREEPORT/LUCAYA

Global Socio-Political Developments and their impact on Tourism

Global Movement Against Racial Discrimination

During the 1960's the tourism sector was still dominated by Caucasians and racial discrimination throughout the industry was widespread. In the United States, the civil rights movement accelerated, led by Georgia-born African American, Dr. Martin Luther King, Jr. (1929-68), son of a Baptist minister, who held a doctorate degree in Theology. He organized the first major protest of the civil rights movement—the successful Montgomery Bus Boycott. A powerful orator, he appealed to Christian and American ideals and achieved growing support from the federal government and northern whites. In 1963, he led his massive March on Washington, at which he delivered his famous "I Have a Dream" address. In 1964, the civil rights movement achieved two of its greatest successes: the ratification of the 24th Amendment, which abolished the poll tax, and the Civil Rights Act of 1964, which prohibited racial discrimination in employment and education and outlawed racial segregation in public facilities.

In 1964, Dr. King, after receiving word that he would receive the Nobel Peace Prize, visited Bimini, the Big Game Fishing Capital of The Bahamas, along with several associates. While on Bimini he not only relaxed and refreshed himself but he also wrote his acceptance speech for the award. It speaks well that Dr. King would select the tiny island of Bimini for quiet solitude and rest. Dr. King also went fishing on the Bimini flats with one of the premier Bahamian fishing guides, Captain Ansil Saunders. Ansil spent a great amount of time with Dr. King while he visited Bimini. The Bimini Historical Society and the Bimini Museum later formed a committee to organize annual events to mark the anniversary of Dr. Martin Luther King's visit to Bimini[1].

In October of 1964, nearly four years before his assassination in Memphis, King was awarded the Nobel Peace Prize for his non-violent resistance to racial prejudice in America.

Global efforts to remove racial discrimination also affected the tourism industry. By 1963, desegregation in American hotels had started. The winds of change were also slowly impacting The Bahamas.

Internal Self Government—Birth of a New Bahamian

In January 1964, The Bahamas achieved full **internal self government** after more than 200 years of British rule. Sir Randol Fawkes, Bahamian labour leader, politician and freedom fighter, in his book *The Faith That Moved the Mountain*,

described its significance: "Just as a New Bahamas was born on 7th January, 1964, so a new Bahamian was also born with the coming into force of the new Constitution. This new Bahamian will no longer accept second-class citizenship. He stands tall with the light of wisdom in his eyes and the flame of freedom in his heart."[2] This was the period when a decline in prejudice could be readily observed as blacks began to assume leading positions in areas previously reserved for whites. Covenants in title deeds restricting subdivisions of land "for whites only" were disappearing. The previous year, Bahamian Sidney Poitier, a native of Cat Island, became the first Black person to win the

In 1963, Bahamian Sir Sidney Poitier (left) makes a special trip to Nassau after winning The Oscar for Lilies of the Field

prestigious Oscar for *Best Male Actor* in a leading role for his performance in *Lilies of the Field*—another great source of pride for Bahamians.

Indeed, Bahamians were ready to take on new responsibility throughout the country, including the tourism industry. That was the prevailing mood when internal self-government was realized.

First Minister of Tourism under the Promotion of Tourism Act

With internal self-government, a ministerial form of government evolved, with Sir Roland Symonette becoming the nation's first Premier. The Promotion of Tourism Act, passed in 1963 and effected in 1964, placed the Ministry of Tourism outside the cadre of the Public Service. This enabled the Ministry to undertake tourism promotional activities with some degree of autonomy.

The Act also allowed the Ministry of Tourism to operate in a more flexible manner, without the rigid procedures and bureaucratic controls traditionally associated with Government Departments (Appendix 6).

Becoming the nation's **first Minister of Tourism** was Stafford Sands, who had effectively led the tourism drive through his chairmanship of the Development Board. Knighted in 1963, Sir Stafford also held the post of Minister of Finance. These dual portfolios gave him the power and the resources to shape the economic development of the country.

Sir Stafford used his clout as Minister of Finance to ensure that adequate resources were made available for marketing the country. During the 1960-66 period, tourism budgets increased by an average of 10.5% per annum, reaching £1,464,580 (B$4.1 million) by 1965 and B$4,992,968 by 1966 (Appendix 4).

Even from a global perspective, the tourism budget was huge, and was even larger than that of the United States. The *Bahamas Handbook* records that in May 1965, Richard Joseph, travel editor of *Esquire* informed the US House Ways and Means Committee that while the US spent $3.5 million to promote tourism, The Bahamas was spending more than $4 million "to sell tourism to a place the size of Connecticut and with a population about the same as South Bend, Ind."[3]

The results of an unbiased independent US research survey underscores the enormity of the growth in the Colony's visitor arrivals. In 1960, the Development Board engaged the First Research Corporation of Miami to conduct a survey on the importance of tourism to the Bahamian economy. The survey forecasted that, by 1970, The Bahamas would welcome 560,000 travellers, who would spend approximately £35,714,286 ($100 million). The study also projected that, to accommodate the expected influx, 10 to 12 first-class resort hotels with at least 6,630 additional tourist beds would be needed. This forecast of the First Research Corporation was conservative.[4] Their 1970 projected arrival figure was achieved as early as 1964.

Commenting in 1965, Sir Stafford stated, "What started fifteen years ago as a small trickle of prosperity has today become a flowing brook. That brook is increasing and will continue to increase so that by the end of the 1960's it will have become a broad and swiftly flowing stream".[5] By 1966, The Bahamas attracted over 800,000 visitors. This success provided much needed funds to improve harbours, infrastructure, medical facilities and social programmes within the country.[6]

Heightened Promotions

The **promotional programme**, directed at an upscale audience, continued to include high-impact, onshore and offshore promotions. In fact, expenditures on publicity and promotions (advertising, public relations, sales aids, films, promotions, subsidies and the cost of maintaining overseas sales offices), represented over 90% of total budget and reached as high as $4 million in 1965 and $4.8 million in 1966. Employment of foreign hospitality workers was the order of the day. Expenditure on local training of the hospitality work force was minimal.

Private flying was targeted as a new niche market. In 1960, the first Flying Treasure Hunt took place. This promotion was designed to attract high-spending private pilots, primarily from North America, to the pleasures of "Island Hopping". It became an annual event and played an important role in the increase of private aircraft visiting The Bahamas from 7,000 in 1960 to 70,000 in 1968.

The Colony remained attractive as an exotic destination for **film production**. In 1965, *Thunderball,* starring Sean Connery and Claudine Auger, was filmed partially at Rock Point House, West Bay Street, Nassau, and at the spectacular marine location of Thunderball Grotto at Staniel Cay, Exuma. The Vulcan bomber used in the movie was built at the old shipyard on Paradise Island and later sunk off Clifton Pier to form an artificial reef. The movie won a "best visual effects" Oscar. That same year the production team for the movie *Help!* came to Nassau/Paradise Island with their popular stars of the Beattles—Ringo Starr, John Lennon, Paul McCartney and George Harrison. Gardner Young, expert local diver, was hired to assist in the underwater scenes.

The **public relations** firm of Kelly Nason continued to manage the public relations account for The Bahamas. Writers employed by them at the local Bahamas News Bureau included a good mix of experienced and creative professionals—Bahamian and foreign—such as Addington Cambridge, Preston Stuart, Hans Groenhoff, Harry Rose, Don McCarthy, Harry Kline, Gordon Lomer, Rose McArdle, Jack Macbeth and P. Anthony White. They developed stories on all aspects of Bahamian life for widespread publicity through the agency's network. The stories were accompanied by black and white photographs produced by an outstanding photographic team of Fred Maura, Roland Rose, Gus Roberts, Howard Glass and Lorenzo Lockhart. Sylvia Perfetti Dupuch, wife of Etienne Dupuch Jr., was an integral member of the News Bureau team, who had been recruited by Carl Livingston, the Publicity Director.

Group travel grew in importance. The biggest group to be accommodated (in three-day segments) by a single hotel (the Emerald Beach) was the "Chevy Isle" sales incentive troupe of auto dealers, sales managers and their wives, in July 1964. Another noteworthy group was the 5,000-member Gibson Refrigerator Sales Corporation, housed at the Emerald Beach and Nassau Beach hotels during September 1963. Peanuts Taylor, Bahamian entertainer, proudly recalls that The Bahamas won the bid after he and a team of local entertainers accompanied Development Board officials to Hawaii at the previous meeting of the Gibson Group and made a strong and entertaining presentation which so impressed the audience that they unanimously voted to make Nassau their next meeting place. Other prominent groups included the Ford Motor Company of England, Bulova Watch Company, Parke Davis & Company, the American Institute of Architects, various chapters of the American Society of Travel Agents, and others. By 1960, group meetings averaged 20 per month.[7]

This period recorded the development of two major tourism destinations—Paradise Island and Freeport/Lucaya—which became the envy of the region, and the image created abroad was one of a millionaire's paradise.

Paradise Island

For many years, Hog Island was the site for popular day trips for vacationers to Nassau who would take a ferry to enjoy the world-famous beach. Only a few homes and a lighthouse dotted Hog Island shortly before World War II, when a Swedish industrialist, Dr. Axel Wenner-Gren, bought 750 acres for an estate and built a lavish home. He saw the possibilities the island offered as a resort, but it was left to American multi-millionaire Huntington Hartford, heir to the Atlantic & Pacific Tea (A&P) grocery fortune, to start the development. Hartford, after acquiring most of the island's 700 acres to achieve his vision of creating a complete resort paradise on Hog Island, renamed it *Paradise Island*. After three years of careful planning, the first phase of the investment, costing $20 million, was underway. He expanded the home into an exclusive club—the Ocean Club—landscaped the island, built new roads, constructed the fabulous *Café Martinique* restaurant on the lagoon, and made Paradise Island a showcase resort of international fame. Construction of other additional less exclusive hotel accommodations commenced in 1962. By winter of 1963, the 18-hole golf course, designed by golf architect Dick Wilson, opened.[8]

Paradise Island Bridge, completed in 1966, links Nassau to Paradise Island by land

Some critics felt that Paradise Island had become too exclusive to be a money-maker. Hartford sold it in January 1966 to Mary Carter Paint Company, which bought 75% interest in Paradise Island. Hartford, who held 25% interest, continued to advise, for a period of time, on further development of the island Shortly after the purchase, the paint company's chairman, James Crosby, and I.G. (Jack) Davis Jr., president, committed $12 million to build a 500-room luxury hotel by December 1967; a toll bridge connecting Paradise Island and Nassau; a $1 million 100-room lodge at Paradise Beach by December 1966; a $3 million theatre-nightclub seating 600 to 1,000, along with a casino housed in the same building; to extend Ocean Club as an exclusive resort with 100-150 rooms; and re-open the 18-hole championship Golf Course. Their vision was a tastefully done resort, but not a millionaire's retreat. The world famous Paradise Beach, with its miles of powdersoft white sand and crystal clear blue ocean water, was upgraded with a modern bath house and restaurant facilities.

Old world charm and the colourful spirit of the Riviera were also recaptured at the new Hurricane Hole marina, with protected anchorage and easy docking for 40 craft. In Nassau, at the foot of Deveaux Street off Bay Street, was Paradise Island's own boat terminal from which a fleet of shuttle boats operated.

26-year-old Glen Wells, sponsored by the Mary Carter Paint Company for the Mr. Universe competition, is congratulated by Mr. Jack Davis (left), President of the company after he captures the Mr. Universe Most Muscular title in Israel in 1967.

In 1969, Mary Carter sold its paint division which became Resorts International and continued to develop Paradise Island as a magnificent and glamorous tourism mecca.

Grand Bahama emerges as an international tourism centre

Around this time, exciting new developments were also taking place on Grand Bahama.

Freeport/Lucaya

The developers of what was originally conceived as an industrial free zone were rapidly moving into the tourism business. In 1961, Wallace Groves, Freeport's developer, formed a partnership with Louis Chesler, a Canadian financier, who owned a controlling interest in Seven Arts, the motion picture studio, and established the

Grand Bahama Development Company, the corporate instrument by which Freeport's status as a major destination was to be achieved. The Development Company's land became known as "Lucaya". After the airport was constructed, Mackey Airlines began regular service to and from Florida in early 1963, and, on New Year's Eve 1963, the luxury *Lucayan Beach Hotel* opened. By 1965, two new hotels opened—the 500-room *Holiday Inn* and the 800-room *King's Inn* (later called Bahamas Princess). Freeport/Lucaya became one of the fastest-growing tourist resort destinations in the world.

Visitor arrivals to Grand Bahama which totalled 26,894 in 1963, representing 5% of total arrivals, jumped to 308,737 in 1968, representing 29% of total arrivals (Appendix 3).

West End

Although Grand Bahama's tourist facilities were concentrated in the Freeport/Lucaya area, there was a sizable resort operation at West End—the well-known *Grand Bahama Hotel and Country Club*, a member of the Jack Tar hotel chain (now Old Bahama Bay). In 1963, a new air terminal opened in West End and, during this period, the Grand Bahama Hotel also completed a new marina and network of canals, ensuring ease of access to the resort by both air and sea.

Jack Tar Hotel, Grand Bahama

The Bahamas competes as a major Casino Destination

As was noted in Chapter 4, the first casino in The Bahamas opened in the Bimini Bay Rod and Gun Club, in Alice Town, Bimini in 1920, and Nassau's first casino, the Bahamian Club, also opened in 1920. These facilities, along with a casino at Cat Cay, were all small and operated on a seasonal basis as entertainment for tourists. By the 1960's The Bahamas could boast major, modern casinos.

Freeport, Grand Bahama was the site of the first major casinos with the opening in 1964 of the *Monte Carlo* casino in the Lucayan Beach Hotel and *El Casino* in 1968. Bahamas Amusements Ltd. initially operated both of these Grand Bahama casinos, which were later taken over by Grand Bahama Management Ltd and Princess Properties. In December 1967, the *Paradise Island Casino* opened after Paradise Enterprises, a subsidiary of Mary Carter Paint Company, was granted a Certificate of Exemption.

The opening of these large casinos became a source of controversy among religious groups because of perceived negative influences (such as money laundering, prostitution, alcoholism) which casinos normally attract. To reduce the negative influences on the local community, Bahamian citizens and residents have always been barred from gambling in any of the casinos and initially Bahamians were not allowed to take employment in the gaming industry. Eventually, Bahamianization of some sectors of the casino operation (Cashiers Cage, Credit, Slots, Food & Beverage, and Security) was accomplished, but employment at gaming tables was reserved for foreigners until 1983. Bahamians have now been trained in all spheres of gaming and presently enjoy lucrative careers in this sector. The Gaming Board, in accordance with the 1969 Lotteries and Gaming Act, was charged with the regulatory oversight of the gaming industry.

Twelve Islands in The Bahamas Boast Hotel Accommodations

The other hotels and guest houses on New Providence and the Family Islands continued to capture their share of the growing tourism business, and several small properties came on stream.

By 1962, 12 islands in The Bahamas chain could boast tourism accommodations, extending the country's competitive advantage as an archipelago with a variety of vacation options.

Bahamas Airway's first BAC 1-11 aircraft (Courtesy: Yvonne Shaw)

Bahamas Airways' first black stewardess, Yvonne Shaw, meets Lady Symonette, wife of the Premier, Sir Roland Symonette

Table 7-1
Hotel Rooms in The Bahamas, by Island
1962 vs. 1957

Island	1957	1962
New Providence/ Paradise Island	1,795	2,233
Abaco	52	187
Andros	43	99
Berry Islands	16	16
Bimini	114	146
Cat Cay	36	36
Eleuthera	95	163
Exuma		28
Grand Bahama	135	397
Harbour Island	78	99
San Salvador		19
Spanish Wells	10	10
Total	**2,374**	**3,433**

Source: 1977 Annual Report, Bahamas Ministry of Tourism

Native Entertainment permeates Bay Street and Over the Hill

The 1960's was an exciting era in Bahamian entertainment. The entire island of New Providence was alive with native entertainment. Bay Street alone boasted nearly a dozen nightspots from which visitors could choose. Those downtown properties included *Blackbeard's Tavern, Junkanoo* (formerly *Spider Web*), *Pino's* and *Sloppy Joe's* both in the Prince George Hotel, the *Big Bamboo, Ba Ma, Parliament Street Club, Imperial Hotel* and *Dirty Dick's*.

A popular "over-the-hill" native nightclub was the *Drumbeat Club*, on the corner of Market and Fleming Streets. Owned by Berkeley "Peanuts" Taylor (who is spotlighted at the end of this book), this club was frequented by tourists and locals alike for 11 years. Peanuts Taylor was no stranger to the entertainment world, having been performing from the age of 4 in the mid 30's. He opened the Tropicana Club on the site of the once-famous Paul Meeres Club on Market Street. Headliners were Richie Delamore, Eloise Lewis, and Pat Rolle. After the Club burned down, he worked for a number of years at other night spots, before building the famous Drumbeat Club in 1964.[9]

Adventurous tourists made their way to other over-the-hill native nightclubs. Veteran entertainer, "Duke" Errol Strachan, recalls that there were numerous such establishments which catered to both locals and visitors. In Oakes Field, there was the *Banana Boat,* operated by American Frank Minaya in the 60's, featuring *Tony Seymour.* When local entrepreneur Teddy Foster took over this club from Frank Minaya, *Ezra and the Polka Dots* became the featured band.

Duke Errol also reminisced that in Oakes Field opposite the Oakes Field airport, several night clubs were housed at the site of the Jimmy Gleco Restaurant; the first night club at the spot was the *Skylark Club.* When Fidel Castro took over Cuba in 1960 a Cuban group was featured there and it became the *Latin Quarters.* In 1964, Freddie Munnings managed that establishment, and called it the *Goombay Club.* For a time, Peanuts leased it from Freddie Munnings. Finally, under Ritchie Delmore it was called the *Lemon Tree* around 1968-69, when it went up in flames[10].

Another popular over-the-hill spot was the *Native Club*, on Poinciana Drive, which later became the *Blue Notes.* Also in the deep South was *Hutch Night Club* on Wulff Road, and *Coconut Palm* (on the property now occupied by Wescar), which became the *Yellow Bird* in the 1960's. *Bird Land* on Mt. Royal Avenue featured Sweet Richard in the 1960's.[11]

A unique entertainer of the period was Sabu Butler. Nicknamed "*Sabu the Great*", he created an indigenous Bahamas culture through his dances and rituals. Dressed in costume, complete with head gear and face painting, he performed incredible feats such as walking on broken glass, eating glass bottle, bending a cutlass under his throat and blowing flames from his mouth. Sabu entered the entertainment field at the old Cat N' Fiddle nightclub and for three decades performed for tourists at night spots in Nassau, Freeport and throughout the United States and Canada. A television film of his performance entitled "Thrill Seeker" was viewed by over 30 million people.[12]

This era recorded the death of Paul Meeres, one of the most brilliant entertainers of the century. The Paul Meeres Club, which he built in the 1930's, and was later run by Peanuts Taylor, had been destroyed by fire in 1958. Meeres was killed in a car accident in 1962, at the age of 60. He left a legacy unparalleled in Bahamian history and a team of entertainers who had benefitted from his generosity and tutelage.

Veteran Bahamian entertainers, such as *George Symonette, "Blind Blake"* and *Ronnie Butler,* travelled across the USA and Canada introducing The Bahamas through their music and song. George Symonette's popular recordings included *Spread Down your Apron Gal, John B. Sail and Little Old Nassau.* Other popular entertainers of the era were *King Eric & His Knights, Tony Seymour and the Nightbeaters*, the *George Moxey Quartet*, Vocalist *Andre Toussaint, Smokey 007* and *Count Bernadino*, among numerous others.

Commenting on the state of local entertainment in the 1950's and 60's, Peanuts Taylor noted that all of the hotels employed at least one band. Live music was offered in hotels on weekdays from 7 p.m. until midnight and on Saturdays at 1 p.m. When bands in the hotels stopped playing for the night, visitors headed to one of the local nightclubs. The Development Board used local bands on its overseas promotional trips. Because the Board subsidized the cruise ships, it was in a position to insist that, while in port, ships should close their shops and casinos and enjoy entertainment in the port. "These were good days in the entertainment industry, with full employment for bands", said Peanuts.[13]

Sir Stafford Sands leads a Development Board promotion in the USA. Miss Bahamas, Leonora Rodgers (left), accompanies the delegation

Delbon Johnson and band entertain travel agents at a special promotion

Sir Stafford Sands (6th from left) employs Count Bernadino's band to greet visitors at the airport (Photo: Courtesy of the Counsellors Ltd)

Tourism Performance

Donald Delahey, President of Tour Operators Association, meets President Nixon at Oakes Field airport

In the 1960's The Bahamas was the tourism leader in the Caribbean with more than twice the number of visitors than its nearest competitor, Jamaica, which catered to approximately 350,000 total visitor arrivals. The other Caribbean countries with slightly over a quarter of a million visitor arrivals were Bermuda and Trinidad & Tobago.

It can be noted from Table 7-2 that the average annual increase in visitor arrivals for The Bahamas during the 1960 to 1966 period was 19%. The United States supplied over three-quarters of the total air visitors, as indicated in Table 7-3, with Florida and New York ranking #1 and #2, respectively, among American states.

January 9, 1967 marked the end of a successful era with Stafford L. Sands, a promotional genius, at the helm. During the 17 years he led Tourism as Development Board Chairman and Minister of Tourism, the country experienced dramatic visitor growth from 32,000 arrivals in 1949 to 822,317 in 1966.

Table 7-2
Tourism Budgets and Visitor Arrivals
1960-66

YEAR	VISITORS TO NASSAU/ PARADISE IS.	VISITORS TO GRAND BAHAMA & FAMILY ISLANDS	TOTAL VISITORS	% INC	DEV. BOARD (TOURISM) BUDGET
1960	305,553	36,424	341,977	40.0	£807,696 ($2,310,000)
1961	314,126	54,085	368,211	7.7	£902,864 ($2,582,000)

1962	335,993	108,877	444,870	20.8	£1,004,130 ($2,872,000)
1963	398,676	147,728	546,404	22.8	£1,136,186 ($3,528,000)
1964	399,907	205,264	605,171	10.8	£1,233,646 ($3,528,000)
1965	494,552	225,868	720,420	19.0	£1,464,580 ($4,179,000)
1966	531,167	291,150	822,317	14.1	$4,992,968**

* Excludes yachtsmen   rate: £ = $2.80

** The Bahamas converted to decimal currency in 1966

Source: Development Board Annual Reports—Courtesy of Department of Archives

Table 7-3
Origin of Visitors by Air
1960-66

Year	USA	CANADA	U.K.	Other
1960	88.3%	6.6%	2.1%	3.0%
1961	86.7%	8.0%	2.2%	3.1%
1962	83.4%	10.4%	2.2%	4.0%
1963	82.2%	12%%	2.2%	3.6%
1964	80.4%	11.8%	2.8%	5.0%
1965	77.9%	10.4%	4.5%	7.2%
1966	82.5%	9.4%	3.0%	5.1%

Source: Development Board Annual Reports—Courtesy of Department of Archives

*   *   *

In the next two chapters tourism growth under leaders possessing a totally different management style from that of Sir Stafford Sands will be explored.

8

BAHAMIANIZATION AND PRODUCT DEVELOPMENT
1967-79

Global Travel Trends

While the late 1960's were booming years, the early 1970's was a slow period for tourism in the region because of high unemployment, the energy crisis, and economic policies of the US Government designed to counter inflation, impacting consumer spending, borrowing and travel. The advent of one-stop inclusive tour charters (OTCs), first from Canada and later from Europe in the early 1970's, helped to reverse the negative trend. By the 1975-76 winter season, the Civil Aeronautics Board in the USA approved OTC's, opening up interior cities in the United States for direct service to The Bahamas and the Caribbean, increasing competition.

The environment received special attention, starting on 22nd April, 1970, when the first *Earth Day*, an event to increase public awareness of the world's environmental problems, was celebrated in the United States for the first time. Millions participated in rallies, marches, and educational programmes, which increased environmental awareness, and, in July of that year, the Environmental Protection Agency (EPA) was established by special executive order to regulate and enforce national pollution legislation in America. Environmental consciousness, which had already gained popularity in Europe, became an issue within the travel industry throughout the world as nations began to acknowledge that the future of the tourism industry will depend on protecting the natural beauty and cultural richness of destinations.

This period also began an era of rapid expansion of technology in the airline industry making remote destinations more accessible. Modernization of the lodging industry continued. For example, in 1969 Westin Hotels became the first hotel chain to implement 24-hour room service.

An important development took place in nearby Florida, a major market for Bahamas visitors, when the $282 million *Walt Disneyworld* amusement park opened in Orlando in 1971 and a few years later the futuristic EPCOT Center opened its doors. By 1983, Disneyworld was catering to 20 million visitors per year, who came from all over the world, thus creating great opportunities for Florida-Bahamas two-centre vacations.

The year 1967 recorded significant historical events for blacks, both in the United States and The Bahamas. One such milestone in the United States was the appointment, under American President Lyndon Johnson, of US Court of Appeals Judge, Thurgood Marshall, as Supreme Court Justice, making him the first African American in history to sit on America's highest court.

Majority Rule in The Bahamas

On 10ᵗʰ January, 1967, political power was delivered into the hands of the black majority. Lynden Oscar Pindling of the Progressive Liberal Party (PLP) became the first black premier of The Bahamas. Following the defeat of his United Bahamian Party government, Sir Stafford Sands left The Bahamas. Sir Stafford died in 1972 while in voluntary exile.

The Bahamas constitution was revised in 1969 to give Government more responsibility for its own affairs and changing the status from British Colony to the Commonwealth of The Bahamas, with Mr. Lynden Pindling becoming the first Prime Minister. The new sense of pride and nationalism, which ran high at the time, found its way into the tourism industry as much as in any other area of life in The Bahamas. Recognizing the importance of tourism to the economy, Premier Pindling assumed the responsibility for the tourism industry himself in January 1967. His government pumped large sums into tourism, with the budget increasing from $5.5 million in 1967 to $15 million in 1979.

Pindling as new Minister of Tourism calls for Attitude Check

After the January '67 election, there was obvious exuberance throughout the country among blacks, who, although representing 80% of the population, had been treated like second-class citizens in their own country. In one of his first radio broadcasts to the nation a week after taking office, Pindling pointed out that he had been "disturbed about reports that in some quarters workers are slacking on their jobs, thinking that they no longer need to work hard". He reminded them that "we need to work harder today than we have ever done before. My government has promised you a square deal, a better life. It will not drop out of the sky. Hard work, honesty and determination are the only things that will do it". He added a special note to the large body of hotel workers: "As Minister of Tourism I hope to visit every Nassau hotel real soon and some in the Family Islands. I want our waiters and maids to smile and be courteous more than ever before because you have something to smile for now. If you fail, you fail me and then I shall fail you."[1]

Look Up, Move Up, The World Is Watching

BAHAMAS MINISTRY OF TOURISM

Lynden Pindling launches Awareness campaign "Look Up, Move Up, The World is Watching"

Despite admonishments by the Minister of Tourism, the excitement turned to arrogance and poor attitudes in the workplace, in some cases directed against white employers. Service by blacks to employers and tourists, who at that time were over 90% white, was viewed, by some, as servitude. The Premier and Minister of Tourism launched a national campaign under the theme "Look Up, Move Up, the World is Watching". Through posters, tent cards, radio broadcasts, a comic book, and a motion picture shown in local cinemas and throughout the community, Premier Pindling made a national and personal appeal to all Bahamians to translate their renewed national pride into good work ethics, commitment to excellence, courtesy and professional service.

To protect the leading industry, special emphasis was placed on reaching tourism workers—waiters, barmen, taxi drivers, hotel employers, and others who interacted with tourists such as shopkeepers, policemen and telephone operators.

Building a Professional Tourism Organization while Maintaining a Competitive Edge

Meanwhile, other measures were taken to ensure the continued success of tourism. Premier Pindling initiated the process of long-term planning, and building a professional organization.

Recruitment began for a qualified Director of Tourism (title later changed to Director General). On 1st September, 1967, Som Nath Chib, an internationally renowned tourism expert, was hired. Of Indian nationality, Chib had served as president of the International Union of Official Travel Organizations (IUOTO) and the Pacific Area Travel Association, Director of the Indian Tourist Board, and co-Chairman of the United Nations Conference on International Travel and Tourism.

As technological advances in the airline industry made remote destinations more accessible, the government realized that offshore promotional campaigns would need to become even more competitive and aggressive to retain market share, while the onshore product would require special attention to ensure guest satisfaction.

Although the country had a well-established image as a result of the successful promotional campaign of the three advertising and P.R. agencies contracted under the previous Minister of Tourism, the new PLP government, in July 1967, decided to consolidate all communication under the Interpublic Group of Companies, the third largest advertising agency in the world, with headquarters in New York. The new agency provided worldwide research, advertising, public relations, and sales support services, through its subsidiaries—Marplan, McCann Erickson, and Infoplan.

Portfolio and Structural Changes

After serving as Minister of Tourism for two years and recognizing that his vast political programme did not allow sufficient time for this important and growing industry, Prime Minister Pindling dropped Tourism from his portfolio, but not before welcoming the one millionth visitor, and putting in place a competent Director of Tourism. The year 1968 closed with a total of 1,072,213 visitors, representing a 17.1% increase over 1967 and exceeding projections.

MR. S. N. CHIB
DIRECTOR OF TOURISM

Som Chib, an internationally recognized expert, recruited as Director of Tourism in 1967. He served until April 1974.

In January 1969, Prime Minister Pindling appointed **Arthur Foulkes** as Minister of Tourism and Telecommunications. A journalist trained by Sir Etienne Dupuch, he had been the founding editor of the PLP newspaper *The Bahamian Times* in 1962. He retained the Tourism portfolio until September 1969. During his short tenure, there were two notable tourism achievements. First, the total number of visitors (1,332,396) and the percentage increase (24.3%) were the highest of the decade. Second, a Feasibility Study for tourism was initiated. Minister Foulkes, an excellent ambassador for the country, was committed to Bahamianization, and he appointed the first Bahamian—Gordon Rolle—to a post of Senior Executive at the head office in Nassau.

In January 1969 Arthur Foulkes replaces Pindling as Minister of Tourism

In September 1969, Premier Pindling replaced Arthur Foulkes with Clement T. Maynard, who was to become one of the longest serving tourism leaders in The Bahamas, and indeed the Caribbean.

The main priority areas identified and pursued by government were: design of an appropriate organizational structure to provide the framework within which tourism could flourish; preparation of a long-term plan to manage tourism growth; targeted research, publicity and promotions; and product development—expansion and control of facilities, amenities and events for the enjoyment, safety and satisfaction of visitors and formal training, involvement and recognition of Bahamians in the industry.

In November of 1969, Mr. Ellison A. Thompson, with vast administrative experience in various government agencies, became the first Permanent Secretary to be appointed in Tourism. His role was to assist the Minister, on the administrative and financial side, and to oversee all matters in his portfolio.

Clement Maynard assumes portfolio of Minister of Tourism in September 1969 and becomes the longest serving Minister of Tourism

Som Chib, as Director of Tourism, remained the technical head of the Department of Tourism until April 1974, when he retired, after serving six years and having created a professional organization. He was succeeded

Basil Atkinson, second professional Director of Tourism 1974-1976

Minister Maynard (right) and Basil Atkinson, Director of Tourism (left)

by *Basil Atkinson*, who was seconded from Australia where he had served as General Manager of the Australian Tourist Commission. Like Mr. Chib, Atkinson was a professional in international tourism and a former president of IUOTO, forerunner of the World Tourism Organization (UNWTO). The final foreign Director of Tourism, *Dan Wallace*, a retired Director of the Canadian Tourist Board, took office in 1976.

Dan Wallace, right, 3rd professional Director of Tourism 1976-1978

Som Chib (centre), first Director of Tourism, is honoured by BHA after being inducted into the Hall of Fame for travel at the annual ASTA Congress in Madrid. From left: Dan Wallace, Director of Tourism; Sir Clement Maynard, Minister of Tourism; Mr. Chib; Mike Wallen, Chairman NPI Promotion Board; and Steve Norton, President of BHA

Clement Maynard, with the assistance of his tourism experts, crafted a professional tourism organization, which became the envy of the Caribbean. This period was characterized by Bahamianization, expansion of tourism facilities and services and general improvement of the tourism product, without reducing the historic emphasis on publicity.

Bahamianization

New administrative procedures were introduced and the relations between head office and overseas offices were systematized. Bahamians were recruited to fill posts in the reorganized Ministry of Tourism and blacks took their place as meaningful participants in the tourism industry. Young Bahamians were recruited for the first time to fill positions in tourist information, market research, sales promotion, and public relations. A proper structure was put in place, patterned after that of the British Travel Authority, and job responsibilities grouped under various Assistant Directors and Managers. Two of the three Assistant Directors of Tourism were Bahamians: John Deleveaux, appointed in 1969, and Basil Albury, in 1971.

John Deleveaux, first Bahamian Assistant Director of Tourism, 1969

Basil Albury appointed Assistant Director in 1971

Bahamians were recruited for Sales and Information positions in Bahamas Tourist Offices (BTO) overseas. The first Bahamian appointed in the overseas offices was Bernard Davis, a Washington resident, who was hired as a Sales Representative. After a recruitment and training programme in 1970, a team of pioneer Bahamians took their place in the tourist offices. They included Athama Bowe, James Catalyn, David Johnson, Arlene Wisdom (Albury), Philip Mortimer,

Van Isaacs—all posted as Sales Representatives. Grace Fountain and Joan Jones (Neely) were the first

First group of Bahamian Sales Trainees—(from left) Van Isaacs, Arlene Wisdom (Albury), Athama Bowe, Philip Mortimer; (back) Joe Delaney and David Johnson. Adel Fahmy, Regional Manager, Bahamas Tourist Office (standing) was the instructor.

First Tourist Information Assistants—Jeanette Thompson, Velda Sands Campbell, Joan Jones, Keva Hanna Lawrence, Beverly Gibbs Allen, Gwen Forbes Kelly, Grace Fountain

Bahamian Tourist Information Officers in the New York BTO, and Sheila Cox was posted to the London BTO. At the end of 1973, 11of the 60 BTO staff (18%) were Bahamians. In 1973, Eugene Gibbs became the first Bahamian to hold a managerial position in a BTO when he was promoted to Regional Manager, Boston in 1973.

Richard Malcolm (left), who served in BTO Washington from 1971 to 1974, and Eugene Gibbs, who became the first Bahamian BTO manager, point to the islands of their birth

Sir Clifford Darling—first Chairman of re-constituted Tourism Advisory Board

The existing Tourism Advisory Board, which had previously consisted of six members appointed in their individual capacity, was reconstituted. In 1967, the board was increased to 13 and became more broad-based with representatives appointed from the key agencies that impacted tourism—Taxicab Union, Airlines, Shipping Agencies, Bahamas Hotel Association, Tour Operators Association, Nightclub Owners and Operators, Straw Vendors Association and the Grand Bahama Tourist & Convention Board. Private citizens representing the Family Islands were also added to the board. The advisory board created a valuable partnership, with all interests and worked tirelessly to produce creative solutions to interrelated problems.

Participation in World Tourism

In 1968, The Bahamas was accepted as a member of the International Union of Official Travel Organizations (IUOTO), which acted on behalf of the United

Nations on matters related to international tourism, becoming the first member country from the Caribbean. Membership in IUOTO provided The Bahamas with access to information on global trends, training opportunities and best practices in tourism. The Ministry of Tourism introduced global standards in research and statistics; tourist information services; tourist amenities; visitor relations; facilitation of entry and departure formalities at ports of entry; and a general dynamic national tourist policy.

The Bahamas hosts the Executive Committee of IUOTO in 1971

In January 1975 when IUOTO was reconstituted as an inter-governmental organization called the World Tourism Organization (UNWTO), each government was taxed based on the number of visitors it received. The Bahamas, though a developing country, was required to pay increased fees similar to those of developed countries who hosted the same number of visitors. Despite petitions, the UNWTO refused to amend the fee structure. Hence, in 1977, The Bahamas withdrew as a member of UNWTO.

Implementation of Modern Planning, Research and Statistics Techniques

Checchi & Company Long-Term Plan

Recognizing the synergistic relationship between planning, research, and marketing methods, The Bahamas engaged professional consultants to introduce the most modern research techniques and market intelligence. In 1969, a Washington company, Checchi and Company, completed a 10-year *Plan for Managing the Growth of Tourism in the Commonwealth of The Bahamas.* The mandate was to inventory capabilities, establish goals and lay out a programme of priorities. The study gave The Bahamas, for the first time, a yardstick for measuring the importance of tourism to the economy. The study revealed that tourism contributed over 70% of the country's Gross National Product and 60% of Government revenue. The Report made many innovative recommendations, including:

- Redesign of the Nassau Waterfront and a new transportation plan for Shirley Street, along with a concept for a new Bahamian vehicular system;
- Linking several of the islands, including development of a causeway to Current, Eleuthera;
- Establishment of an Industry-Government Task Force to prepare a plan for training hotel employees as well as a modern hotel school;
- Establishment of an overall expatriate quota by Cabinet, institution of a Key-Man work permit for two years, a Qualifications Committee as well as improvement of the administrative machinery at Immigration;
- Improvement of Government relations with the private sector by attracting the best brains in the country to serve on an expanded Tourism Board;
- Development of a more effective system of licensing and inspection of tourist accommodations;
- Establishment of a development bank for tourism projects to give loans and technical advice to local entrepreneurs and invest in tourism ventures;
- Involvement in "Social Tourism" by development of beach and park projects and encouragement of low-cost resorts for the indigenous population;
- Establishment of an Out Island Corporation to promote Family Island Tourism and to organize and regulate non-hotel rental accommodations in the Islands;
- Active promotion of group Fly-Ins and an annual Open Race for Pilots to capitalize on the exceptional flying conditions and attractions for the private flier;
- Increase in Government funding of the Bahamas National Trust and empowerment of the Trust to designate structures/sites of historic, scenic or ecological value, maintain museums and operate a "design bank" which would help to finance architectural fees to improve designs for new tourist projects.[2]

Many of the basic recommendations were implemented, in part, over the years but the feasibility of the major proposals was never fully investigated.

Statistics

The source of The Bahamas statistics is the Immigration card, which is completed on arrival in The Bahamas and handed to Immigration Officers at Points of Entry. In the previous decade, these cards were counted by hand, an inaccurate and tedious process. The Ministry of Tourism developed computer programmes to ensure that the IBM punch card yielded adequate information to meet the needs of the main users—hotels, Bahamas Tourist Offices, carriers serving the country, advertising agencies, and developers. The cards were coded, keypunched and sorted by Tourism staff working at the Immigration Department, in accordance with world tourism guidelines. Not only was a head count taken at first port of entry of total foreign arrivals by Air and Sea, Stopover, Cruise and Transit, but computer programmes were fine tuned to better pinpoint visitors' origin by sales region, major media markets, points of residence, age, length of stay, and mode of accommodation. The detailed breakdown enabled the Ministry of Tourism to better target its communication campaign and to give incentives to high producers of visitors.

The Immigration card, though providing vital statistics, yielded insufficient information on the characteristics or profile of visitors. In light of the importance of tourism to the economy, such information was considered essential for developing a sustainable tourism policy and introducing product improvements. Marplan, the research arm of the Interpublic Group of companies, was contracted to develop a series of studies in the major tourism markets—United States, Canada and the United Kingdom—to determine the attitudes and motivations of recent visitors, potential of the ethnic market and opinions on Bahamas advertising. A special study among travel agents was subsequently carried out. Simultaneously, a year-round Exit Survey was initiated in Nassau, Freeport, and later in key Family Islands. Through interviews of departing visitors at airports and cruise ports, national statistics were obtained on visitor expenditure, repeat business, expectations and satisfaction level with the facilities, amenities, and service. For the first time, accurate statistics were published showing actual earnings from tourism and the segments of the economy which benefitted directly from tourist dollars.

Air Service

Tourism success is directly related to air access from important markets. The major international carriers serving The Bahamas at the beginning of this period were Pan American, Eastern, Air Canada, British Overseas Airways Corporation (BOAC), and Qantas. Chalk's continued to service The Bahamas, although its founder, Arthur B. Chalk, passed away in 1977 at the age of 88. During the decade, there were many new developments in air service. The most significant of these developments was the inauguration of new direct service on 15th May, 1968 from New York/Boston by Northeast Airlines, which was acquired by Delta in 1972.

Joining BOAC in opening up the European market was International Air Bahama (IAB). International Air Bahama was unique in the annals of Bahamian civil aviation. Created in 1968 in Miami, Florida to fly transatlantic passengers at highly discounted fares, IAB operated one route with one plane—between Nassau and Luxembourg. Although IAB was officially a Bahamian carrier, it had little presence in Nassau. Its plane was registered in the USA and, for most of the airline's history, flown by U.S. pilots who lived in the USA and commuted to Nassau to go to work. It did, however, an excellent job of moving people—mostly on time—through Nassau International Airport. Initially they used a Boeing 707-355C but they soon switched to a DC-8F-55. After the company was taken over by Loftleidir Icelandic Airlines they settled on a DC-8-63CF. During most of the 1970s, IAB and Loftleidir became the most economical ways to travel between the USA & Europe. Once travellers no longer needed to travel via Nassau and Luxembourg, IAB could no longer fill the 246 seats on its 6-times-a-week schedule and it eventually discontinued service.

Bahamas World Airline (BWA) was another Bahamian player on the international scene. Everette Bannister led BWA and they operated Boeing 720 jets with scheduled services to Frankfurt, Germany and Brussels, Belgium and they also operated charter flights as far afield as Hong Kong. Their financial viability seemed to be tied to Robert Vesco and they left the scene at about the same time that he did.[3]

In 1973, Lufthansa offered service to Germany. Pan American Airlines, which pioneered air travel to The Bahamas in 1929, dropped its Caribbean routes, including The Bahamas, in 1976. The most far reaching development in air service during this period involved the sale and subsequent liquidation of Bahamas Airways.

Eastern Airlines brings an 85-member group which is welcomed to The Bahamas by Roy Davis, Eastern's Manager, and Sammy Gardiner, MOT

Permanent Secretary of Ministry of Tourism, Basil O'Brien (centre), congratulates Air Canada on its 30th anniversary of Bahamas Service. Air Canada commenced service to The Bahamas in 1948

International Air Bahama commenced service to The Bahamas in 1968. Stewardesses show off their new uniforms

International Air Bahama aircraft—Douglas DC.8 (Courtesy: Paul Aranha)

Frank Bartlett, Undersecretary Ministry of Tourism, with responsibility for Civil Aviation (right) welcomes winners of an Eastern promotion as Roy Davis (left), Eastern Airlines Manager, looks on

Bahamian officials welcome Air Canada's new 747 jet

Out Island Airways helps to fill the gap after the demise of Bahamas Airways

Bahamasair, the national carrier, starts service to all of the Islands in 1973

Bahamasair stewardesses

The Demise of Bahamas Airways

Before its demise, Bahamas Airways Limited (BAL), a BOAC subsidiary, was the main national carrier linking the Family Islands with Nassau and Freeport, and competing with Eastern Airlines and Pan Am on the Nassau-Miami route.

On 1st October, 1968, the Swire Group (who operated Cathay Pacific) acquired Bahamas Airways from BOAC. Its shareholders, over the next two years, reportedly spent $8.5 million for expansion of the airline to improve its competitiveness. It introduced the flamingo insignia, expanded service, opened offices in the United States, and commenced construction of a $250,000 headquarters at Nassau International Airport. To expand its long-haul markets, BAL ordered a new jet and made application in early 1970 to commence service from Nassau to New York and to Jamaica. BAL at that time owned three BAC-111 aircraft, five Hawker-Siddeley Avro 747 turbojets and some D.C.3's, with a total investment of $14 million.

Even though, over the years, the company had established a good image and reputation, when Swire took over the Company it was losing $1 million annually. BAL lost $4.75 million in 1969 and $2.5 million in the first six months of 1970. Despite its losses, the company's efficiency rate had reportedly improved. Nevertheless the shareholders of BAL concluded that they could not sustain the losses. Hence, on 28th July, 1970, the Company wrote to Prime Minister Pindling informing him that the shareholders of BAL were no longer willing to pump cash into BAL, and invited Government to take over all, or at least the majority, shareholding in the airline. Government expressed a positive interest in the offer. The Government agreed to enter into negotiations with BAL for four basic reasons: Firstly, it hoped to protect the jobs of Bahamas Airways' 753 employees, 590 of whom were Bahamians. Secondly, it recognized the importance of BAL to the economy of the Commonwealth. Thirdly, it envisioned the creation of a strong inter-island air link—an essential element of communications for a country with a land mass and population scattered over 100,000 square miles of ocean. Lastly, as The Bahamas approached nationhood, a true airline flag carrier, with Government and other Bahamian participation, was necessary and desirable.[4]

In order to safeguard the public interest and protect public funds, Government requested that BAL agree to an analysis of the administration and operational machinery of BAL including its present and future routes, its existing financial commitments, cash needs for the next 5-10 years and an official audit.

According to Prime Minister Pindling, who addressed the nation on this topic, Government's willingness to take a majority position in the Company was frustrated by the shareholders' insistence that the following three basic subjects were non-negotiable:

1) Agreement by Government that BAL would continue to operate for a period of at least 18 months in accordance with the existing policies and plans of the present management, with sufficient additional capital from

Government to maintain the company's present scale of operations and any
previously agreed expansion.

2)   Agreement that Government would unconditionally indemnify John Swire
     & Sons Limited, and its subsidiaries against any liability, costs, claims or
     expenses arising directly or indirectly from the leases or proposed leases of
     BAL's jet aircraft and spares, such guarantees not exceeding B$2,500,000
     in total.

3)   Government to guarantee obligations incurred by BAL in regard to a
     mortgage for an "aircraft package", which was backed by Lloyds Limited.[5]

The Government's understanding of these demands was that BAL was asking
that the airline be run in exactly the same way as it had been in the past, with the
same plans for expansion and management until March 1972, despite its losing
position. There was also concern that, even though the Government was buying
only one percent more than half of the Company, BAL shareholders demanded that
Government be responsible for all of the company's bills up to $2 ½ million. It also
meant agreeing in advance to keep the BAC-111 aircraft, even if Government found
they were not best suited for the service.[6]

According to Pindling, since BAL's non-negotiable three points could have
subjected the Government to huge liabilities, a counter proposal was made to BAL
which would have enabled the Government, in 90 days, to make its own thorough
study of the company's financial position and other necessary details about the whole
operation. BAL was prepared to allow only four weeks. Pindling, in his broadcast, had
also commented that BAL was not a true flag carrier in the internationally recognized
sense, in that a substantial proportion of its shares were not owned by Bahamians,
and, furthermore, management decisions were based upon the interests of foreign
shareholders living abroad, with the welfare of Bahamians taking second place.[7]

Without an outright Government assurance as to the possibility of a satisfactory
outcome of Government's "study", the shareholders of BAL could not continue what
would have amounted to another three months' underwriting of the company. It
was then that BAL gave Government notice of termination.

In making the announcement of the closure of the airline, BAL's managing
director, Duncan R. Bluck, who in two dynamic years had introduced jets and an
international image, said that, like many airlines operating in the North American
market, BAL's planned development had been "seriously affected by the current
US recession and its effect on tourism to The Bahamas".[8] The previous Thursday,
Pan American World Airways had announced suspension of its Freeport-Miami
flights from 25th October due to lack of passengers and the previous month Eastern
Airlines cancelled their flights from Florida to West End, Grand Bahama for the
same reason. Bluck explained that it was because of this 'recession" that BAL had
begun discussions with Government in late July to arrive at a basis upon which the
Government would participate in the airline.

The news that the multi-million dollar airline would be "put into liquidation forthwith", was received in disbelief by the 800 stunned BAL staff members, who, overnight, were out of a job. The airline, which had been paying out $8.5 million in salaries every year, had just acquired a new BAC-111 stretch jet to inaugurate its New York and Jamaica services, scheduled to start on 12th November of that year.

There were many critics of the Government's position on these negotiations. The Tribune, in its 13th October, 1970 editorial, questioned whether Government meant what they said when they told Bahamas Airways they were "definitely interested in taking over the airline". They pointed out that Government made no positive approach to BAL to help in what must have been for them a most painful decision. The editorial also pointed out that Government had contributed to BAL's losses by awarding Bahamas World Transport nearly all the route licences under which BAL then operated. The whole country mourned the folding of an airline which had been the largest single carrier of tourists to The Bahamas and had, for 35 years, serviced the Bahama Islands without any major disaster or loss of life. It was suggested by many that the Bahamas Government lost a golden opportunity to acquire, at a low cost, an efficient airline with a good image.[9]

Aftermath: While BAL's loss was felt for many years, Colony Airlines, Out Island Airways and Mackey Airlines reacted swiftly to fill the gap and a new carrier, Flamingo Airlines, established inter-island service in 1971; also Mackey Airlines expanded its routes from Miami and Fort Lauderdale direct to 15 Family Islands. The gap left by BAL's demise led to serious discussion about the establishment of a National Air Carrier with exclusive rights to operate domestic scheduled services.[10]

Bahamasair—the National Flag Carrier

Following the recommendations of a 1971 report, the amalgamation of assets of existing small carriers led to the formation of Bahamasair, as the national flag carrier. On 18th June, 1973, shortly before Independence, Bahamasair commenced operations over domestic and Florida routes formerly served by the smaller airlines. From the outset the airline was under-funded, over-staffed and in financial difficulty. Over the years it added new international routes, all of which proved to be unprofitable. Because of its poor financial status, it had difficulty upgrading its fleet or even maintaining its regular aircraft to keep on schedule. Government was forced to vote large sums to supplement the airline's budget to keep it flying. However, the airline maintained, and continues to maintain, an impeccable safety record, with no fatal accidents, and provides a vital service to Family Islands.[11]

Sea Travel

At the beginning of this period there were four ships on the Miami run—*Bahama Star, Ariadne, Sunward* and *Miami*. Home Lines' *SS Oceanic* and *SS Homeric* provided service out of New York. Nassau's popularity as a port of call was strengthened by the opening of the new wharf and the deepening of the harbour facilities in 1969, making it possible for the largest cruise ships to dock. This expansion signalled the onset of phenomenal growth in cruise holidays globally. New vessels were being constructed and based in Miami and Port Everglades and both Nassau and Freeport were added to the ports of call on their multi-island itineraries. In addition, many cruise lines—such as Eastern Steamship, Costa Lines, Holland America Lines and Norwegian Caribbean Cruise Lines out of Florida—operated weekly and twice-weekly Nassau-only cruises. Freeport's cruise service expanded in 1968 with the introduction of Bahama Cruise Lines' Miami-Freeport daily service on the *M/V Freeport*.

With the Nassau Harbour expansion, up to 9 of the world's largest cruise ships dock in Nassau at one time

Marketing The Bahamas

Effective 1st July, 1968, the Interpublic Group of Companies began its contract with the Ministry of Tourism for global communications. Emerging from their research was the broad concept that The Bahamas was not one product, but three, each appealing to a different segment of the travel market: *Nassau* with its "foreign" flavour; *Freeport, Grand Bahama*, a swinging casino destination; and the *Family Islands*—remote, undeveloped, and unspoiled. A media strategy was developed with this in mind. The Bahamas employed the medium of television for the first time in the United States and Canada in 1967. An innovation in 1971 was the mention of specific Family Islands in mass media messages to familiarize the public with names such as Eleuthera, Abaco, Andros, and Exuma, and special in-depth brochures were developed for these four major islands to be used in support of the advertising. Market segments identified for special emphasis were Fishing, Private Flying, Yachting, and Golf.

New collaterals and sales aids for Bahamas Tourist Offices to use in the travel trade

Separate brochures produced for four Family Islands

New posters

ARE YOU BIG ENOUGH FOR THE BAHAMAS?

Bahama Islands
700 twenty tropical islands.

An inexpensive plane ticket buys you a hot wind in your face,
A cool blue ocean at your feet.
Nobody breathing down your neck.
And a chance to think things over.

Hurry hurry hurry.
The world is fast running out of islands like this.

Just 2½ hours from Times Square.

Bahama Out Islands
You to there. So near. And yet so far.

Magazine ads

The Bahamas seized the opportunity to lure many of the Disney visitors from Orlando, Florida, by beefing up publicity, developing Florida/Bahamas packages, and introducing new and exciting onshore promotions such as Goombay Summer, Son et Lumiere, Dolphin Experience, and sporting promotions.

Sun, sand and sea continued to be the main drawing card for northern visitors. However, the country's reputation as a sunny winter resort was challenged, when on 19th January, 1977, snow flakes fell on parts of the northern Bahamas for the first time in history.

The publicity arm of Interpublic—Infoplan—and the local Bahamas News Bureau, provided good press coverage for the country by arranging press trips to The Bahamas for hundreds of journalists each year, and distribution of film clips, stories and photographs to all of the media. Special events such as golf tournaments, powerboat racing and treasure hunts generated headlines and articles throughout the world. Communications (advertising, public relations, sales aids, publications), the largest single item in the Ministry of Tourism's budget, has averaged 60% over the years. The Bahamas received a good return on investment on its communications budget.

During the decade, the sales offices were reorganized. Mr. O.B. Cloudman, an American with wide marketing experience, was appointed General Sales Manager for North America on 1st May, 1967. In 1967, sales offices were opened in Detroit, Dallas, Boston, and Washington, and new sales representatives hired in Toronto, a growing winter market. The St. Louis office was closed. Offices were grouped by region, headed by a Regional Sales Manager.

With the advent of low-cost charter flights, the cost of transportation from the United Kingdom and Europe was no longer as important a factor. Hence, greater investment was made in targeting Europeans, who stayed longer. In light of the dramatic increase in the number of visitors from Continental Europe, an office was opened in Frankfurt, Germany, in 1970.

In 1969, the modern concept of joint promotions between the Ministry of Tourism and the Bahamas Hotel Association began. An attempt was also made to coordinate the advertising, public relations and marketing efforts. Recognizing the importance of travel agents in selling the destination, a unique programme of workshops, called "Teach-Ins", were held, embracing hundreds of agents in major cities.

To open new markets, the Ministry of Tourism embarked upon an aggressive campaign to market the Islands through sales promotions directed at private plane flyers in North America and Europe. This market segment played a significant role in the development of Family Island tourism. In 1970, the highlight of the aviation activities was the 20th Women's International Air Race, "Angel Derby", which terminated in Nassau. A record number of airplanes piloted by all women crews registered for the contest and hundreds of followers flew to Nassau to witness the exciting finish at Prince George Dock in May 1970.

Golf rose to new prominence when The Bahamas Open was staged in Freeport in 1970. The $130,000 tournament was the largest event of its kind ever to be conducted in the Islands and was sanctioned by the Tournament Players Division of the Professional

Golfers Association of America. Top name golfers, including Arnold Palmer, competed. By 1973, the country could boast fifteen 18-hole golf courses. Yachting events which continued to be popular were the world-famous Bahamas 500, the Miami-Nassau Races, the Family Island Regatta, the Yachtsmen's Piloted Cruise, and the Southern Ocean Racing Conference races. Auto Racing, which had previously been staged in Nassau, was moved to Freeport and sponsored by the Grand Bahama Tourist and Convention Board.

Bahamas booth for International Boat Show, London

Anthony Roberts, High Commissioner presents representatives from Association of British Travel Agents (ABTA) with Bahamian gifts, while Director for Europe, Hans Borghardt, (left) and Basil Albury (right) look on

Minister of Tourism Livingstone Coakley (third from left) and Tourism team meet with Adventure Tours to negotiate new charter service from Dallas to Exuma

Jacqueline Kennedy Onassis (left) and mother-in-law Rose Kennedy visit downtown Nassau

Governor Reuben Askew and family visit Straw Market

Greg Barrett (left), BTO, and Pam Richardson (second from right), Nassau/PI
Promotion Board escort travel agents on a familiarization trip

Flip Wilson performs in Nassau. At right is Prime Minister Pindling and his daughter, little Monique Pindling

Cordell Thompson (centre) presents Miss Nassau/Paradise Island with a special gift

Joe Delaney (left) and Athama Bowe (second from right) at a Freeport promotion

BTO staff at Dallas promotion

Randy Clare and Diana Johnson promote The Bahamas in New York

Count Bernadino (on steel pans) and his band perform at a special promotion for Private Flyers. Hans Groenhoff, MOT's Consultant for Private Flying, is at left

James Catalyn (left) at Town Crier promotion in Canada

Bahamas Tourist Office managers and sales representatives on Family Island familiarization

Netica Symonette (left) hosts U.S. Senator Shirley Chisholm (centre)

Singer Isaac Hayes (right) explores Eleuthera with Preston Albury in search of a site for a second home

Tourism leaders meet to discuss 1978 Marketing Plan. From left: John Walsh, Director of the Bahama Out Islands Promotion Board; Dan Wallace, Director General of Tourism; Bill Naughton, president of BHA; Baltron Bethel, P.S., Ministry of Tourism; Mike Wallen, Chairman of Nassau/Paradise Island Promotion Board; Buddy Goodwin, GM of Freeport Inn, Freeport; and Albert Miller, Chairman of the Freeport/Lucaya Promotion Board

Promoting The Bahamas at the 48th ASTA World Congress in Acapulco—From left: Henry Ross, NPI Promotion Board; Sella Hatfield, Hanna Travel, Oregon; George Myers, Paradise Island Ltd.; and Corinne Graham of Boca Raton Travel, Florida

As the promotional campaign drew large numbers of international visitors, it also sparked local interest. A massive Domestic Tourism Campaign under the theme "It's a Family Affair", was launched in 1972, targeting Bahamians and local residents. Through partnership with the local airlines, hotels, and travel agents, attractive weekend packages were offered.

Film Promotions: The Bahamas was a spectacular natural setting for two films that effectively showcased the country's marine life. *The Day of the Dolphins*, with George C. Scott and local diver, Willie Meyers, as a villain, was filmed at Treasure Cay, Abaco and the dolphin pens at Clifton Pier. *Salty,* the story of a lovable sea lion, was filmed near the Montagu Beach Hotel, Nassau.

In 1977, *The Spy Who Loved Me,* starring Roger Moore as James Bond, was shot north of Goulding Cay. The tanker that swallowed the submarine and the underwater city were built at Coral Harbour. The movie earned Academy Award nominations for best art direction/set decoration and best song. These productions pumped large sums into the local economy and generated much publicity for the destination.

The Onshore "Experience"—Product Development

Government introduced product initiatives with special emphasis on improvement and regulation of the physical product and enhancement of the visitor welcome through cultural development as well as training, incentives and empowerment of locals.

The Hotel Sector

The period 1967 to 1972 recorded much expansion in the hotel industry. The Paradise Island plant increased significantly with the construction of the 503-room *Paradise Island Hotel and Villas*, the 300-room *Britannia Beach Hotel*, the 250-room *Flagler Inn*, the 100-room *Beach Inn*, and the 17-storey 535-room *Holiday Inn*. New hotels on New Providence included the 400-room *Sonesta Beach Hotel & Golf Club*, (which later became the Ambassador Beach and then SuperClub Breezes) and the 120-room *South Ocean Beach Hotel & Golf Club* near Nassau International Airport. Smaller properties which opened on New Providence included the 80-room *Blue Vista Club*, the 26-room *El Greco* and the 32-room *Ocean Spray* on the Western Esplanade. In Freeport, Grand Bahama, new hotels included the 400-room luxury *International Hotel* adjacent to El Casino and the International Bazaar, with its sister hotel, *King's Inn* (subsequently Princess hotels and later Royal Oasis) across the street on the highway, the 200-room *Shalimar* with kitchenettes, the 140 room *Indies Hotel* and the 140-room *Sheraton Oceanus*.

In the Family Islands, new quaint and popular resorts opened. In South Eleuthera were the 20-room *Island Inn*, Windermere Island, as well as the *Arnold Palmer Inn*, and *Arawak Cove Club*, each with 100 rooms. In the Cays, the *Great*

Harbour Club on the Berry Islands, and the *Walker's Cay Club* on Abaco became popular with boaters.

In 1967, the *Balmoral Club*, which from its inception had catered to the sophisticated and elite society, added a six-floor tower, with a walk-up penthouse on the seventh floor, greatly increasing the resort's capacity. With its new European-styled rooms and suites, and its private Balmoral Island, the resort changed its name to the Balmoral Beach Hotel (now Sandals Royal Bahamian),and maintained its reputation as an exclusive and charming hotel with Bahamian setting, drawing patrons such as The Beatles, US Presidents, and members of various European Royal Houses.

New Providence gets its first Holiday Inn, a 17-storey 535-room hotel on P.I.

Netica Symonette (right) Assistant Innkeeper at the Holiday Inn, Paradise Island, works with front desk employees to keep visitors to the new hotel satisfied. Here she chats with Glenda Granger, recording artist, who was on a two-week engagement at the hotel. Looking on are (left to right) Heinz Higgs and Paul Thompson

In 1970 hotel construction was at an all-time high

The 400-room Sonesta Beach Hotel on Cable Beach (renamed Ambassador Beach and now the site of SuperClubs Breezes)

Managerial staff of the three government-owned hotels chat with John Micklewhite, Secretary and treasurer of BHA. From left—Robert Souers, Ambassador Beach, Mr. Micklewhite; Netica Symonette, Balmoral Beach Hotel; and Klaus "Nick" Pattusch, Emerald Beach Hotel

Netica Symonette (centre) is surrounded by well-wishers as she opens her own hotel, Casuarinas on Cable Beach in 1977. Prime Minister Pindling (right) gave the keynote address

Agriculture and BHA officials meet to discuss linkages between the hotel sector and Tourism. Left to right—Willamae Salkey, Permanent Secretary, Ministry of Agriculture & Fisheries (formerly with Tourism); Hon. Pierre Dupuch, Minister of Agriculture & Fisheries; Robert Sands, President of BHA; and John Deleveaux, Executive Vice President of BHA

Overall essay winner in Adopt-A-School competition, Sabrina Robinson of Aquinas College, accepts a plaque from Minister of Education Hon. Ivy Dumont (second from left). Also pictured from left: Max Belin of American Express (one of the sponsors of the programme); Calvin Johnson, Parliamentary Secretary, Ministry of Tourism; and Robert Sands, BHA President (right)

BHA's Annual Skills Day—hotels compete for fun awards

When the PLP came to power in 1967, there was a consensus for amending the Hawksbill Creek Agreement which created the nation's second city, because it was felt that the exclusion of Bahamians from the social and economic mainstream of a foreign enclave was intolerable as was the surrender of governmental control over immigration and other administrative functions. However, the Government recognized the great potential of Freeport to provide employment and professional and commercial opportunities for tens of thousands of Bahamians, thus relieving the population pressure on New Providence. They concluded that the necessary changes could be made without destroying the economy of Freeport; but the amendments led to a slowdown in the economic fortunes of the island that was to last for many years.

Hotels which closed during this period included the 75-room French Leave, in Governor's Harbour in 1970, and the Rock Sound Club, in Rock Sound, Eleuthera, in 1973. One of the historic relics of the past, the Royal Victoria Hotel, began to suffer from neglect. The once luxuriant gardens had become cement-covered walks in a stripped-down public "park". The Royal Vic closed its doors in 1971. As Henry Villard reminisced of the hotel: "Few could boast such a rich heritage of memories: riotous headquarters of blockade runners in the American Civil War; pioneer haven for invalids and refugees from wintry blasts; oasis for Americans in the Prohibition era; cherished retreat of important personages from across the seas"[12]. The Bahamas Government acquired the hotel site in 1972.

The most significant event in the hotel industry was Government's acquisition in August 1974 of three major hotels on Cable Beach—the Hyatt Emerald Beach, the Balmoral and the Sonesta Beach Hotel. The Government established the Hotel Corporation of The Bahamas in October 1974 "to extend and improve the resort industry for the benefit of the people as a whole". Prime Minister Pinding, as the Corporation's first Chairman, optimistically announced that, once the Corporation was on a firm financial footing, the Bahamian public would be able to buy shares in it. However, Government quickly learned that, despite its best efforts, running of hotels was unprofitable. The only hotels easy to acquire were those in financial difficulty. Government was forced to make expensive concessions to attract further investment. "The Hotel Corporation had to weigh and juggle the cost to the Treasury against the benefits of import duty concessions, the advantages against the disadvantages of levying a government tax on rooms, the problem of keeping the owners and managers happy with the level of the wages bill while keeping the workers contented with pay and working conditions, the acceptable balance between Bahamian expatriate employment."[13]

As many large properties came on stream, hoteliers were now in the mass tourism business and had to devote much attention to marketing their properties through wholesalers and tour operators in order to keep occupancies high and avoid losses. One problem was the relationship between Association member hotels and travel wholesalers over room rates. Many resorts still refused to sell rooms to some wholesalers at net (bulk) rates, fearing a loss of profits and the financial instability of the wholesalers. This problem was resolved in 1973 when, in conjunction with the Ministry of Tourism, the BHA began requesting Letters of Credit drawn on the wholesalers' banks to cover three months of business in The Bahamas. This strict requirement was enforced over the objections of some wholesalers and thus provided BHA member hotels with tremendous financial security and paved the way for an even greater volume of tourists. In 1974, the Bahamas Hotel Association joined the Caribbean Hotel Association and began to benefit from the exchange of ideas within the organization and its annual trade show, *Caribbean Market Place*, which brought major suppliers, tour operators and travel agents to the region. Three local Promotion Boards, *Nassau/ Paradise Island Promotion Board*, *Grand Bahama Island Promotion Board* and the *Bahama Out Islands Promotion Board*, were formed to coordinate marketing activities for New Providence, Grand Bahama, and the Family Islands

(Out Islands), respectively. In addition to the work of these boards, the Bahamas Hotel Association continued to undertake joint offshore promotions each year with the Ministry of Tourism.

Bahamas Reservations Service (BRS) was formed by the Nassau/Paradise Island Promotion Board in 1977, to provide a cost efficient reservations service for all licensed hotels in The Bahamas, through toll-free information and reservations. This especially helped smaller properties and Family Island hotels that did not have the resources to contract their own reservations agents.

The creation of an **overbooking policy**, under the presidency of Ron Overend in 1978, was another important development for BHA members. The new policy eliminated the fear of overbooking for prepaid guests by outlining standard procedures and compensation for hotels to follow in the event that overbooking occurred.

Licensing of Hotels

Before the 1970's, hotels in The Bahamas operated without regulation or controls. Even though the Bahamas Hotel Association attempted to provide some guidelines for operation, their primary role was that of promotion; furthermore, less than half of the hotels in the country were members of the Association. This created great difficulty in taking inventory, securing hotel rates in order to promote the properties, and, most important, ensuring that properties met acceptable standards of safety, hygiene, and comfort of guests. On the recommendation of the Ministry of Tourism, Government passed the *Hotels Act 1970,* which made it mandatory for lodging establishments of four rooms or more to undergo regular inspections and to be licensed annually as hotels by the Hotel Licensing Board, a statutory autonomous body. This Act also introduced a hotel guest tax to be collected from hotel guests and paid to Government. The Bahamas was the first country in the Caribbean to introduce such a licensing system.

First Black-owned tour operation

In September 1967, the first local black-owned tour operation came into existence when Pleasure Travel, headed by Harcourt Bastian, with years of experience as a taxi-driver, was established in Nassau. Mr. Bastian adopted as his motto *Travelling with Pleasure,* and promised to offer his patrons well-organized, accurate city and country tours and extended island tours. Shortly after opening his company, he began to forge international relationships and to establish affiliation with travel agencies in the United States and Canada. Bastian immediately joined the Bahamas Sightseeing and Tour Operators Association, and, like the other member tour operators, was able to make advance arrangements for package tours, including hotel accommodations, airport transfers, night club tours and other facilities.

In 1987 Harcourt Bastian (centre) becomes the first black owner of a tour company

Harcourt Bastian (right) welcomes two new tour operators into the Tour Operators Association

Harcourt Bastian and staff greet President Reagan during his Nassau visit

Local tour operators meet regularly to discuss improvements in ground tour operations

Members of Bahamas Sightseeing and Tour Operators Association pose with Robert Sands (2nd from right)

Local Entertainment

This period recorded the construction of two new night clubs in Nassau with the opening of the *King & Knights Club*, owned by King Eric Gibson and the 400-seat *Ronnie's Rebel Room*, featuring Ronnie Butler's band in the Anchorage Hotel. However it also marked a gradual decline in popularity of native night clubs with the hotel expansion and popularity of casino entertainment. One group which continued to grow in popularity was the *Royal Bahamas Police Force Band.*

Peanuts Taylor (centre), who signs a contract to perform on the SS Norway, is congratulated by Berlin Key, representative for the cruise line

Police Band performs in Nassau, to the delight of locals and visitors

In the 1960's and 1970's, the Royal Bahamas Police Force Band cemented its role as important goodwill ambassadors for The Bahamas. In 1962, the band had travelled abroad, for the first time, with the Development Board, performing in Las Vegas, Nevada, for the American Society of Travel Agents (ASTA) convention, where it had been well received. At the 1964 World's Fair in New York and the 38th Annual ASTA Convention in San Juan, Puerto Rico, held in September 1968, which was the scene of the largest cooperative promotional effort in the history of The Bahamas tourist industry, with nearly 100 representatives, including hoteliers, tour operators, airlines, steamship companies and tourist board officials, the Police Band again made a strong impact. The music of the Band so captivated the crowd at the 1968 Olympic Games in Mexico that band members were almost mobbed for autographs. The band also took over the spotlight in performances in Canada and Europe and at *Carifesta* in Barbados. In Washington, the band won first prize for *best marching and playing* in the Elks parade.

During the 1970's, members of the Police Band were sent abroad for in-service training in music and bandmaster courses, resulting in the composition of new marches. In 1978, Mr. Dustin Babb, Superintendent of Police, succeeded Mr. Dennis Morgan as Director of Music. During Babb's tenure, the scope of the band broadened, as it began to play more contemporary and pop music.[14]

Son et Lumiere—an idea ahead of its time

In 1968, to create new attractions for visitors, the Director of Tourism, Som Chib, invited an expert in the production of Son et Lumiere (sound and light) spectacles to produce a show in The Bahamas. Thus, in 1968, Fort Charlotte was converted into a Sound and Light Theatre. With the help of intricate electronic equipment and hundreds of projectors, the colourful history of The Bahamas was reenacted and given reality. The scenario, played against an original musical score by Edwin Astly, began with the suffering of an Arawak slave at the hands of the Spanish Conquistadors, discovery of the island of San Salvador by Christopher Columbus, the days of the pirate, Blackbeard, Lord Dunmore and other historical characters. No actors appeared on the scene; only their voices were heard. Yet, through the power of suggestion, the visitor was taken into the past to meet villains and victims. The show, entitled "The Silent Guns", was designed by Emile de Harven, who produced the world's leading Sound and Light dramas at the Acropolis in Athens, Red Fort in Delhi, the Forum in Rome, The Tower of London and the Pyramids in Cairo. Even though Son et Lumiere attractions were popular in Europe, the Fort Charlotte, Nassau, spectacle never became a financial success. Because it became a drain on the Public Treasury, local newspapers dubbed the spectacle "Chib's Folly". Son et Lumiere closed to the public in 1973. In later decades, new groups have explored the feasibility of reviving Son et Lumiere, which was considered ahead of its time.

Improving the Welcome

The results of marketing research revealed an absence of a cultural identity for The Bahamas. The Islands for years had been the preferred destination for sun, sand and sea, but the people and culture played little role in the marketing of the destination. During this era, fresh new programmes were introduced to expose visitors to Bahamian culture, to showcase the friendliness of the local people, and to ensure that tourists would return year after year.

Goombay Summer

The year 1971 heralded the inauguration of Bahamas Goombay Summer—a 13-week festival staged in Nassau and Freeport. This popular onshore promotion was conceived to boost tourism arrivals after the 1970 recession, while exposing visitors to Bahamian culture. The main feature was the closure of Bay Street, Nassau, for one day a week for local entertainment, a cultural shopping mall, and a taste of Junkanoo. What in concept had been a planned festival became a spontaneous event, with the involvement of both tourists and Bahamians in the Goombay Parade, Jump-in Dancers and goatskin drummers, vendors selling native delicacies, and performances by the Police Band and other local bands. Goombay events staged on other days included a Folklore show, Fashion shows at hotels, and art exhibitions. Goombay Summer specials, featuring attractive package tours and on-shore bargains, were offered through the travel trade. All sectors of the hospitality industry, including hotels, Promotion Boards, tour operators, taxicabs and retail stores, cooperated to make the event a success. August 1991 broke all records for visitors to The Bahamas in a single month, and it was therefore decided to make Goombay Summer an annual event. Lasting for twenty years, Goombay Summer turned out to be the most effective and long-lasting promotion ever staged by the Ministry of Tourism.

John "Chippie" Chipman teaches a visitor dance steps during Goombay Summer

Goombay Summer

People-to-People Programme

An important innovation in improving the visitor experience was the ***People-to-People*** programme, launched in December 1975, by Sir Clement Maynard, Minister of

Tourism. The programme was patterned after Jamaica's "Meet the People" programme which their Tourist Board had introduced a few years earlier to enhance that island's profile as a hospitable destination. The Bahamas quickly took the programme and expanded it, creating several People-to-People products. The goal of the programme is to enable visitors of varied interests to experience the country's lifestyle and culture through its people. *People-to-People at Home* is the main programme in which volunteers were recruited and vetted to become a part of an official register of approved "hosts" who were willing to invite visitors into their homes. By linking visitors with Bahamians for a cultural outing or an afternoon at home, it played a major role in winning of life-long friends of The Bahamas. The *People-to-People at Sea* programme, a cooperative partnership with cruise ships, involved selecting Bahamian couples for a complimentary cruise on the Oceanic to New York (and later the Sunward II was added to the programme). The Bahamian couple would be given a special briefing time on the ship when they would address passengers on Bahamian history and culture and invite them to participate in the People-to-People programme when they arrived in the port of Nassau. This also served as a vehicle through which volunteers could be thanked for their warm hospitality to guests over the years. The third programme, *Home Away from Home*, enables foreign students studying at one of the local colleges to be "adopted" by Bahamian families, thus providing them with needed support during their stay in the country.

Visitors who participate in a People-to-People experience leave enriched with an appreciation of the destination and hospitality. It has turned out to be an extremely successful public relations vehicle for The Bahamas. Dozens of visitors regularly write glowing letters of appreciation after being hosted by a local volunteer, and the many interactions have created life-long bonds and repeat visits.

Through the People-to-People at Sea programme, local volunteers interact with visitors on cruise ships

Melanie Farrington, Ministry of Tourism's People-to-People Coordinator, presents plaque to Home Lines for partnering with Tourism in hosting outstanding Volunteers

Minister Coakley presents plaque to a participating cruise line in the People-to-People At Sea programme

The wedding of a British couple is arranged through People-to-People

Mrs. Jeanette Bethel, Permanent Secretary Ministry of Tourism, presents plaque to Sylvia Cole, for unselfish and dedicated service as Coordinator, People-to-People

In December 2005, Acting Governor Paul Adderley addresses long-serving People-to-People Volunteers on the 30th anniversary of the programme

Bahamahost

The industry training programme *Bahamahost,* also a brainchild of Minister Clement Maynard, was another major achievement. Introduced in 1978 in response to the industry's need for better informed, and more highly skilled, taxi drivers, the programme was later extended to the entire hospitality industry—hotel workers, retail store personnel, ferry boat operators, beach and straw vendors, and everyone else who came into contact with visitors. The programme includes 60 hours of lectures and practical training in the History, Geography, Culture, Economy, Points of Interest and all aspects of the country about which a visitor might ask, along with practical instruction and role-play on guest interaction. Winn Dixie/City Markets donated $25,000 to the initial programme in 1978 and additional amounts, in later years, enabled lectures to be converted to videotape technology. Other benefactors, such as John Bull, contributed towards the success of the programme.

Minister of Tourism, Hon. Clement Maynard, Bahamahost founder (seated 4th from left), with graduates

Bahamahost graduates—Seated: Athama Bowe, Coordinator (right), Permanent Secretary Basil O'Brien (3rd from right); Undersecretary Willamae Salkey (2nd from left)

Top Bahamahost graduates receive special awards from Minister of Tourism Livingstone Coakley (2nd from left)

Top Bahamahost graduates in Freeport, Grand Bahama, accept awards

Top Bahamahost graduates in Eleuthera receive awards from Deputy Director General of Tourism, John Deleveaux (centre), and Hon. Philip Bethel, MP for South Eleuthera (3rd from right)

National Tourism Achievement Awards

As local Bahamians excelled in tourism, the Ministry of Tourism launched the *National Tourism Achievement Awards* (NTAA) to recognize exceptional service. The objective of this programme, launched in 1976 as part of a tourism awareness campaign, was to reward individuals who, by a single act or through continuous efforts, had exhibited qualities of responsibility, sensitivity, expertise and friendliness to tourists and, by so doing, had enhanced the reputation of The Bahamas as a tourist destination.

NTAA recipients are people who work in ordinary jobs but who reject mediocrity and choose instead to incorporate high standards of professionalism into their working lives. During this period, they included taxi and tour drivers like Vernon Bullard, Doris Toote, Lloyd Delancy and Romeo Farrington, who went beyond the call of duty for their passengers' comfort and convenience; operators of guest houses like Mamie Worrell, Flo Major and Pearl Cox, who made their guests feel like part of their families; straw vendors like Ivy Simms, Diana Thompson and Telator Strachan, who excelled in their craft and in organizing the straw industry; outstanding hosts such as Sylvia Cole, Chena Gibson and Mildred Sands who began entertaining visitors in their homes long before the People-to-People programme started; entertainers like Blake "Blind Blake" Higgs, Ronnie Butler, John Chipman, Eddie Minnis, Naomi Taylor, King Eric Gibson and Tony McKay, among others, who gave their audiences superb entertainment with a distinct Bahamian flavour. The Awards Ceremony was held at Government House annually, beginning on 12th October, 1976.

In subsequent decades, the NTAA programme became a most prestigious award because it was an honour that could not be gained through social or other status, but earned through excellent performance at one's chosen job or vocation. Bahamians were nominated by their employers, fellow workers and associates within a wide spectrum of the tourism industry. Nominations were screened by a selection panel appointed by the Minister of Tourism. The panel, which included the Commissioner of Police, President of the Chamber of Commerce, the Director of the Bahamas Hotel Training College and representatives from each of the Promotion Boards, was chaired by the President of the Bahamas Christian Council. It became an acknowledgement that one had made a significant contribution and one's efforts had been appreciated. (A full listing of NTAA recipients is shown at the end of this book.)

Visitor Information and Tourist Police

In an attempt to ensure that visitors received accurate information on the destination, a well staffed Information Unit was established, comprehensive sales aids were produced, including a detailed Industry Travel Guide, which became a single source of reference for travel agents and airlines. Tourist

Information Booths were erected at the Nassau International Airport and on Prince George Dock. The downtown information centre, which had been in existence for many years, was moved to a more spacious and attractive building in Parliament Square. Standardized tours were produced and plaques were erected at major historic sites, in cooperation with the Department of Archives.

Tourist Information Booth on Bay Street, Nassau in the 1960's

Minister of Tourism Clement Maynard opens new Tourist Information Booth in Rawson Square in the early 1970's

Starting in the early 1970's, Ministry of Tourism boasts Bilingual Tourist Information
Assistants, and multi-language brochures in Spanish, French, Italian and German

In 1975, The Bahamas took additional steps to enhance the visitor experience
by introducing a special unit of tourist police, called **Beach Wardens**. These
wardens had powers of arrest, were trained by both the Police Department and
the Ministry of Tourism, and had as their majority responsibility the patrolling
of popular beaches, public areas and tourist attractions. While they had powers
of arrest, they were also trained to give tourist information and assist visitors in
enjoying their stay.

Nassau Surreys and Straw Market

Another product improvement during this era was the replacement of the aging
horse-drawn surreys, long a featured attraction. Tourism contributed the down
payments for a brand-new fleet of 12 carriages, and negotiated a financing plan
with a bank whereby the individual surrey owner could pay off the balance over a
period of time.

In the year 1973, the popular Bay Street Straw Market burned to the ground.
Temporary stalls to house straw vendors were set up at several locations in the
downtown area until a new modern facility was constructed in the 1980's.

Clement Maynard moves on and the first Bahamian Director General is appointed

After completing a decade in the Tourism portfolio, Sir Clement Maynard was replaced as Minister of Tourism by Livingstone Coakley in November 1979. Baltron B. Bethel became the first Bahamian Director General of Tourism in May 1978.

Tourism Performance—Statistical Analysis

The late 1960's were good years. However, the year 1970 marked the first time in more than a decade that The Bahamas did not show an increase in the number of visitors over the previous year, but The Bahamas fared better than most of its neighbours. The following year saw the growth trend continue with a 12.7% increase in arrivals in 1971. There was a further decline in 1974, and the slow growth continued until 1977. In 1978 the market rebounded, as shown in Table 8-1. Approximately 60% of visitors travelled to Nassau, 28% to Grand Bahama and 12% to the Family Islands.

In 1975, hoteliers took a bold step to counteract the negative economic climate by establishing Bahama Island Tours (BIT) as a travel wholesaler. Formed by member hotels of the Bahamas Hotel Association with the object of selling only Bahamian packages, BIT put together interesting programmes combining several destinations within the country. BIT worked closely with the Bahamas Hotel Reservation Service, based in Miami, which provided a Bahamas information service using toll-free numbers.

1968 was the first year that The Bahamas welcomed 1 million visitors in a single year. The one-millionth visitor is welcomed to Nassau in 1968 by Minister of Tourism, PM Pindling (right)

Table 8-1
Visitor Performance
1967-79

YEAR	STOP-OVERS (% of Total)	CRUISE (% of Total)	DAY & TRANSIT (% of Total)	TOTAL. FOREIGN ARRIVALS	% INC or DEC.	AIR (% of Total)	SEA (% of Total)
1967				**915,273**	11.3	649,388	265,885
1968				**1,072,213**	17.1	818,994	253,219
1969				**1,332,396**	24	970,325	362,071
1970	891,480	351,865		**1,298,344**	-2.6	916,479	381,865
1971	960,820	435,825		**1,463,591**	12.7	970,965	492,626
1972	1,015,320	420,860	67,060	**1,511,860**	3.3	1,044,970	466,890
1973	976,760	462,390	71,200	**1,520,010**	0.5	1,021,840	498,170
1974	876,080	386,680	116,072	**1,378,310**	-8.7	966,560	421,480
1975	827,760	421,280	127,030	**1,376,070**	-0.5	917,670	463,190
1976	818,720	404,620	176,270	**1,399,610**	1.6	953,930	449,710
1977	891,260	352,945	135,550	**1,379,755**	-1.6	982,220	399,190
1978	1,083,180	449,625	160,940	**1,693,745**	23.6	1,181,580	525,360
1979	1,129,430	476,159	160,200	**1,765,789**	4.8	1,252,270	537,150

Source: Research Department, Ministry of Tourism

Table 8-2
Foreign Arrivals by first Port of Entry In The Bahamas
1967 versus 1979

	New Providence/ Paradise		Grand Bahama		Family Islands		Total Foreign Arrivals	
	No.	%	No.	%	No.	%	No	%
1967	576,846	63	231,382	25	107,045	12	915,273	100
1979	1,060,550	59	508,170	28	220,700	12	1,789,420	100

Source: Research Department, Ministry of Tourism

Until the Exit Study was initiated in 1968 there was no accurate information on what visitors were contributing to the Gross National Product of The Bahamas or which segments of the economy were benefiting, and to what extent.

The expenditures by stopover visitors versus cruise visitors are listed in Table 8-3 and Appendix 11 at back. Hotels were the largest beneficiary of the expenditure. The second largest item of tourist expenditure was meals and beverages.

How the Tourist Dollar was Spent in 1970

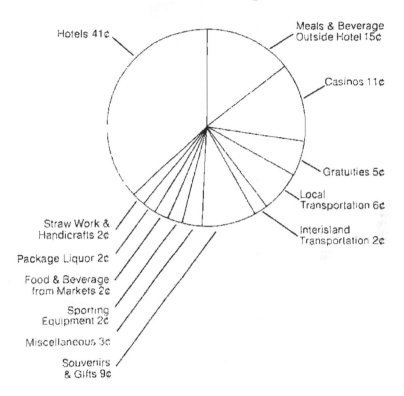

Hotels 41¢

Meals & Beverage Outside Hotel 15¢

Casinos 11¢

Gratuities 5¢

Local Transportation 6¢

Interisland Transportation 2¢

Straw Work & Handicrafts 2¢

Package Liquor 2¢

Food & Beverage from Markets 2¢

Sporting Equipment 2¢

Miscellaneous 3¢

Souvenirs & Gifts 9¢

Table 8-3
Visitor Expenditure
1968-79

	Expenditure By		
Year	Stopover Visitors	Cruise Visitors	Total Expenditure
1968	$168,726,000	$11,668,000	$180,329,926
1973	$281,219,000	$20,808,000	$302,027,000
1979	$536,907,510	$24,760,760	$561,667,830

Source: Ministry of Tourism 1979 Statistical Report

Table 8-4
Stopover Visitors by Country of Residence
1973 versus 1979

	USA	%	CANADA	%	TOT. EUROPE	%	UK	Germany	REST OF WORLD	TOTAL
1973	793,010		113,440		42,620		12,270	11,880	27,680	976,760
1979	851,590		134,710		101,880		18,290	83,590	30,540	1,129,430

Source: Annual Reports of the Ministry of Tourism, 1973 and 1979

The United States accounted for about 87% of total visitors, with ten states of the USA (Florida, New York, New Jersey, Illinois, Pennsylvania, Michigan, Ohio, Massachusetts, Connecticut and California) contributing about 79% of the US total. The USA continued to comprise as much as 80% of visitors to The Bahamas. With the opening of a tourist office in Frankfurt, the number of visitors from Germany increased gradually, and by 1985 was equal to the number from the UK. As a result, a number of hotels and restaurants began to print menus in German and the Ministry of Tourism and several hotels hired bilingual personnel to assist foreign-speaking visitors (with emphasis on German, French and Spanish).

In 1968, three out of every 10 travellers to The Bahamas were **repeat visitors**. It was found that repeat visitors who came by air spent $221.56 during their stay as against $200.76 spent by first-time visitors coming by air. The same trend was noticed in the case of repeat sea visitors who spent more than the number of first-time sea visitors.

Competition from the British Commonwealth Caribbean

Until the post-1970 era, tourism was not considered a viable industry by most countries in the British Commonwealth Caribbean, except for The Bahamas and Bermuda, in which tourism was the principal industry, accounting for 70% of the GDP in both cases, compared to 25% or less for the other countries. As can be seen from Table 8-5, The Bahamas and Bermuda were allocating huge budgets for tourism promotion, and by 1969 annual visitors to these small countries had reached a figure of seven times the population.

Table 8-5
Comparative Visitor Statistics for British Commonwealth Caribbean Countries
1967-1970

Country	Size (Sq. Miles)	Population 1970	Tourism Budget 1970 US$	No. of Hotel Rooms 1969	TOTAL VISITORS			
					1967	1968	1969	1970
Antigua	108	65,000	50,000	1,169	59,174	55,838	61,262	65,369
Bahamas	5,382	168,838	6,697,000	9,503	915,273	1,072,213	1,332,396	1,298,344
Barbados	166	238,100	725,000	6,290*	91,565	115,697	137,632	
Bermuda	20	53,000	3,185,000	6,904*	281,167	331,379	370,920	388,914
British V.I.	59	10,500	18,000	262	18,934	22,793	29,513	33,128
Dominica	305	70,300	12,500	133	7,465	9,977	8,246	
Grenada	133	94,500	61,900	600	37,033	49,664	68,745	71,697
Jamaica	4,412	1,861,400	3,960,000	7,000	332,838	396,347	407,105	414,500
St Kitts Nevis	153	52,000	30,000	322	15,193	16,984	18,712	
St. Vincent	150	89,100	43,000	356	7,242	12,472	15,569	17,586
Trinidad & Tobago	1,980	945,200	778,000	1,200	230,160	257,860	283,240	

* Hotel beds

Source: The Organization of the Tourist Industry in the Commonwealth Caribbean, June 1971 (paper presented by Angela B. Cleare as a requirement for the university programme in Management—UWI Library, Kingston, Jamaica p. 65, 67-70)

Indeed, most Caribbean countries, while allocating token amounts towards tourism development, did not, at that time, consider tourism to be a serious business. In his book *Growth of he Modern West Indies*, Gordon K. Lewis suggests that the political apathy of the people of The Bahamas and Bermuda may be largely responsible for their positive attitude towards tourism. He further suggests that, because of the proximity of these two territories to the United States, the inhabitants have never really had to work hard for a living—their prosperity being largely accidental. Tourism, he said, allowed these countries to continue this carefree existence![15]

*   *   *

During succeeding decades, this negative attitude towards tourism would change dramatically, with all countries of the Caribbean coming to recognize that tourism is a viable business with tremendous economic, social and environmental benefits.

9

EFFORTS TO CONSOLIDATE AND IMPROVE THE BAHAMIAN TOURISM INDUSTRY FROM 1980 TO 1991

External Factors Impacting Bahamas Tourism

Deregulation in the United States

A factor which significantly affected the United States travel sector was **deregulation**. In October 1978, President Jimmy Carter had signed into law the Airline Deregulation Act of 1978, which led to cut-throat competition in the 1980's, as thousands of new domestic and international routes were awarded. Fare experimentation reached unprecedented levels. The new smaller airlines, with lower costs, were able to compete successfully, at least for a period, on the basis of price. Carriers once limited to charters began flying scheduled services. Deregulation resulted in a huge number of companies, not just airlines, searching for a clear positioning and marketing direction. A disillusioned travelling public was presented with a confusing array of products and services. In an attempt to develop brand loyalty, many established airlines introduced frequent flyer programmes, rewarding travellers with bonus points redeemable for future travel.

Amid the confusion, advocates of deregulation asserted that the former regulated environment had inhibited the progressive, imaginative operator, and that the new era of liberalization and competition would benefit consumers and the trade in the long term.[1]

During the first six months of 1980, scheduled airlines suffered an operating loss of $500 million—around $3 million per day. One formerly powerful airline that played a vital role in Bahamas tourism, and which experienced severe financial problems following deregulation, was Eastern Airlines.

The History and Liquidation of Eastern Airlines

The birth of Eastern Airlines is associated with the name of Clement Keys, a former financial editor of *The Wall Street Journal* and promoter of multimillion-dollar aviation corporations in the 1920's and 1930's. In 1929, Keys purchased

Pitcairn Aviation, Inc., a small Philadelphia-based airline, that had been formed in September 1927. Keys later sold Pitcairn to North American Aviation, then a holding company for a number of aircraft companies in which he was a key shareholder. In 1930, Pitcairn's name was changed to Eastern Air Transport, Inc., and to Eastern Airlines in 1934. World War I ace, Eddie Rickenbacker, served as general manager of Eastern at that time.

While most major airlines were focusing on transcontinental flights, Eastern established a near monopoly on the East Coast through 1933, acquiring contracts for routes spanning from New York to Miami. In 1938, Rickenbacker and several associates bought Eastern from North American Aviation. He set up Eastern's *Great Silver Fleet* of DC-2 aircraft. In 1950, Eastern acquired the new Lockheed L.1049 Super Constellation airplanes and enjoyed high profits until the 1950's. Although the airline experienced low growth rates in the early 1960's, profits improved in the late 1970's. In 1964, Eastern was the first of the "Big Four" domestic airlines to use the Boeing 727 jet that would revolutionize air travel. Eastern diversified into Canada in 1956, Mexico in July 1957, **The Bahamas** in 1967, and the Caribbean in 1971. After Rickenbacker's retirement in 1963, Eastern's growth slowed. In 1978, after Airbus offered a very generous deal, Eastern's new president, former NASA astronaut, Frank Borman, agreed to buy 23 of the new European Airbus A-300 jets in the spring of 1978. For Airbus, this was one of the most important breakthroughs into the US market. Eastern, however, did not fare well in the 1980's and recorded annual losses. In late 1985, when it had an accumulated debt of $3.5 billion, Frank Lorenzo, the airline powerbroker who controlled Continental Airlines, bought the airline for only $615 million. Lorenzo used Eastern's core assets for his other airlines—People's Express, Frontier Airlines, Texas Air, and New York Air. To survive, Eastern had to sell off aircraft and lay off workers in large numbers. As tensions mounted with the labour unions, Lorenzo began to dismantle Eastern and sell off its parts. When the unions struck in March 1989, he filed for bankruptcy. In January 1991, the airline went into liquidation. Thus ended the life of one of America's greatest domestic airlines, and one of the biggest suppliers of business to The Bahamas.[2]

Tourism becomes the World's Largest Industry

Global tourism—despite effects of deregulation, recession, oil crisis and widespread changes in the industry—resumed its growth between 1984 and 1990, but at a slower rate than in the 1950's and 1960's. By 1988, when total international tourist arrivals reached 390 million and international receipts exceeded $200 billion, tourism took its place as the world's largest industry. Travel, which had long been viewed as a fickle industry, was now an indispensable factor in household planning. On 9th November, 1989, the collapse of the Berlin Wall heralded the end of communism and further removal of travel barriers. Even the Gulf War at the end of this period did not permanently halt travel demand.

Gulf War

On 2nd August, 1990, Iraq invaded and occupied Kuwait, its tiny oil-rich neighbour. Three months later, the United Nations Security Council passed a resolution authorizing the use of force against Iraq if it failed to withdraw from Kuwait. In January 1991, *Operation Desert Storm*, a massive international coalition with forces from 32 nations, began in the Persian Gulf. On 24th February, a massive coalition ground offensive began, and Iraq's outdated and poorly supplied armed forces were rapidly overwhelmed. By the end of the day, the Iraqi army had effectively folded, 10,000 of its troops were held as prisoners, and a US air base had been established deep inside Iraq. After less than four days, Kuwait was liberated, and a majority of Iraq's armed forces had either been destroyed or had surrendered or retreated. On 28th February, US President George Bush declared a cease-fire, and Iraq pledged to honour future UN peace terms. The war had a dampening effect on the travel market since people were reluctant to travel due to uncertainty about the world economy. Globally, airlines, hotels, cruise ships, car rental companies and tour operators slashed prices to attract customers. During the four-year period following the war, international tourism grew at a rate of only 3.7%, compared to the growth rate of 6.9% during the 1985-90 period.

Caribbean Tourism Integration

In January 1989, two well-established tourism organizations, Caribbean Tourism Association (CTA) and the Caribbean Travel Research Centre, merged. Thus, the Caribbean Tourism Organization (CTO) was officially chartered, with headquarters in Barbados, and offices in New York and London. CTA had been established as far back as 1951 as the *Caribbean Travel Association*, a regional body mandated to promote Caribbean tourism. Its headquarters moved from Antigua to New York in 1955, since the association's marketing efforts were focused primarily on the United States market. In 1959, in response to a lobby by hoteliers, Caribbean Travel Association formed a hotel committee, made up of individual hotels, which evolved into the *Caribbean Hotel Association* (CHA) in 1962. In 1975, the Caribbean Travel Association's name was changed to the *Caribbean Tourism Association*, and was headed by Audrey Palmer Hawks, a Grenadian graduate of Cornell University who managed the office until her death in 1987. Also in 1975, the first Caribbean Tourism Association Allied Chapter was formed with the assistance of Michael Youngman, an airline and marketing executive, and Chapters were later established throughout the United States and Canada. In response to the need for credible research data to guide the marketing effort, the *Caribbean Tourism Research and Development Centre* (CTRC) came into existence in 1974, with headquarters in Barbados, and initial funding of the Inter-American Foundation. Jean Holder, a career diplomat, became its Chief Executive Officer and created a regional agency focusing on tourism planning, research, statistics, product and environmental issues. With the amalgamation of CTA and CTRC into a single organization—the Caribbean Tourism Organization (CTO). Promotional, educational, training and research activities to better serve the interests of the region were broadened, Allied Chapters were expanded, a stronger travel trade network was forged in North America and Europe, a sophisticated tourism database and specialized divisions for Sustainable Development and Human Resources were established. The Director General of Tourism for The Bahamas, Baltron Bethel, became the first Chairman of the new CTO, and spearheaded the growth and development of regional tourism. Through CTO, Caribbean countries made great strides in realizing the benefits of collaboration and joint promotion. CTO became an important marketing tool for the entire Caribbean, especially the smaller Caribbean countries which could not afford to launch individual marketing campaigns.

Response to Heightened Consumer Expectations

As travel demand grew, governments throughout the world responded with policy changes. In the USA, the National Tourism Policy Act was passed in 1981, creating the *United States Travel and Tourism Administration* as the national coordinating body on international tourism. Also local tourism jurisdictions, US carriers, hotel chains and the travel trade pumped large sums into tourism. The early 1980's also saw more package tours and a special drive to increase efficiency through technology. Important developments in the hotel industry centred on market segmentation. Hotel chains began developing new products for different types of people. Marriott, for example, encompassed mega hotels of 1,000 rooms or more through its Marriott Marquis brand and its low-rise lodging product through its Marriott Courtyard. The Holiday Corporation catered to various clientele through its Holiday Inns, Hampton Inns, Crowne Plaza Hotels and Embassy Suites. The high quality *Porche* or *Jaguar* concept in hotels was achieved through brands like Four Seasons and Ritz Carlton. In 1984, Choice Hotels, responding to consumer demand, was the first to offer non-smoking rooms, in compliance with health and environmental concerns of consumers. In the leisure segment of the lodging industry, a big innovation, more marked in Jamaica, moved beyond segmentation based on physical buildings but on lifestyle experiences, with hotels catering exclusively to families, couples, health/fitness enthusiasts, and hedonists, as well as cash-less all-inclusives. Attempts to pamper guests became widespread with the introduction of added complimentary conveniences such as continental breakfast, fitness spas, or shuttle services. It was the Hampton Inns chain that first introduced the 100% satisfaction guarantee.[3] These trends also became evident in Nassau hotels in the 1980's.

Unpreprecedented Growth in the Cruise Industry

With increasing demand for an all-inclusive vacation alternative, the cruise industry experienced tremendous growth in the 1980's, with expansion in 3- and

4-day cruises, and a new recognition by travel agents of the simplicity and ease of selling cruises. By 1987, total cruise bed nights globally reached 20.3 million with the Caribbean capturing the lion's share, as shown in Table 9-1. The Bahamas, shown as a separate destination from the Caribbean in this table, ranked fourth in the world in total cruise bed nights.

Table 9-1
Global Distribution of the 20,376,994 Total Cruise Bed Nights in 1987

Caribbean	8,828,791	Trans Canal	970,191	Hawaii	602,728	Far East (Orient)	465,608
Mediterranean	841,051	Mexico West	1,131,462	South Pacific	352,983	Mississippi	231,392
Alaska	1,715,197	Europe	357,516	S.E. Asia	272,592	S. America	620,396
Bahamas	**1,922,386**	Transatlantic	339,388	Canada	283,714	USCoastal West	64,444
Trans Pacific	17,904	US Coastal East	132,794	Party Cruises	85,336		

Source: *Cruise Lines International Association*

According to the Cruise Lines International Association (CLIA), the cruise industry recorded a growth rate of 8.4% per year during the decade of the 1980's, as cruising became an important vehicle for sampling destination areas to which passengers may return. Cruise travel in North America increased from 1.4 million passengers in 1980 to close to 4 million passengers in 1991, as shown in Table 9-2. The cruise industry constantly responded to market and consumer research by adding new destinations, new ship design concepts, activities and themes. The cruise experience consistently exceeded expectations on a wide range of vacation attributes.[4]

Table 9-2
Growth in North American Cruise Travel

Year	Cruise Passengers (000)	Year	Cruise Passengers (000)
1980	1,431	1986	2,624
1981	1,453	1987	2,898
1982	1,471	1988	3,175
1983	1,755	1989	3,286
1984	1,859	1990	3,640
1985	2,152	1991	3,979

Source: Cruise Lines International Association

Portfolio Changes and New Tourism Goals in The Bahamas

Livingstone N. Coakley, who took over from Sir Clement Maynard in 1979, served as Minister of Tourism until 1982. Following the 10th June,

1982 General Election, Prime Minister Lynden Pindling appointed Perry G. Christie as Minister of Tourism, a position he held until October 1984. During the period 1982 to 1984, emphasis was placed on special promotions and product development to strengthen the image of The Bahamas, in light of the strong competition from neighbouring Caribbean islands. An impressive public speaker, Christie became an enthusiastic

Hon. Perry Christie, Minister of Tourism (centre), chats with Fred Mitchell, a law student, at a reception in London for members of the Bahamian Association in March 1983. Basil Albury, GM BTO Europe is at left.

ambassador for The Bahamas within the travel industry. His aim was to involve as many Bahamians in tourism as possible and to expose visitors to every facet of The Bahamas, particularly its culture and history, through special promotions. During his tenure, the culture of The Bahamas was projected in promotions with local bands and Junkanoo taking centre stage. Junkanoo was integrated into tourism advertising and promotion, both offshore and onshore, and new avenues were created for this cultural expression in an attempt to differentiate the country from the competition.

On 8th October, 1984, Sir Clement Maynard began his second term as Minister of Tourism and held the portfolio for five years, consolidating his position as the longest serving Minister of Tourism in the region. The industry, which he described as his "first love", achieved the three million milestone under his leadership.

In 1990, Prime Minister Pindling took over the Tourism portfolio for a second term. He was Minister of Tourism at the time of his party's defeat in the 1992 General Elections.

During the term of Hon. Perry Christie, a member of one of the major Junkanoo groups, the culture of The Bahamas was fully integrated into tourism promotions

Government continued to place high priority on Tourism, with annual budgets voted for the Ministry of Tourism increasing from $18 million in 1979 to $42 million in 1991. Expenditure by the Bahamas Government on tourism ranked fourth in terms of budget allocations. However, expenditure by the government was supplemented by large amounts spent by the private sector on promotion. This private sector contribution enabled the government to concentrate its limited resources in the areas of Education and Health, which were then considered items on which priority should be placed.

Baltron Bethel remained at the helm as Director General of Tourism, and, in addition to this important responsibility, was appointed CEO of the Hotel Corporation of The Bahamas in 1985 by Prime Minister Pindling. During this period, Bethel fostered a strong and close working relationship between the Ministry of Tourism, the Caribbean Tourism Association, other international and regional groups, the overseas travel trade, and local private sector. He capitalized on the deregulation of the industry by negotiating with carriers to increase airlift to Nassau, Freeport, and the Family Islands and achieved tremendous success. His accomplishments in hotel expansion and promotion are also noteworthy.

Director General Baltron Bethel (left) is featured on the cover of Black Enterprise for outstanding contributions to tourism development in The Bahamas and the Caribbean

Assisting the Director General were two Deputy Directors General—John Deleveaux and Basil Albury—a team of Consultants (including George Suhr), Directors (Angela Cleare, Gregory Barrett, Craig Woods) and General Managers (including Cordell Thompson) for specific divisions.

It was acknowledged by the political and technical leaders that during the decade of the 1980's, The Bahamas faced major challenges, including the urgency of attracting new investment, revitalizing Family Island economies by encouraging cruise ship calls and direct airlift, educating and training to meet the higher expectations of the traveller and strengthening marketing initiatives in a very competitive marketplace, including diversifying into new markets.

Additional staff move up to "Director" posts in Ministry of Tourism

To guide the communications strategy, there were large injections of capital into product and market research.

Planning and Research

To ensure orderly tourism growth, the Ministry of Tourism commissioned a ten-year Tourism Master Plan, to be conducted by a US-based consulting group, Dames & Moore. What was impressive about this process was that qualified Bahamian companies were integrated into the planning process to ensure relevance of the final outcome and exposure to Bahamian counterparts.

A fully functional Planning and Research Unit was established which included foreign and highly skilled local professional staff. Targeted research on a sustained basis—both offshore and onshore—was carried out to determine the competition, potential markets, the success of marketing strategies, as well as tourists' perception of the Bahamian product—all in an attempt to improve market intelligence and the ability to respond to trends and opportunities. Surveys confirmed the importance of tourism to The Bahamas economy, and emphasized the urgency of innovative marketing and product initiatives.

The Minister of Tourism, Hon. Livingstone Coakley, signs contract with a US based company, Dames & Moore, for a 10-year Tourism Development Plan

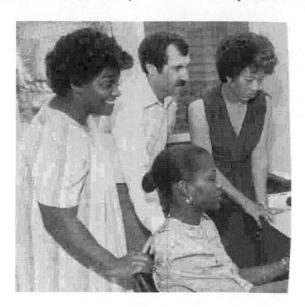

Research staff at Ministry of Tourism in the 1980's, headed by Dr. James Hepple, Consultant

In 1986, with the support of the Inter-American Development Bank (IDB), the Ministry of Tourism undertook a *Survey of the US Vacation Market* to identify market segments with greatest potential for The Bahamas.[5] Recent visitors to Hawaii, Mexico, Bermuda, Jamaica, Puerto Rico, and other Caribbean islands, were compared with those who had recently visited The Bahamas. Warm weather vacationers, although broadly similar, did show key differences, particularly related to length of stay, lead time for travel, and expenditure habits.

As would be expected, in light of the proximity of The Bahamas to the United States, the study revealed that the average length of stay of the visitor to The Bahamas tended to be shortest—at 4.3 nights; the longest being Hawaii at 9.8 nights, followed by Puerto Rico at 7.8 nights. The length of stay for Jamaica, Mexico and the US Virgin Islands (USVI) was six nights, and Bermuda five nights. While visitors to most destinations started planning their trips at least a month ahead of time, 23% (compared with an average of 13%) planned a trip to The Bahamas within one month of departure.

Hawaii had the largest amount spent per trip of $3,000, while Mexico had the least, $1,500. The Bahamas was second lowest at $1,580, followed by Jamaica, $1,627, Bermuda and Puerto Rico, $1,850 and those to USVI spent $2,530.

The US Vacation Market study also probed into visitor attitudes and perceptions. It revealed that the number one concern when choosing a destination was *safety*; visitors also want destinations that offer: the *best value for money*; fairly constant *good weather, rest and relaxation, friendly local people, a good vacation package* and *a variety of things to* see and do. Visitors perceived The Bahamas as having the following **strengths**: *casino gambling, water sports* and *nightlife*. **Weaknesses** were perceived as: *poor value for money, sightseeing, attitudes, service* and *food*. Hawaii was ranked best in all but two criteria, Mexico ranked best for value for money, and USVI for rest and relaxation. The Bahamas was only ranked best for casinos/gambling.[6]

With 70% of Bahamas business booked by travel agents, Tourism also commissioned special studies to determine attitudes in the trade. A 1984 survey of 550 US travel agents showed that, while the agents ranked The Bahamas as superior to other warm weather destinations for beaches, water, gambling and packages, there was considerable dissatisfaction with the price of meals, surcharges and taxes in The Bahamas.[7]

Tourists' comments on the Ministry of Tourism's own Exit Surveys collaborated these findings. The surveys indicated satisfaction with the weather, people and beaches, but the primary complaint was *value for money*. There was strong dissatisfaction with onshore prices (especially meals) and with the quality of hotels (particularly on New Providence and Grand Bahama) and service.

These findings served as a wake-up call, and prompted the Bahamas Government to place even more emphasis on product development and service improvement, and to strengthen its promotional strategy.

The Communications and Promotional Thrust

Advertising and Public Relations

Top award-winning advertising, public relations and promotional campaigns were implemented through advertising agencies such as N.W. Ayer and McKinney and Silver, public relations firms of Manning Selvage and Lee (USA) and PIR (Canada). Bernard Marko and Associates was the contracted collaterals agency. In May 1985, the Counsellors Ltd, the Nassau public relations firm which had been operating the Bahamas News Bureau for the Ministry of Tourism under the direction of William Kalis and Joe Edwards, with Eric Wilmott as Vice President, was taken over by a Bahamian group headed by Mrs. Joan Albury, formerly General Manager, Marketing, with the Ministry of Tourism.

Strong advertising campaigns were developed using magazines, radio, television, and newspapers. Cooperative advertising with wholesalers and retail travel agents was increased to facilitate greater exposure in smaller markets. State-of-the-art collaterals were produced and made available to the trade and consumers through Bahamas Tourist Offices (BTOs).

In addition to expanding the traditional markets of the United States, Canada, and the United Kingdom, new markets in Europe (Germany, France, and Italy) were successfully targeted. In an attempt to reduce duplication of effort and to achieve synergy, a Promotions Coordinating Committee was established, enabling government and the private sector to pool resources, make joint decisions on promotional strategies, thus presenting a united thrust in the marketplace.

To fill the void in European traffic, as a result of reduced direct air service and currency fluctuations, a Latin American division was established in the Bahamas Tourist Office, Coral Gables, Florida and intensive marketing was carried out in Colombia, Venezuela, Ecuador, Chile and Brazil, with special competitive packages. Representation in Japan was coordinated through the Ministry of Tourism's P.R. agency and efforts were made to attract this lucrative market.

Negotiations took place with numerous new tour operators and incentive travel companies to establish Bahamas travel packages out of Europe, Canada, US, Latin America and the Far East. The 3-4 day vacations in US and Canadian markets and two-centre European/Caribbean market were pioneered. In 1984, a sophisticated IBM computer system was installed in the Bahamas Reservations Service in Coral Gables, Florida to improve the efficiency in which agents and consumers could receive information and book reservations. The service handled up to 10,000 calls weekly.

To emphasize the variety of islands and things to do, the advertising by-lines adopted at one stage was *"In The Bahamas, you never run out of things to do . . . ."*

until you want to" and *"You may not want to do it all, but it's nice to know it's there"*. In addition to Freeport, Grand Bahama, the islands of Abaco, Eleuthera and Exuma received special promotion as separate destinations. The signature line *"It's Better*

Advertisements in the 1980's

in The Bahamas" remained unchanged until 1987, when it was slightly amended as follows: "It's Better in Our Country . . . The Bahamas", but the original by-line was later restored.

Public relations activities were geared towards building the image of The Bahamas as a stable, safe, culturally rich and diverse multi-destination. In 1981, The Bahamas received the Silver Anvil Award, the highest award bestowed by the American Public Relations Society for excellence in public relations, and for professional and results-oriented promotional activities. High impact specials that took centre stage included the *Bob Hope Easter Special* for NBC Prime Time television, the *Walt Disney Easter Special* as part of Premier Cruise Line's Abacodabra Cruise services to Abaco, the ABC-Television special on the Harlem Globetrotters shown on the Wide World Sports in 1990. Many popular television shows, such as *Life Styles of the Rich and Famous* and *Good Morning America,* were filmed in The Bahamas. Recognizing the increased importance of the electronic media, The Bahamas was one of the first countries in the region to produce and distribute electronic news releases.

Ministry of Tourism team display the Silver Anvil awarded in 1981 to The Bahamas for excellence in public relations. From left: Cordell Thompson, GM PR; Baltron Bethel, Director General, Minister Livingstone Coakley, and John Deleveaux, Deputy Director General

Sales Promotions

To increase support to the travel trade, the Ministry of Tourism opened additional tourist offices in Philadelphia, Atlanta, Houston, San Francisco, Vancouver, Paris and Milan, bringing total sales offices to 22, 15 in the United States, three in Canada and four in Europe. Professional development programmes were introduced to train sales staff. The Ministry of Tourism and the hotel industry continued its series of onshore and offshore promotions. Very close alliances were formed with the world's most influential travel associations like ASTA (American Society of Travel Agents), ACTA (Canadian Association of Travel Agents), ABTA (British Association of Travel Agents), and SATW (the Society of American Travel Writers). National and regional meetings of these associations were held in The Bahamas.

Group Departments were established and group and convention business to The Bahamas flourished. In October 1985, Tourism joined forces with the Bahamas Government to host the most important conference ever held in the country—the Commonwealth Heads of Government Meeting (CHOGM). The host hotel was the Cable Beach Hotel and Casino. The 45 Presidents/Prime Ministers, along with other delegations from former British territories all over the globe, were led by Her Majesty Queen Elizabeth II of England. Another high-level celebrity who visited for a convention was Dr. Henry Kissinger, former US Secretary of State and co-winner of the 1973 Nobel Peace Prize, who was the keynote speaker at the June 1985 Caribbean Hotel Industry Conference (CHIC) held on Paradise Island, attracting over 6,000 registrants.

Among the promotions hosted in The Bahamas was the Muhammad Ali versus Trevor Berbick fight on 1st December, 1981 at the Queen Elizabeth Sports Centre. Billed as the "Drama in Bahama", the event generated much local publicity among Bahamians and visiting tourists. The actual fight was perhaps less exciting than the preliminaries on Paradise Island when spectators could enjoy the charisma of the ex-champion during his sparring sessions when he displayed his "Ali Shuffle", or his horseback riding, jogging, or swimming escapades. After a poor showing which lasted for the full ten rounds, Ali's boxing career came to an end as the three judges gave Berbick the victory.

A Sports and Aviation Information Centre was established in the BTO in Florida. Sports promotions were centred around sports consumer trade shows, fishing, golf, boating and flying tournaments, regattas, sports videos, Bahamas "Learn to Dive" and "Learn to Golf" programmes and high-impact events.

Among the innovative sporting events was the 1984 *Bahamas Diamond Triathlon of the Stars,* which attracted hundreds of celebrities and up to one thousand top international athletes for the swimming, biking and running competitions. Also in 1984, motor racing was revived, when the Grand Bahama Vintage Speed Week was hosted. Although the previous Bahamas Speed Weeks took place as far back as 1967, many of the classic cars that raced then returned for the 1984 event, which was headquartered at the Bahamas Princess Resort & Casino in Freeport. Other familiar and time tested events continued to be featured on the sports calendar, such as the Southern Ocean Racing Conference, Bahamas Billfish Championships, Windsurfing Regatta, Regatta Time in Abaco, fishing tournaments and the Bahamas Grand Prix of powerboat racing.

To give visitors a taste of the local culture, while encouraging domestic tourism, a number of new onshore promotions were introduced. One such event was the Pineapple Festival, which was inaugurated in Gregory Town, Eleuthera, in 1988 by Jackie Gibson of the Eleuthera Tourist Office. Goombay Summer became the longest running local promotion and the festivities spread to the major islands. While the Family Island Regatta on Exuma continued to serve as the "national" regatta of The Bahamas, nearly every island introduced their own regattas during this period, such as the All

Bob Hope (centre) records the Bob Hope Easter Special in The Bahamas. He is pictured with Romeo Farrington, limousine driver (left)

Eleuthera Regatta, North Eleuthera Regatta, Long Island Regatta, among others.

Hon. Perry Christie, Minister of Tourism (right), and Bob Hope (2nd from left) share a light moment.

Hon. Perry Christie Minister of Tourism (2nd from right) presents Joseph Stone, Chairman and CEO of ASTA with a gift of a sailing vessel in a bottle at 52nd ASTA Congress. Mr. Stone was honoured for his years of cooperative service to The Bahamas Also pictured—from left: Baltron Bethel (Director General of Tourism), Mrs. Stone, and George Myers (GM & President of Resorts International)

First minority contract awarded to NY-based Carolyn Jones Agency Carolyn Jones
is second from right. Ministry staff present from left include Greg Barrett, Director,
Marketing, Angela Cleare, Director PR, and Baltron Bethel, Director General of
Tourism (right)

Carolyn Jones agency unveils its new campaign for the black American market. Left
to right—Angela Cleare, Baltron Bethel, Carolyn Jones, Minister Clement Maynard
and Robert Sands

Discovery Season promotion coordinated by Joint Promotions Committee chaired by James Catalyn (left). At right is Emmett Saunders, BOIPB, and Bill Volk, N.PI Promotion Board

NBA superstar Magic Johnson visits Nassau for a youth basketball camp. Left to right: Dwight Jackson of New York, Angela Cleare, Earvin "Magic" Johnson, Mr. & Mrs. Charles Marzouca (at left) Gail Moaney (right) of Manning Selvage and Lee PR Agency.

The Bahamas booth at ASTA Convention, Tokyo, Japan (Pictured: Angela Cleare and Juanita Gonzales, Ministry of Tourism)

Familiarization trip for British travel agents. Ellison Thompson (left) of the London Tourist Office and Pam Richardson (2nd from left) of the NPI Promotion Board accompany the group

Bahamas poster captures first prize at World Travel Mart, London. Left to right: Bernie Marco, President of the Collaterals agency which produced the poster, Baltron Bethel, Nalini Bethel, Minister Perry Christie and Basil Albury

Destination seminar for Groups Specialists coordinated by Ingrid Davis Bartlett (right), Groups Manager. At left is Van Isaacs of Bahamas Tourist Office and Baltron Bethel, DG (2nd from left)

Fred Kassner, President of Gogo Tours (2nd from left), one of The Bahamas' top wholesalers, arranges a Bahamas Seminar at Sea for 300 US travel agents. Also in photo: Bob Burke, N/PI Promotion Board—(left) and Bill Naughton, Sheraton BC Hotel (right)

Goombay symbol takes on a new look at the Henry Davis Travel Industry Trade Show in New York as Nassau hoteliers promote One Stop Inclusive Tour Charters (OTCs). From left: Lavern Lockhart (South Ocean Beach Hotel), George Myers (Paradise Island, Ltd.), Ricci Riccardi (Flagler Inn), Jill Grant (Nassau Harbour Club), Mike Williams (Nassau Beach Hotel).

Herve Villachez, Fantasy Island star, enjoys a fishing trip in The Bahamas

Danielle Knowles, Sales Representative, BTO, makes a presentation to agents

Dick Birch (2nd from right) of Small Hope Bay Lodge, Andros, and Chairman BOIPB, promotes The Bahamas with Ministry of Tourism staff.

After a hero's welcome, including a motorcade through the streets of his hometown, Nassau, Prime Minister Pindling presents a plaque to NBA superstar Mychal Thompson celebrating LA Lakers '87 Championship

Discussing new Delta Dream Vacation packages to the Family Islands were: from left—Carol Jones and Paul Mercer (Certified Tours) and Joan Albury (Marketing MOT); standing - Emmett Saunders (BOIPB), George Suhr (MOT Consultant), and David Johnson (BTO)

MOT Executives, Priscilla Williams, Vernice Walkine and Velda Campbell, brief Nashville tour operators, Mr. & Mrs. Charles Marzouca

Queen Elizabeth who visited The Bahamas for 1985 Commonwealth Heads of Government Meeting (CHOGM) chats with local Bahamians

BTO staff in Europe join forces with industry leaders to entertain travel agents following a reception in London. Left to right: Anthony Conyars, BTO UK; Jane Salter, Trust House Forte; Jan Hutchins, Bahama Holidays; H.E. Anthony Roberts, Bahamas High Commissioner; Ellison Thompson, BTO UK; Hans Borghardt, BTO Sales Director, Europe; and Linda Pryke, Princess Hotels

At 1989 ASTA Conference in Florida, the Bahamas team is shown dressed in pirate costumes, depicting the country's colourful history. From left: Henry Ross, Richard McDaniel, Greg Barrett, Craig Woods, Ms. Bahamas 1989—Lisa Sawyer, Bill Volk, Angela Cleare, Baltron Bethel, James Catalyn, Tommy Thompson and Cordell Thompson

Dan McVicar (2nd from right) who plays the role of Clark Garrison on the soap The Bold and the Beautiful poses with staff at Government House following a reception

Sir Clement Maynard (right) enjoys a round of golf with US Secretary of State George Shultz

Film Promotion

Films and television commercials poured millions of dollars into the local economy. The James Bond producers, having achieved success in their previous Bahamas productions, brought two more films to the country. In 1981, *For Your Eyes Only* featured underwater scenes shot off New Providence. Local divers, Gavin McKinney and Franny Young, doubled in the underwater action scenes for Roger Moore and Carole Bouquet. The film earned an Academy Award nomination for the title song. Two years later, *Never Say Never Again,* the popular *Thunderball* remake, marked Sean Connery's return to the James Bond role after 12 years.

Encouraged by the increased interest in film production, the Ministry of Tourism established a *Film Promotion Bureau* in 1985, to promote The Bahamas as a film location and to facilitate and support filmmakers. John Deleveaux, who served as the first Film Commissioner, was successful in bringing many more movies, television specials, and commercials to The Bahamas. Other major movies filmed in The Bahamas during this period were *Splash* in 1984, *Cocoon* in 1985 (starring golden oldies like Don Ameche and Jessica Tandy), which created magical underwater sequences near Clifton Pier and won an Academy Award for best visual effects and best supporting actor, *Jaws IV: The Revenge* in 1987, and *Silence of the Lambs* in 1991 (starring Anthony Hopkins and Jodie Foster), which won numerous awards, including best actress, best actor, best adapted screen play and best picture, and used Bimini for the final scene.

The Film Bureau was successful in convincing the popular syndicated comedy game show "Hollywood Squares" to tape 10 of their shows on Paradise Island. Apart from the publicity, this production pumped thousands of dollars into the local economy.

Eugene Gibbs (left), Bahamas Film Bureau, Ministry of Tourism, and Jonathan Demme during shooting of last scene of Silence of the Lambs on Bimini, Bahamas

Junkanoo is staged for the movie Jaws, the Revenge

John Deleveaux (left), Bahamas Film Commissioner MOT, presents a gift to Michael Caine after the shooting of Jaws, the Revenge

At World Travel Mart, John Deleveaux (2nd from right), Eugene Gibbs (right) and Grace Hart-Hill (left) promote The Bahamas as the premier location for filming

Kurt Jergens (2ⁿᵈ from left) on location in The Bahamas

John Deleveaux (centre) and Ivan James (left) welcome Philip Michael Thomas to Nassau to shoot an episode of *Miami Vice*

Academy award actor, Sir Sidney Poitier (right), meet with Bahamas Film Bureau executives, John Deleveaux and Darlene Davis

Celebrities arrived on Paradise Island on Chalk's Airline for shooting of 10 episodes of Hollywood Squares

Craig Clarke and Brynda Knowles, on the set of Hollywood Squares, taped on Paradise Island

British Actress Jane Seymour, star of Dr. Quinn, Medicine Woman, with photographer Derek Smith

Actress Jane Kennedy learns the limbo from Dr. Bernard Nottage, Minister of Consumer Affairs

Product Improvement

Among the main challenges being faced during the 1980's were product issues, including service and attitude as well as the need for infrastructure and hotel expansion/refurbishment, as new, modern facilities were being constructed by the competition.

Gaming

In 1978, the Bahamas Government amended the 1969 Lotteries and Gaming Act to allow for casinos to be taken into public ownership, with the Hotel Corporation as the agency for granting of gaming licences of any type and on any premises in The Bahamas. The Hotel Corporation, in consultation with the Gaming Board, also was given responsibility for the grant of a licence to an operator to manage a casino.

In 1978, the Playboy Casino opened in the Ambassador Beach Hotel, West Bay Street, Nassau, but closed in 1983 when the Cable Beach Casino (later called the Crystal Palace Casino) opened.

Investment in Hotels and Tourist Attractions

This period recorded the construction or expansion of several hotels, with a total investment of over $700 million.

Cable Beach and West Bay Street Rejuvenation

Major development took place on Cable Beach, which took on the name *Bahamian Riviera.* Government, through the Hotel Corporation of The Bahamas, took a bold step by building the *Cable Beach Hotel and Casino* complex, which opened in 1984. In 1987, the Hotel Corporation leased 8½ acres of land on the site of the Emerald Beach Hotel to Carnival Leisure Industries, to construct and manage the *Carnival Crystal Palace Resort & Casino*, comprising five towers housing 759 rooms and convention facilities, costing $85-$100 million. Ted Arison, chairman of Carnival Leisure Industries, also undertook to refurbish and redecorate the existing Cable Beach Hotel's theatre, adjacent to both the Cable Beach and Carnival hotels, and to extend the balcony to create additional seating. By 1989, the Cable Beach Hotel had been acquired by the Carnival Crystal Palace Corporation under a long lease. After Carnival completed all phases of its development, the Crystal Palace Hotel and Casino boasted 1,650 rooms and 14 restaurants. To support their projects, Carnival established a tour company and an airline, Carnival Air, and promoted its vast onshore empire in conjunction with its cruise business. By fall 1989, Carnival's new 2,600-passenger ship, the Fantasy, joined its fleet, which made weekly calls to Nassau.

Complementing the Cable Beach Hotel rejuvenation was the establishment, in 1988, of a picturesque village built around a network of waterways, called *Sandyport.* Modelled after Port Grimaud, Venice of the Côte d'Azur in the south of France, Sandyport became an exclusive resort community of luxurious waterfront homes. The Sandyport developers later constructed an attractive shopping complex, a village square featuring musicians, artists and restaurants, catering not just to its own clientele but to the local community and the tourism industry.

A stone's throw from Cable Beach, the *Coral World Underwater Observatory and Marine Park,* opened on 3rd April, 1986. Located on Silver Cay, accessible by a short bridge, north of Arawak Cay, it featured a unique underwater observatory and a distinctive tower with panoramic views, a shark tank, ocean-front restaurant and bar, nature path, a marine garden and aquarium, and sea turtle pool. At the end of 1987, Coral World opened a 22-room hotel. The resort closed in the late 1990's after Atlantis developed its marine theme park.

There were major changes in other New Providence hotels. The exclusive Balmoral Beach Hotel, on Cable Beach, owned by Government, was renovated and re-opened in 1984 as the Royal Bahamian Hotel. The Hotel Corporation contracted the Wyndham Hotels to manage the Royal Bahamian as well as the Cable Beach Hotel & Casino and the Ambassador Beach. Royal Bahamian was later taken over by the Meridien hotel chain and renamed Le Meriden Royal Bahamian Hotel. The South Ocean resort, southwest of the Nassau International Airport, underwent several expansion programmes and changed management several times in an attempt to increase profitability.

$100 million Government-owned Cable Beach Resort and Casino

Cable Beach Resort and Casino dedicated January 1984
In January 1984, Lady Pindling, wife of Prime Minister Pindling, cuts the ribbon at
the opening celebration for the Hotel Corp's new $100 million Cable Beach Resort.
Left to right: Peter Streit and Trammeli Crow (Wyndham Hotels), Prime Minister and
Lady Pindling, Ted Arison (Carnival Cruise Lines), Hon. A.D. Hanna (Deputy Prime
Minister), and Mickey Arison (Carnival Cruise Lines)

Port Lucaya opened in 1988, with 85 shops, restaurants and bars overlooking a 50-slip marina. A waterfront board walk links the complex with the Underwater Explorers Society and the Dolphin Experience

Director General of Tourism opens a workshop on security for the hospitality industry. From left to right: Arthur Barnett (BHA Executive Director), Vincent D'Aguilar (Chairman, security committee, BHA), Baltron Bethel (Director General), Mike Williams (BHA president), and William Dean who served as co-coordinator with Mr. Barnett

Resorts International on Paradise Island Changes Hands Twice in Two Years

Meanwhile, Paradise Island properties, for the first time, were in competition with the invigorated Cable Beach properties as the largest resort complex in the Caribbean. Paradise Island properties included the 1,200-room Paradise Island Resort and Casino with a 30,000 square-foot casino; Club Paradise, a 125-room all-inclusive facility; the 100-room Paradise Beach Resort; the elegant 71-room Ocean Club,12 gourmet restaurants and an 18-hole championship golf course.

On 21ˢᵗ July, 1987, Donald R. Trump, New York developer, real estate tycoon and owner of the Trump Towers, took control of Resorts International and was elected Chairman of the Board. He met with Government officials in 1987 to seek approval to build a new air strip on Paradise Island. He publicised his vision for Paradise Island to become the Number One island resort in the entire world. A year later, in 1988, Merv Griffin, billionaire entertainment entrepreneur, purchased control of Resorts International properties from Donald Trump. Merv Griffin attempted to give the island a lush tropical flavour, by adding palms, flowers and a magnificent fountain. On 16ᵗʰ April, 1990, it was announced that Resorts International would sell its Paradise Island properties, valued at about $350 million, after completion of a reorganization plan before the US Bankruptcy Court in New Jersey. Resorts' Atlantic City holdings, and not its Paradise Island properties, were responsible for its net loss of $302 million in 1989.

The hotel inventory on Paradise Island expanded further, with the opening in April 1982 of the 340-room *Paradise Grand Resort*, located on the beach, just east of the Paradise Island Hotel and Villas. Also on Paradise Island, the 151-room *Comfort Suites*, opposite the Paradise Island Casino, opened in 1991, and entered into an arrangement with the Paradise Island Resort and Casino for access to all facilities along with full charge/sign privileges. Comfort Suites, after initiatives by its General Manager, Jeremy MacVean, to install solar panels and other energy, water, and landscape conservation features, soon became known as the most environmentally sensitive property in Nassau/Paradise Island. The Holiday Inn, Paradise Island, was upgraded, and *Paradise Harbour Club & Marina* became an important hotel for boaters.

Blue Lagoon Island, accessible by boat from Paradise Island, became a favourite spot for visitors seeking an entertaining day-retreat on a private island.

Grand Bahama Facelift

On **Grand Bahama**, the two luxury *Princess* hotels—Princess Tower and the Princess Country Club with a total of 965 rooms—completed a multimillion dollar refurbishment of its rooms and casino. The *Lucayan Beach Hotel*, an old favourite, was rebuilt and re-opened in 1984, with a brand new 20,000 sq. ft. casino. The 148-room Lucayan Harbour Club re-opened in 1986 as the *Lucayan Marina Hotel & Spa*. The 2000-acre Grand Bahama Hotel and Country Club at West End, which had closed in 1991-92, re-opened in January 1993, after renovations, as the all-inclusive Jack Tar Village. Other resorts experiencing improvements or expansion on Grand Bahama included Club Fortuna and Port Lucaya Club & Marina.

In 1988, Freeport celebrated the opening of The Bahamas' first waterfront festival marketplace in 1988 when the $7 million *Port Lucaya* opened with 85 shops, restaurants and bars overlooking a 50-slip marina. Located just across the street from the Lucayan Beach Hotel, Port Lucaya offered live entertainment, fabulous day and night dining and shopping, rivalling popular state-side marketplaces such as Bayside in Miami and Harborplace in Baltimore. A waterfront board walk linked the complex with the famous Underwater Explorers Society (UNEXSO) and the new Dolphin Experience, where swimmers could enjoy the company of dolphins as they frolick in the water.

Investment by the Hotel Corporation in the Family Islands

In the **Family Islands**, the Hotel Corporation of The Bahamas constructed the *Lighthouse Beach Hotel and Marina* at Fresh Creek, Andros and renovated the former Las Palmas Hotel in South Andros. The third Bahamas Club Med resort, a 375-room facility located on San Salvador, was completed in early 1992. Numerous other small hotels and marinas were built in the Family Islands, including the upscale *Spanish Cay Resort* on Abaco. Other hotels, such as Winding Bay, Cotton Bay and Windermere on Eleuthera, and the Great Abaco Beach Resort on Abaco, were refurbished.

While a Freeport tourist office had been established in the 1970's, it was during this era that the Ministry of Tourism began to establish branch offices in the Family Islands, the first being in North Andros in January 1986 under the management of Jeritzan Outten, and in Governor's Harbour Eleuthera in March 1987, managed by Jacqueline Gibson.

During this period the Bahamas Government acquired several failing hotels, which were on the brink of closure, in an attempt to safeguard jobs. By the end of the period, the Hotel Corporation owned six hotels representing 20% of total room inventory.

While new resorts were created, two Nassau landmarks disappeared. The 129-year-old Royal Victoria Hotel was gutted by fire in 1989. Henry Villard's epitaph, written ten years earlier, was most fitting: "Like John Brown's body, she lies a mouldr'ing in the grave—of Britain's colonial past—but her soul goes marching on in the romantic pages of history".[8] Another historic relic, the abandoned Montagu Beach Hotel, was demolished four years later, on 25th April, 1993.

First native Bahamian President of BHA

The Bahamas Hotel Association continued its coordinating role for the accommodations sector, under the presidency of seasoned professional hoteliers. In 1983, Berkeley Evans became the first native Bahamian President of the BHA. In 1987, the BHA marked its 35th anniversary by initiating a special awards scheme to motivate and reward employees in the tourist industry. The duho, a ceremonial stool of Lucayan chiefs, was adopted by the BHA to recognize outstanding contributions to the hospitality industry. Bahamian artist, Quentin Minnis developed the duho symbol.

Berkeley Evans—first native Bahamian president of BHA

The beginning of the 1980's was also a period of adjustment for hoteliers, due to the introduction of the net rate system in 1982. Under the new system, travel wholesalers could purchase rooms at rates that were 20% to 40% lower than the previous "rack" or standard guest rates. The immediate effect was a dilution of the average room rate. Profits fell and it took several years for the industry to adjust to the system.

Hotel Rooms surpass 13,000

Hotel rooms in The Bahamas during this period are shown in Appendix 7. There were 11,427 hotel rooms in 1980 of which 5,333 were in Nassau/Paradise Island, 3,880 on Grand Bahama and 2,214 in the Family Islands. By 1991 the number of hotel rooms had increased to 13,475 (7,797 in Nassau/Paradise Island, 3,211 on Grand Bahama and 2,174 on the Family Islands). However, hotels suffered low occupancies—averaging 69% in Nassau, 62% on Grand Bahama and 46% on the Family Islands. To improve profitability hoteliers agreed to offer a wider range of room prices at the lower end of their rates. Attractive packages were offered, based on economy airfares during low week-day traffic days, and low group fares were negotiated with airlines.

Government Initiatives

Complementing the private sector investment, Government invested heavily in airport and other infrastructure expansion. In addition to the Prince George Dock and Nassau International Airport developments, $80 million was expended on improvement of international airports at Moss Town (Exuma), San Salvador, and

Governor's Harbour (Eleuthera). In January 1983, to help pay for some of these investments, Government increased the departure tax for persons leaving the country for a foreign destination by $1 to $5 for adults and $2.50 for children, and by 1991 the tax had been further increased to $7 for everybody, except children under three years of age. New straw markets opened in Market Plaza, Bay Street, Cable Beach and Lucaya, on Grand Bahama.

The Bahamas Telecommunications Corporation (BaTelCo, now BTC) modernized its communications network, investing heavily in direct-distance dialling to most islands of The Bahamas and cellular phone system, which greatly benefitted the boating community.

Despite the Government's stated objective of creating a genuine Bahamian character for the industry, within most of the large hotels the number of local bands diminished. Hoteliers cited budgetary considerations for their cutbacks, and entertainers complained bitterly to the Prime Minister and Minister of Tourism. Speaking at the third annual Hospitality Leadership Conference at Workers House, Nassau, in September 1991, Prime Minister Pindling pointed out that "hotels in Nassau and Freeport have systematically frozen out Bahamian musicians and entertainers. Too many of the top musicians in Nassau today are unemployed. It is my view that Bahamian and Caribbean music should permeate the air at every hotel in The Bahamas". He went on to say that even if budget considerations are the determining factor, it cannot hold good for the casino hotel or for hotels with over 200 rooms.

In response to proposals by local merchants to boost sales in a sagging economy, Government approved duty free shopping for 11 categories of items at the end of 1991, prompting merchants to form the Duty Free Promotion Board (later changed to Nassau Tourism and Development Board) to advertise the competitive shopping opportunities.

Attitudes within the Industry

Exit surveys revealed that poor attitudes within the Tourism industry remained at the top of the listing of negative comments from departing visitors.

Prime Minister Pindling exemplifies Pride in Service

Prime Minister, the Right Honourable Sir Lynden Pindling, issued a challenge for the Ministry of Tourism and the industry to put in place a top-level conference to bring together owners, managers, unions, and decision makers along with the Government to develop a plan to address the problems facing the industry. The first Hospitality Conference was held in November 1988, when over 400 hospitality workers used this forum to exchange views and experiences. The second conference, primarily for management, was held in May 1990 under the theme "Teaming Up to Keep it Better in The Bahamas". The participants developed over 100 recommendations to improve various elements of the "product". The third and fourth conferences in 1991 and 1992, delved into root causes of attitude and service problems, identified task forces to spearhead action, and featured world renowned presenters, including experts from the Disney organization. An initiative of the Bahamas Hotel Catering and Allied Workers Union, the Bahamas Hotel Employers Association and the Ministry of Tourism, under the chairmanship of Angela Cleare, these conclaves played a key role in improving the industry and in visitor satisfaction. In 1991, a similar conference was staged on Grand Bahama.

Prime Minister Pindling, on assuming his second term as Minister of Tourism on 1st October, 1990, set as a goal the injection of Pride into hospitality jobs. "Tourism was in trouble and needed an injection of new energy and encouragement from the top." "Countering those who believed that tourism was a inferior enterprise, retarding other forms of economic activity and engendering a lackey mentality, Pindling had to show that it was both an essential and irreplaceable element of the Bahamian economy, bringing prosperity to all, and that far from being demeaning, it succeeded best if those involved took pride in giving good and cheerful service. It was not a new message but badly needed reiteration".[9] On 1st October, 1990, Pindling took time from his schedule to exemplify dignity in all levels of jobs, by working first as a bellman at Resorts International on Paradise Island and later as a houseman at the Crystal Palace Resort on Cable Beach. Visitors were indeed shocked to see the Prime Minister making their beds, navigating the laundry cart, vacuuming floors, carrying visitors' luggage and welcoming guests—jobs he carried out with pride and diligence. After his shift was over, along with Thomas Bastian, President of the Bahamas Hotel Catering and Allied Workers Union, he lunched with and addressed the staff in the cafeteria. "I did manage to buck up with the luggage trolley about three times before I got the hang of it and earned myself a tip," he told them, to laughter and applause, before going on to deliver a more pointed message.[10] In commenting on the experience, the Prime Minister stated that the "sampling" of jobs in the industry was more than symbolic; it marked the beginning of a new era for The Bahamas—one that would embrace each and every Bahamian and impress on them like never before the importance of a job well done.

Having set the example, the Prime Minister appointed the New York-based Carolyn Jones Agency to produce an onshore tourism awareness campaign. The campaign, which adopted the theme *Bahamas: Our Pride and Joy,* focused on the importance of having pride in everything one does—from working to living to treating others with kindness and consideration. The campaign comprised print, radio and television advertising, citing exemplary hospitality employees and role models. A Careers Day was organized and Seminars also took place focusing specifically on Professionalism and Dignity in Service.

Prime Minister Pindling exemplifies dignity in service by spending the day working at the Cable Beach Hotel

Visitors are thrilled when Prime Minister Pindling (centre) serves as porter for the day at Paradise Island Hotel & Villas

Bahamas: Our Pride and Joy awareness campaign features exemplary hospitality workers

Minister Maynard presents a Pride and Joy certificate to taxi driver Lloyd Delaney (centre) for earning high praise from visitors for exemplary service

Richard McCombe of Nassau Cruises (2nd from left) presents a check to Director General of Tourism to assist in funding the Pride and Joy campaign. Angela Cleare (right) and Velda Campbell (left) coordinated the campaign

The goal of bringing hospitality training institutions under one umbrella and improving professionalism was pursued when construction began on the Bahamas Tourism Training Centre—the finest and most extensive tourism and hotel training facilities in the Caribbean—to embrace the Bahamas Hotel Training College, University of the West Indies Hotel Management Division and the Ministry of Tourism's Industry Training Unit. The facility opened in 1994.

The Ministry of Tourism's attitudinal training programme *Bahamahost* was further strengthened by a further injection of capital by Winn Dixie/City Markets, and local private institutions like the Royal Bank of Canada and John Bull Ltd., which gave generous donations. The private sector funding was used to produce additional video tapes and audio visuals to further modernise the programme, which was cited by Organization of American States (OAS) as the most effective training programme of its kind in the region. Bahamahost became a core training programme for hospitality workers throughout The Bahamas. Many employers in the tourism industry emphasized Bahamahost as a requirement for their staff.

Bahamahost lecturers, led by Iris Dean (seated) during Planning Workshop

Prime Minister Pindling (2nd from left) was the keynote speaker at the Bahamahost graduation in Long Island

First Bahamahost course for Andros. Pictured with some of the participants are Jeritzan Outten (right), Manager of the North Andros Tourist Office and Iris Dean, Coordinator for Bahamahost (2nd from left)

Iris Dean (2nd from right) is presented with a bouquet for outstanding service to Bahamahost

Permanent Secretary Jeanette Bethel (2nd from left) presents Winn-Dixie/City Markets with a plaque for generosity in supporting the Bahamahost programme. The donations were used to upgrade the programme and digitalize the lectures.

Bahamahost combined graduating class—Permanent Secretary Basil O'Brien
(3rd from right); Willamae Salkey, Undersecretary (later PS—2nd from left). Athama
Bowe (right) Coordinator.

Changes in the Airline and Cruise Industry

Recognizing that tourism growth is directly related to accessibility, Director
General of Tourism, Baltron Bethel, was in continuous negotiation with carriers.
He vigorously pursued cooperative marketing initiatives with airlines, and, despite
escalating air transportation costs, was successful in opening up new routes.
Bahamasair introduced non-stop jet service to several US cities including Tampa,
Orlando, and Philadelphia. In 1982 Pan American World Airways resumed
its service from New York and Miami to both Nassau and Freeport; the airline
was later bought by Delta. Carnival Airlines initiated service, offering up to 30
flights per week from eight or nine US cities. Paradise Island Airlines offered 5
flights per day to Miami and to Ft. Lauderdale using its new 3,000 feet airstrip
on Paradise Island. New or upgraded service was also introduced by many other
carriers including Trans World Airlines, Eastern, Piedmont, Midway, Delta, Air
Florida, Western (acquired by Delta Airlines in 1987), USAir, American/American
Eagle, Air Canada, Trans American, Laker Airlines, Comair, United, Midway,
Paradise Island Express (formerly Bahamas Express), Apple Tours (UK) plus at
least a dozen other Canadian and US charter airlines and commuter airlines.

This period witnessed a loss in European business, especially from Germany, with
the reduction in spending power due to the strengthening of the US dollar against

European currencies. The reduction in demand for passenger seats from Germany to Nassau led Lufthansa to cancel its Frankfurt-Nassau flights in April 1981 and, about the same time, International Air Bahama, which for years had been an important carrier out of Luxembourg, went out of business. British Airways stopped its non-stop services into Nassau as well as its weekly London-Nassau-Bermuda-London flights in April 1991; however, the airline introduced special promotional fares to The Bahamas via Miami. The reduction in direct service also prompted the Ministry of Tourism to actively negotiate and promote other airlinks to major cities in Europe, the Far East and Latin America via direct connections over Florida and East Coast gateways.

A major blow to tourism in the region involved the 1989 strike, the retrenchment and final demise of Eastern Airlines in 1991 and bankruptcy of one of the major wholesalers—Flyfaire. Braniff Airlines also went into bankruptcy in 1989. Bahamasair and charter operators moved quickly to add new service to fill the shortfall in seats.

Resorts International purchased Chalk's Airlines and made significant initiatives to upgrade the airline's fleet, thus ushering in a new standard of scheduled seaplane service. The 17-passenger Grumman G-73 Mallard had its old piston engines removed and replaced with modern P&W PT-6 turbo prop engines. Airline amenities such as flight attendants, in-flight snack service and lavatories were also added. With the addition of 30-passenger Grumman G-111 Albatross aircraft, Chalk's became the primary carrier to Paradise Island until Paradise Island Airways was established by Merv Griffin. Paradise Island Airways flew the DeHavilland Dash 7 land planes on the new Paradise Island airstrip, but this service disappeared when the Paradise Island Airport closed. However, Chalk's survived under the name Chalk's Ocean Airways and continued to offer regular service from Florida to Bimini.

United Airlines inaugural guests hosted at Ocean Club, Paradise Island

Delta inaugurates Dallas service

Craig Woods, Director Sales (centre), presents a plaque to Paradise Island Airways for innovative marketing

Air Canada celebrates 50th anniversary in 1967

Bahamasair and Ministry of Tourism officials during a planning workshop

Delta inaugurates Nassau-Orlando service

The Family Island destinations of Abaco, Eleuthera and Exuma were on the threshold of major tourism development with improvements to airports, making it possible for them to accept wide-bodied jet aircraft from all the major gateways in North America. Additionally, all three islands enjoyed multi-level scheduled commuter service from three gateways in South Florida—Miami, Fort Lauderdale, and West Palm Beach—by carriers such as American Eagle, USAir and Comair.

The outdated airport at Windsor Field was totally inadequate for the increased air traffic. In 1990, a $50 million contract for the massive expansion of the airport was awarded to Mosko United Construction Company and Andrade Gutierrez of Brazil. The new 167,000 square-foot terminal included greatly expanded US Immigration and preclearance facilities, with boarding fingers, enabling passengers to board aircraft in air-conditioned comfort. The facility was completed in late 1992.

Christening of Premier Cruise Lines' Oceanic cruise ship. Lois Symonette, Permanent Secretary, Transport (centre) and John Deleveaux (Deputy Director General—to her right) accept a plaque for the Bahamas Government.

Responding to the resurgence in global cruise travel, the $45 million Nassau harbour project, completed in 1990, accommodated up to nine of the world's largest ships at one time. Of particular significance was the structure of the Grand Bahama cruise business. The cruise stopover market on Grand Bahama developed to as much as 30% of that island's total stopovers. New ships were attracted to the Family Islands, with regular stops on Bimini, Great Stirrup Cay, Little Stirrup Cay (renamed Coco Cay), Eleuthera and Abaco. Premier Cruise Line's Abacodabra cruise to Abaco became an instant success. The Bahamas was established as the world's leader in cruise travel with 25 ships making regular calls to the various ports.

With direct or connecting air or cruise service from all of the major cities, travellers to The Bahamas had many options open to them.

Tourist Performance—the Numbers Game

The Bahamas' performance must be evaluated in the context of both international and local economic conditions. The global market was depressed. This was a period of slow growth and consolidation for the industry. While The Bahamas was boasting

The Bahamas welcomes the 2-millionth visitor in 1983

3-millionth visitor toasted in 1986

annual increases in visitor arrivals—2 million by 1983 and 3 million by 1986—an examination of more relevant indicators of tourism performance, such as stopover visitors and visitor nights, revealed disturbing trends, as summarized in Tables 9-3 to 9-6.

1) **Tourism arrivals** nearly doubled from 1,904,560 in 1980 to 3,621,889 in 1991, but the increase was largely due to the burgeoning cruise industry.

2) The percentage of **air visitors** declined from close to 66% of total visitors in 1980 to 36% in 1991, with adverse implications for visitor nights and income.

3) **Stopover visitors** increased slightly from 1.1 million in 1980 to 1.4 million in 1991. As a percentage of total arrivals, stopovers declined significantly from 62% in 1980 to 39% in 1991.

4) **Cruise visitors** increased dramatically from ½ million in 1980 to 2 million in 1991. In 1986, cruise visitors to The Bahamas exceeded stopover visitors for the first time in history. Cruise passengers increased from 30% in 1980 to 56% of total arrivals in 1991.

5) Total **hotel nights** in The Bahamas dropped by 8% from 5.9 million in 1980 to 5.7 million in 1991.

6) Total **Visitor Nights** declined slightly from 8,436,140 nights in 1980 to 8,401,925 visitor nights in 1991, with Grand Bahama experiencing 12 lean years of decline. There was growth, however, on New Providence and a modest increase in the Family Islands.

7) The weak performance in visitor nights was reflected in **visitor expenditure** figures. Between 1986 and 1991, total expenditure became stagnant at $1.1 billion. The average stopover visitor spent roughly $720 in The Bahamas in 1987, while a cruise ship visitor spent, on average, $60.

8) During the period 1980-91, The Bahamas increased its share of the US market from 65% to 75%, and lost market share in other traditional markets. In the Canadian market, where visitor nights fell from 1.2 million to 700,000, this was caused by twin negative factors of inadequate lift and an unfavourable exchange rate on the Canadian dollar. European travel, which is highly cyclical, varied with the strength/weakness of the US dollar. The Bahamas' share of European visitor nights fell from 14.4% in 1980 to 5.7% in 1985, but recovered to 12% by 1991.

9) An even more disturbing trend was that visitor satisfaction was declining and many expressed their disagreement with Tourism's slogan "It's Better in The Bahamas".

Table 9-3
Summary Table of Visitor Performance—1980 vs. 1991

YEAR	STOP-OVERS	CRUISE	DAY & TRANSIT	TOTAL FOREIGN ARRIVALS	BY AIR % of Total	BY SEA % of Total	HOTEL NIGHTS	VISITOR NIGHTS
1980	1,181,260	577,631	145,960	**1,904,560**	1,262,330	642,230	5,905,070	8,436,140
	62%	30.3%	7.7%	**100%**	66.3%	33.7%		
1991	1,427,035	2,019,964	174,890	**3,621,889**	1,303,318	2,318,900	5,724,965	8,401,925
	39.4%	55.8%	4.9%	**100%**	35.9%	64.0%		

Source: Annual Statistical Reports of the Research Department, Ministry of Tourism

Table 9-4
Visitor Nights by Destination in The Bahamas
1980 vs. 1991

	New Providence/ Paradise Island		Grand Bahama		Family Islands		Total Visitor Nights	
	No.	%	No.	%	No.	%	No	%
1980	3,849,200	45.6	2,613,620	30.9	1,973,320	23.4	8,436,140	100
1991	4,197,680	49.9	2,094,160	24.9	2,110,085	25.1	8,401,925	100

Source: Annual Statistical Reports of the Research Department, Ministry of Tourism

Table 9-5
Visitor Nights and Average Length of Stay (In Nights)
In The Bahamas 1980 vs. 1991
By US, Canadian and European Residents

YEAR	UNITED STATES			CANADA			EUROPE		
	LENGTH OF STAY (Nights)	VISITOR NIGHTS	%	LENGTH OF STAY (Nights)	VISITOR NIGHTS	%	LENGTH OF STAY (Nights)	VISITOR NIGHTS	%
1980	6.25	5,527,390	65	9.0	1,213,010	14	11.0	1,216,760	14
1991	5.36	6,304,555	75	8.0	742,720	9	9.24	1,035,540	12

Source: Annual Statistical Reports of the Research Department, Ministry of Tourism

Table 9-6
Expenditure by Visitors to The Bahamas
1980 vs. 1991

YEAR	STOPOVER VISITORS	PER CAPITA	CRUISE VISITORS	DAY VISITORS	TOTAL
1980	$ 558,000,000	$472.38	$ 31,000,000	$ 5,000,000	$ 595,453,490
1991	$1,082,047,732	$758.25	$129,969,153	$10,377,000	$1,222,393,867

Source: *Annual Statistical Reports of the Research Department, Ministry of Tourism*

The Bahamas loses ground to Competitive Destinations in the Caribbean

Despite the promotional and onshore initiatives, it became increasingly more difficult to protect market share, as competition stiffened. The entire region of the Americas had now begun to develop a new and realistic appreciation of tourism as an economic engine. Mexico had undergone massive expansion of its tourism plant and, with successive devaluations, had become a major competitor. The neighbouring Caribbean islands, many of which initially despised tourism, began aggressive marketing campaigns in an attempt to earn foreign exchange and create jobs. Like Mexico, their comparatively lower labour and energy costs, combined with their local currencies, which were valued well below the US dollar, made them attractive bargain destinations.

Caribbean stopover arrivals increased from close to 7 million in 1980 to 12 million in 1990, representing an average annual increase of 6%. Three markets—the USA, Canada, and Europe—generated over 6 million of these stopover visitors, 70% of the total. Growth from the USA slowed significantly; growth from Canada was less than 3% per annum. Only after 1985, with the decline in the value of the US dollar against major European currencies, was there growth from Europe. Growth in developmental markets, like Japan, was not sufficient to compensate for the slowing down of US stopover traffic. Cruise business, by comparison, recorded a 10% p.a. growth rate to the Caribbean during the 1980's.

With the large number of competing destinations, the top tourism earners lost market share. In 1974, the five leading destinations—The Bahamas, Bermuda, Jamaica, Puerto Rico and the US Virgin Islands—accounted for 82.2% of all US arrivals in the region. By 1984, their share had fallen to 68%. Many of the smaller islands increased their share of the overall Caribbean market. While The Bahamas suffered a decline in share from 17.8% in 1980 to 13.2% in 1990, Anguilla, Dominican Republic, Turks & Caicos, Belize, St. Maarten, Dominica, Grenada, St. Kitts & Nevis, Antigua, and Aruba each experienced growth rates of over 120% over the decade. Jamaica recorded a 112.7% increase. In 1980, only seven countries could boast annual stopovers in excess of 250,000, but, by 1990, 12 of the 22 Caribbean countries listed in Appendix 1D had joined the "big league" with annual stopovers of over a quarter of a million.

*   *   *

Such was the dismal status of the industry at the end of the period under review. It was crystal clear that to remain competitive in tourism, drastic new measures would be needed—in 1992 and beyond.

10

ENVIRONMENT, TECHNOLOGY AND INNOVATION
1992-2004

External Developments Impacting Bahamas Tourism

Hotel Trends

While in the 1980's pampering the hotel guest was the strategy, in the 1990's quality service was the differentiating factor. Hotels implemented quality assurance programmes and referred to the quality of their service in their advertising. For the first time, a hotel company—The Ritz-Carlton—won the prestigious Malcolm Baldrige National Quality Award. Between 1990 and the beginning of the 21st century, mergers, acquisitions and joint ventures changed the competitive environment of the lodging industry worldwide.

The EEC and Japan

In 1992, the *European Economic Community* (EEC) was transformed into a single market. With the freedom of travel, stable currencies, reduced costs and airline deregulation, travel within the EEC became attractive. Member EEC states—Belgium, France, Germany, Greece, Ireland, Italy, Luxembourg, Netherlands, Portugal, Spain and the United Kingdom—with a per capita income of $14,140, represented strong competition for the rest of the world. An American entity that tried to quickly capitalize on this major development was Disney World which opened Euro Disney in France in 1992. A new Channel Tunnel ("Chunnel") in 1993 made it possible to drive from the United Kingdom to France.

By the 1990's, Japan could boast the second highest GDP in the world (second only to the USA) and the highest per capita income. During the first five years of the decade, Japanese overseas travel increased at an average rate of 10% per annum, compared to 4% worldwide, with total overseas travellers reaching 15 million per annum by 1995. Caribbean travel by the Japanese had started in 1990, with airlines such as All Nippon, Japan Airlines and American Airlines promoting the Japanese-Caribbean market, with concentration on

Jamaica, Cancun and The Bahamas, creating a welcome, though small, boost to these economies.

Emphasis on the Environment

The 1990's recorded the most significant environmental event, the historic United Nations Conference on Environment and Development, referred to as the *Earth Summit*. At this important forum, *Agenda 21*, a comprehensive programme of action was adopted by 182 governments, including The Bahamas, on 14th June, 1992, at Rio de Janeiro, Brazil. The first document of its kind to achieve international consensus, it provided a blueprint for securing the sustainable future of the planet. From the Earth Summit evolved many other important conventions and environmental initiatives such as the Convention on Biological Diversity. The Bahamas had the honour of hosting the first meeting of the Conference of the Parties of the Convention of Biological Diversity. Held in Nassau, from 28th November to 9th December, 1994, this United Nations parley brought to The Bahamas leaders from all over the world.

The tourism industry, recognizing its huge stake in the environment, put together its own guiding principles for protecting the natural and cultural resources, the core of its business. Three international organizations—the World Travel & Tourism Council (WTTC), the World Tourism Organization (UNWTO) and the Earth Council—launched *"Agenda 21 for the Travel & Tourism Industry: Towards Environmentally Sustainable Development"*, which contains priority areas for action by government, the private sector, and non-government organizations (NGO's).[1]

These landmark conferences prompted governments all over the world to develop sustainable tourism plans. To guide countries in the sustainable process, environmental groups like the United Nations Environment Program (UNEP), Earth Watch and Green Globe have produced numerous handbooks such as *Environmental Codes of Conduct for Tourists* and *Indicators of Sustainable Tourism Development*. To offer incentives for countries and organizations to take action, regional and international groups such as CTA, CHA, Conservation International, National Geographic Traveler, British Airways, ASTA, and many others, have introduced annual award schemes to celebrate and promote outstanding sustainable tourism initiatives across the globe.

2001 Attack on America (9/11)

While there was steady global growth in travel during the first nine years of the decade under review, the year 2001 recorded one of the most disastrous events in the tourism industry.

On Tuesday, 11th September, 2001, an American Airlines Boeing 767, loaded with 20,000 gallons of jet fuel, crashed into the north tower of the World Trade Center in New York City, instantly killing or trapping hundreds of people. As the evacuation of the tower got underway, television cameras broadcast live images of what initially appeared to be a freak accident. Just 18 minutes after the first plane hit, a second Boeing 767—United Airlines Flight 175—exploded into the south tower of the World Trade Center, showering burning debris over surrounding buildings. America was under attack.

The attackers, Islamic terrorists from Arab nations, reportedly financed by Saudi fugitive Osama bin Laden's al Qaeda terrorist organization, were allegedly acting in retaliation of America's support of Israel, its involvement in the Persian Gulf War, and its continued military presence in the Middle East.

As millions watched in horror the events unfolding in New York, American Airlines Flight 77 circled over downtown Washington and slammed into the Pentagon military headquarters, killing all 64 people aboard the airliner. Less than 15 minutes after the Pentagon attack, the two World Trade Center towers collapsed in a massive cloud of dust and smoke. Close to 3,000 people died, including 366 firefighters and policemen who were struggling to evacuate the buildings. Only six people in the towers at the time of their collapse survived unscathed. Almost 10,000 other people were treated for injuries.

Meanwhile, a fourth California-bound plane—United Flight 93—was hijacked about 40 minutes after leaving Newark International Airport. Passengers on board learned of events in New York and Washington via cellular phone. The passengers are suspected to have fought the four hijackers before the plane crashed in a rural field in western Pennsylvania. All 45 people aboard were killed.

Operation Enduring Freedom, the US-led international effort to oust the Taliban regime in Afghanistan and destroy Osama bin Laden's terrorist network, began on 7th October, 2001. These events dealt a devastating blow to confidence in air travel and increased security and waiting time at all airports throughout the world. Global travel took a nose dive, and it was predicted in many quarters that the travel industry would not recover for several years.[2]

Global Travel Performance and Outlook since 9/11

While the United States was hardest hit by the events of 9/11, all countries of the world were affected. But, according to the 2002 US Travel Industry Survey, the events of 9/11 were not as devastating as had been expected. A reduction in air travel was evident as 8% of leisure travellers reduced their flying, and travel by car increased. Because more travel was closer to home, The Bahamas capitalized on its proximity to North America in its promotions.

After a decline in global tourism in 2001 of 0.6%, the first decline in a decade, global travel grew by 3% in 2002, in keeping with predictions by both WTTC and UNWTO. The Americas was the only region that experienced a decline in 2002. International tourism arrivals fell by 1.2 per cent in 2003, the biggest annual drop ever. This decline was a result of three negative factors: the Iraq conflict, SARS

(Severe Acute Respiratory Syndrome) outbreak, and a weak economy, causing a high level of uncertainty. Despite a series of difficult years, from 2001 to 2003, the number of international tourist arrivals had still managed to show an overall increase of seven million, equivalent to a rise of one per cent, over the "millennium" year of 2000, commented the Secretary-General of UNWTO, Mr. Francesco Frangialli. "In such a hostile environment this very fact confirms the resilience of tourism, based on the incompressible need for travel and leisure that characterizes consumers in post-industrial societies," he added. [3]

The Air Transport Association, the umbrella body for US airlines, reported that, since 9/11, airlines lost $18 billion. Many large airlines filed for bankruptcy or were forced to reorganize. It was also noted that, while the region benefitted from increased visitors during the first Gulf War, the terror factor following 9/11 "could make US and British tourists feel that they would not be safe even in the Caribbean"[4].Recognizing that regional partnership was the best method of dealing with the global competition, governments of the Caribbean joined forces to launch a marketing campaign under the theme, *Life Needs the Caribbean*. The US$16 million campaign, administered by the Caribbean Hotel Association Charitable Trust, featured four advertisements showing a range of Caribbean vacation experiences—from the traditional beach and sun vacations to the more eco-oriented destinations. Shown first in North America, juxtaposing the pressures and sounds of urban life in North America against the tranquillity of vacation life in the Caribbean, the advertisements had a positive impact of "branding" the Caribbean.

Timeshare Hotels

While the airline and accommodations sector experienced lean times following 9/ll, the multi-billion-dollar timeshare sector recorded growth and has proven to be resilient to economic downturns.

Timeshare is a "vacation ownership" concept based on the premise that a group of people share the purchase cost of a vacation accommodation, in increments of one week, or more, per year of use, thus guaranteeing each buyer the ability to use that accommodation during the period of choice, either for life or for a specified number of years. In the 1960's the timeshare industry began in Europe as a way of making the vacation pleasures of a "second home" accessible to families who did not want the financial burdens of year-round second property ownership. Timesharing was introduced into the United States and the Caribbean in the 1970's. As more and more units were constructed, some consumers complained about low-quality construction, high-pressure sales tactics, and scams run by unscrupulous real estate dealers. As a result, the industry suffered from negative perceptions during its "adolescence".

In the 1980's, Marriott entered the timeshare industry and began providing *Vacation Ownership—the Marriott Way*. Other hotel chains and corporations, such as Sheraton and Walt Disney Productions, entered the industry, and well managed and modern timeshare resorts became the norm throughout the world.[5] In the 1990's, timeshare resorts became highly organized and regulated. Trade bodies, such as the American Resort Development Association and the Organization for Timeshare in Europe, began to apply codes of conduct and to ensure that expansion was based on sound commercial and ethical standards.[6] By 2002, timeshare resorts were located in 95 countries and 47 states in the US. Some of the world's biggest names in the hospitality sector now have timeshare interests—Hilton, Sheraton, Disney, Ramada, Four Seasons, Hyatt, Westin, Ritz-Carlton, and others. At the same time, well-known European companies with timeshare interests has also grown. Over 1,600 of the 5,300 total timeshare resorts worldwide are in the United States, with the majority in Florida and California. Timeshare has been experiencing phenomenal annual growth (approximately 15%).

The Bahamas is currently third in the Caribbean in timeshare sales (behind Aruba and St. Maarten), with over $1 million in revenue since 2000. The Vacation Plan and Timeshare Act in The Bahamas was passed in 1984 and updated in 1999. The cornerstone of the legislation is that it also provides consumer protection, particularly by way of disclosure by developers of various matters affecting the project. Proposed legislative changes provide for additional consumer protection, plus legal mechanisms in regard to defaulting purchasers who have acquired an ownership interest in timeshare. It also provides for the right, as compared to the discretion of the Government, for the developer to offer a timeshare product with an ownership component. There are approximately 40,000 owners of timeshare weeks, in about 34 resorts, the majority of which are on Grand Bahama and New Providence, with a small number on Abaco, Exuma and San Salvador.[7]

With the passage of the proposed amendments to the legislation, the continued support of the Bahamas Government, and the interest expressed by major United States developers, it is anticipated that the timeshare industry in The Bahamas will continue to grow over the next ten years.

From the 1990's, the **Internet** has transformed marketing and booking capabilities within the hospitality sector. In 1994, the first online hotel catalog, TravelWeb.com, was launched. Hyatt Hotels was one of the first chains to establish a site on the Internet, while Choice Hotels International and Holiday Inn became the first to introduce online booking capability in 1995. In 1999, Choice Hotels was also the first chain to test in-room PCs as a standard amenity for guests. With the Internet increasing in importance as a method of booking vacations, travel agency locations decreased gradually over the years, with a decline as high as 16% in the 1999-2001 period.[8] Online travel became widespread. It was predicted that Internet bookings would reach $60 billion by 2006.

Local Political Changes and their Impact on Tourism

In the general election of August 1992, the Honourable Hubert Alexander Ingraham led the Free National Movement (FNM) party to a victory, capturing 55%

of the vote and 32 of the then 49 seats in the House of Assembly. This brought to an end almost 26 years of Progressive Liberal Party (PLP) rule under Prime Minister Lynden Pindling.

Before joining the FNM, Mr. Ingraham, a practising attorney, had served in the Cabinet of Prime Minister Pindling from 1982 to 1984. In 1984, Mr. Ingraham and then Minister of Tourism, the Honourable Perry Christie, had been dismissed from the Cabinet and the PLP, following their criticisms of Government's inaction in the face of damaging allegations of widespread corruption, as documented in the 1984 Commission of Inquiry. Ingraham joined the opposition FNM in March 1990 and was elected leader of that party. The FNM, under Prime Minister Ingraham's leadership, had a second landslide victory in 1997, winning 34 of the reduced 40-seat House of Assembly.

Sir Lynden Pindling died on 26th August, 2000. Despite their political divorce, Prime Minister Ingraham gave credit to Sir Lynden Pindling for the significant part he played in the country's economic development and growth. Another tribute to Sir Lynden highlighted one of his major contributions as that of "freeing the Bahamian spirit and allowing it to fly".

The FNM's first term in office was marked by a deliberate attempt to revitalize the economy, which was suffering from the effects of the US recession and the war in the Persian Gulf. They sought to create new jobs, setting as a goal the reduction of unemployment from 14% to 10%. Tourism, as the chief employer, was clearly identified as the industry that could contribute greatest to achievement of that goal.

The new Government immediately set to work studying the tourism industry, including exit surveys, and market studies. The state of the tourism product in 1992 had been clearly described in a Hill and Knowlton report.[9] The study, commissioned by the PLP government, was conducted during the period April through July 1992 but the report was not completed until August 1992, when the new Government had taken office. The report discussed reasons for the decline in stopover visitors. It concluded that, while the recession and stiff competition played a role, the real problems of the industry included the very high cost of doing business, coupled with a lack of "value for money", "spotty service", dissatisfied visitors, inadequately maintained hotels, and unwillingness to recognize major tourism trends such as selling "experiences", all-inclusive vacations, development of new markets, Ecotourism, upscale emphasis, visitor loyalty and controlled development. The study outlined major strategic recommendations for improving the tourism product.

A further analysis by the new administration led to the conclusion that Nassau/Paradise Island and Grand Bahama had lost their charm and had become associated with mass tourism, "low class" visitors and low visitor satisfaction. Furthermore, larger properties, through price-cutting, had encroached on the territory of the small properties, in some cases putting them out of business. Because most of the selling focus had been on features of larger hotels, the history and culture of The Bahamas had received little exposure, leaving the destination without personality.

These findings led to the conclusion that far too little investment had been made in the product. Within the hotel sector, more than 20% of rooms were owned by Government, hotels were run down, and room rates and occupancies were low; there was deterioration in the environment, and the product in general was in a state of decay.

Among the immediate priorities identified by the FNM government were encouragement of tourism investment and divestment of government-owned hotels. In Nassau, the entire landscape underwent a makeover—Bay Street, the Harbour, Wharf, Cable Beach Strip, and Arawak Cay—and there was general infrastructure improvement.

Hon. Brent Symonette—Minister of Tourism 1992-1995

The first Minister of Tourism appointed by the FNM government was attorney Brent Symonette, son of the first Premier of The Bahamas, Sir Roland Symonette. The new Minister took office in August 1992 and he appointed a task force to review the structure of the tourism industry in The Bahamas. He took advantage of the autonomy granted to a Minister of Tourism under the Promotion of Tourism Act to engender change within the Ministry by causing it to function less like a government entity and more like a private sector enterprise. He forged closer partnerships with the Promotion Boards, NGOs and other private sector agencies. A Trinidadian named Roy Boyke was hired as Communications Consultant. Boyke conceived the short-lived "Hip to Hop" promotion concept replacing "It's Better in The Bahamas". A decentralized reporting system was implemented, and it was publicly announced that market forces should take precedence over Government intervention. In December 1994, Mr. Symonette left office to pursue personal interests. Between January 1995 and May 2002, three different Ministers held the portfolio of Minister of Tourism, namely the Honourable Frank Watson, the Honourable Cornelius Smith and the Honourable Orville "Tommy" Turnquest. During this period, the previous decentralized structure was abandoned. The governmental structure of the Ministry reverted to the more traditional pattern with the Director General of Tourism functioning as the technical head of the Ministry, fully empowered to make policy decisions on its behalf. During this period, much of the infrastructural development of Bay Street was carried out, including the beautification of the thoroughfare, improvement to the Nassau International Airport and harbour, and the development of Arawak Cay as a heritage site.

Hip to Hop advertisement

Ministers of Tourism January 1995 to May 2002:

DPM Hon. Frank Watson 1995-1997

Hon. Cornelius Smith 1997-2001

Hon. Orville "Tommy" Turnquest 2001-2002

Product Refurbishment

During the years 1992 to 2002, a great deal of attention was paid to product refurbishment. In 1995, a $1.2 million Prince George Wharf redevelopment programme began. The design called for new buildings to showcase picturesque, tropical-island architecture and a functional Welcome Centre, "Festival Place", a colourful Junkanoo Expo, and modern taxi call-up system for cruise passengers. The Architects Partnership team, headed by Master Bahamian artist/architect Jackson Burnside, was appointed to design and oversee the project, which was to have been completed in 2000. However the project experienced many financial problems. Festival Place finally opened in 2003.

Festival Place

The downtown area received a facelift. Bay Street underwent a $1.5 million beautification, which involved repaving, landscaping, and enhancement of Colonial-style architecture. Improved tourism infrastructure in the Rawson Square area included a surrey shelter parallel to Woodes Rogers Walk to accommodate 20 horse-drawn carriages, and a new Hair Braiders station to provide a clean, organized facility from which the young entrepreneurs could conduct their trade. Government's programme to restore public buildings included a $3.2 million refurbishment of the Adderley and Churchill Buildings and a $900,000 exterior refurbishment of the General Post Office on East Hill Street.

Hotel Development and Branding

During this period, the FNM Government divested itself of all publicly owned hotel properties, except the Radisson Cable Beach and the Lighthouse Yacht Club, Andros, facilitating their upgrade by successful hotel chains. John Issa, Super Clubs, purchased the Government-owned Ambassador Beach Hotel for $8 million and invested $24 million over the next 18 months into a 396-room all-inclusive resort, *SuperClubs Breezes,* and Sandals' Butch Stuart purchased the Royal Bahamian and converted it into its flag ship property, *Sandals Royal Bahamian.* These Jamaican-owned properties boasted a quality experience and high visitor returns.

Butch Stuart's Sandals Royal Bahamian—winner of the prestigious 5-star Diamond award—the premier resort for couples

One of the most significant investments of this period was the creation of *Atlantis* on Paradise Island by South African born Sol Kerzner, president of Sun International Ltd., for a total investment of US$1 billion. After acquiring Resorts International, which owned three large hotels, an airport, golf course, marina, along with the 564-room Holiday Inn hotel, the transformation began in 1994 in several phases. The first phase was completed in 1996 and the second in 1998. The result was a magnificent theme park beach resort complex, depicting the lost continent of Atlantis, with 2,300 guest rooms, 38 restaurants, the Caribbean's largest casino and more than 11 million gallons of water activities including lagoons, cascading waterfalls, water slides, rides, swimming pools, and fountains. Its centrepiece, the 34-acre waterscape park, boasts the world's largest aquarium with 50,000 spectacular marine animals.

Atlantis, Paradise Island, created by Sol Kerzner

In 1997, the Canada RHK Group purchased the run-down British Colonial Hotel on Bay Street, and invested millions of dollars in painstakingly transforming it to a more elegant version of its original design. The new upscale British Colonial Hilton in the historic district of Nassau, a favourite spot for businessmen, comprises 291 rooms, 21 suites, 7,500 square feet of state-of-the-art function space, two restaurants, three bars/lounges, a fresh water swimming pool, tropical gardens and a health club. The second phase of the redevelopment of the site included a banking and business office complex.

British Colonial Hilton restored to its original splendour in 1997

The RHK Group also completed a multimillion dollar upgrade to the South Ocean Beach Hotel and Golf Club, at the southwestern end of New Providence.

Among the other properties added to the inventory on New Providence were the quaint Compass Point Resort, Love Beach, West Bay Street, and Graycliff's new suites on West Hill Street and restaurant "Humidor", on the site of the new Cigar Factory, which produces 1,500 hand-rolled cigars a day.

On **Grand Bahama,** in 1995, Hutchinson Whampoa, the Hong Kong-based conglomerate, invested US$78 million in a container port project with the Grand Bahama Port Authority and acquired a 50% interest in Freeport International Airport. In 1998, another subsidiary, Hutchinson Lucaya Ltd. embarked on construction of a large hotel complex in Freeport—*Our Lucaya*, later becoming *Westin* and *Sheraton* brands.

Hutchinson Whompoa's Our Lucaya

To increase investment in the **Family Islands**, the Government amended the Hotels Encouragement Act in 1993, making it possible for hotels with as little as four rooms to become eligible for customs duty concessions. With the introduction of Local Government in 1996, Family Island Administrators and Councillors began to play a more active role in the hotel licensing process.

Among the new or refurbished properties that came on stream were the deluxe *Pink Sands Hotel* on Harbour Island, the *Tiamo Resort* in South Andros, *Musha Cay* resort in the Exuma Cays, and *Different of Abaco* in Casuarina Point, Abaco. A number of new bonefishing and bed and breakfast properties throughout the Islands were established, many of them owned by Bahamians.

The island of Exuma received a massive economic injection with the entry of the upscale Four Seasons brand to The Bahamas. The 200-room 60-suite Four Seasons Resort at Emerald Bay, which opened in Fall 2003 in Great Exuma, boasts a Greg Norman designed 18-hole par-72, 6,880-yard golf course, featuring six ocean-side

Four Seasons at Emerald Bay, Exuma, under construction

The 200-room 60-suite Four Seasons resort at Emerald Bay, Exuma, opened in fall 2003 and has revitalized the island's economy

holes with spectacular views and innovative, environmentally friendly seashore fairways, a plush spa and fitness centre, a 17-acre 100-slip full-service marina, three fresh water pools, two ocean-front restaurants, four tennis courts and full water sports. Employing over 400 people, many of whom are housed in the resort's 320-room staff housing complex, Four Seasons has created numerous economic linkages throughout the island. Even with an average room rate of $600 per night, the resort has had high occupancies from the day it opened its doors.

On the debit side, Club Med in Governor's Harbour, Eleuthera, which employed hundreds of Eleutherans, closed its doors in November 2001, shortly after the devastation of Hurricane Michelle. This began a long period of depression for that island.

During the 1992-2002 period, there was no increase in total available hotel rooms, as can be noted from Appendix 7, because many older properties were demolished or taken out of service for refurbishing. However, this massive upgrading exercise, particularly on New Providence, Abaco and Exuma, has led to a reversal of the image, an increase in room rates and occupancy in Nassau/Paradise Island, translating into higher visitor expenditure.

The PLP, headed by Prime Minister Perry Christie, re-elected in 2002, announced its determination to maintain tourism as the primary engine of economic growth and source of employment in the country. As a result, investment further accelerated, with the Family Islands taking centre stage, starting with the re-opening of Club Med on San Salvador.

Club Med, San Salvador

Under its new Minister, the Honourable Obediah Wilchcombe, the Ministry of Tourism was required to address the negative impact of the 9/11 crisis, which had severely hampered travel to The Bahamas, as well as deal with the effect of the war of Iraq on the travel industry. Luckily, the result was not as severe as anticipated, as The Bahamas was able to capitalize on its proximity to North America.

The Ministry of Tourism began restructuring to take advantage of marketing opportunities and revamp the product. Emphasis was placed on the Florida-Bahamas and Latin American markets, sports, religious and other niche markets.

Goals were set to improve the distribution of tourism income to Grand Bahama and the Family Islands, while creating greater linkages between tourism and other sectors. Steps were taken to accelerate the availability of market data derived from the Immigration card so that the Ministry could make informed marketing decisions. Attempts were also made to improve the effectiveness of online booking agents, and to aggressively target the film industry. A Czar was to be empowered to improve all aspects of the product and to integrate local culture into the tourism experience.

Development of tourist facilities continued to take place throughout The Bahamas. On the island of Abaco, Peter de Savary, resort developer, began construction of the $160 million Abaco Club on Winding Bay. The new resort consists of 70 environmentally friendly two- and three-bedroom cottages, each with a view of the incredibly beautiful bay and beach and amenities, such as a large circular club house, ultra modern spa and exercise facility, stable, golf course and golf academy. The first phase of the resort was completed in December 2004, and attempts are being made to provide its members and visitors with a true Bahamian experience, in terms of architecture, cuisine, landscaping, and culture. Navigation of the 500-acre property is by golf carts or on foot. When completed, it is projected that the Club will employ 250 persons, 98% of whom are expected to be Bahamian.

In 2004, Prime Minister Christie announced the signing of a Heads of Agreement with the owners of the Atlantis resort, Paradise Island, for the completion of Phase III of that hotel development. The addition to the Atlantis facility includes a new 1,200 room hotel at Pirate's Cove, along with three new villas at the Ocean Club, 20,000 square feet of additional restaurant and retail facilities, 120 two-bedroom timeshare units fronting on Nassau Harbour, 50,000 square feet of additional convention facilities and a world-class ecologically sensitive golf course. Scheduled for completion in December 2006, this expansion will create an additional 2,000 jobs and will constitute an increase to $1.7 billion total investment by this group in The Bahamas.

The effect of Hurricanes and Fire Damage on Tourism Infrastructure

Between 1992 and 2004, The Bahamas experienced several major natural disasters. This was the most active period ever recorded for hurricanes—*Hurricane Andrew* in August 1992, *Floyd* in 1999, and *Michelle* in 2001 caused severe damage to homes, other buildings, roads, seawalls, marinas, causeways, bridges, and shorelines. While most of the hotels were spared, there was much disruption in the tourism industry, primarily in the Family Islands, as a result of damage from storm surges. Potential visitors were also deterred from coming to the country because of misperceptions as to the true nature of the hurricane damage.

In 2004, the hospitality industry suffered the most devastating blow. As a result of two Category 3 and 4 hurricanes, *Frances* and *Jeanne*, hotels on Abaco, Grand Bahama and San Salvador suffered extensive damages, while properties on other islands experienced some damage.

Boats swept into the streets of Abaco during Hurricane Jeanne in 2004

After Bonefish Foley's home (West End, Grand Bahama) was totally destroyed in the hurricane, the American Ambassador, John Rood, spearheaded the drive to construct a new home for him

In 2001, a fire which started in the Straw Market, destroys the entire complex including the office of the Ministry of Tourism. Photo by Vincent Vanderpool Wallace

Only a shell remains after the Straw Market/Ministry of Tourism fire in 2001

The tourist infrastructure was also disrupted when fire destroyed the Nassau Straw Market and the Ministry of Tourism building in 2001, the Exuma International Airport in 2004 and the San Andros Airport in 2005. The Nassau Straw Market was moved to a large tent on Bay Street, and Ministry of Tourism's head office was housed for four years in the Business Centre of the British Colonial Hotel, and various other buildings throughout New Providence. Modular buildings were acquired as temporary air terminals for those damaged at Exuma and San Andros.

Fire destroys Exuma International Air Terminal in May 2004

International carriers continue to land following the Airport fire thanks to the cooperation of Immigration and Customs officers

New modular buildings completed to house Exuma Air Terminal

San Andros Airport burns to the ground in 2004

Policy Changes at the Ministry of Tourism over the period 1993 to 2004

In January 1993, Harvard-educated Vincent Vanderpool Wallace, then Vice President of Resorts International, Paradise Island, was appointed Director General of Tourism. He replaced Baltron Bethel, the first Bahamian Director General of Tourism, who had been his mentor when he started his career in both the Ministries of Education and Tourism.

The new Director General put in place the following new **Mission** statement for the Ministry of Tourism:

> *To make it increasingly easier to create, sell, and deliver satisfying vacations to the individual Islands of The Bahamas; satisfying to those who work in the tourism industry and live in The Bahamas; satisfying to those who invest in the industry; and satisfying to our visitors.*

The mission statement was intended to reflect the need to emphasize that the main purpose and overriding goal of the Ministry must be the provision of a satisfying visitor experience. A satisfied visitor is more likely to return year after year, to spend generously and thereby contribute to the success of the tourism industry.

Under the new leadership, a business plan was developed. The plan, which would be updated annually, would identify key factors critical to Tourism's success as well as fresh new strategies and tactics for dealing with major issues.

Of greatest importance would be the establishment of the "closer Caribbean", thus marketing the country as a diverse multi-island region, with a variety of highly differentiated vacations, thereby eliminating the perception that once you have seen one island in The Bahamas, you have seen them all.

Other priorities included increasing the availability of low-

Vincent Vanderpool Wallace lauded by Travel Agent magazine for his Innovative initiatives as Director General of Tourism in The Bahamas

cost, quality transportation to and within the islands, providing a more positive experience for cruise passengers, initiating direct-marketing programmes to past visitors, and the restoration of group business.

To assist him in carrying out these objectives, a small team was mobilized within the Ministry and included, among others, Ms. Vernice Walkine, who was appointed Deputy Director General of Tourism.

New management team—Turnquest, Vanderpool Wallace, Walkine featured on cover of travel Agent magazine

Marketing the diverse products

Marketing of The Islands of The Bahamas was contracted to advertising agencies Bozell, New York, and Irma S. Mann, Boston, on a fee basis.

Recognizing that product, services, and promotion must all work together, the role of the agencies was expanded to include participation in the development of the overall tourism business plan, and not simply to develop advertising and promotion plans. The private sector became an even more active partner in the planning process. Selected Tourism employees were given exposure, through secondment to advertising agencies, offshore and onshore public relations agencies, the Bahamas Hotel Association, the three promotion Boards, and various hotels.

It Just Keeps Getting Better—The New Communications Programme

With the improvements, which were anticipated in The Bahamas tourism product, an integrated marketing communications plan was launched to convey a more positive, realistic image for The Bahamas. Recognizing that the slogan "It's Better in The Bahamas" continued to enjoy high awareness in the marketplace, the slogan was initially reinstated in a tag line but with a more realistic and credible twist: ***The Islands of The Bahamas: It Just Keeps Getting Better.***

There were several other marketing achievements which created a competitive edge. The first involved the buy-out in 1994 of the toll free number 1-800-BAHAMAS, which many years ago had been secured by another agency. This ***1-800-Bahamas*** toll free number now appears on all advertising related to Bahamas tourism, increasing the ease with which a visitor or travel trade partner can contact a Bahamas representative.

To further improve the probability of converting an information call to a sale, a second initiative was introduced, namely the establishment of a special Bahamas tour operator, *Destination Bahamas.* The main objective here was to prevent leakage of business to competing destinations, to reduce the number of cases of excessive markup on Bahamas packages and to expand the number of properties, destinations and features which could be instantly sold, with special attention to small hotels and resorts.

With the increase in Internet usage, the Ministry of Tourism's new Web site *bahamas.com* was launched. All the major tourism related businesses were represented on the site and invited to update their own content. Agents and consumers could now access updated Bahamas information or packages from their office or home at any time of the day or night. The Ministry of Tourism was on the cutting edge of the new technology. It became the first Caribbean organization to introduce the various computer networks throughout its worldwide system, thus greatly improving communication and effectiveness. *Tourismbahamas.org,* the Internet site designed primarily for use by tourism employees, investors and industry partners, was launched in 2004.

Promoting Individual Islands

Trade marketing research revealed that, in addition to the negative commercial image of The Bahamas, travel professionals and the media seem to be more acquainted with two of The Bahamas tourist destinations, namely, Nassau/Paradise Island and Grand Bahama. The brand *The Islands of The Bahamas* was introduced, to create awareness in the marketplace that The Bahamas was a destination of many islands, a mini-Caribbean without the hassles of border restrictions. This message was effectively portrayed through ads as well as a series of well choreographed and entertaining "Preview" Shows for the travel trade throughout North America. While "Family Islands" was the term used within the country, the magical name "Out Islands", with which the trade was familiar, was restored in the market place; in addition, promotions and communications campaigns attempted to move beyond "Family Islands" to create awareness for individual islands.

In 1995, Weber Shandwick, New York, was engaged to create a comprehensive public relations campaign to market The Bahamas to US travellers. The agency developed many programmes, one of which was The **Bahamas Weather Conference.**

Recognizing that hurricanes are the number one threat to the continued growth and stability of tourism in The Bahamas, and that meteorologists, in their television coverage, often referred to "The Bahamas" rather than the individual islands in the archipelago, it was decided to educate the media about the multiplicity of islands so that they could better inform their audience that a threat to one island in The Bahamas or the Caribbean does not necessarily pose a threat to the entire region. In other words, while the Ministry of Tourism cannot control the weather, it can attempt to educate the media, travel professionals and the public so that travel decisions can be made based on accurate, precise information.

In establishing the Weather Conference, the strategy was to use meteorologists to call attention to The Bahamas by instilling in them an island-specific vocabulary and perspective when reporting on hurricanes, while developing an alumni meteorologist network in The Bahamas' top US markets. Because the event was organized in partnership with the National Weather Association and the National Hurricane Center, its credibility was ensured.

Planning for this event involved creating a production-friendly "uplink island" with all the technical equipment and crew needed to work directly with local stations and allowing the meteorologists and their producers to set up the right interviews, activities and background materials to develop unscripted and entertaining weather segments.

The Bahamas' choice to address hurricanes directly has developed an impressive list of historical results. For example, direct communication from the Bahamas News Bureau during *Hurricane Dennis* prompted *USA Today* to change its hurricane coverage from the Associated Press story to be more detailed, specific and accurate. Jack Williams, Weather Page Editor of *USA Today*, added Nassau to the weather map after attending an early Bahamas Weather Conference. Weather Conference alumni like Bryan Norcross, meteorologist for WFOR-CBS in Miami, now identify specific Bahamian islands when covering hurricanes, as during *Hurricane Michelle*.

On 2-6 April, 2003, with tanks 15 miles outside of Baghdad and advancing, meteorologists at the 7th Bahamas Weather Conference produced 127 live and taped segments from the peaceful sands of Atlantis, Paradise Island. If converted to advertising time, these segments would equal more than 500 30-second commercials.

Indeed, the *Bahamas Weather Conference* created resounding third-party endorsements of the destination, delivered by the favourite television personality of millions of viewers and vacationers across North America—the weatherperson.

Weather conference: Top weather personalities from network and cable stations broadcast from The Bahamas throughout the weather conference

Film Promotion

The natural beauty of The Islands of The Bahamas, combined with the warm hospitality and excellent service of the Bahamas Film Bureau, continued to provide the essential ingredients for the attraction of films, commercials and catalogue fashion shoots.

Production crews from Europe, the United States and Canada visited The Islands of The Bahamas and produced a wide variety of shows, including CBS' *60 Minutes*, which profiled Sean Connery, British actor, at his home in Lyford Cay and the Oprah Winfrey Show.

Various segments of movies were shot in The Bahamas, such as My *Father the Hero*, in 1993; *Flipper,* 1996; *Zeus and Roxanne, Speed 2* and *Cruise Control,* which had originally been slated for production in St. Maarten in 1997 and the James Bond movie *The World is Not Enough*. Other productions included the British Broadcasting Corporation's documentary *Navy in Action* shot on Eleuthera, *Weddings of a Lifetime* one-hour television documentary, and Emmy Award winning *Victory Gardens* filmed on Eleuthera. Al Roker of the *Today Show* highlighted his island roots through the production of an interesting feature story on Exuma.

E-Marketing

One of the most significant marketing initiatives during the new millennium was the decision, in late 2003, to partner with Expedia as the booking agent for the Ministry of Tourism's Web site *bahamas.com*. Because Expedia, the leading online travel provider in the world and one of the top 75 visited Web sites on the Internet, also serves as the booking engine for approximately 20,000 affiliate sites (such as MSN.com and Delta.com), it has a wide reach. Expedia spends over $250 million dollars on marketing each year to drive consumers to the site. With a dedicated staff of telesales agents, Expedia provides a low-cost way to market one's product to consumers in weekly merchandising and special promotions and through a five-page electronic brochure with space for up to 20 photographs, which it supplies to its partners. The partnership with Expedia enables The Bahamas to be on the cutting edge of technology and market all of The Islands of The Bahamas to millions of people each day.

The Bahamas at Smithsonian

The promotion of The Bahamas received an added boost when the country's culture was displayed at the Smithsonian Institution's Festival of American Folklife in Washington, D.C. from July 1-10, 1994. The annual festival, initiated by Smithsonian in 1967, is the national and international model for research-based presentations of living culture throughout the world. It is Smithsonian's "museum without walls", staged outdoors at the National Mall, between the Washington Monument and the US capital.

The objective of this annual cultural exhibition of traditional music, craft, occupational skills, verbal arts and foods, is to encourage the research, preservation and conservation of culture. The Bahamas was invited to participate in the Festival as a result of discussions and meetings initiated by the Bahamas Embassy in Washington, headed by Ambassador Baswell Donaldson. Cabinet approved The Bahamas' participation and designated the Ministry of Tourism as the lead agency. Angela Cleare served as the Administrative Coordinator and Dr. Gail Saunders, Director or Archives, was named Bahamas Curator for the project. Dr. Saunders selected scholars and artists to produce research broken down in four clusters—Music and Dance; Junkanoo; Craft, Food, Boatbuilding and other Traditional Occupations; and Narrative and Ethnic Groups. Following detailed research throughout The Islands of The Bahamas, a 100-member team of presenters and artisans were selected to represent the traditional culture of The Bahamas.

Temporary replicas of various elements of the Bahamian community— traditional church, rock oven, clapboard house, a "big yard", story porch, Junkanoo shack—erected on the National Mall—provided natural settings in which participants demonstrated their arts and craft skills, Junkanoo costume design and construction, boat-building, farming, basket-weaving, plaiting, quilting, story telling, food preparation, bush medicine, music and dance. In addition to the daily demonstrations and performances, there was a spectacular Junkanoo "Rush Out" on the Washington Mall on 4th July holiday, which attracted huge crowds.

An estimated 1½ million persons visited the Folklife Exhibition in Washington during the eight days of the Festival and approximately 40 million were reached through the media. It is estimated that the Festival generated exposure equivalent to $8-12 million in paid advertising. The event was so spectacular that the Junkanoo contingent was invited two years later to perform at the festival on the occasion of the 150th anniversary of the Smithsonian Institution. This 1996 performance again made a huge impact.

The Smithsonian experience, in particular, the tremendous success of the delegation, evoked renewed national pride back home and a greater interest in authentic culture. The event resulted in the production of a Culture workbook for schools, as well as a full array of archival records, documents, photographs and educational material which adhered to the high standards of Smithsonian.

Bahamas Government dignitaries, led by the curator, watch a bush medicine demonstration by Daisy Nottage (Andros). Left to right: Hon. Theresa Moxey Ingraham (Minister of Social Development), Kirk Ingraham, Mrs. Algernon Allen, Hon. Brent Symonette (Minister of Tourism), Dr. Gail Saunders (Director of Archives and Curator for The Bahamas), and Mrs. Brent Symonette

Henry Wallace (right), woodcarver from Andros, demonstrates his craft

Hon. Brent Symonette, Minister of Tourism (right), whose Ministry spearheaded The Bahamas exhibit in Washington, and James C. Early from the Smithsonian

Dr. Gail Saunders (right) who served as curator for The Bahamas presentation at Smithsonian, leads a walkabout after the Opening Ceremony. To her right is Hon. Algernon Allen, Minister of Youth and Culture

Folk artist Amos Ferguson demonstrates his painting. His wife, Bloneva, is at right. In conjunction with this event, a full exhibition of Amos Ferguson's paintings was also staged at one of Smithsonian's galleries

Israel Forbes (from Andros) plays tunes on his guitar reminiscent of Joseph Spence

Boatbuilding area. Among the tradition bearers representing The Bahamas in boatbuilding were Joseph Albury (Abaco), Kingston Brown (Andros), and Bertis Knowles (Long Island)

Cat Island Mites, led by Osborne King, thrill the crowds in the Music and Dance tent

John "Chippie" Chipman, on stage at the Smithsonian

On the Craft porch, Eloise Smith (left) along with Lorna Kemp, Peggy and William Colebrook, Viola Collie, Wendy Kelly Elsie Knowles and Olga Major demonstrated various types of straw craft found in the various Islands of The Bahamas

The Dicey Doh group performs a capella on the music stage

Old Story Time with Dr. Cleveland Eneas (on porch). Dr. Eneas was a hit on the Story Porch, along with other story tellers such as Derek Burrows, Sheddie Cox (Inagua) and Mabel Williams (San Salvador). The researchers/presenters included Tracey Thompson (on porch—left) Kim Outten, and Grace Turner

Derek Burrows performing on the Story Porch

Junkanoo at Smithsonian. The performance was coordinated by a team from the Junkanoo Leaders Association—Gus Cooper, Vola Francis, Stan Burnside and Ronald Simms

At Smithsonian—Angela Cleare of Ministry of Tourism and Harry Cooper. Harry Cooper was also a graduate of the first birdwatching course and became an accredited birdwatching tour guide

The team from the Ministry of Tourism who handled the administration of the Festival. From left: Andrea Coakley, Angela Cleare, Project Coordinator/Chief Administrator, Valerie Gaitor, Frederica Cartwright and Adrian Archer

The Onshore Experience

Arawak Cay—a Meeting Place for Down-Home Native Food and Culture

Following the Smithsonian experience, the Arawak Cay *Fish Fry* was developed into a heritage site. The *Fish Fry* had evolved over the years as young entrepreneurs built vending outlets on the Arawak Cay property for cooked-to-order native seafood dishes and conch salad.

Arawak Cay, West Bay Street

At the initiative of the Honourable Frank Watson, then Deputy Prime Minister and Minister of Tourism, $3 million was invested in Arawak Cay to construct a permanent stage, changing rooms, modern toilet facilities, an attractive narrative porch for small intimate productions and story telling, a rock oven, an administrative building in the style of a quaint Island house, proper landscaping, parking facilities, sidewalks, and a Police Station. The objective of the park was to create a safe cultural village where Bahamians and tourists could gather for a "taste of the real Bahamas", and provide a venue for artisans to market their products and skills, thus, exposing the rich culture of The Bahamas, while creating income for local Bahamians.

The Heritage Village at Arawak Cay became a popular site for annual festivals and special events organized by the Ministry of Tourism, the Ministry of Youth Sports & Culture and the Bahamas Agricultural and Industrial Corporation

(BAIC)—*BahamArts & Seafood Festival, Junkanoo in June, Bahamas Heritage Festival*, among others. The "Fish Fry" concept soon began to spread to several Family Islands.

Baking bread in the rock oven at Exuma Music and Heritage Festival, Exuma

Authentically Bahamian Gifts and Souvenirs

Recognizing that visitors to The Bahamas spend approximately $150 million annually on souvenirs, with a large proportion being expended on imported items, a concerted effort was made to increase local employment opportunities through an *Authentically Bahamian* Unit within the Ministry of Tourism. The Unit promotes locally made craft and souvenir items through trade shows, craft fairs, joint promotions with hotels, Bahamas Tourist Offices throughout the world, brochures, competitions, and the Web site. Additionally, these items are promoted at major conferences and have become preferred gifts for VIP's.

The Unit also organizes an annual workshop for Artisans to improve their skills in presenting and marketing their products. As a result of this initiative, there has been a marked increase in the quality and quantity of souvenir products available for sale in the country. In addition to the Ministry of Tourism's initiatives, BAIC, in conjunction with Atlantis, opened a Craft Market on Paradise Island, to showcase local products.

Rowena Rolle (2nd from right) introduces Prime Minister Christie to an artisan at annual Authentically Bahamian trade show

Bernadette Christie (front right), wife of the Prime Minister, tours booths after opening the 2005 Authentically Bahamian trade show

Straw craft in The Bahamas has become the best in the region

Angela Cleare, Sr. Director Product and Vernice Walkine, Director General (left), view Artisans' displays with Governor General, Dame Ivy Dumont (right), at 2004 Authentically Bahamian Trade Show

Traditional straw craft at Red Bays, North Andros

Indigenous Culinary Arts gain international exposure

During the decade of the 1990's, authentic Bahamian cuisine gained in popularity among visitors and Bahamians. In an article on *Foodways*, Julia Burnside, head of the Ministry of Tourism's Culinary Arts division, traces the evolution of local dishes and describes how each island has been able to lay claim to specific dishes (such as wild hog on Inagua, pigeon peas soup on Exuma, flour cake on Cat Island, coconut/pineapple tarts on Eleuthera, crab and coconut dishes on Andros, bonnevis soup on Grand Bahama).[10]

Through the Culinary Arts division of the Ministry of Tourism, in cooperation with the Bahamas Culinary Association and the School of Hospitality of the College of The Bahamas, which organized the Great Bahamas Seafood Festival and the annual Bahamas Culinary Classic, local foods are now presented in most creative ways.

The *Bahamas Culinary Classic,* a three-day event designed to raise culinary standards and introduce greater creativity in the use of local products in hotel and restaurant menus, consists of culinary competitions involving top chefs from the major hotels in the country, with judges and certification provided by the American Culinary Federation.

Bahamas Culinary Classic—winning entries in the Signature Dish category

Culinary Arts—A winning entry in the Showpiece category by chef Tracey Sweeting

Judges from American Culinary Federation and Bahamas Culinary Association review entries from top chefs throughout the country

A winner in the 2002 Culinary Classic is congratulated by Minister of Tourism, Obie Wilchcombe (3rd from right) and Minister of Agriculture & Fisheries, Alfred Gray (right)

Julia Burnside, coordinator of the Culinary Classic from Ministry of Tourism and Head Judge Kensella announce winners

Edwin Johnson, Master chef, one of the instructors and judges for the prestigious culinary awards, points out that, even though most chefs in major hotels were imported until the 1980's, the influence of Bahamian "cooks" has been significant as far back as the 1800's when Bahamian specialties such as turtle pie and turtle soup could be found on menus at the Royal Victoria Hotel.

He further asserts that as local Bahamians received training as chefs following the establishment of the Bahamian Hotel Training College, creativity in local foods became more evident and Bahamians qualified for the top positions as chefs in the various hotels and restaurants.

Berkeley Williamson became the first qualified Bahamian sommelier (wine steward) in 1971 at the Nassau Technical College and Highbury Technical College, Portsmouth, England. He headed the Food and Beverage departments of several hotels, and later became the first Bahamian Chief Training Officer at the Bahamas Hotel Training College and at the University of the West Indies, Bahamas campus.

Berkeley Williamson (left), first Chief Training Officer at the Bahamas Hotel Training College, played an important role in the upgrading of chefs

During his presidency of the Bahamas Hotel Association, Robert Sands placed special emphasis on the introduction of Bahamian dishes on hotel menus, as new creative specialties, such as blackened conch, became standard favourites.

Local bartenders also established specialty drinks. Supplementing the traditional *Rum Punch, Gin & Coconut Water*, and *Pina Colada*, were new additions, such as *Goombay Smash, Yellow Bird, Bahama Mama*, and *Bahamian Delight*, blending Caribbean rums, juices, syrups and garnish into potent island drinks.

By the 1990's, The Bahamas was one of the main contenders in regional and international culinary competitions, capturing annual awards. In 2004, an all-Bahamian team of chefs competed successfully in the Culinary Olympics in Germany, bringing home two culinary Olympic Bronze medals.

One of the showpieces displayed by Bahamian chefs at the Culinary Olympics In Germany

Bahamas team at Culinary Olympics in Germany

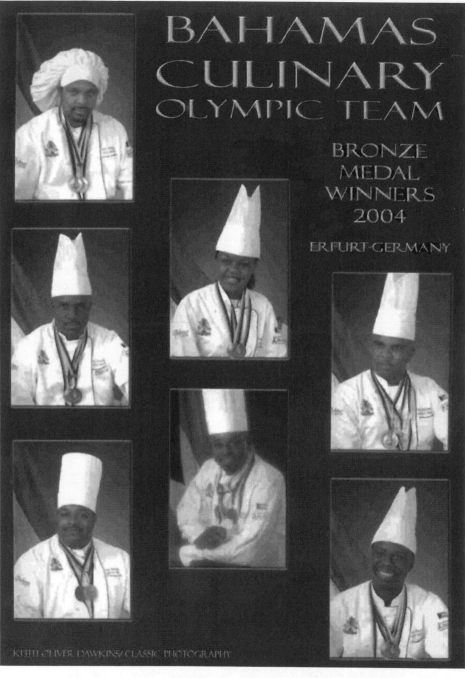

Chefs on The Bahamas team proudly show off their bronze medals at the Culinary Olympics in Germany. The National Olympic team consisted of Tracey Sweeting, Wayne Munroe, Jason McBride, Basil Dean, Emmanuel Gibson, Jasmine Young and Alpheus Ramsey.

Small Treasures—a new hotel brand

With well-known large hotel brands—Sandals, SuperClubs, Hilton, Marriott, Radisson—operating in The Bahamas—an attempt was made to develop a special brand of distinctive, charming small hotels through the *Small Treasures* programme.

Guided by regulations set by the Nassau/Paradise Island Small Hotels Committee, hotels were required to undergo inspection by an independent Travel Agent Advisory Board, which selected hotels for inclusion under the brand name. Those properties which qualified, based on both facilities and service, were promoted internationally through the Ministry of Tourism's marketing network.

The revitalization of Bay Street

In keeping with Government's revitalization of Bay Street, several Bay Street stores improved their facilities. John Bull led the way in expanding its operation. With the closure of the Nassau Shop, the Hazlewood family acquired the prime location, 284 Bay Street, in 1996 and completed major refurbishment before re-opening its flagship store, John Bull, with six departments including Leather, Perfume & Cosmetics, Tobacco, Jewellery, Watches and Cameras, and world-renowned designer products. John Bull described itself as the "Shopping Paradise of the Islands".

John Bull has an interesting history. In 1929, Asa Pritchard (later knighted) opened an Old English Tobacco House "*John Bull*", on Bay Street north, just east of East Street. It was named after a character in the British satire, "Law is a Bottomless Pit", written in 1712. John Bull represented a stout Englishman wearing a top hat, waistcoat, knickers and high boots. At that time, when England was known for its famous Woodbine cigarettes and Briar pipes, John Bull Tobacconist prospered, catering to local residents and tourists. John Bull in downtown Nassau continued as

John Bull—the centrepiece of Bay Street

a tobacco shop until the 1950's, when Sir Asa's children and their families injected new ideas, capital and product lines into the business. John Bull has become the centrepiece of Bay Street.[11]

Recognizing deteriorating conditions in general in the downtown Nassau, in 2004 the Prime Minister engaged EDAW, a renowned international land planning and design firm, to develop a Master plan for the area. The charge given to EDAW was to recapture the vitality and romance of the Nassau of yesteryear. The first phase of the master planning process was launched as part of EDAW's internationally renowned intern programme. The 19-member group of professional interns addressed the relocation of the commercial shipping port and identified regeneration strategies for multiple areas of downtown with unique character along the waterfront. The concept developed by the students was fine-tuned by EDAW's professional staff in cooperation with Bahamian professionals. The planning process involved active and continuous consultation with stakeholder groups including the Nassau Economic Development Council, the Nassau Tourism Development Board, the Ministries of Tourism and Works, and the Hotel Corporation of The Bahamas.

Envisioned in the master plan are pedestrian-friendly Bahamian spaces, full of life and culture, resort uses and Bahamian businesses. The natural and man-made boundaries of the study suggested seven distinct districts. Seven catalyst projects, one for each district, were identified, representing the initial steps towards translating the vision into tangible results. The objective was to transform historic Nassau, from Fort Montagu to Arawak Cay, into one of the most attractive harbour cities in the hemisphere. The seven projects—the Government Green, Downtown Waterfront,

The National Art Gallery opens during the 30th Anniversary of Independence Celebrations in 2003, adding significantly to the cultural treasures of downtown Nassau

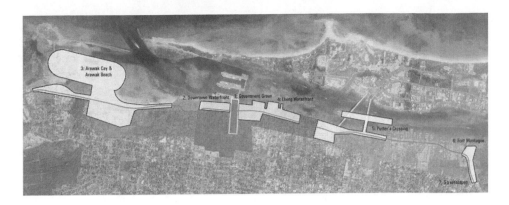

The 7 projects identified in EDAW's Plan for Downtown Nassau

Arawak Cay and Beach, Living Waterfront, Potters Crossing, Fort Montagu Harbour and Streetscapes—seek to increase property values, tourist spending and entrepreneurial opportunities. By mid 2006, negotiations were underway for the port relocation to southwest New Providence, establishment of a Business Improvement District and a Downtown Improvement District, with accompanying duty exemptions, code enforcement strategies and incentives.[12]

Lynn Holowesko becomes the first Ambassador for the Environment in 1995. Photo shows Holowesko (centre) as Chair of the Quincentennial Commission celebrating, Christopher Columbus' landfall in San Salvador, Bahamas in 1492

Ecotourism and Sustainable Tourism Development

Following participation in the Earth Summit, The Bahamas became a key player, like other countries, in sustainable initiatives. In 1995, the Government established a special agency—the *Bahamas Environment Science and Technology* (BEST) *Commission,* and named an Ambassador for the Environment. Though not a regulatory agency, BEST coordinates environmental initiatives of the Bahamas Government and ensures that the country complies with international regulations on environmental protection. The Ministry of Tourism is one of the agencies that serves on the Board of Directors which governs the Commission.

Another indication of Government's full commitment to the environment was the doubling of the national park network. In April 2002, the Prime Minister announced the addition of national parks to be placed under the management of the Bahamas National Trust, increasing the total acreage of parks from 320,000 to 644,000 acres.

The Bahamas National Trust receives the 1988 Cacique Award for its achievements in managing the national parks system and conservation of natural resources. Glenn Bannister, President of BNT, accepts the award on behalf of the Trust.

Pericles Maillis leads a tour of the primeval forest in New Providence

Harrold and Wilson Pond, Nassau, one of the new national parks announced by the Prime Minister in 2002, and developed by BNT in 2006

The Department of Fisheries became more proactive in environmental and biodiversity protection by establishing the first five of a network of marine protected areas and protecting spawning aggregations of the Nassau Grouper.

The Ministry of Tourism established a Sustainable Tourism and Ecotourism division. This division coordinated a Sustainable Tourism strategy for the Family Islands, in cooperation with the Organisation of American States (OAS), awareness programmes including annual Ecotourism Awareness and Coastal Awareness Months, environmental education seminars for segments of the community, including hoteliers, students and the general public, in cooperation with the Bahamas National Trust, the Bahamas Hotel Association, and the Caribbean Association for Sustainable Tourism (CAST). Environmentally friendly Bahamian hotels such as Higgins Landing on Exuma, Tiamo Resort on South Andros and Comfort Suites on Paradise Island have qualified for international sustainable tourism awards.

Environmentally friendly hotel—Tiamo Resort, South Andros—has received numerous sustainable tourism awards

Prime Minister Perry Christie (left) chats with the Hartmans at Tiamo Resort

A representative from National Geographic Traveller visits Tiamo to present Sustainable tourism award

In an attempt to develop Ecotourism as a niche market, the Ministry of Tourism also established a certification programme for birdwatching tour guides in cooperation with the Bahamas National Trust and the National Audubon Society. In recognition of some of its environmental planning initiatives, the Ministry of Tourism received a World Travel and Tourism Council (WTTC) Green Globe award.

A birding field trip

Birding Experts: From right—Paul Dean, Sandy Sprunt and Lynn Gape of the Bahamas National Trust serve as instructors in birding certification course sponsored by Ministry of Tourism. Sandra Buckner (left), past President of the Bahamas National Trust, is also an ardent birder

Legends in Bahamian conservation (from left) Pericles Maillis, Oris Russell and Alexander Sprunt III, receive a special award from the Society for the Conservation and Study of Bahamian Birds

A student, Anithia Butler, from Xavier's wins 1996 International Marine Life Poster Contest for Youth, supported by the United Nations. Pictured at the award presentation from left: Diane Cepero, Headmistress, Xavier's Lower School, Anithia, Angela Cleare, Ministry of Tourism and Sir Nicholas Nuttall, Bahamas Reef Environment Educational Foundation (BREEF)

Earlston McPhee (centre) is presented an award for his initiatives in sustainable tourism development. Also pictured, from left, are Frank Comito (Bahamas Hotel Associatrion), Vernice Walkine (Director General of Tourism), Jeremy McVean (Chair of BHA's environmental committee) and Colin Higgs, Permanent Secretary, Tourism

Cacique Awards

In 1995, the Cacique Award programme was inaugurated to honour "Tourism's finest". Replacing the National Tourism Achievement Awards, the objective was to use a prestigious academy-award format to recognize the leadership roles played by those individuals and organizations whose performance or products have consistently made a positive impact on the quality and the growth of tourism in The Bahamas.

The use of the name *Cacique* pays tribute to the original inhabitants of The Bahamas, the Lucayan Indians, who called their leader "Cacique", and who greeted European visitors with great warmth. As the supreme figure of authority, the Cacique would administer justice, resolve disputes, and receive visitors in much the same way as a leader today.

The Cacique Awards ceremony is now recognized as the highest honour for tourism in The Bahamas. Winners receive a mounted trophy and a pin in the shape of a duho, the seat of power of the Lucayans, the original inhabitants of The Bahamas. The original design of the duho portion of the trophy was the work of the talented Bahamian artist, Quentin Minnis. The expertly carved mahogany base, upon which Cacique Awards are mounted, is the work of Gilbert Elliston of Hopedale Centre, Highbury Park, Nassau. The Bahamas Hotel Association contributed the design of the duho to the Cacique Awards when the hotel industry awards were incorporated into the national awards.

The Lifetime recipient receives a special duho ring, a cash prize of $1,500 and an equal amount is donated to the charity of the recipient's choice, courtesy of the Royal Bank of Canada, the major sponsor of the award from its inception to 2004. Some of the national heroes selected by the Blue Ribbon Panel are spotlighted at the end of this book.

Contributions of Athletes and Musicians to awareness of The Bahamas in the outside world

Tommy Robinson, veteran sprinter, and Andre Rodgers, baseball player, were the first to place The Bahamas on the world track and field and baseball map in the 1950's and early 1960's. Robinson won a gold medal in the 220-yard dash in the 1958 Commonwealth Games, and he set a world record for the indoor 300 yards at a meet in Saskatchewan, Canada. Rodgers achieved a major league fielding record as a member of the Chicago Cubs.

Other noteworthy athletic successes for The Bahamas, prior to the 1990's, were a gold medal in yachting earned by Durward Knowles in the 1964 Olympics in Tokyo, and Elisha Obed's Junior Middleweight World Boxing Championship in Paris in 1975.

Starting in the 1990's, unprecedented international recognition was recorded for Bahamian athletes and entertainers. Mychal Thompson made the Los Angeles Lakers team and played in several NBA championships during the period, taking every opportunity to promote his country while in the spotlight. Rick Fox signed a $10 million contract with the Boston Celtics in 1994. In 1996, Mark Knowles, tennis professional, became the first Bahamian to rank in the top 10 in the world for tennis in both singles and doubles. He competed at the US Open in 1994 and won the RCA Championship doubles title in 1995. In 1994, Roger Smith, tennis professional, was the only player at the US Open to take a set from Pete Sampres, the number one ranked player.

Bahamian athletes captured Olympic Games track and field medals. Frank Rutherford was a bronze medalist in 1992, and the 4 x 100 women's relay team won the silver medal at the 1996 Olympics. At the 1995 World Track and Field Championships in Göteborg, Sweden, Troy Kemp won a gold medal and Pauline Davis-Thompson a silver medal.

The greatest athletic triumphs for The Bahamas took place in August 1999, 2000 and 2004. The relay team of Sevatheda Fynes, Chandra Sturrup, Pauline Davis-Thompson, Debbie Ferguson and Eldece Clarke-Lewis captured a gold medal at the World Championships in Seville, Spain, in 1999 and at the Olympic Games in Sydney, Australia, 2000, earning themselves the title of "The Golden Girls". At the 2004 Olympic Games in Athens, Greece, Tonique Williams-Darling achieved a stunning victory when she captured the gold medal in the women's 400-meter competition, and Debbie Ferguson came away with a bronze medal in the women's 200-meter race.

Golden Girls pose after winning medals

Golden Girls at 2000 Olympics in Sydney Australia

In the musical field, the group *BahaMen* captured the attention of the world with their release "*Who Let the Dogs Out*" in July 2000. BahaMen's album dominated the U.S. Top Ten for the rest of 2000, reaching triple platinum status in only four months while also achieving Top Ten status in no less then twelve countries. The song won a Grammy Award for Best Dance Recording in 2000, and was included in the soundtrack of several movies including *Rug Rats in Paris*. The group also received a Billboard Award for World Music Album of the Year as well as a Nickelodeon Kids Choice Award for "Favorite Song". The song rang out mightily in Shea Stadium, New York, in 2001 when the New York Mets won the National League pennant. The success of BahaMen, as well as that of the Golden Girls and other athletes, generated tremendous publicity for The Bahamas.

BahaMen wins a Grammy for Best Song—Who Let the Dogs Out

Tourism Performance—Quality versus Quantity

In the mid 1990's, extensive work was carried out on the redesign of the Immigration card to deliver greater market intelligence. At the time, a huge backlog of unprocessed cards led to a delay in the publishing of visitor statistics for the guidance of tourist offices and agencies. When this problem was corrected in 2003, The Bahamas again became the undisputed leader in market research.

From 1993, in an attempt to measure the success of the new initiatives designed to encourage higher visitor spending, the tourism statistics reported to the public and in the press placed greater emphasis on visitor nights and visitor revenue than on "head count" or total visitor arrivals. While visitor arrivals continued to climb, emphasis was placed on attracting upscale visitors and ensuring that a quality product was in place to satisfy visitor demand. The investment in the facilities, events and new marketing programmes led to the attraction of a higher quality visitor. In 1993, 28% of visitors to The Bahamas had annual household incomes of more than $80,000 per year. By the year 2001, more than 60% of visitors to The Bahamas had household incomes of more than $80,000 per year. In fact, every year since 1992, The Bahamas attracted a more affluent visitor.

As Appendices 8, 10 and 11 show:

1. Visitor arrivals increased from 3.6 million in 1992 to 5 million in 2004.
2. Air visitors, as a percentage of total arrivals, increased from 1,227,703 (33% of total visitors) in 1992 to 1,368,107 (40% of total visitors) in 1997. This upward movement of air visitors continued until 2001, when global air travel sharply declined because of 9/11.
3. The Bahamas remained dependant on the United States market, with visitor nights from the United States jumping from 74% of total visitor nights in 1992 to 84% by 2004.
4. One non-traditional market that recorded success for a period, with little promotional effort, was Japan. Annual visitors jumped from approximately 500 in the 1980's to a high of 24,000 in 1997, comparable to the number of visitors from Italy, France and Latin America, as shown in Table 10-1.

Table 10-1
Japanese Stopover Visitors to The Bahamas in the 1990's compared to European and Latin American Visitors

	Latin America	Italy	France	Germany	Japan
1980	18,440	3,240	9,670	39,060	570
1994	17,215	19,675	12,450	28,490	13,725
1995	17,980	17,335	15,865	25,100	18,240
1997	24,095	18,390	13,690	20,685	18,750

5. There was a sharp decline in sea visitors starting in 1994. The 1992 level of sea visitors was not surpassed until the year 2000.
6. There was a 1½ million increase in visitor nights from 8.1 million in 1992 to 9.6 million in 1997. By 2004, total visitor nights had reached 9,898,181.
7. Total expenditures by visitors in The Bahamas increased from $1.2 billion in 1992 to $1.8 billion in 2004. The average per visitor stopover

expenditure increased from $809 in 1992 to $1,061 in 2002. While, there was an increase in the per capita visitor expenditure in all three destinations—Nassau/Paradise Island, Grand Bahama, and the Family Islands—the lion's share of the increase was driven by Nassau/Paradise Island, specifically the Atlantis, Paradise Island resort, which attracted a high quality visitor.

Table 10-2
Expenditure by Visitors to The Bahamas
1992 vs. 2002

YEAR	STOPOVER VISITORS	PER CAPITA	CRUISE VISITORS	DAY VISITORS	TOTAL
1992	$1,132,040,949	$809	$102,577,088	$8,934,300	$1,243,552,337
1997	$1,307,443,107	$808	$105,203,398	$3,452,100	$1,416,098,605
2002	$1,605,405,547	$1,061	$151,232,382	$6,022,980	$1,762,660,909

Table 10-3
Average Expenditure Per Visit by Destination in The Bahamas

	Nassau/ P.I	Grand Bahama	Family Islands	Average All Bahamas
1997	$983	$505	$840	$808
2002	$1,256	$664	$1,006	$1,061

Exit surveys also revealed an improvement in visitor satisfaction. During this period, there was an increase in the employment of Bahamians in the industry, since hotels, in order to meet the higher service standards demanded by their upscale guests, increased the number of employees per hotel room.

New efforts devoted to further development of tourism in The Bahamas

Since 2002, the present Minister of Tourism, the Honourable Obie Wilchcombe, has built on the many achievements of his predecessors by emphasizing new initiatives, placing greater emphasis on the Family Islands, diversifying the overseas marketing initiatives and improving the on-shore Product. In June 2005, Vernice Walkine replaced Vincent Vanderpool Wallace as Director General of Tourism, becoming the first female to hold this important post.

Vernice Walkine is handed the baton from Vincent Vanderpool Wallace and becomes
the first female Director General of Tourism. Minister of Tourism, Obie Wilchcombe
(centre), announces the appointment.

Despite the three devastating hurricanes, tourism investment in the individual
Family Islands appears to be at an all-time high. In addition to the Abaco Club
on Winding Bay, Abaco, additional new anchor tourism projects are underway on
Bimini, Abaco, Cat Island, Eleuthera and Mayaguana. Smaller developments are
also planned for other Family Islands.

Abaco Club on Winding Bay, Abaco—now a Ritz Carlton brand

Bimini Bay

The marketing campaign is being refocused and diversified. In 2005, a strong promotional campaign was unveiled in New York, the top market for stopover visitors, when The Bahamas broke through the advertising clutter by placing impactful advertisements in train stations.

Advertising in Grand Central train station, New York.

Bahamas new advertising

Bozell Advertising, NY, account executives who produced Bahamas ads. along with MOT executives Stephanie Toote (GM Advertising, standing right) and Basil Smith (Director Communications, sitting right)

Director General of Tourism, Vernice Walkine (centre) accepts the Ministry of Tourism's Adrian Award for excellence in adverting in 2006

For the first time, the Islands of The Bahamas television advertisements captured the multiple islands of the destination and sent a message to the world that The Bahamas is more than one island and offers more than sun, sand and sea, but a vacation dream with varying enchanting experiences.

Web site marketing was being revolutionized, to benefit the smaller properties, placing them on a level playing field with larger properties. Overseas markets are being expanded beyond the traditional emphasis on the United States, with renewed marketing in Canada and emerging markets such as China and Latin America. Renewed focus is being placed on the religious market, and the advantage of The Bahamas as a group-friendly destination was reestablished. Hi-impact public relations projects have taken centre stage and the onshore public relations effort was strengthened with the unveiling of a new, impactful *My Bahamas: Movement for Improvement* national campaign.

Minister of Tourism, Hon. Obie Wilchcombe (left) shakes the cowbells with a Junkanoo group during an overseas promotion

Royal Bahamas Police Force Band performs outside the Apollo in New York

Tourism representatives, headed by Carla Stuart (left), Director Cruise Development, attended Seatrade 2006 Cruise Shipping Convention and Trade Show at the Miami Beach Convention Center. Seatrade is the leading cruise industry trade show and a meeting place for cruise line visitors and cruise line suppliers

Director General of Tourism presents the Baxter Award in Canada
In photo: Mark Linton (Royal Bank Travel Insurance), Edith Baxter (Baxter Publications) Judd Buchanan (William H. Baxter Lifetime Achievement Honoree), Vernice Walkine (Director General), Marc Rosenburg (Air Canada)

Under the campaign My Bahamas—Movement for Improvement, the importance of preserving local culture is emphazised, with Elon Moxey, a local entertainer

Director General, Vernice Walkine (centre) at press conference in New York in June 2006 announcing new initiatives. Deputy Director General Ellison Thompson is at left

To meet the increased demand for air seats as a result of the new marketing thrust by hotels, an Airlift division was established at the Ministry of Tourism. Airlift has already significantly improved with the introduction of low-fare airlines such as *Spirit, Jet Blue* and *Song*, serving New York and Florida markets. The introduction of service by Virgin Airlines from UK was a major boost for the European market.

Inaugural ceremonies at Airport for Jet Blue new low-cost airline

Inaugural ceremony for Virgin Atlantic's new service from the United Kingdom to The Bahamas

On 7th July, 2006 at a special ceremony, the Nassau International Airport was renamed the Lynden Pindling International Airport. Lady Marguerite Pindling (now Dame Marguerite), spouse of the late Sir Lynden Pindling, is pictured

Attention was given to cruise ports, as more cruise companies repositioned ships from other parts of the world to North America to take advantage of the trend for shorter and more frequent vacations. Cruise ports were improved at Princess Cay (Bannerman Town), Eleuthera, as well as the ports at Great Stirrup and Coco Cay (Little Stirrup Cay), in the Berry Islands, thus providing additional jobs for Bahamians.

Cruise line and Bahamas Government officials meet to discuss improvement of linkages and benefits to the South Eleuthera community from the cruise line (Steve Neilson, VP Princess Cruises, Mr. Oswald Ingraham, MP for South Eleuthera, Angela Cleare, Sr. Director for Family Islands along with Raymond Harrison, GM, Eleuthera Tourist office and Local Government officials)

Cruise Ports—Princess Cay, Bannerman Town, South Eleuthera

From 2003, under Craig Woods as Film Commissioner, film production accelerated. Among the various achievements were several full-length movies such as *After the Sunset,* and *Into the Blue*, employing up to 100 Bahamians and an estimated expenditure of $5 million, and Disney Productions' ***Pirates of the Caribbean***. Filming of *Pirates of the Caribbean* is expected to benefit the Grand Bahama economy by more than $20,000. The first Film Festival, held on Paradise Island in December 2004, was so successful that it has become an annual event.

Hi-impact promotions were staged both overseas and on-island, including a highly acclaimed Bahamian review at Apollo Theatre, New York.

Pirates of the Caribbean—Reception in Freeport, GBI

Celebrating the launch of After The Sunset

In the words of Minister Wilchcombe, "It would be foolish to believe that the industry would, or could grow without ensuring that our product is better than, or equal to, the competition, particularly the Hispanic nations of Cuba, the Dominican

Republic and Mexico". He began revolutionary measures to monitor and improve the on-shore experience.

Details of the visitor satisfaction index are being shared with the community through the "Voice of the Visitor", a regular feature in local publications of visitor feedback, giving Bahamians a greater appreciation for the role they play in the day-to-day visitor experience.

Product improvement was undertaken with the restoration of historic sites, such as Preacher's Cave on Eleuthera, the Forts in Nassau, and other sites frequented by visitors, in cooperation with Antiquities Monuments & Museums Corporation. Also, a new signage programme was initiated, with Exuma as the model.

Scientists, members of the North Eleuthera Historical Society, and tourism officials, discuss Preacher's Cave development.

Remains of a Lucayan are unearthed at Preacher's Cave, North Eleuthera

Environmental initiatives were strengthened through Blue Flag certification for marinas which meet international environmental standards.

A signature heritage festival was established in every island, along with Junkanoo Summer in Nassau, to showcase the rich and diversified culture. Other upscale events were launched throughout the country.

Andros Crabfest, held annually in June, is the top domestic tourism Festival, attracting hundreds of locals and international visitors

Exuma Music and Heritage Festival established in March, 2005, has become one of the major signature events

Straw booth at Long Island Cornfest

Abaco office staff, headed by Jeritzan Outten (4th from right), at Abaco Country and Western Festival

Janet Johnson (centre), Events Director, along with Permanent Secretary of Tourism, Colin Higgs, review the festival site in preparation for Junkanoo Summer 2006

A member of the Chinese delegation, on a special familiarization trip, participate in Junkanoo Summer in June 2006

Recognition for employees within the industry and within the Ministry of
Tourism was emphasized through a re-vamped Tourism Week that encompassed
a National Tourism Conference, Careers Fair and the Cacique programmes as
well as the first ever *"Men and Women of Excellence"* awards within the Ministry of
Tourism.

Men and Women of Excellence: Long serving staff honoured by Ministry of
Tourism. Minister of Tourism, Hon. Obie Wilchcombe, presented the awards
and Sir Clement Maynard (former Minister of Tourism, seated at centre) was the
keynote speaker

Recognizing the need to generate a talent pool of bilingual young professionals
who can converse with foreign guests, a Foreign Language Cadets programme was
launched in 2004, providing high school students with exciting opportunities for
immersion in foreign language programmes. Each year, schools throughout the
country present candidates to sit the qualifying examination. Successful applicants
participate in a three-phase programme of workshops, field trips, excursions and
internships conducted in either Spanish or French, culminating with study abroad
to cities like Costa Rica and Paris, for a month of immersion.

Despite the ravages of the three hurricanes which cost the country well in excess
of $100 million in visitor spending, the record 5 million visitors in 2004 spent $1.9
billion, which represents a huge per capita visitor expenditure of $6,000 for every
Bahamian, and is among the highest in the world. A major challenge still being faced

relates to the Grand Bahama product, much of which was devastated by Hurricanes Jeanne and Frances in 2004 and Wilma in 2005. An attempt is being made to address this issue through additional incentives for new hotel operators, increased airlift, and supplementary attractions.

High School Foreign Language Cadet Programme, coordinated by Sheena Newton, (second from left) helps to generate a pool of bilingual young professionals who can converse with foreign guests

Another tragedy in the Bahamas tourism industry, this time in Bimini, took place on Monday 19th December, 2005, when Chalk's Ocean Airways' Grumman G-73T Turbine Mallard seaplane, enroute from Miami to Bimini, crashed, killing all 19 persons (17 passengers and two crew members) on board. The wing of this vintage seaplane, built in 1947, separated from the aircraft before landing in the ocean off Miami. According to the National Transportation Safety Board (NTSB), there were cracks in the wing span of the mallard. There were eleven Biminites who died in the crash, creating much pain and suffering within the close-knit community in Bimini. Although Chalks had experienced a few accidents previously, including a crash in March 1994 near Key West, Florida, killing two pilots, NTSB records confirmed that that the airline had never had a fatal accident with passengers on board before the December 2005 crash. Chalks Ocean Airways has since grounded its entire sea plane fleet.

Famous Visitors

Terry Waite, Advisor to the Archbishop of Canterbury, Peace Envoy and former hostage, visited The Bahamas in the 1990s after his release from a prison in Lebanon, where he was held captive for 1,763 days

Nelson Mandella shakes hands with officers in the Public Service, as Prime Minister Hubert Ingraham looks on (left—Lois Symonette, Permanent Secretary, Ministry of Transport)

Marla Gibbs (left) and Sir Sydney Poitier, with Angela Cleare, Senior Director, Product, Ministry of Tourism

President Bill Clinton. on a visit to Nassau, congratulates The Bahamas on its effective AIDS prevention campaign

*   *   *

The previous chapters have traced the history of tourism in The Bahamas up to 2005. The following chapter will measure the positive and negative impact of tourism both from an economic and social perspective.

11

SOCIOECONOMIC IMPACT OF TOURISM ON THE BAHAMAS—POSITIVE AND NEGATIVE

Tourism is recognized throughout the world as a human activity with tremendous economic impact, resulting from the demand for goods and services purchased by travellers. Also of significance is tourism's far-reaching social, cultural, political and educational impact.

Globally, the systematic measurement of tourism began only in the 20th century after the volume of international travellers increased following the first and second World Wars. The World Tourism Organization has played an important role in establishing guidelines for the standardization of tourism statistics for better measurement and comparison.

The Bahamas has been the leader in the region in the accurate compilation of tourism statistics, using Immigration card data and visitor expenditure data through surveys of departing visitors at airports and cruise terminals. These statistics have periodically been supplemented by research studies to measure the contribution of visitor expenditure on Gross Domestic Product, Balance of Payments, Government revenue, and employment. Studies have also analyzed linkages, along with the social, cultural, and political impact, both positive and negative, of tourism on local communities.

Economic Impact of Tourism

Table 11.1 shows that visitor arrivals have increased from 32,000 in 1949 to five million in 2004, due, in part, to the huge sums invested in marketing the industry by the public and private sectors. The Exit Surveys revealed that, by 2005, visitors spent $2 billion in The Bahamas.

Table 11-1
Summary Table of Visitor Arrivals and Expenditure

Year	Visitor Breakdown		Total Arrivals	Visitor Expenditure	Tourism Budget
	Air	Sea			
1949	21,722	10,296	**32,018**		£94,031*
1954	67,122	42,483	**109,605**	£340,386*	£340,386*
1964	364,611	240,560	**605,171**	£1,233,656*	£1,233,656*
1974	966,560	421,480	**1,378,310**	B$327,959,000	B$8,500,000
1984	1,321,330	1,003,920	**2,325,250**	B$801,500,000	B$26,200,000
1994	1,332,280	2,114,096	**3,446,376**	B$1,334,097,901	B$35,500,000
2004	1,450,037	3,553,654	**5,003,691**	B$1,884,481,507	B$76,000,000
2005	1,514,532	3,264,885	**4,779,411**	B$2,068,858,768	B$78,000,000

Source: Statistics of the Development Board and Research Department, Ministry of Tourism
* The Bahamas converted to decimal currency in 1966. Exchange rate £ = B$2.80

The first survey to determine the impact of tourism was conducted in 1960, when Sir Stafford Sands, Minister of Tourism, engaged The *First Research Corporation of Miami* to develop economic estimates. Among their findings were that direct employment of Bahamians by hotels climbed from 916 in 1950 to 4,454 in 1959 (with additional thousands employed in other direct tourist industry occupations), and that the average visitor in 1959 spent £71 (US$200) during his Bahamas visit with approximately £25 (US$70) of the amount being returned to the Public Treasury.[1] In 1968, when the Ministry of Tourism began interviewing departing visitors on a random sampling basis throughout the year, it was confirmed that the average expenditure by visitors by air was US$207 and US$46 per person by cruise visitors.

While additional data on the socio-economic importance of tourism were published in the 1969 Checchi Report[2], the most detailed empirical research tracing the flow of tourist dollars was conducted between 1974 and 1976 when Dr. Brian Archer of the University of North Wales, United Kingdom, assisted by the Ministry of Tourism's Research Department, then headed by Mrs. Joan Albury, now President of the Counsellors Ltd., completed two studies "Employment and Tourism in The Bahamas" and "The Impact of the Tourist Dollar."[3] In 1974, tourism expenditure in The Bahamas generated over 64% of all Customs duties, 56% of total government revenue from all sources, and 65% of all non-fuel imports[4].

Brian Archer's study was updated several times by other organizations. The 1988 update[5] reported that revenue from tourism was equivalent to 50% of GDP and that a 1% rise in tourist arrivals was associated with a 0.7% rise in real GDP. In 1987, more than 70% of the government revenue base was directly (through casino tax, room levy and departure tax), and indirectly, linked to tourism.

A Caribbean Tourism Organization study, funded by the European Union in 1997, also reported that visitor expenditure has a significant impact on the balance of payments. In 1997, it accounted for 79.9% of total inflows of receipts from the export of goods. These inflows were partially offset by outflows to purchase imports of goods and services required to produce the output demanded by visitors.[6]

Tourism's Role in Job Creation

Tourism, a service industry that is the world's greatest creator of jobs, is also by far the greatest employer in The Bahamas, accounting for one in three workers. The findings of the Brian Archer study on Employment and Tourism in The Bahamas were that, in the 1970's, Tourism created about 44% of all employment in The Bahamas; it estimated that 28,850 jobs (two-thirds of jobs in the country) would be unlikely to be maintained in the absence of tourism. The hotels sustained 30% of these jobs, 49% of the jobs were in other commercial establishments, and 21% in the private sector. An average of 350 cruise passengers created one additional job.[7] The 1997 CTO study estimated that tourism accounted for 49,250 jobs, or 38.41% of total employment in The Bahamas (representing 35 jobs for every $1 million of visitor expenditure). The largest share of employment was at the direct impact level with 27,796 jobs being supported in industries such as hotels, restaurants, casinos, taxis and duty free establishments. The indirect impact employment amounted to 12,867, or 9.5% of total employment, and a further 8,587 jobs was generated at the induced impact level by 1997 visitor expenditure.[8]

As in other Caribbean countries, tourism is the major creator of opportunities for employment throughout the economy, providing jobs for unskilled labour, and both sexes, regardless of age. Many hair braiders, straw vendors, taxi drivers, and artisans with successful businesses would have no market for their products or services without the tourism industry. Furthermore, many of these entrepreneurs have limited formal education and, without tourism, would have few opportunities for alternative employment.

Improvements to Infrastructure stimulated by the Needs of the Tourism Industry

Proper development of the infrastructure is necessary in any country reliant on tourism. Visitors demand that telephones work, that there are reliable electricity supplies and that roads and airports function efficiently. Nowhere in the region has tourism had a more positive impact on improvements in infrastructure than The Bahamas. Evidence of this can be found in Nassau/Paradise Island, and, to a lesser extent, on Grand Bahama, Abaco, Exuma, and Eleuthera.

It is interesting to contrast The Bahamas today with The Bahamas at the beginning of the 20th century before the development of the tourism industry.

> *At the beginning of the 20th century, the Colony was devoid of electricity, running water, telephones, radio, motor cars and many other amenities. Men known as lamplighters made their living lighting the oil lamps on Bay Street in the evenings. The only mode of inter-island travel was by mailboat. Donkey carts and horse-drawn drays were the principal means of transportation for people and goods[9].*

Because of demands of the tourist industry, Grand Bahama can now boast one of the most modern airport facilities in the region. In Nassau, the cruise terminal at Prince George Dock can accommodate as many as nine mega cruise ships at a time. San Salvador's modern airport was constructed in time for the opening of Club Med in 1992. The Rock Sound Airport was built as a result of new hotels constructed on South Eleuthera. The improvements on Exuma to the George Town Airport in 2003 were driven by the Four Seasons at Emerald Bay resort, to the benefit of local inhabitants as well as local businesses.

The major tourism island destinations in The Bahamas have all profited from a good network of roads, electricity, telephones, satellite, cable and Internet service. They are also served by international air links to North America and Europe. In return, more than half of the funds used by Government to pay for the infrastructure, national health and education programmes is obtained from revenue generated by activity in the tourism industry.

Private Investment in Tourism

During the 1930's, The Bahamas first became known internationally as a tax haven, attracting foreign investment. Many foreign hotel owners first came to the country as tourists, and, while vacationing, discovered investment opportunities. Sir Harry Oakes in the 1930's became a major hotel investor on New Providence after having been invited by Sir Harold Christie to visit The Bahamas. In the 1950's, actor Craig Kelly purchased and operated the French Leave resort in Governor's Harbour, Eleuthera, after falling in love with the island while on vacation.

The increase in investment in vacation homes throughout The Islands of The Bahamas is a direct result of the tourism industry. Modern hotels, golf courses, museums, parks, tennis courts, and shopping centres have been constructed because of tourist demand. They, in turn, have become important venues used not only by foreigners, but also by Bahamians.

On the negative side, some tourism investors have worked to the detriment of developing countries like The Bahamas. Before the establishment of the Bahamas Environment Science and Technology (BEST) Commission, with its stringent requirement for objective Environmental Impact Assessments, and the Bahamas

Investment Authority, with its complement of experts, foreign investors may have obtained agreements which, while favourable to the investor, need not fully consider the needs of The Bahamas to preserve its environment from long-term degradation.

Economic Benefits from Tourism—Dependence on a Single Market and the Need for Diversification

The proximity of The Bahamas to the United States is reflected in the large US market share of tourism arrivals.

Table 11-2 shows that Stopover Visitors from the United States have been increasing steadily over the past three decades, climbing to 87% of total arrivals in 2004, while the number of visitors from other countries has been declining. On the other hand, Table 11-3, that deals with Visitor Nights, presents a slightly more positive picture, taking into account the length of stay, which is higher for Canadian and European visitors. Dependence on a single market is dangerous, and, while business from the United States will continue to represent the bulk of visitors to The Bahamas, a conscious effort is being made to diversify by targeting other important markets.

Table 11-2
Stopover Visitors by Country of Residence

Year	USA	%	Canada	%	Total Europe	%	Other	%	Total
1980	884,030	75	129,780	11	114,070	10	53,390	4	1,181,260
1990	1,321,930	85	96,755	6	96,625	6	46,355	3	1,561,665
2000	1,294,295	84	82,840	5	104,610	7	62,214	4	1,543,959
2004	1,360,912	87	68,462	4	83,590	5	48,348	3	1,561,312
2005	1,380,083	86	75,643	5	85,276	5	67,150	4	1,608,153

Table 11-3
Visitor Nights by Country of Residence

	USA	%	CANADA	%	EUROPE	%	OTHER	TOTAL
1977	3,766,070	65%	1,144,760	20%	593,610	10%	249,980	5,754,420
1980	5,527,390	65%	1,213,010	14%	1,216,760	14%	478,980	8,436,140
1990	6,939,085	77%	795,830	9%	920,830	10%	307,110	8,962,855
2000	7,005,453	77%	640,575	7%	973,979	11%	428,354	9,048,361
2004	8,012,064	81%	618,772	6%	859,719	9%	407,628	9,898,181
2005	8,176,385	79%	667,310	6.5%	900,251	9%	553,381	10,297,327

Linkages—A Missed Opportunity in The Bahamas

Tourism has a high multiplier effect with opportunities for linkages to many other sectors. However, the full economic benefits of the $2 billion spent in The Bahamas by the 5 million annual visitors are not being realized because of the high level of imports and the leakage of foreign exchange back to the suppliers of those imports.

Surveys show that 80 cents of every dollar leave the country to pay for imports. Despite the demand created by the 300 hotels for seafood, meats, fruits and vegetables to serve visitors, that demand is largely being satisfied by foreign produce. As old farmers die off, their descendants prefer employment in the more sophisticated and lucrative white collar and blue collar service sectors.

While many local businesses now make a good living supplying products to major hotels in The Bahamas, few effective linkages have been established between the consumers in the hotel industry and local producers of food and other non-service products.

Some inroads are now being made into the souvenir business through the efforts of the Ministry of Tourism's Authentically Bahamian Unit and the Bahamas Agricultural and Industrial Corporation (BAIC). There will, however, continue to be the need for Government to work closely with the private sector to determine areas of demand, as well as to offer incentives and training programmes to increase local expertise, with work permits only granted to supplement needs in those areas where there is insufficient local experience.

Expenditure by Cruise Visitors

Brian Archer's studies "Employment and Tourism in The Bahamas" and "The Impact of the Tourist Dollar,"[10] completed in 1974, reported that stopover visitors made the largest contribution to the economy—94.7% of overall tourism expenditure, over 61% of all Customs duties, 53% of government revenue, 61% of non-fuel imports, and almost 96% of tourism expenditures in restaurants and nightclubs. Although cruise visitors were responsible for only 5.31% of tourism expenditure, the report noted that cruise spending accounted for a disproportionately high expenditure in casinos, on shopping (handicraft, souvenirs and gifts) and local transport. This observation applies only to cruise visitors to Nassau.

Table 11-4
Expenditure by Cruise Visitors vs. Stopover Visitors
1989-2004

	No. of Cruise Visitors—Total Bahamas	Expenditure by Cruise Visitors	No. of Stopover Visitors Total Bahamas	Expenditure by Stopover Visitors
1989	1,644,583	$93,000,000	1,575,070	$1,205,924,150
1993	2,047,030	$96,360,481	1,488,680	$1,199,189,895
1997	1,751,140	$105,203,398	1,617,596	$1,307,443,107
2001	2,551,673	$147,579,684	1,537,780	$1,496,814,452
2004	3,360,012	$185,817,482	1,561,312	$1,693,486,565

Source: Research Department, Ministry of Tourism

Since Brian Archer's studies were presented, cruise ship visits were initiated to Little San Salvador in 1980 and later to the Berry Islands, Abaco, Eleuthera and Bimini. As will be noted from Appendix 8B, in 1979 82% of cruise passengers to The Bahamas travelled to Nassau, with only 5% to the Family Islands. By 1995, Nassau only accounted for 57% of cruise passengers, with 34% travelling to the Family Islands and 9% to Grand Bahama. The ships to the Family Islands dock on remote islands or cays, and, while they boosted visitor arrival numbers to the Family Islands from a mere 26,810 cruise arrivals in 1979 to 1,076,390 in 2005, they make a minimal contribution to the local community. In 2005, the average expenditure by cruise ship passengers was $73 in Nassau, $58 in Grand Bahama and $28 in the Family Islands.

While it may be possible to establish trade linkages between the cruise ships and the local communities living in proximity to these cays, amendments would be required to the existing Heads of Agreement signed with cruise lines, as well as a programme of extensive training and financial help to enable the local entrepreneurs to be successful.

Visitor Distribution among the Various Family Islands

Prior to the 1950's, tourism was concentrated in Nassau, with a few smaller resorts on Bimini and West End, Grand Bahama. Even though new hotels were constructed on Eleuthera, Abaco, Andros and Exuma in the 1950's, and many local Family Islanders were making a good living through tourism, there was no statistical breakdown for visitors to each island until the 1960's.

As Table 11-5 shows, visitors to the various Family Islands represented as much as 22% of total arrivals in the 1960's. Also in the 1960's, with the opening of the

Lucayan Beach Hotel, Holiday Inn and King's Inn in Freeport, and the Grand Bahama Country Club in West End, along with further resorts in Freeport in the 1970's, Grand Bahama became the fastest growing tourist destination in the world, capturing as much as 38% of total foreign arrivals in the 1970's. Grand Bahama, throughout the decades, continued to record a disproportionately high level of tourism arrivals compared to its population, attracting skilled labour from Nassau to service the hospitality industry.

Table 11-5
Percentage of Tourist Arrivals vs. Population
1953-2000

	New Providence/Paradise Is.				Grand Bahama				Family Islands			
Year	Popu-lation	% Total Popu-lation	Total Arrivals	% Tourist Arri-val	Popu-lation	% Total Popu-lation	Total Arrivals	% Tourist Arri-vals	Popu-lation	% Total Popu-lation	Total Arrivals	% Tour. Arri-vals
1953	46,125	54.4	90,485		4,095	4.8	-		34,621	40.8	-	
1963	80,907	62.1	398,676	73.0	8,230	6.3	26,894	4.9	41,081	31.5	120,834	22.1
1970	101,507	60.1	730,611	56.3	25,859	15.3	496,040	38.2	41,446	24.5	71,700	5.5
1980	135,437	64.6	1,090,900	49.3	33,102	15.8	540,040	32.3	40,966	19.5	273,620	18.3
1990	172,196	67.5	1,957,913	54.0	40,898	16.0	1,175,537	31.0	41,955	16.5	495,069	15.0
2000	210,832	69.4	2,685,819	63.9	46,994	15.5	676,098	16.1	45,872	20.0	841,917	16.2

Table 11.6, showing Visitor Nights, gives a more accurate picture of the benefits accruing to Nassau/Paradise Island, Grand Bahama and the Family Islands from tourism. Visitors to the Family Islands stay longer than those to Nassau and Grand Bahama.

Table 11-6
Visitor Nights by Destination in The Bahamas
1977-2005

	Nassau/Paradise Is.		Grand Bahama		Family Islands		Total Visitor Nights	
	No.	%	No.	%	No.	%	No	%
1977	2,558,070	44	1,822,030	32	1,374,330	24	5,754,430	100
1987	4,192,850	48	2,334,645	27	2,157,810	25	8,685,305	100
1997	4,946,245	51	2,142,400	22	2,548,730	26	9,637,375	100
2005	5,744,901	56	1,963,513	19	2,588,913	25	10,297,327	100

In the decade of the 1990's, the individual Family Islands were promoted separately. With the introduction of Internet online bookings, the establishment of anchor flagship resorts on various islands in the new millennium, and more direct air service, each island began to take on its own identity.

By 2005, as Table 11-7 below shows, the number of foreign arrivals to Abaco had nearly reached ¼ million. As the island economy grew, and other new investments came on stream, a Director of Tourism for Abaco was appointed. With the opening of the Four Seasons Resort in 2003 on Exuma, that island is poised to give Abaco strong competition. In 2005 Exuma recorded the second highest number of Air Arrivals, jumping from 11,256 air arrivals in 1990 to 35,712 in 2005.

Although by 2005 the Family Islands could boast 68% of total resorts in The Bahamas (and 21% of total hotel rooms), 50% of these small hotels do not have staff trained in modern marketing techniques, and, as a result, they are not able to enjoy the potential benefits to be derived from using the latest available technology.

Table 11-7
Distribution of Visitors—Family Islands

	Visitors by Air			TOTAL AIR AND SEA VISITORS			
	1950	2000	2005	1950	1990	2000	2005
Abaco	56,990	89,354	94,715	58,990	157,904	145,215	202,939
Andros	8,180	8,749	8,799	8,270	6,833	9,480	9,965
Berry Islands	9,180	10,009	9,790	19,610	157,128	247,584	319,262
Bimini	24,210	12,894	14,512	51,410	92,974	48,270	45,804
Eleuthera, HI	40,990	34,511	34,511	41,200	47,086	164,717	300,318
Exuma	5,870	11,256	35,712	6,210	8,419	11,851	36,284
Other Family Is.	8,390	19,199	24,893	87,930	24,725	214,800	244,348
Total Family Is.	153,810	185,972	222,932	273,620	495,069	841,917	1,156,134

The Sustainability of the Tourism Sector—Myth or Reality?

The economic benefits of tourism to the gross national product, balance of payments, government revenue and employment sector, as borne out by statistics presented in this report, are undisputable.

Nevertheless, many countries in the region were originally reluctant to invest funds in tourism because the industry is subject to uncontrollable conditions such as recessions, wars, social unrest, hurricanes and environmental incidents, or even rumours of disasters or disturbances. There was also the perception that tourism is unstable, since the travel budget is usually the first item which a family is likely to sacrifice if funds are scarce. While it is true that tourism is influenced by uncontrollable socio-economic and environmental factors, historic evidence suggests that consumer shifts in expenditure following disasters and recessions are temporary. With increased industrialization and pressures on today's modern citizens, travel, for many, is now considered a necessity.

The economic downtown following the 9/11 events in the United States has shown that tourism is, indeed, vulnerable to external conditions. However, the rapid rebound of some of those countries most hurt by the reduction in visitor arrivals after the tragedy clearly demonstrated the resilience of tourism and its importance as a legitimate and viable industry.

In The Bahamas, there were job losses following 9/11 and the 2004 and 2005 hurricanes, but the country responded rapidly, putting in place increased safety measures at ports of entry. There was also extensive use of the Ministry of Tourism's Web site and its international public relations contacts to post credible information on the state of the country. As a result, while there was some reduction in the number of visitors, the adverse impact was greatly reduced.

Negative Social and Cultural Impact of Tourism

Tourism should not be discussed solely in terms of its economic benefits. There are important social and cultural impacts—both positive and negative—on a host country.

James Stark's account of Nassau in the early 20th century, before the influx of tourists, describes a totally different Bahamian society:

> *"Nassau was a very quiet and orderly city where scenes of violence, drunken brawls, profane, abusive and irritating language in public streets and places were absent. Life was slow moving but pleasant and the people were noted for their kindness, hospitality, and grace".*[11]

A letter written to the Tribune as far back as March 1930 complained about the behaviour of visitors at the New Colonial Hotel. The Bahamian resident noted:

> *What an example for our girls to see stockingless painted half-drunken dissipated young men and women displaying to all around how far they have fallen into a state of utter depravity and disgrace.*[12]

Another letter to The Tribune on 4th October, 1933 stated that Nassau, under the influence of American culture, had gone mad. The writer remarked that young people of Nassau had become frivolous, "dancing, drinking and living a sporting life, in and out of season"[13].

Evidence suggests that the country has undergone some important changes in values since James Stark's day.

In an article, *The Changing Face of Nassau: The Impact of Tourism on Bahamian Society in the 1920's and 1930's*,[14] Dr. Gail Saunders discusses the embryonic stages of the tourism industry, emphasizing tourism's overall effect on society, and its negative impact on the culture and value system within the local community.

Dr. Saunders has maintained that tourism, which made liquor so accessible after Prohibition, had a profound impact on Bahamian drinking habits and the growth of alcoholism.

Dr. Sandra Dean Patterson, Bahamian Psychotherapist, in her study *Changes in Bahamian Drinking during the period 1969-77*, referred to the profound effect on local Bahamians in constant contact with people on holiday "full of joie de vivre, enjoying the two-week holiday with the sun, sea and booze".[15] Her study also revealed that, unlike the United States where those in the higher income groups drink more heavily than those in lower income groups, most of the heavy drinkers in The Bahamas were males in the lower income category.

The behaviour of visitors on vacation and their demand for illegal substances may, in some cases, have influenced Bahamians in a negative way. Alcoholism in The Bahamas is cause for concern, and some have suggested that the exposure of impressionable Bahamians to the drinking and carousing of tourists may have influenced, to some extent, drinking habits in The Bahamas. The casual attitudes seem to be patterned on this lifestyle, without regard to the fact that for 50 weeks of the year, most of these carefree vacationers work very hard and saved diligently to be able to afford a short vacation in The Bahamas.

There is also evidence that casinos attract prostitutes and undesirables to a destination and that they create negative values within a society. Although casinos are an integral part of the tourism infrastructure of The Bahamas, it should be noted that, since the 1960's, Bahamians are not allowed to gamble in them.

Of concern also is the growing cultural influence of the United States. The large influx of United States visitors demanding American products in the form of food and entertainment, has resulted in the Americanization of Nassau and Freeport, with merchants and hotels catering to this major market. Franchises, such as KFC, McDonalds, Burger King, Wendy's and Subway, cater to that demand and American music is prominently featured in hotels. It is doubtful that these trends can be blamed on tourism alone since our closeness to the United States permits us to be aware, through television, of all the latest trends in music and fashion, and this would probably be the case even if no American visitors ever came to our shores.

Historically, the Christian community has blamed tourism for interference in religious worship. As far back as the 1930's, some Bahamians, according to Dr. Gail Saunders, were critical of the ruling elite's concentration on tourists and on making money to the detriment of locals. An anonymous writer in protest wrote:

"I can only come to the conclusion that we really need a thorough change among our so-called leaders today. They have sold Sunday for the almighty

dollar; they have sold themselves for a mess of pottage and now they are
trying to sell the last and only privilege that Bahamians have and pride,
our walks along the waterfront".[16]

Christian leaders also openly opposed the decision by the Bahamas Government to
allow stores to open on Sundays.

In describing the social impact of tourism in The Bahamas, frequent mention
is made of the racist policies that prevailed in the early days of the tourism industry
in The Bahamas and in other Caribbean countries. Prior to 1930, most hotels and
boarding houses, as well as some winter residents, imported their staff to perform
housekeeping, bartending and other domestic services.

Blacks could not work in, nor patronize, hotels. According to Dr. Saunders, if
black musicians wished to hear a foreign orchestra, they had to seek permission to
enter the outside premises and listen at the windows.[17]

In the 1930's, after Lady Dundas (the wife of the Honourable Charles Dundas,
Colonial Secretary who later served as Governor) established the Nassau Improvement
Society, that later evolved into the Dundas Civic Centre, blacks received domestic
training and were recruited within hotels. Hotels and nightclubs hired American
bands during the tourist season in Nassau in the 1930's and 1940's, and the benefit
of tourism to the majority of the local people was minimal.

When all jobs within the hotel industry became available to Bahamians, tourism
became an employment of last resort, and viewed as an occupation of "servitude".
Children who were not academically gifted were steered towards domestic careers
or employment in tourism, either within hotels as waiters, housekeepers or porters,
or as taxi drivers or straw vendors. Even a qualified accountant or secretary would
choose a job in a bank or law firm before answering an advertisement for such a
position in a hotel.

The relationship between the visitor and tourism service employee was perceived,
in many circles, as an extension of the master-slave syndrome. While racism is no
longer an issue and the servile stigma has diminished, tourism is still not a preferred
career choice, unlike in European and Asian countries where a job in the tourist
sector carries little or no stigma and is highly regarded with a diverse cadre of trained
staff serving their guests with pride, dignity and professionalism.

Dr. Patterson, in her study, previously cited, maintains that in the decade of the
1950's the tourism industry did little to profit the masses, noting that the cost of
living index rose by 100% between 1950-60, but the wages of most black Bahamians
changed little, and, as late as 1966, the hourly rate of unskilled workers was 78 cents
and maids were earning only $17.00 per week. She recommended diversification
of the economy to decrease the country's reliance on tourism and "all the social
dislocations associated with a leisure industry".[18] Happily, this economic picture
has now dramatically changed. Bahamians in all socio-economic groups have equal
opportunity to earn attractive wages in tourism, and are reaping such benefits.

Positive Contributions made by the Tourist Industry

Apart from the negative effects of the predominance of tourism in our economy, the many positive contributions made by the tourist industry to the cultural life of the community should not be forgotten.

Prior to the 1980's, politicians of many Caribbean countries criticized The Bahamas for "packaging" indigenous culture for special tourist events, such as *Goombay Summer*, considered by some as a "bastardization" of authentic culture. The conduct of little boys who would dive for coins from cruise ships, to the amusement of visitors, was also considered degrading.

However, many of the improvements to the country's cultural landmarks—Fort Charlotte upgrade, Pompey Museum, new National Art Gallery, Arawak Cay Fish Fry, Museums on Green Turtle Cay (Abaco), Long Island, Spanish Wells, San Salvador, and many others—were prompted by tourist demand, but have enriched the lives of both residents and visitors. Similarly, special events such as *Bahamas at Smithsonian, Junkanoo in June, Pineapple Festival, Bahamas Heritage Festival, Goombay Summer, Crabfest, Coconutfest,* and *Cat Island Rake and Scrape Festival*, were created and funded by the Ministry of Tourism to showcase local culture for the tourist market and to serve as a source of enjoyment and pride for Bahamians.

Local entertainers and artists have gained international fame and local acceptance because of tourism. Paul Meeres did not become famous until he had performed for visitors in Paris. Bahamians did not value the work of Amos Ferguson, folk artist, until foreign visitors praised Ferguson's work and publicized his talent overseas. Nor did they properly acknowledge Joseph Spence's work until it received high acclaim at the Smithsonian Institution in the United States.

In addition, tourism has had an important effect on the development of arts and craft in the region. Straw work throughout The Islands of The Bahamas has become a thriving industry with creativity in straw plaiting and finished straw goods among the highest in the region, and improving each year to meet tastes and demands of upscale visitors. Also of significance is the creativity displayed by young artisans who now produce a variety of Authentically Bahamian products from local marine and plant by-products such as sand, shells and sisal, demonstrating how the "trash to treasure" concept can reap extraordinary rewards.

The Ministry of Tourism and the Bahamas Culinary Association have also fostered high achievement and success in the culinary arts. Local chefs from the major hotels now compete annually on the world stage, winning regional and Olympic medals for their creative local dishes. Their standards improve each year in response to tourism demand.

As a country which, for the foreseeable future, will continue to be dependent on tourism, we can take heart from the fact that tourism not only guarantees our economic well-being but it is an industry that can make a contribution to world peace.

The UNWTO has asserted that the greatest benefit of tourism is not a tangible one. At the World Tourism Forum for Peace and Sustainable Development held in Brasilia in 2003, Kofi Annan, Secretary-General of the United Nations, expressed a similar point of view. He noted that "by promoting greater awareness of the rich heritage of various civilizations, tourism can contribute to better understanding among peoples, and help foster a culture of peace that is essential to development."[19]

The UN Secretary-General added that the sustainable development of tourism is needed to prevent a wide range of harmful effects that are becoming all too visible in popular destinations "including destruction of natural heritage through overbuilding; ever-higher demands on scarce water and energy resources; damage to ecologically fragile areas caused by irresponsible development; threats to indigenous cultures; exploitation of workers; organized sex tourism, and—most tragic of all—child sex tourism, which affects millions of children each year".[20]

The positive influence of travel is much more powerful than any negative by-products. Tourism, which brings people of different nationalities, traditions and beliefs face to face, can help to foster better understanding and eliminate prejudices, thus contributing to world peace. With progress come costs. The challenge is to manage development so that economic benefits for both investors and residents are maximized and social costs are kept at a minimum.

*   *   *

When all factors are considered, the overall impact of tourism is a positive one. As Baron Thomas Macaulay, the noted British historian and political activist, asserted as far back as 1849, the greatest "inventions" of mankind are those that have facilitated travel:

> *"The chief cause which made the fusion of the different elements of society so imperfect was the extreme difficulty which our ancestors found in passing from place to place. Of all inventions . . . those which abridge distance have done most for the civilization of our species. Every improvement of the means of locomotion benefits mankind, morally and intellectually as well as materially, and not only facilitates the interchange of the various productions of nature and art but tends to remove national and provincial antipathies, and to bind together all the branches of the great human family."[21]*

The last chapter will discuss the Way Forward, and share trends, challenges and outlook.

12

OVERVIEW, OUTLOOK AND TRENDS

An Historical Overview

At the beginning of the 21st century, The Bahamas is still one of the most prosperous countries within the Caribbean, with a GDP of around US$16,400, and one of the lowest unemployment rates in the region.

The success of Bahamian tourism is as much the product of external events, as it is the result of the conscious decision made during the last century to promote the country as a year-round tourist destination.

Steam-powered vessels in the 1800's and aeroplanes in the early 1900's provided the means whereby visitors from many distant destinations were able to visit The Bahamas. The era of blockade-running in the 1860's gave way to the development of a modern tourism product and led to the emergence of travel agents or brokers, whose job it was to serve as distribution channels for the destination. As travel became more reliable, efficient and comfortable, greater attention could then be paid to marketing the country's considerable natural assets and setting the stage for the emergence of tourism, as we know it today.

Although the Bahamas Development Board was established since 1914 to promote tourism, the years preceding 1920 can be described as the Period of Unsolicited Visitors. No significant promotional funds were expended by either the Government or the private sector to target visitors. It was not until the 1950's that the Government seriously considered the development of tourism to be an important economic goal. Then, during the tenure of Sir Stafford Sands at the Development Board, the necessary funds were provided for the first time to support a full-fledged marketing campaign that would actively promote The Bahamas as a major tourist destination.

As Table 12-1 shows, the budget for tourism in the 1950's represented about 12% of Government revenue, with the allocations to Health and Education being 9% and 7%, respectively. Starting in 1968, Tourism moved to third and then to fourth place in the budget allocations (7% of Government revenue), with Education receiving between 16% and 19% annually of the revenue, followed by Health.

Table 12-1
Government Expenditure on Tourism vs. Education and Health
For selected years 1956-59 and 1969-71

YEAR	BUDGET ALLOCATED TO EDUCATION AS A % OF GOVT REVENUE		BUDGET ALLOCATED TO HEALTH AS A % OF GOVT REVENUE		BUDGET ALLOCATED TO TOURISM AS A % OF GOVT REVENUE		TOTAL GOVT REVENUE
1956	£305,571	7.5	£352,070	8.6	£475,242	11.6	£4,078,921
1957	£324,624	6.6	£413,610	8.4	£556,813	11.3	£4,938,958
1958	£361,526	6.9	£469,340	9.0	£658,482	12.7	£5,198,975
1959	£484,317	7.5	£593,733	9.2	£730,250	11.3	£6,456,795
1969	B$13,245,990	15.7	B$ 9,030,144	10.7	B$6,499,400	7.7	B$ 84,504.022
1970	B$17,075,827	17.5	B$10,091,403	10.1	B$6,696,636	6.7	B$ 97,587,191
1971	B$19,305,073	19.1	B$12,731,812	12.7	B$6,879,713	6.9	B$101,160,540

Source: Bahamas Handbook and Businessman's Annual
and Ministry of Tourism Annual Reports

After the attainment of Independence in 1973, and with the shift from minority to majority rule, there was a clearer understanding of the importance of tourism to the local economy and, with greater emphasis being placed on its development, Bahamians were better able to participate in making policy as it affected the industry, as well as participate in decisions regarding media advertising and overseas promotional activity.

The three decades that followed can be characterized as a period of rapid development of people and product in keeping with the goal of distributing the benefits of tourism more equitably within the various island communities.

Trends

Burgeoning Cruise industry

One of the most important developments impacting local tourism since the 1980's is the explosive growth of the cruise industry, which has grown globally at a rate of 8.4% per annum (versus 4% for global air and sea travel combined). However, recent high-profile problems on the high seas, including a passenger disappearance and food poisonings, have prompted concerns among would-be travellers about cruise safety. This, along with memories of the 2004 and 2005 brutal hurricane seasons in the Caribbean, could make the next few years the most challenging for cruise lines. According to *Ferri & Partners Marketing & Tourism Trends*, some cruise lines are already experiencing softer bookings and are beginning to cut prices.[1]

In The Bahamas, the number of cruise visitors outnumbered stopovers for the first time in 1986, and since that time cruise visitors have recorded increases nearly every year. However, there is the need to establish additional linkages, as earlier discussed, to increase cruise visitor expenditure on island, thus improving the economic impact on local communities.

It is also important to ensure that the growth of the cruise market does not result in the pollution of the sea in the Caribbean or in the destruction of the marine environment, while contributing only marginally to increasing cruise revenue to Caribbean governments. Unlike hotels, the cruise industry in the Caribbean has not been taxed, nor do cruise ships have to pay an environmental levy if they engage in pollution of the sea.

To ensure the competitiveness of land-based tourism, the Caribbean Tourism Organization has put forward a proposal for the levy of a head tax on arriving cruise passengers throughout the Caribbean. CTO has also proposed that individual governments should examine their tax structures to ensure that tourism, which is essentially an industry utilizing the pristine waters and beautiful beaches of the region, makes a greater contribution to the overall revenue. Thought is also being given to the establishment of a Tourism Investment Fund to harness regional capital and to make it available for development of the tourism industry.

Competition from the Region and the World

There are two other trends that are cause for some concern. The first is that of increased competition from other Caribbean countries. While total arrivals to The Bahamas soared from 1.5 million in 1973 to 3.6 million in 1991 and to 5.0 million in 2004, total stopovers and tourist expenditure have not shown a similar relative increase. In contrast, many neighbouring Caribbean countries, which had earlier failed to realize the economic importance of tourism, have now begun aggressive marketing campaigns to attract visitors to their shores. The result has been that, in some cases, they have increased their share of the US, Canadian and European markets at the expense of The Bahamas. This necessitates a product renaissance and re-vamping of The Bahamas image as a tourist destination to differentiate it, in a positive way, from its competitors.

As a result of these new pressures, and the changes taking place in world tourism, the years 1992 to 2005 emerged as a period in which great emphasis was placed in The Bahamas on hotel transformation, product branding, airlift strengthening, and the increased use of technology by the more successful hotel chains. The Bahamas had no choice but to take full advantage of the Internet for advertising purposes. In addition, the normal press and magazine advertising continued with added emphasis on creative advertising, special promotions and distinctive product initiatives, in order to place the destination in a more competitive position.

The second noteworthy trend is the challenge posed by the spectacular growth of world tourism. Over the past 50 years, international tourist arrivals have risen dramatically from 25 million in 1950 to 808 million worldwide in 2005. Travel and Tourism remains the world's largest industry, contributing over 10% in global GDP. In 2002, international tourism and related activities generated an estimated 199 million jobs—one in every 13 jobs worldwide. Despite an unstable travel environment caused by the 9/11 events in the United States, the SARS threat, and fears of terrorism, world tourist arrivals registered only a small decline of 1.5% in 2003.[2] The year 2004 marked a resurgence of international travel, as overall tourist arrivals showed a 10% increase, after three years of sluggish performance. Consumer confidence is clearly reflected in the soaring demand, with leisure tourism still performing stronger than business tourism. In addition, the years 2004 and 2005 showed a gradual recovery of long-haul traffic, with stronger demand for air transport on overseas routes, premium accommodation, and by visits to world capitals.[3] Although 2005 was a tumultuous year, with various terrorist attacks and natural disasters, such as the aftermath of the Indian Ocean tsunami and an extraordinarily long and strong hurricane season, the recovery, that started in 2004, continued firmly through 2005. According to the World Tourism Organization, the number of international tourist arrivals in 2005 is estimated at 808 million, up by 5.5%. Although growth was more moderate than in 2004, it was still almost 1.5 percentage points above the long-term average annual growth rate of 4.1%.[4]

UNWTO's *Tourism 2020 Vision* forecasts that international arrivals are expected to grow by an average 4.1% per annum, to reach over 1.56 billion by the year 2020. Of these worldwide arrivals in 2020, 1.2 billion will be intra-regional and 0.4 billion will be long-haul travellers.[5] Although the fear factor has faded, inflation contained, and the long-term forecast is positive, it is still not business as usual. UNWTO research has confirmed that the crisis of 2001-2003 has led to accelerating changes in consumer habits and has transformed the fabric of the industry, encouraging the creation of new operators such as low-cost airlines. "It has led to restructuring and regrouping, the implementation of new technologies, the modernization of marketing techniques, the strengthening of co-operation between the private and public sectors with a renewed focus on product development, training and promotion, to the benefit of all involved. Even though many threats remain, including high oil prices, the threats appear to have far less impact on tourism than before".[6]

Although, overall, the growth of tourism will continue, it is clear that some countries will experience more growth than others. For this reason The Bahamas must take into consideration the latest countries who have entered the market and who will be competing with The Bahamas for a share of the tourist market.

Established markets such as the United States, Japan and Western Europe have strengthened considerably since the 9/11 event in the United States. Europe remained the top tourist destination, capturing 58% of arrivals in 2002. However, its share of the world's tourists continued to fall from a high of 75% in 1964, as emerging markets such as China and India increase their share of the tourism pie. As more destinations aggressively market their modern tourism products, an even more competitive arena will emerge.

Of particular interest is China. China's inbound and outbound tourism industry is growing rapidly. In 2004, arrivals to China totalled 109 million, 60 times the number in 1978. Overnight tourists accounted for 41 million and tourism receipts reached US$25.5 billion. In 2004, China was ranked as the best tourism destination by TTG ASIA magazine.

In terms of outbound tourism, China has become the fastest-growing tourist generating market in the world, gaining almost 17 million international tourist arrivals in the period 1995-2002. China grew at an average rate of 9% per year during this period and reached a total of almost 37 million tourist arrivals in 2002.

In 1997, outbound group travel of Chinese citizens had officially started, with the total numbering 5.32 million. Prior to 2004, the approved tourist destinations for outbound travel of Chinese citizens included Thailand, Singapore, Malaysia, the Philippines, Hong Kong and Macao. In 2002, the total of outbound travel of Chinese citizens reached 16.6 million. By 2003, it had reached 22 million, surpassing Japan, the biggest outbound tourist generating country in Asia, and climbed even further in 2004 to 28 million. Now that Chinese citizens will be able to travel in tour groups to 63 countries with Approved Destination Status (ADS)—30 countries in Europe, 18 countries in Asia, 10 countries in Africa, 2 countries in the Oceanic, 1 country in America and two in the Caribbean (The Bahamas and Jamaica)—tourism generated by China will continue to increase rapidly.[7]

The Internet Transforms Marketing Capabilities

One of the most noteworthy trends is the transformation of the marketing capabilities through the use of the Internet. From the 1990's, the Internet has transformed the promotional and booking capabilities within the hospitality sector, with online travel becoming widespread. Nearly 64 million online travellers, 30% of the US adult population, used the Internet in 2004 to get travel and destination information. Of that group, 44.6 million actually booked at least one travel service or product online in the past year, up nearly 6% from over the previous year. The number of Americans using the Internet for travel planning remains stable at 63.8 million, reflecting slower growth in general Internet use among the travelling population. Those who do all of their travel booking online grew from 29% in 2003 to 40% in 2004. PhoCusWright's "*Online Travel Overview: Market Size and Forecasts 2004-06*" projects a continuing shift of travel bookings to the Internet. Key findings were that the United States online travel sales reached US$39.4 billion in 2003, up 37% from 2002, increasing to $52.8 billion in 2004. Expedia, Travelocity and Orbitz represent nearly one-third of all Internet-driven hotel sales.[8]

In the same way that travel marketers have engaged in market segmentation for traditional advertising and promotions, the Internet provides opportunities for targeting specific generational segments, which vary dramatically in terms of behaviour and preferences. A 2005 travel study, "*Online Travel Comes of Age*," conducted by *Compete, Inc.*, revealed that Baby Boomers (age 45 to 64) are more likely to book on line. Over 10% of the 17 million Baby Boomers who research travel online each month will also book online, considerably more than Young Travellers (18-24) who tend to window-shop, and Seniors (65+) who may be uncomfortable purchasing over the Web. The study also revealed that Young Travellers are influenced by the flashy marketing campaigns of online agencies and consequently spend more time on agency sites, especially price focused Web destinations. Seniors prefer booking directly with airlines and hotels, particularly with suppliers that offer low-rate guarantees and other perks. Nearly 80% of the flights booked online by Seniors are done at supplier sites, compared to 72% for 25-34 year olds. Similarly, 68% of hotel bookings made by Seniors are at supplier direct sites, compared to 58% for the 25-34 age group. Baby Boomers view an average of 36 pages of travel content when researching online. This is 15% more than Young Travellers and 25% more than Seniors.[9]

It is also imperative for destinations serious about attracting European, Asian and Latin American business via the Internet to develop and manage foreign language Web sites. For example, an *eMarketer* report, *Hispanic Youth Online: Language and Culture Define Usage*, revealed that the 15.7 million Hispanic Internet users in the US in 2005 will increase to 16.7 million in 2006 and to nearly 21 million, by 2010, approaching the number of African-American users. In addition, the US Hispanic population is composed many of young people, who use the Internet more than older Hispanic Americans. By 2010, when the median age of the US population is expected to be 36, the Hispanic median age will be just over 27, and in 2010, one-third of all Hispanic people in the US will be under 18.[10]

Such research provides agencies and marketing managers of tourist offices with data needed to better manage online distribution strategies. Also, persons in the travel trade in The Bahamas must be equipped to handle requests for information about The Bahamas from overseas clients in an efficient and timely fashion. Proper and thorough training of staff is critical for success in this competitive area.

The Future for Caribbean Tourism

The recovery of the Caribbean tourist industry after the 9/11 events in the United States began somewhat earlier than in other parts of the world. Based upon the available returns from its member countries, the Caribbean Tourism Organization estimates that for the two-year period 2003-04, tourist arrivals to the Caribbean grew by almost 15%, compared to a 10% increase for world tourism. Tourist arrivals to the region in 2004 grew by 7% to reach 21.8 million. During this period, cruise passenger visits to Caribbean destinations increased by an estimated 13% to reach 20.5 million.

In terms of major markets for 2004, tourist arrivals from the United States grew by just over 7%; arrivals from Canada were up by some 16%, although most of these Canadians travelled to Cuba and the Dominican Republic, while arrivals from Europe grew by just over 4%. The active hurricane season in late 2004 negatively impacted travel to the region during the fall of 2004, but the decline was temporary.

At the Fifth Caribbean Media Exchange on Sustainable Tourism (CMEx) held in Barbados on 30th December, 2003, Simón Suárez, president of the Caribbean Hotel Association (CHA) projected that, based on current growth rates, tourism to the region over the next decade will grow from US$34.6 billion to $78.4 billion, and employment in the sector will grow from 1.8 million to 2.9 million jobs.[11]

Although the tourism sector seems poised for continued growth, it is important to bear in mind that because of safety concerns of Americans, who constitute our major market for travel to the area, the stability of the Caribbean region is of great importance in maintaining the desirability of the area as a tourist destination for visitors from North America, faced as we are with stiff competition from long-haul destinations in Europe and the Far East.

Jean Holder, former secretary-general of the CTO, in commenting on regional challenges in the next decade, noted that the Caribbean was "at the mercy of a consolidated and changing distribution system that tightens its grip on the decision-making process of filling our rooms", with many regional carriers on the brink of bankruptcy or liquidation. He noted that resources must be found to keep planes in the air.[12]

Speaking at a meeting of the Caribbean Leadership forum of the International Downtown Association in Willemstad, Curacao,[13] Vincent Vanderpool Wallace, who assumed the post of Secretary General of the Caribbean Tourism Organization (CTO) in 2005, emphasized that the Caribbean is more dependent on tourism than any other region in the world. He indicated that during the next five years CTO will concentrate on the firm establishment of a Caribbean brand focus on seven areas in that quest:

(1) Better data management;
(2) Improved training and development;
(3) Establishment of a world class consumer Web site;
(4) Establishment of a single membership site on "best practices" for the Caribbean tourism industry;
(5) Promotion of the Web addresses for the consumer and membership sites;
(6) Public relations;
(7) Public/Private Sector cooperation, coordination and sustainable development in all that we do.

A key component in all of the areas was an increase in the use of technology in executing programmes. He described the Internet as the most important tool for the tourism industry since jet airplanes and talked about ways in which this technology enables the Caribbean to be much more competitive in a global marketplace. Vanderpool Wallace reminded the group that vacationers do not buy hotel rates; they buy destination experiences, and that much of the data management will concentrate on providing information on what leads to the greatest visitor satisfaction with a destination. He stressed that in future CTO will use such information to focus more on outcomes and constantly adjust inputs and processes until the outcomes are attained.[14]

Vanderpool Wallace further noted that CTO cannot be successful unless the peoples of the Caribbean identify proudly and simultaneously with "the Caribbean" as well as with their national identities. That is why, he said, ". . . we believe in the existence, in principle, of "the United States of the Caribbean". Public relations will emphasize the positive aspects of the Caribbean to all markets and encourage members of the Caribbean Diaspora to maintain an interest in their own country of origin and in the Caribbean in general.[15]

Discussing the need for a renewed approach to education and training as well as a professional approach to tourism, he pointed out that tourism is not a career but a collection of careers all of which would still exist even if no visitors came to our countries on vacation. Hence, the principal overriding skill required for success in tourism is a sound background in business principles, with a bias toward those principles required in the hospitality industry. The tourism industry in the Caribbean, he continued, will thrive when sound business principles are applied through the artful delivery of goods and services by persons properly selected and trained to satisfy the needs of our visitors. In fact, Vanderpool Wallace suggests that we might consider avoiding the stigma still attached to tourism by focusing on its business aspects, in order to attract to the industry our region's best and brightest.[16]

Regional market integration through the Caribbean Single Market and Economy (CSME) has long been a subject of active discussion in tourism development circles in the Caribbean. Such integration has been suggested as a means whereby the region could compete successfully with other integrated areas such as the European Economic Community (EEC).

The result has been pressure to create the CSME, which, according to the Prime Minister of Barbados, who visited The Bahamas for meetings on the subject, would transform the respective Caribbean nations into a single market space by removing barriers not only to trade in goods, but also to trade in services, the flow of capital, the movement of people and skills, and the right of Caribbean nationals to establish enterprises and engage in non-wage earning activities throughout the region.[17]

While the hospitality industry in the region is anxious to further explore the concept of a regional market, it is unlikely that The Bahamas will join CSME as presently constituted.

Whether The Bahamas joins the CSME or not, it is necessary that local tourist businesses should be structured so as to take full advantage of the new liberalized global economy, including the opportunities afforded by the growth of inter-regional Caribbean companies. Some Caribbean companies, such as Sandals and SuperClubs, have been able to develop their own brand to ensure marketing success.

Bahamian companies, including restaurateurs and artisans, must also look to the wider world for export success and, where necessary, use franchising and other methods of branding to differentiate their products from those of their overseas competitors. To do so, it would be necessary to examine the quality of those products and, where necessary, upgrade them to international standards.

The Impact of Changes in Airline Travel and Port Security

David Johnson, Deputy Director General for the Bahamas Ministry of Tourism, who has had wide travel trade experience in both North America and The Bahamas, and who has always been closely associated with airline trends and innovations, noted that, since 9/11, airlines worldwide, and especially the major carriers in the United States, have experienced tremendous losses, with almost each major carrier—American Airlines, Delta, United and US Airways—being forced to reorganize or file for bankruptcy.

Mr. Johnson predicted that while the major traditional carriers struggle with high cost and low productivity and produced over $10 billion in losses since 9/11 alone, this environment has enabled low-cost carriers such as Southwest, Jet Blue, Air Tran and Spirit Airlines to gain market share at the expense of the majors.

The low-cost, low-fare carriers have taken advantage of the Internet as a distribution arm to sell to customers via their Web site directly using their customized virtual private network (VPN) in order to avoid high distribution costs associated with dependency on travel agents and GDS (Global Distribution Systems). Nassau/Paradise Island became the recipient of some 200,000 low-fare seats generated by Spirit and Jet Blue Airlines, reducing the cost of the Nassau-packaged vacation product and, simultaneously, resulted in a shortage of rooms to meet the increased seat capacity and overall demand in the short term.

The Bahamas' tourism air stopover market reflects a pattern whereby over 75% of traffic is generated from markets where the air travel time is 'short-haul', that is less than three hours from origin (departure destination) to destination (arriving destination). This trend is likely to continue, especially with the incremental growth fuelled by the low-fare carriers that operated mostly point-to-point service short-haul flights using narrow body aircraft with 120 to 160 seat capacity.

It is expected that the Florida market will continue to be the principal source market for The Bahamas due to its proximity and its position as the preferred global connecting gateway for air travel to The Islands of The Bahamas. A strong and growing network of commuter services provided by AA Eagle, Bahamasair and

Continental Connection also enhances the Florida market. Some 35% to 40% of all air seats to the Family Islands of The Bahamas originate in the Florida markets of Miami, Ft. Lauderdale, West Palm Beach, Orlando and Tampa.

One new development that could have a major impact on the development of tourism in warm weather destinations in Asia, which are competitive with The Bahamas, is the A380 super-jumbo jet. This twin-deck aircraft capable of carrying 555 passengers, unnveiled in early 2005, is a milestone in air travel.[18]

The new aircraft was designed in collaboration with 60 major airports and input from airlines, aviation authorities and air traffic regulatory bodies. With air travel continuing to grow, the radical A380 could offer a solution to the problem of airport congestion. A key economic benefit is the ability to fly more people on long-haul trips without having to pay for more landing and take-off slots.

The A380 boasts enhanced passenger comfort and environmental advantages. It has significantly reduced noise and emission levels. Airbus claims that the A380 will be the first long-haul jet to consume less than three litres of fuel per passenger over 100 kilometers, which is a rate comparable to an economical family car.

The A380 aircraft will be deployed, in the first instance, in the long haul, high density markets, such as London/Hong Kong, NY/Tokyo, Sydney/LA markets and not into The Bahamas or the Caribbean. It was expected that by 2006, 23 airports would be ready to handle the new aircraft, increasing to 60 by 2010. By the end of 2005, Airbus had confirmed orders from 16 airlines around the world for 150 of its A380 super jumbos, with a delivery schedule of 25 in 2007, 35 in 2008 and 45 in 2009. However, the company announced in 2006 that there would be delays in delivery.[19] It might also be feasible, in the long run, for Airbus to migrate to higher density leisure markets in North America and the Caribbean.

Security Issues

There are two factors which could curtail future travel in The Bahamas, at least temporarily. The first relates to the port security rules imposed, since 9/11, by the Federal Aviation Administration (FAA), International Civil Aviation Organization (ICAO) and the Transportation Security Administration (TSA). The new rules make it mandatory for all ports of entry, including the small Family Island airports, to introduce scanning procedures, to hire the necessary security staff and implement additional new measures or risk being closed to direct traffic from the United States. The Bahamas Government, recognizing the importance of direct service to its 28 Airports and its cruise ports, has already expended millions of dollars since 9/11 to upgrade airports and cruise ports, retrofitting them with new screening equipment and employing additional security staff. Night landing capabilities have also been improved.

The second critical factor relates to the new rules requiring all U.S. citizens travelling by air or sea to or from the Caribbean, as well as Central and South

America, to have passports to re-enter the United States. This new rule could affect the Caribbean, in particular The Bahamas, which because of its proximity to the United States, currently enjoys a higher level of Impulse Travel. It could discourage U.S. citizens without passports from taking quick jaunts to the various Islands.

It was reported that approximately 70 million U.S. citizens held valid passports in 2006, representing only 25% of the eligible population, and prior to 9/11 there was little incentive for them to acquire passports since they could travel within the hemisphere with only a driver's licence. United States' officials report, however, that the number of new passports issued within the past five years has increased dramatically and is expected to continue to escalate. The Bahamas has made an official appeal for the deadline for mandatory passports to be extended but, meanwhile, the Ministry of Tourism, in cooperation with the private sector, has launched an awareness campaign directed at current and potential visitors through its Web sites, posters, brochures and other collateral material.

While it is appreciated that new policies are needed to tighten security for travellers around the Western Hemisphere in light of heightened terrorist threats, these rules have the potential to severely impact local economies dependent on tourism traffic from the United States.

Other Challenges Facing The Bahamas

The Bahamas is pricing itself out of the market and must move quickly to address this issue, as lower cost destinations, such as Cuba and the Dominican Republic, compete aggressively. Many of the high costs, such as labour and electricity, are fixed; therefore, strategies being explored, particularly in other regions of the Caribbean, relate to retrofitting resorts with alternative energy such as wind or solar power, and low energy appliances.

Since many visitors are prepared to pay a high price, once the package is perceived as offering value for money, it is also imperative for destinations to pay special attention to upgrading every element of the visitor experience, with emphasis on service. Recruitment, selection, training and incentive programmes must be carefully examined and enhanced.

A related issue is that of linkages. An improved programme of incentives and training opportunities to assist local Bahamians in taking advantage of the numerous opportunities for linkages is a matter of urgency. Of particular urgency is the need to invest in new attractions and tours, that is new adventures, sights, and experiences outside the hotel. Such attractions should take into consideration new trends and emphasize events that meet customers' needs for entertainment, education, fitness and spiritual upliftment.

Of the 300 hotels in The Bahamas in 2004, 200 are Family Island resorts, the majority of which are small owner-operated establishments. More than 50% of the locally owned tourist establishments are experiencing low occupancy and financial difficulty. Many such entrepreneurs were granted crown land or financial assistance under Government's loan guarantee plan. However, no accompanying mechanism was put in place to guide these local entrepreneurs so that their businesses could become viable. It is urgent for hands-on advisory services to be made available to local entrepreneurs from the inception of the business idea to the final marketing of their establishments.

As noted earlier, all new initiatives must take into consideration the importance of sustainable development. The need to preserve the world's assets for future generations is becoming an important goal, not only for the travel industry but also for all other industries that use the earth's natural resources.

*   *   *

While the outlook for tourism appears positive, the challenge is for Government and private sector organizations to move from the existing ad hoc approach to tourism development to a systematic sustainable development strategy that integrates economic, social, and environmental programmes, so that tourism truly becomes a catalyst for positive transformation and growth.

TOURISM GIANTS
OF THE CENTURY

Sir Stafford Sands
The first Minister of Tourism (1913-72)

Stafford Lofthouse Sands was born on 23rd September, 1913, in Nassau, Bahamas. Of Spanish ancestry, his maternal great-grandfather, Manuel Ramon Menendez y Alonzo, came to Nassau in the mid-1800's. Manuel established himself as a merchant, married Elizabeth Ann Holmes, the young widow of a prominent Bahamian. The fifth daughter of Manuel and Elizabeth Menendez married Thomas Lofthouse, a merchant and legislator. Stafford Sands was the son of Enid Rosalie Lofthouse, the eldest daughter of Thomas and Elizabeth Lofthouse.

Stafford Sands attended Queen's College and the Government High School in Nassau, and Winnwood School, Lake Grove in New York State, from 1926 to 1929. Following the loss of an eye at the age of 12, he developed a phenomenal memory, with enormous powers of concentration, which baffled many of his colleagues.[1] In 1929, at the age of 16, he was articled in the law chambers of Sir A. Kenneth Solomon where he received his legal training. He opened his own law chambers at 309 Bay Street, Nassau, in 1935. He also demonstrated great business acumen and eventually became one of the most influential local businessmen of his era. He owned a chain of liquor stores, the Bahamas Gas & Fuel Company, the Nassau Market grocery chain, which he later sold to the American Winn-Dixie Corporation, and other businesses.

Stafford Sands entered politics in 1936, when he won the seat left vacant on the death of the Honourable Harcourt Malcolm, member for the *City* constituency. He represented the City for three decades. In an interview for the ***Bahamas Handbook and Businessman's Annual***, Sir Roland Symonette, former Premier, reminisced that from the time Sir Stafford made his maiden speech in the House, he was tough, forceful, determined, and very capable, and not afraid to oppose even the older conservative members, many of whom resented his brashness, terrifying cleverness, arrogance and devastating powers of argument.[2] But he was a born leader and eventually gained the support and admiration of his new, younger contemporaries. In October 1937, he was appointed a member of the powerful Finance Committee.[3] He was further described as possessing qualities of superb diligence, brilliance, and tenacity of purpose. In 1945, Governor Sir William Murphy appointed Sands a member of Executive Council and Leader for Government, but he resigned as Leader in less than a year because "he could not get his way".[4]

In 1949, a delegation comprising Bobby Symonette, Roy Solomon and Donald McKinney, called on the Acting Governor, Derek Evans, to urge for Stafford Sands' appointment as the Development Board Chairman. Sands became the Development Board Chairman in 1950 and went on to become the first Minister of Tourism in 1964. He also held the portfolio of Finance, which not only guaranteed that adequate budgets were allocated to Tourism each year, but also led the way for The Bahamas to become one of the world's leading offshore banking centres. As Minister of Finance, he also introduced the Bahamian dollar in 1966, fixing it against the US dollar, enabling tourists from The Bahamas' largest market to avoid burdensome conversion rates.

Tourism Achievements

From his appointment as Chairman of the Development Board in 1950 to the time he left office as Minister of Tourism in 1967, Stafford Sands exercised his genius to develop a brilliant promotional strategy that would differentiate The Bahamas from its competitors. To ensure that there were modern hotels to house the expected influx of visitors, the Hotels Encouragement Act was passed in 1954, offering incentives for new developers. In 1955, the Hawksbill Creek Agreement created Freeport, which soon began to rival Nassau as the main city, with modern infrastructure, luxurious hotels, a casino and golf courses. The Family Islands were added to the tourism product, with new resorts on Eleuthera, Abaco, Andros and Exuma. Before that time, resort development existed only on Bimini and Grand Bahama. The Family Island Regatta, inaugurated in 1954, became an annual event, bolstering arrivals to Exuma.

Stafford Sands' major legacy was his visionary marketing. The tourism budget was spent nearly exclusively on newspaper and magazine advertising, a massive public relations campaign in North America and England, and an effective sales promotion campaign, with high impact events such as fishing tournaments, sports car racing, Nassau-Miami Power Boat Races, sailing regattas, annual Speed Week, even "Junkanoo in June". He was the first tourism leader in the Caribbean to introduce a home-town newspaper public relations campaign and incentive travel for large corporations. His aggressive group and incentive strategy helped the country to become a year-round tourist destination since many of the meetings were scheduled during the traditionally slow periods of summer and fall. When he learned that the American Society of Travel Agents (ASTA) would be meeting in Miami, he organized such an impactful promotional programme to target these influential agents that two ASTA Chapters chose The Bahamas for their area meeting, the first time in history that the ASTA chapters had ever met outside the United States. The President of ASTA, at a concluding banquet, noted that "we in the travel business have come to realize that the Bahamas Development Board has done more in a short time to sell travel than any other country or area in the world".[5]

He opened sales offices in North America and the United Kingdom, and with the assistance of a General Sales Manager, directed the strategy. He capitalized on the country's spectacular marine attributes to attract filmmakers such as the 1954 Academy Award winning epic *Twenty Thousand Leagues under the Sea*.

To accommodate the increased level of air visitors, he spearheaded the construction of the Windsor Field airport and new Customs facilities at Prince George Wharf for cruise passengers. In response to his promotional thrust, Pan American expanded its service to Miami and inaugurated Nassau-New York daily service in 1957. Other new airlines, such as British Overseas Airways Corporation, inaugurated London Service in 1956, Trans-Canada Airlines provided service to Toronto and Montreal. Cubana Airlines began Havana-Nassau service.

During this regime, the relationship between tourism and the environment was recognized and important steps were taken by his Government to preserve natural resources. In 1958, the Inagua National Park and the Exuma Cays Land and Sea Park (the world's first land and sea park) were established; and the Bahamas National Trust came into existence by Act of Parliament in 1959.

In summer, 1954, Stafford Sands was singled out for special recognition. In an unprecedented gesture, the Florida State Chamber of Commerce awarded an engraved plaque to Sands "in appreciation of the cooperation in making the Florida-Bahamas area an outstanding vacation playground".

The decade of the 1950's saw The Bahamas' tourist industry jump from a 32,000 per year seasonal industry to a prosperous business attracting nearly a quarter of a million visitors annually—an increase of about 700% in ten years. The only year in which visitor arrivals did not increase was in 1958, and this was a direct result of the 1958 Strike. The unprecedented growth was concentrated in

Nassau, with the bulk of the tourist accommodation. Stafford Sands' achievements can also be attributed to other members of the Development Board, comprising persons such as "Bobby" Symonette, Trevor Kelly, Charlie Bethel and Sir Harold Christie.

He was appointed a Commander of the Order of the British Empire in 1955 and knighted in 1963. Posthumously, he was honoured by the Free National Movement government by placing his portrait on the new $10 Bahamian bill, which created some controversy.

Sir Clement T. Maynard, who later held the post of Minister of Tourism, stated that he contemplates Sir Stafford's career "with a certain amount of admiration for his single-minded devotion to the tested theory that substantial increases in promotional spending would surely result in corresponding rises in the numbers. He marketed and sold the Bahamian product—sun, sand, sea—and some of the giant footprints he left in the Bahamian sands are still there to be seen".[6]

Following the defeat of his United Bahamian Party government in 1967, Sir Stafford went into voluntary exile in Spain. He died on 25th January, 1972 in London. On the occasion of the first meeting of the House after Sir Stafford's death, Prime Minister Lynden Pindling commented: "There may be members of this House who might not agree with what Sir Stafford did or why he did it, but one can still say that for many years a great Bahamian stood in this chamber and gave service to his country in the manner he thought best". He added that in the view of some of government members, Sir Stafford was the "blue-eyed baby of the classes, and the arch-enemy of the masses".[7]

Footnote on Sir Stafford's style and accomplishments

Sir Stafford was indeed a visionary, but autocratic, leader. His view was that "the only way a small country could be run effectively and efficiently and with a progressive economy from which all would benefit was by a benign dictatorship . . . there was no doubt . . . that Sir Stafford saw himself as being ideally cast for such a role". [8] Many of the managers who worked in Bahamas Tourist offices in North America during Sands' regime spoke of him as flamboyant, demanding and often extravagant. Sir Stafford Sands was not a democratic leader nor was he a student of organization. Yet, he earned the respect and loyalty of his staff.[9]

The tourist industry, like other businesses during this era, was controlled and managed by whites, nearly all of whom were non-Bahamians. The Nassau operation was insignificant. Sales staff were all non-Bahamian. The six local staff working in the Development Board in Nassau were primarily responsible for administration and servicing the trade, with no input for the overall marketing programme and strategy. Sands spearheaded regular briefings with his sales team and advertising agencies to review promotional campaigns. Matters related to the hotel industry were coordinated through the Bahamas Hotel Association, established in 1952. All managers of hotels were also non-Bahamian. In fact, the entire tourist industry was controlled and managed by non-Bahamians.[10]

Despite his autocratic and exclusionary management style, Sir Stafford achieved unparalleled success as a tourism minister. He was a shrewd promoter. He nearly single-handedly guided the tourism industry from a mere 32,018 visitors in 1949 to a healthy 822,317 visitors in 1966, a 2,466% increase over 1949. He pioneered the country's transition to a year-round successful, tourist resort—the envy of the region.

In the year 2000, there was much controversy surrounding the issue of placing the image of Sir Stafford Sands on the Bahamian $10 bill. While many objected because of his racist attitude, others pointed to Sir Stafford's tremendous contributions to the prosperity of the country. Grassroot supporters of Sir Stafford include Berkeley "Peanuts" Taylor and Rev. Dr. J. Emmette Weir, a Methodist minister.

In an interview with this writer in August 2002, Peanuts Taylor, described how he had been invited by Sir Stafford throughout the 1950's and 1960's to represent The Bahamas both locally and abroad. He affirmed that Sir Stafford showed his admiration, respect and appreciation for his talent and hard work. Sir Stafford's tenure, stated Taylor, was one of the most prosperous periods for local nightclubs and entertainers.

In a commentary in the *Nassau Guardian*, Rev. Dr. Emmette Weir applauded the success of Sir Stafford in pioneering major initiatives in tourism and financial services. Dr. Weir stated: "The writer is old enough to remember the critical economic challenges which faced The Bahamas after World War II . . . With the sponge industry dead, the military bases declining, and very little going on in agriculture and fisheries, the main factor in the Bahamian economy proved to be the remittances from Bahamian farm labourers working in the United States . . . Enter the late Sir Stafford Sands, who conceived of and promoted the idea of making tourism into a year-round industry and who promoted the development of The Bahamas as a tax haven . . ." Recognizing Sir Stafford's faults, Rev. Weir continued: "Sir Stafford was no saint. Indeed, one got the impression that he was coldly efficient, lacking in kindness or compassion at the personal level and, indeed, rather distant. He appeared to be hard working and success oriented, capable of forcing all others who were associated with him also to perform to the best of their ability. And while branded as a racist who did not like black people, his personality was such that he did not endear himself to white people either, many of whom appeared as deferential to him as the working man from Over-The-Hill! No, Sir Stafford was no saint, nor, considering his major contributions in the field of economic development, was he the greatest of sinners."[11]

Oswald Brown, a seasoned reporter, in an article printed in the *Nassau Guardian*, made the case for Sir Stafford to be recognized in a short list of national heroes, along with Sir Lynden Pindling, Sir Milo Butler, Sir Etienne Dupuch and

Sir Roland Symonette. He pointed out that, although Sir Stafford was perceived as a racist, "the fact remains that he was the architect of the economic system that is the foundation for the strength and solvency of the Bahamian dollar, which is responsible for the high standard of living that Bahamians currently enjoy. What is more, even now, more than 35 years later, his visionary approach to the promotion of tourism is still the template being used by the government to ensure that the country's tourism industry as major source of income remains vibrant." [12]

While the debate on Sir Stafford's character continues,
his tremendous contribution in laying the foundation for the
successful tourism industry we enjoy today is a matter of record.

Sir Clement T. Maynard

The longest serving Minister of Tourism

Born in Nassau on 11th September, 1928, Clement T. Maynard was named for his father, a Barbadian, who came to The Bahamas in 1922 during the reconstruction of the British Colonial Hotel. His mother was Georgiana K. Symonette of Wemyss' Bight, Eleuthera. He was educated at Eastern Secondary School in Nassau, Franklin School of Science and Arts, Philadelphia, and the London School of Hygiene and Tropical Medicine, London University.

Starting as an assistant technician, Mr. Maynard moved up to Chief Medical Technologist at the Princess Margaret Hospital. He was founder and first president of the Bahamas Civil Service Union in 1959.

Mr. Maynard began to take an active interest in PLP affairs in 1953, the year the party was formed, and was vice-chairman of the party when it formed the Government in January 1967. He was named Leader of the Senate, Minister without Portfolio and Minister of State. In the April 1968 General Elections, Senator Maynard won the House of Assembly seat in his home constituency of Gambier. He was named Minister of Works in April 1968, and in October 1969, he was named Minister of Tourism and Telecommunications.

Minister Maynard's first term as Minister of Tourism lasted a full decade. He placed emphasis on professionalism for the industry and for his own staff. New administrative procedures were introduced and the entire working of the Ministry of Tourism and its relations with the overseas offices was systematized. A proper structure, patterned after that of the British Tourist Authority, was introduced and job responsibilities grouped under various Assistant Directors and Managers. Professionals were recruited in the Nassau office to fill positions in the new structure. Bahamians were also recruited and trained for Sales and Information positions in Bahamas Tourist Offices overseas. Prior to 1967, there were no Bahamians in the overseas sales operation. At the end of 1973, eleven of the 60 BTO staff (i.e. 18%) were Bahamians and at headquarters 75 of the 78 employees were Bahamian. Although Bahamians were recruited and trained for sales and managerial posts in Bahamas Tourist Offices abroad, Sir Clement maintained a balance between Bahamian staff and qualified foreign sales staff, knowledgeable about the market which The Bahamas was targeting.

Minister Maynard ensured that a comprehensive marketing plan was in place for the orderly growth of tourism that involved not only overseas promotion, which continued to be a major focus, but careful attention to market research, onshore product, safety and satisfaction of guests, formal training, as well as involvement and recognition of Bahamians in the industry. The Headquarters operation was modernized, and new units established such as a Visitor Relations Department to deal with tourist complaints, new Tourist Information offices were opened at ports of entry and downtown on New Providence and Grand Bahama and offices were opened in the Family Islands, starting with North Andros and Eleuthera. An Information Unit was established to deal with written visitor queries and produce collaterals for tourists. Recognizing the importance of safety for visitors, he initiated a unit of Beach Wardens, trained by both Tourism and the Police, with powers of arrest, whose only job was to patrol beaches, and other sites frequented by tourists, to protect visitors from harassment, while extending a warm welcome. A fully functional Research Department was established, with the assistance of world-renowned consultants, and this unit was considered the best in the region. Key Bahamians in the new structure were given exposure in established BTOs in the United Kingdom and Europe. A broad-based advisory board, with representatives from all of the key agencies that impact tourism, was appointed and became partners to produce workable solutions to problems facing the industry.

Minister Maynard was exceptionally dedicated and personally initiated innovative programmes. The Bahamahost and People-to-People programmes, National Tourism Achievement Awards, designed to improve standards of service and visitor satisfaction and to recognize outstanding contributions to tourism, are just a few of his notable achievements. Each year, Tourism Awareness campaigns were launched to ensure that the entire community was sensitized to the importance of tourism and the need for good attitudes. The drive to increase domestic tourism and the hugely successful Goombay Summer festival were initiated during his tenure, along with the winning marketing theme "It's Better in The Bahamas". The national flag carrier, Bahamasair, was formed while aviation and tourism were in his portfolio.

During his first term in office, visitor arrivals increased from 1,332,396 in 1969 to 1,789,420 in 1979. By the time he completed his second term as Minister of Tourism in 1989, visitor arrivals had reached 3.3 million per year. He succeeded in making The Bahamas the envy of the Caribbean. But his greatest legacy is that Bahamians at all levels, formerly excluded, took their rightful place in this important industry. Apart from his success in Bahamianizing the Ministry of Tourism, grass root Bahamians from the community were seen in media advertising, and they participated in overseas promotions and in policy decisions affecting the industry through representation in the new broad-based Tourism Advisory Committee. In the hotel industry, he initiated an exchange programme with foreign countries enabling young Bahamian hotel employees to get the necessary expertise. All stake holders, whether straw vendors, taxi drivers, entertainers, hoteliers, airline personnel, or trade were embraced as important partners in the Number One industry.

Minister Clement Maynard built a professional organization, leaving behind a record of unparalleled success. He turned over the Tourism portfolio to Livingstone Coakley in October 1979. Five years later, Maynard was reappointed as Minister of Tourism which he described as his "first love" and served until 1989, consolidating his position as the longest serving Minister of Tourism in the region.

He was knighted by Her Majesty, the Queen, in her birthday honours, 1989. Also, he received the Grand Prix Mondial award in Paris, for outstanding achievement in tourism. The Bahamas tourism industry established a scholarship for tertiary studies in tourism in his name. The prestigious Cacique Award for Lifetime Achievement was named in his honour in 2005.

Mr. Maynard married Zoe' Cumberbatch, daughter of Dr. & Mrs. Roland Cumberbatch, Nassau, in 1947. They are the parents of four sons, one deceased, and a daughter, the Honourable Allyson Maynard Gibson, a Cabinet Minister.

SPOTLIGHT ON

TOURISM STALWARTS

OF

THE 1930'S AND 1940'S

Bert Cambridge

Leader of the First Band of Professional Musicians

Bert Cambridge, born in February 1901, was the son of Nathaniel and Florence Cambridge. He attended Boys Central School in Nassau and studied in New York at the Holland Conservatory of Music from 1919 to 1921. A gifted musician, he specialized in organ playing. In 1919, he entered the New York Conservatory of Music, obtaining a Bachelor of Music Degree two years later. Cambridge's music was the very first heard on ZNS, as he played at the opening of the studio. In 1922, he organized the Dundas Musical Association, out of which came the Cambridge Orchestra, established in 1923. He has made a tremendous contribution to the music industry.

Said to be the first band of professional musicians in The Bahamas, the Cambridge Orchestra was versatile, and played liturgical dance and concert music. The ensemble, though small, competed with bands imported from the USA to perform at the Royal Victoria and British Colonial Hotels for the winter season. Because local bands were often bypassed in favour of foreign bands, Bert Cambridge discussed the matter with Governor Bede Clifford, who agreed that this was unfair. The Governor ordered that all hotels requiring permission to bring a foreign band must employ also a native group. This served as an incentive for bands and other entertainers to study music and play professionally, demanding the respect that the art deserved.[13]

Cambridge's Orchestra played during Nassau's first international radio broadcast which took place in the foyer of the British Colonial Hotel, and was sponsored by the Bahamas Development Board. His was also the very first band of black musicians to broadcast in Miami, Florida, which opened the way for black bands into broadcasting in their own homeland.

Cambridge set the music to many Bahamian songs including "Peas and Rice and Coconut Oil", "My Lima Beans", "Hoist up the John B. Sail".

Members of the Orchestra included Bert Cambridge, pianist (leader); Harold Curry, violinist; John "Sir Coke" Coakley, saxophonist; Oliver Mason, trumpetist; Mannaseh "Massa" Strachan, bass; Arthur Pinder, trombonist and Harold "Baby Face" Deveaux, drummer.

Mr. Cambridge won a seat for the Southern District in the House of Assembly in the 1942 General Election, and served until 1956. He is remembered for his stand against racial discrimination, when, in 1956, he seconded Sir Etienne Dupuch's anti-discrimination resolution, which was instrumental in opening public places to all Bahamians, regardless of colour.

He served for many years on various Government committees and boards, including the Finance Committee, Electrical Board and the Public Establishments Committee.

Sir Harold G. Christie

Pioneer in Tourism Investment

A visionary Bahamian who deserves much credit for tourism investment and promotion is Sir Harold G. Christie, CBE. His name is synonymous with real estate in The Bahamas. He founded H.G. Christie Ltd. in 1922 and was the greatest promoter of Bahamas real estate and tourism from the 1920's until his death in 1973.

Sir Harold's early life is best described in a brief article on him in the Lyford Cay Property Owners Association newsletter, written by Arthur Haley.

A native born Bahamian, he loved his country with a passion. Christie was also an active social figure of his times, gregarious, affable, and with wide-ranging friendships at every social level. Stories and rumors still revolve around his vibrant private life.

His life began modestly, however, in a home with a large family and very little money. The father of Harold Christie, and two younger brothers and five sisters was Henry Christopher Christie, an eccentric poet and evangelist who according to his second son, Percy, was "uninterested in money and simply decided that he wasn't going to work." Instead, he went on preaching trips in The Bahamas lasting for weeks, though he must have been home a good deal since the ***Bahamas Handbook*** of 1979 notes that Henry's wife, Margaret Alice, "endured 21 pregnancies."

Margaret Christie was a practical woman who determinedly supported her family, first with a straw-basket business, then by buying and selling real estate in Nassau and Florida. Harold, it is recorded, adored his mother.

Harold Christie attended school in Nassau, and later described himself as "not a bad student, but not a particularly bright one". In 1912, at age 16, he went to New York where he found temporary but uninteresting work, and a year later moved to Canada. He enlisted in the Canadian Air Force, and was briefly a cadet pilot, but did not gain his wings. The experience, though, gave him a lifelong interest in aviation, and he was involved in the forming of Bahamas Airways in 1935. In 1921, however, he returned to Nassau, reportedly as broke as when he left nine years earlier, but within a year, his fortunes had reversed. After he formed H.G. Christie Real Estate in 1922, the business dominated the remainder of his life.

Sir Harold Christie and
Frank Christie at
309 Bay Street

Through his real estate business, he achieved notable success in promoting property investment. When there was a boom in land sales in Florida in the 1930's, Christie used his charm to secure introductions to the rich and famous and was successful in luring many of them to The Bahamas to invest in winter homes, businesses and tourism establishments. According to his personal assistant, Reginald Walker, "he could look at a piece of real estate and immediately visualize what it could become if sufficient capital were invested in it. He believed wholeheartedly in the concept that the best export trade a country can develop is selling land which could not be turned to agricultural use. The purchaser can't take it away with him—it's always there—and whatever he spends on it directly benefits the country".

In late 1934, when Harold Christie learned that Harry Oakes, discoverer of the Canadian Lake Shore Mines, had arrived in Palm Beach Florida, he immediately put a plan in place to lure this multi-millionaire to Nassau. He arranged a meeting with him in Florida, and brought him and his wife to Nassau at his expense. Christie arranged for Oakes' residency papers and, in the winter of 1936-37, Harold Oakes and his wife came to Nassau with their lawyer, Walter Foskett, as house guests of

Harold Christie. Oakes invested in the tourism industry and became a new force in the country until his mysterious murder on 8th July, 1943.

After the liquor business ceased, leaving the country in deep depression, Christie is said to have invited the "Bay Street Boys" to his office to reveal his plan for developing a stable economic base for the island. He explained to the merchants that The Bahamas had a great opportunity to exploit its natural assets to the world. He urged them to adopt a long-range plan for the tourist trade.

Harold Christie travelled to England, Canada and the United States on promotional trips. He achieved much success in luring wealthy businessmen to Nassau, starting with Britain's Frederick Sigrist, who designed England's modern fighter plane, the Spitfire, Canadian Sir Frederick William Taylor, president of the Royal Bank of Canada and American Mr. Lynch of the investment firm of Merrill, Lynch, Pierce, Fenner and Beane. Christie and his partners purchased land cheaply "from the natives and sold it to the newcomers at a substantial profit"[14].

While Harold Christie liked to earn money, "he was generous to a fault", according to his friend, the Honourable Godfrey W. Higgs, CBE. Another friend, Prince Hepburn, described him as "one of the most unselfish and generous men I ever met".

Harold Christie was a member of the House of Assembly for Abaco from 1927 to 1935. When he won a seat on Cat Island in 1935, he began a life-long interest in the people of Cat Island, whom he served until his retirement in 1966, and who fondly acknowledged him as "Papa Christie". Christie also served on the Executive Council from 1939 to 1948. The Honourable Godfrey Higgs noted that "although he was active in politics all his life, the only matters which interested him were those involving the development of The Bahamas—land, tourism, agriculture and the like. In such matters he would give his all and was tireless in his efforts". [15]

For much of his life, while enjoying women's company, Christie remained a committed bachelor, but in 1960 married Mrs. Virginia Johnson, an interior designer.

Christie was awarded the Commander of the British Empire (CBE) in 1949, and a knighthood in 1964. He died of a heart attack on 27th September, 1973, in Hamburg, Germany, while setting up an office intended to attract German investors to The Bahamas.

Due, in great part, to Harold Christie's efforts in attracting visitors and investors, Nassau became a thriving winter resort.

Alphonso "Blind Blake" Higgs

Musician, Songwriter, and Father of Bahamian Music

Alphonso "Blind Blake" Higgs (centre)—Musician, Songwriter, and Legendary
Entertainer

Among the many local entertainers whose music was used to promote the country was Alphonso Blake Higgs, commonly known as "Blind Blake". Blake Higgs was born at Matthew Town, Inagua, in 1915. He became interested in music at an early age. He was adept at string instruments—ukulele, banjo, tenor banjo, six-string guitar—and he also played the piano.

After losing his eyesight at the age of sixteen, he did not allow this affliction to deter him, but continued to pursue his music career. He was dubbed "Blind Blake".

Higgs began his musical career in earnest in 1933, and as early as 1935, recorded for Philco Radio, long before recording was even thought of in The Bahamas. He wrote many songs on the political and social life of The Bahamas. One of his more popular songs was "It was Love, Love Alone, Cause King Edward to Leave The Throne", based on the love affair of King Edward VIII with Wallis Simpson. He was forbidden to play the song upon the arrival of the Duke and Duchess of Windsor to the Colony. However, he was invited to play the song by the Duke at Government House and he received a standing ovation by the Duke and his party.

Blind Blake wrote about sixty Goombay songs starting in the 1920's including "Run Come See Jerusalem", based on the effects of the 1929 Hurricane, "Jones Oh Jones", "Noise in the Market", "Conch Ain't Got No Bone", "Mame had a Rooster, She took it for a Hen" and "J.P. Morgan".

He performed for many Heads of State, royalty and international celebrities such as President John F. Kennedy and Prime Minister Harold Macmillan. He performed for tourists at the Royal Victoria Hotel, Dirty Dicks, Blackbeard's and many other hotels and clubs throughout New Providence. Internationally, he gave live performances in Philadelphia, Boston, Florida, New York, Maryland and Washington D.C.

Over the years, many visiting celebrities, such as Mahalia Jackson, Louis Armstrong and "Duke" Ellington, praised Blind Blake for his pure Bahamian flavour and originality. In 1980, Blind Blake was one of the Bahamian artists interviewed for a Perry Como television special on The Bahamas.

In an interview with a Tribune reporter in 1980, Blake talked about how his songwriting changed over the years because of politics. "In these days, in writing about certain events, you must be very careful because there is so much politics in this town today. You gotta watch yourself. You don't want to be seen to be landing on one side or another. You want to be a man in the middle. Now, when I write my song, I circulate it just to certain people to get their feelings before I attempt to publish it."[16]

In the 1970's, Blind Blake's band was employed by the Ministry of Tourism to play at the Nassau International Airport, giving a musical welcome to arriving visitors—a job he performed for almost two decades.

Dubbed the "Father of Bahamian Music", he was awarded the Bahamas Chamber of Commerce's Distinguished Citizens Award in 1973 and the Ministry of Tourism's National Tourism Achievement Award in 1979.

Blake Higgs—musician, songwriter, and legendary entertainer—died in November 1985, at the age of 71.

Paul Meeres

Pioneer Entertainer

The 1930's signaled the beginning of the most significant chapter in Bahamian entertainment, with the rise to popularity of Paul Meeres, who built the first over-the-hill theatre and became the role model and protégé of future local entertainers.

Paul Meeres was born in 1902. His father was Frenchman, Paul Meeres, and his mother, an Abaconian, Victoria Gilbert, was described by Berkeley "Peanuts" Taylor as a "tall, black, beautiful woman". As a talented dancer and entertainer, his name dominated the Paris theatrical circles for years. He gave a command performance at Buckingham Palace in the 1930's. At one time he was a partner of Josephine Baker, a famous Negro singer and Paris nightclub entertainer. He was a star performer with the Folies Bergère, a famous nightspot in Paris.[17]

Paul Meeres returned to Nassau at the height of his career in the 1930's to share his success with his people. He built a fabulous theatre and 50-room hotel, Chez Paul Meeres, in the heart of Market Street near the neighbourhood in which he was born. He was a handsome, generous, brilliant performer, often described as the most colourful entertainer of the 20th century. Paul Meeres was a pioneer who became the role model for many upcoming local performers. Among the entertainers whom he mentored and trained were Peanuts Taylor and John "Chippie" Chipman. He was ahead of his time because few people went over the hill in the 1930's; but he was not discouraged. Meeres later left Nassau to return to the Big Theatre circuit, where he continued to earn a good living, but his example and success continued to inspire young Bahamian entertainers.

(Photo and historical information—Courtesy of Duke Errol Strachan)

Mary Moseley 1878-1960

Historian and pioneer in Tourism Communications
(Adapted from article in Nassau Magazine—Mid-Season, 1960)

Born in 1878, Mary Moseley was the granddaughter of Edwin Charles Moseley, the founder and first editor of the *Nassau Guardian*, and the daughter of Mr. And Mrs. Alfred Edwin Moseley. She was educated in Nassau and privately tutored, learning the newspaper business at an early age.

She undertook the management and editorship of the *Nassau Guardian* in 1904, upon the death of her father. In 1907, she acquired the actual business from the estate of the late Percival James Moseley.

In 1914, Miss Moseley went to England to engage in war work. During her stay in London she formed the Ladies Committee of the West Indian Contingent. She was awarded a Member of the Most Excellent Order of the British Empire (MBE) for her work on behalf of the men in the armed forces from the West Indies.

Returning to Nassau after World War I, she resumed the editorship of The *Nassau Guardian* until 1952 when the newspaper was sold, but continued in an advisory capacity. She was also a keen Bahamian historian. She was nominated a Trustee for the Nassau Public Library and Museum and later became Chairman of the Trusteeship Committee. ***Bahamas Handbook***, written by Miss Moseley in 1926, was the first authoritative account of the history of The Bahamas at the time of its publication.

Miss Moseley served as a member of the Bahamas Development Board for many years. Noting the dearth of tourism information, in 1934 she started a tourist publication NASSAU magazine, which became the official source of Bahamas travel news. The magazine was circulated throughout the travel trade in North America and Europe. When she sold the magazine in 1948, she continued to contribute articles to that magazine and to other publications.

In 1944, on the eve of the centenary of the ***Nassau Guardian***, the House of Assembly presented Miss Moseley with a scroll recording a resolution passed by the House on 27th July, 1944, expressing appreciation for her dedication and excellent reporting of House proceedings as editor of the ***Nassau Guardian***:

> . . . "The ***Nassau Guardian*** will celebrate its centenary on 23rd day of November, 1944
>
> And whereas the said Newspaper has been for many years the Official Newspaper of the Government and the Legislature, and whenever the occasion demanded has carefully pointed out and emphasized the importance of the House and its rightful place in the Colony's Constitution and has also wholeheartedly supported and upheld its traditions, precedents, privileges and ancient rights. And whereas, the present Editor, Miss Mary Moseley, MBE, has taken a very keen interest in all matters pertaining to the House for a period of nearly fifty years by regularly attending its Sessions and voluntarily reporting its debates, Resolved, Therefore, that this House desires to place on record its high and grateful appreciation of the services rendered by *The **Nassau Guardian*** and its Editor, Miss Mary Moseley, MBE.
>
> Dated at the House of Assembly, Nassau, New Providence, Bahamas, this 20th November, 1944
>
> Kenneth Solomon, Speaker"

Miss Moseley's contribution to journalism and documentation of Bahamian history has been noteworthy. It was suggested that hardly anyone has ever published anything worthwhile about The Bahamas without reference to the authority of Miss Moseley, either in person or from her writings. She suffered from raids upon her work by literary pirates, and it was typical of her that she usually faced these incidents with humour rather than resentment.[18] The tourism industry is indebted to her for pioneering the first tourist publication and publishing noteworthy travel information. She died on 19th January, 1960 at the age of 81.

Sir Harry Oakes

Benefactor and Investor
1874-1943

Harry Oakes, born on 23rd December, 1874, to Edith and William Pitt Oakes of Sangerville, Maine, United States, was the third of five children. The Oakes family had lived in Sangerville since at least 1808, but in the 1880's William Oakes moved to a nearby town, Dover-Foxcroft, so his sons could attend Foxcroft Academy, reportedly the best high school in the country at that time. After Foxcroft, Harry attended Bowdoin College and then Syracuse Medical School, but left before completing the course of study. He was restless and uninterested in the medical world, and wanted to head off on his own and strike it rich. Harry was 23 when he set out on a 16-year journey that took him to Australia, Africa, the Yukon, California, Central America and Canada, among other far-flung places. During his college years he predicted to a classmate that he would become a millionaire and die a violent death with his boots on. He did both.

Oakes' quest for wealth began in the Yukon where he chipped rock at temperatures which plunged to 60-degrees below zero. At the other extreme he tried the Belgian Congo and by 1906 he was back where he started—Alaska. In 1910, he turned up in Ontario and got a new miner's licence. In 1912, in Kirkland Lake,

Ontario, Harry finally struck gold. Along with four partners (the Tough brothers), he made a significant strike, and the money finally started to pour in. In 1916, he sold his interest in the mine, opened his own mine nearby, and by 1921 had a fortune, becoming among the richest men in Canada. It is estimated that his mine then netted over US$10 million per year and that he made hundreds of millions of US dollars during his lifetime, in the billions in current dollars.

In 1923, he celebrated his new-found wealth with a world tour, during which he met a shy, quiet Australian lady named Eunice MacIntyre, the daughter of a government official. She was twenty-four, six inches taller than stubby Oakes, and 26 years younger. The couple married in Australia and moved to Ontario, becoming Canadian citizens, mainly for tax purposes. During this time they purchased *The Willows*, a grand Bar Harbour cottage, which became Eunice's favourite place to summer.

Harry made extremely generous contributions to the Canadian Liberal Party, hoping that a Liberal victory would offer him a lifetime senatorial appointment. When the Liberals lost, the opposition passed a new tax that was clearly aimed to punish Harry. Because of these new stringent taxes, Harry left Canada with his wife, and five children.

For the next few years they spent the bulk of their time in London, England, and Nassau, Bahamas, with summers in Bar Harbor and wherever else they fancied. The Oakes became British citizens and Harry again zeroed in on politics, joining the best clubs and making huge contributions where it counted most. His philanthropy paid off. On 8th June, 1939, King George included him on the Birthday Honours list and Harry Oakes became a Baronet.

Harry Oakes was introduced to The Bahamas by real estate tycoon Harold Christie. In late 1934, when Harold Christie learned that Harry Oakes was in Palm Beach, Florida, he immediately put a plan in place to lure this multi-millionaire to Nassau. He arranged a meeting with him in Florida, and invited him and his wife to Nassau at his expense. Oakes' interest grew as Christie explained his vision of placing Nassau on the map as a tourist centre. Having been attracted by the absence of taxes and the charms of Nassau, Oakes agreed to move to The Bahamas. In the winter of 1936-37, Mr. & Mrs. Harold Oakes came to Nassau with their lawyer, Walter Foskett, as house guests of Harold Christie. He acquired "Westbourne", a magnificent home west of the city of Nassau and huge tracts of land all over the island. He also built the Bahamas Country Club, first golf course in The Bahamas and Oakes Field, Nassau's first airport.

Oakes was described by many as a crude, coarse, bitter, angry, abrasive and hardened man, difficult to work for, and given to sudden outbursts of temper. His wife, Eunice, reportedly, was the one person who could make him behave civilly, at least in her presence. He was also famous for seeking vengeance on any whom he thought had wronged him. One story has it that when Oakes visited the British Colonial Hotel and was turned away because of his appearance, he bought the hotel shortly thereafter and fired the employee who had embarrassed him.

Oakes also became renowned for his generosity. He paid for parks and numerous public projects wherever he lived, and is remembered fondly, especially by those who did not know him, throughout Canada and The Bahamas.

After spending six months in London, England, he returned permanently to Nassau. He invested in the tourism industry in Nassau and relieved unemployment through his many projects, becoming a new force in the country. He built a waterworks, a golf course, set up a bus service, an airplane service for emergency illnesses, free milk for children and a fund for unwed mothers. He was elected a member of the House of Assembly in 1938, and later was named to the Legislative Council.

It all came to end on a rainy night on 7th July, 1943, when Sir Harry Oakes was brutally and mysteriously murdered in the bedroom of his Nassau home. At the time, Sir Harry's wife and four of their five children were vacationing at their summer home in Bar Harbor. Oakes was to join them there the following day. His mutilated body was found in the bedroom of his Nassau estate on the morning of 8th July. His body, which was bludgeoned and bloodied, was covered with feathers from his ripped pillow that had been doused with gasoline, and set aflame. According to the autopsy, death had been caused by a blow or blows from a blunt instrument. His remains were buried in the East Dover cemetery in Dover-Foxcroft, Canada.

Although the husband of his oldest daughter, playboy Count Marie Alfred Fouquereaux de Marigny, was tried for the crime, he was acquitted in November of 1943, and the crime remains unsolved. Years later, Alfred de Marigny went public and made a number of accusations concerning the murder. He later published a book on the subject.

The unsolved tragic murder dealt a blow to the image of the Colony as a tranquil, peaceful haven, and some of the events and rumours were a lasting embarrassment to the Duke of Windsor, then Governor of The Bahamas, a personal friend of Sir Harry Oakes.

Harry Oakes left a personal fortune valued at slightly under $12 million, not counting his shares in Lake Shore Mine, or his numerous houses.

Sources: http://www.barharbor.com/sirharry.html
www.sangerville.lib.me.us/oakes.html
http://www.crimelibrary.com/notorious_murders/celebrity/harry_oakes/5.htm

Mamie Irlene Worrell

Pioneer in Hospitality for People of Colour
(Contributed by Beverly Wallace Whitfield)

Mamie Irlene Worrell nee Wright was born on the 28th May, 1893, in Norfolk, Virginia, to parents of Afro-American and Native American descent—parents who tragically died within 48 hours of each other in a terrible 'flu epidemic.

Mamie was one of the fortunate young ladies of her day to be able to go off to College, in Winston Salem, North Carolina, to study Domestic Science. It was here, on holiday, that she met the handsome Barbadian medical student, Gascoygne St. Pierre Worrell, fell in love with him and became his wife.

Gascoygne, who had settled in The Bahamas, sent for his wife. They started a family—a daughter, Beverly and son, Phillip. Over the next few decades, it became abundantly clear to Mamie that persons of colour who visited the Colony from the United States were denied accommodation at the local hotels. She was so perturbed by this that she decided that visitors from the land of her birth would always have a home, in her home. As simply as that, *Worrell's Guest House* was born! The transition from home to Guest House was made easier by the fact that the children had "flown the coop", hence there was much space in the three-storey home to offer visitors. Mamie pioneered this adjunct to the tourism industry of the day.

Many of the guests, who were professionals in their own right, came originally from the Southern United States (mainly Florida and Georgia), to play in The Bahamas' sun. Their "play" was to take part in the tennis matches at the Gym Tennis Club, which was then located at the foot of Mackey Street, where they won many trophies to take back home. These visitors were truly "repeat visitors" as they forged lasting friendships, and subsequently visited often. There is currently one widower from that era who has retired to a home in Sea Breeze—such is the love he experienced from the people of The Bahamas.

Mamie was not short on friendship and hospitality in her Guest House business because each guest was considered a member of the family. Wherever she went, so did the guests: to teas, dinners, dances, bridge, garden club meetings and exhibitions, the theatre, or simply to visit another friend. Members of Mamie's family were often pressed into service as a waiter, chauffeur, tour guide or escort, which enhanced the guest's feeling of being "part of a family". And, of course, these "friends" sent other friends and this created a demand for additional guest houses, with similar professional people coming to them from further afield.

As black Americans realized there was a "special home" for them in The Bahamas, they soon came from all points to enjoy the "at home" atmosphere of Worrell's and other guest houses. It was not unusual for groups of friends (for example, The Links) to gather on the upstairs porch of Worrell's Guest House and share spirited fun as they watched the passing parade both on the main street below and the waterfront across the street. Their enjoyment was infectious, and Mamie and household looked forward to the return each year of these and other fun-loving friends from the North.

Some of the names of visitors to Worrell's Guest House would read like a "Black Who's Who": Dr. & Mrs. Ernest Alexander of New York, Dr. Kelsey Pharr of Miami, Dr. and Mrs. E.G. Bowden of Atlanta and the well-known Mr. & Mrs. W.E.B. Dubois, to name a few. Black entertainers like Roy Hamilton, Etta Moten, Sydney Poitier and Harry Belafonte also came through the portals of Worrell's Guest House as day-time guests. All these persons brought with them class and culture—let alone their accompanying largesse which boosted The Bahamas economy!

Because of Mamie's cosmopolitan nature, George Harrison of "The Beatles" fame also spent a night at Worrell's, and would have stayed longer but fans threatened to descend on him for autographs, so he had to move.

The decision to open her home to visiting Americans was never one that Mamie regretted. Even after Afro-Americans could enjoy the accommodation of local hotels, Worrell's Guest House continued to be a "home away from home" for many West Indians, particularly surveyors and educators, who came on contract, many of whom later settled in Nassau.

So Worrell's Guest House was born out of discrimination of a certain sector of visitors to The Bahamas and went on to become a way-station for others.

Mamie Irlene's contribution to the tourism industry of The Bahamas was recognized by the Government when she was awarded the National Tourism

Achievement Award in the first Awards Ceremony in 1976. A year later she died. Although the Guest House survived her passing, the true spirit—hers—was gone, so the doors officially closed a few years later, and with that the era of the small Guest House virtually vanished as well.

The house, which still stands on East Shirley Street, has been identified as an historic building under the Antiquities & Monuments Act.

TOURISM STALWARTS

OF THE 1950'S

Lou Adams

Pioneer Band leader and Trumpeter

Lou Adams Jr. was born in Nassau on 13th September, 1922. He studied at Eastern Junior and Eastern Senior Schools. In the early 1930's, Lou was impressed by a gentleman by the name of Bill Moore, the first black trumpeter to play with the many white foreign bands that performed at the big hotels on New Providence.

He was tutored for a year by Bill Moore and practiced religiously. He started his career playing with the Chocolate Dandies and The Melody Makers.

Lou acknowledges that prior to the 1950's all of the serious work in big hotels was given to foreign bands, while local bands were relegated to poolside engagements until Sidney Oakes, son of Sir Harry Oakes, used his influence and secured a job for The Lou Adams Orchestra at The Prince George Hotel in the early1940's. The original members of the orchestra were Morris Harvey (piano), Bruce Coakley (saxophone), Eric Cash (saxophone), Leonard Perpall (Drums), Fred Henfield (bass), and Lou Adams on trumpet. They later moved on to the Royal Victoria Hotel. The fact that Lou and his band members knew how to read music worked strongly in their favour.

The band catered mostly to a tourist audience, as it was rare to have blacks socializing in a Bay Street establishment during the early years.

Lou noted that one advantage of having the many foreign bands was that after completing their hotel engagements, they would flock to the "Over The Hill" dances and perform with the local musicians. This exposed the locals to many styles and the high standard of performance needed to be in the business. The Silver Slippers was one of the favourite night spots for musicians to gather during the after hours.

Sir Oliver Simmons, a wealthy landowner, helped The Lou Adams Orchestra to become the first Bahamian band to perform in the dining room of the British Colonial Hotel, at a time when it was unheard of for local bands to perform in the dining room of any hotel in The Bahamas. The band played at the La' Cage Room of British Colonial for 13 years. In the 1960's the orchestra performed at the Fort Montagu Hotel and in the 1970's they moved to the Lyford Cay Club.

The Lou Adams band played for the opening of the Zanzibar and the Balmoral Hotel in 1940's.

Lou and his band also shared the stage with many international celebrities including James Brown and B.B. King while on tour in America. The many years of quality music provided by them are credited with bringing many tourists back to the country.

Lou Adams, as one of the pioneers in the entertainment field, opened many doors for Bahamian musicians. He is a recipient of numerous honours and awards, including the Ministry of Tourism's National Tourism Achievement Award, in recognition of his contribution the music and entertainment industry.

Sir Clifford Darling

Taxi Union chief, Human Rights Advocate and Chairman of the Tourism Advisory Committee

Sir Clifford Darling was born on Acklins, Bahamas, on 6th February, 1922. When his father, Charles, died when he was 11, he moved to Nassau to live with his older brother, Mervin, an electrician. He learned the electrical trade and became a professional barber. When war started, he joined the home defense. He spent three years on the Contract working in Florida, beginning in 1943. He experienced much racial discrimination in the United States and, in 1946, returned to Nassau, where racial discrimination was also being practised. He joined the Taxicab Union because this group was independent and not affected by the victimization of the *Bay Street Boys*. The Union was weak at that time, and he became fully involved, serving for eight years as General Secretary of the Bahamas Taxicab Union and President for ten years, taking over from Prince Huyler. In 1955, Mr. Darling and several associates were instrumental in founding Taxico Limited on Wulff Road, which became a meeting place for taxi drivers.

Sir Clifford starting fighting for majority rule in 1949, at which time there were no political parties. His first step was to educate the members of his own taxicab union about the importance of voting for their own people. After a difficult campaign, they won a few seats in Parliament in 1949 in Nassau, but had no money to extend the campaign to the Family Islands.

Bill Saunders of Majestic Tours and Don Delahey of Playtours recall that Sir Clifford brought discipline and order to the taxi drivers. He introduced a strict dress code and rules of conduct. Unprofessional behaviour, especially towards visitors, was not tolerated. A typical complaint involved taxi drivers who, having been retained for a round trip to take a visitor to a nightclub, would leave the visitor stranded, while seeking other jobs. Anyone violating the principles and rules set by the union was subject to a heavy fine. Money collected from fines was donated to charity. Some of the beneficiaries of this pot of money were the Bahamas Brotherhood, of which C.H. Reeves was President at that time, the Eye Wing of the Princess Margaret Hospital, which was given a donation of £2000 (a large sum in those days), the Ranfurly Home for Children, as well as underprivileged school children and the elderly. Every Christmas, the Ranfurly Home could expect a check from the Union, and approximately 100 old people would get 10 shillings each. The Union would also buy cases of exercise books which would be distributed among the school children.[19]

Sir Clifford played a prominent role in the closure of the Nassau airport in 1957 and the General Strike of 1958. In an interview, Sir Clifford related the events leading to the industrial action. Because the main source of business was airport transfers, taxi drivers would go to Oakes Field, the only airfield at that time, as early as 2 a.m. to be first in line for transferring tourists arriving on the 9 a.m. Pan Am flight, the only service operating at that time. Very often, the hotels would send their own limousines to collect guests and choose a few taxi drivers at random to handle the surplus, with the majority of the taxi drivers without work.[20]

As President of the Taxi Cab Union, Sir Clifford made representation to the Bahamas Hotel Association and Sir Raynor Arthur, the Governor. The Governor intervened and gave taxi drivers the privilege of transporting passengers from the airport for two months while negotiations took place. Lynden Pindling served as the legal advisor for the union, as they negotiated 20 points of disagreement. Nineteen of the 20 points were resolved. The last unresolved point, which led to the General Strike in January 1958, related to the first-come first-served system at the airport. The Union used a bulletin board at the airport to record the names of taxi drivers as they arrived, to ensure fairness in allocating jobs. When the 8-week period of transportation of visitors by the Union, as mandated by the Governor, had expired, the first-come first-served principle was no longer respected and the old system of doing business prevailed. The Taxi Union, joined by the Federation of Labour, led by Randol Fawkes, and Lynden Pindling, called a strike which lasted for 19 days and included all hotel workers, airlines, longshoremen, teachers, et cetera. The tourism industry came to a standstill and the whole country was affected. This was a difficult period for the Union which had to provide three meals a day for all of the striking workers. Sir Clifford further recalled that he, along with many others, had to use their personal savings to supplement the funds of the Union to assist workers, many of whom faced the possibility of eviction from rented homes because of the inability to pay the rent. After the strike, the first-come first-served system went into force. It was made clear, however, that a taxi-driver next on line would not be eligible to take passengers if he did not adhere to the Union rules. A fund was started to bring relief to the workers. Sir Clifford recalls that this 1958 Strike, despite the tremendous sacrifice, united black Bahamians from all walks of life and led to majority rule in 1967. [21]

In the 1950's, Sir Clifford led a delegation to see Sir Stafford Sands, Chairman of the Development Board, requesting a change in the promotional strategy to include black models and publications. This intervention led the way for inter-racial advertising and eventual breakdown of discrimination in hotels.

Sir Clifford was appointed Senator in the Opposition PLP from January 1964 to January 1967. In 1967, when the PLP won the Government, Sir Clifford became Deputy Speaker of the House of Assembly and Chairman of the Tourism Advisory Board. In his role as Chairman of the Tourism Advisory Board, he brought together all the major stakeholders to discuss ways of improving tourism in The Bahamas. He travelled on many promotional trips. In October 1969, he was appointed to the Cabinet as Minister of State and, in November 1971, became Minister of Labour and Welfare, when he put the National Insurance scheme into effect. He served as Speaker of the House of Assembly for 14 years before resigning to become Governor General in 1991.

In an interview, Sir Clifford described the pride he felt to have come from such humble beginnings to hold the highest post in the nation. The walls of his den are covered with plaques and citations from local and foreign organizations, applauding him for his outstanding contribution to the growth and development of the country.

He is married to the former Ingrid Smith. He was knighted by Her Majesty the Queen in 1977.

We salute Sir Clifford Darling for his contribution to the development of tourism as an industry for all races, and for unselfish dedication to the principles of human rights and justice.

Donald Delahey
Pioneer Ground Tour Operator

Donald Delahey—Pioneer Ground Tour Operator

Donald Delahey came to The Bahamas from Canada in 1943 at the age of 17 with the Royal Air Force Transport Command. During World War II, the Transport Command, based in Canada and known as the Ferry Command, flew planes from Nassau to the European war theatre, via South America and the Azores, for use by the allies. After the war, he returned to Nassau in 1946 and worked briefly as a desk clerk at the Royal Victoria Hotel before marrying Loree Kelly, a Bahamian. In that same year, he established Playtours, Bahamas Tourist Company, the first travel and sightseeing company in The Bahamas, which pioneered many of the travel services in the country.

Delahey was instrumental in starting group travel to The Bahamas. He aggressively solicited this business throughout the United States. Noteworthy groups which he successfully negotiated were the 6,000-person J.I. Case Co. sales meeting in 1958, the biggest group to be accommodated (in three-day segments) by a single hotel, and the Fedder-Quiggan incentive group of 5,000 persons. Because of his company's efforts, by 1959 group travel represented 9% of total tourists. The group and incentive business helped the country to become a year-round tourist destination since many of the meetings were scheduled during the traditionally slow periods of summer and fall.

In 1957, he founded the Bahamas Sightseeing and Tour Operators Association and became its first President. This association helped in developing proper rates and in forging a closer working relationship with taxi drivers.

From 1960 to 1964 he also operated United Tours in Miami, Florida, which was one of the largest wholesalers in the United States for tours to The Bahamas. He commuted between the USA and Nassau as he managed his two companies, while developing excellent contacts which helped him to further increase business to The Bahamas. He was American Express Company's representative in The Bahamas from 1946 to 1972. Some of the other wholesalers with which he developed a good business relationship were Thomas Cook and Ask Mr. Foster—to name a few.

Delahay was directly involved in all aspects of the travel industry. A sports promoter, Delahay was a founding member of the Bahamas Angling Club. Along with Red Crise and Sir Sydney Oakes, he promoted Speed Weeks, and also served on the committee of the Miami-Nassau Yacht Race for many years. He owned and operated the *Tropic Bird*, a catamaran offering daily sightseeing excursions from 1957 to 1972 and the *Tropic Rover*, the world's largest catamaran, which offered 10-day cruises through the Bahama Islands from 1962 to 1964, when it was destroyed at the entrance to Nassau by a freak storm. The Tropic Rover was featured in Life Magazine and in the movie *Thunderball*.

He was one of the founding members of the Bahamas Hotel Association, the Skal Club in The Bahamas, and Nassau Air Dispatch Limited. Along with his father, Murray Delahey, who followed him to The Bahamas, he was involved in operating the Prince George Hotel and Coral Harbour Hotel.

In 1972, he left the travel business and went into semi retirement, to work in a less stressful business and to enjoy his family—wife and four children. In an interview at his Eastern Road home, Delehay reminisced about the good times in the industry, where he had the opportunity to meet many people—from movie stars to Presidents. When asked what advice he would give to young travel industry professionals, he responded that they should keep foremost in their minds that good service and attitude are of paramount importance. "Remember", he said "that you are not doing the customer a favour".[22]

The country owes Donald Delahey a debt of gratitude for his contribution in pioneering the tour operation and group business, so vital to the success of Bahamas tourism.

Wallace Groves

Freeport Investor

Wallace Groves was a Virginian financier who settled and invested heavily in The Bahamas during World War II. He later became an important investor on Grand Bahama. Groves acquired and developed Little Whale Cay in the Berry Islands, and, in 1946, bought the ailing Abaco Lumber Company, which had lumbering rights in both Abaco and Grand Bahama. He set to work modernizing and mechanizing the operation, and greatly increased the output.[23] Peter Barratt, in his book on Grand Bahama, reported that Abaco Lumber Company in Pine Ridge, Grand Bahama was, in its heyday, the largest single employer in The Bahamas with nearly 1,800 people on the payroll. In the early 1950's, Groves sold the Grand Bahama lumbering rights, in order to concentrate on a much bigger project—the creation of Freeport.[24]

Groves approached Stafford Sands, who was his lawyer, about his ambitious plan for the development of a "free port" community in the pine barrens of Grand Bahama. Sands was able to convince the Government of the feasibility of the plan, and, on 4th August, 1955, the Hawksbill Creek Agreement between the Honourable A.G.H. Gardner-Brown, Acting Governor of The Bahamas, and Wallace Groves, President of the Grand Bahama Port Authority Limited, was signed. In this original agreement, Government conveyed 50,000 acres of land, with an option for an additional 50,000 acres, to the Port Authority, and promised freedom from customs duty, excise, export and stamp taxes for 99 years. The Agreement further guaranteed exemption from real property and personal taxes for 30 years (later extended to 2015). The developers agreed to create a deep water harbour and to convert the scrubland into a lucrative industrial area, encouraging industries.

Between 1955 and 1960 Phase 1 was completed. This stage focused on the harbour and involved surveying, site planning, dredging, and completion of a deep-water harbour. At Freeport Harbour, all but the largest tankers, cargo ships and cruise ships could anchor offshore in 50 feet of water, with space for five ships to be fuelled at once. At least £6 million was sunk into Freeport by Wallace Groves, along with shipbuilding tycoon D.K. Ludwig (who invested in the harbour).

The developers of what was originally conceived as an industrial free zone were rapidly moving into the tourism business. In 1961, Wallace Groves formed a partnership with Louis Chesler, a Canadian financier, who owned a controlling interest in Seven Arts, the motion picture studio, and established the Grand Bahama Development Company, the corporate instrument by which Freeport's status as a major tourist destination was to be achieved. The Development Company's land became known as "Lucaya". On New Year's Eve 1963, the luxury Lucayan Beach Hotel opened. By 1965, two new hotels opened—the 500-room Holiday Inn and the 800-room King's Inn (later called Bahamas Princess). Freeport/Lucaya became one of the fastest-growing tourist resort destinations in the world.

Visitor arrivals to Grand Bahama, which totalled 26,894 in 1963, representing 5% of total arrivals, jumped to 308,737 in 1968, representing 29% of total arrivals.

Fred Maura
Veteran Photographer

Photographer Fred Maura's extensive work in promoting The Bahamas stretches back as far as the end of World War II. On leaving school, he opened his own studio on Bay Street which he closed when he was asked to join the Bahamas Development Board, the precursor of the Ministry of Tourism.

As the world re-adjusted to peacetime, The Bahamas became an ideal spot for travellers who wanted to enjoy the end of the war. Many of them had an encounter with Mr. Maura in Nassau while he worked as a news photographer.

Mr. Maura joined the Bahamas Development Board in 1947. In those days, tourism was only a three-month industry that lasted during the winter. However, Mr. Maura and his colleagues did everything possible to maximize exposure for The Bahamas in the news media.

Three times per week he would visit the Nassau hotels—Montagu Beach, British Colonial and Royal Victoria. Hotel hostesses would line up their guests for Mr. Maura to photograph them. Afterward, Mr. Maura would mail the photographs to the visitors' hometowns. The strategy was to get photographs and captions of The

Bahamas in as many publications as possible. The publication of photographs and captions of Nassau and the rest of The Bahamas produced invaluable publicity for the country.

"If you had to pay for that kind of advertising, it would just be astronomical," Mr. Maura said of his work. "But the minute you sent a free photograph to the Society Editor of a newspaper, it was very easy to get them to put it in the newspaper. Every time you mentioned The Bahamas or Nassau, it was free advertising."

Mr. Maura dedicated 45 years to the promotion of tourism through his photography at the Bahamas Development Board and Bahamas News Bureau. His contribution and that of other photographers such as Ronald Rose have been invaluable. He was awarded the prestigious 1995 Lifetime Achievement Award by the Ministry of Tourism at the Cacique Awards.

He died on 30th May, 2003 at the age of 82. He and his wife, Joanne, to whom he was married for 48 years, had two sons, Peter and David and three grandchildren.

Freddie L. Munnings, OBE
Entertainer and Composer

The most exciting entertainer, by far, in the 1950's was Frederick Alfred Munnings, Sr. Freddie was born on 20th October, 1921 at Pure Gold, Andros to parents John Ralph and Mary Ellen Munnings. He migrated to Nassau in 1926. From youth he showed musical talent, and attended music lessons locally. Freddie's musical gift was extraordinary: master of the clarinet and saxophone, accomplished jazz pianist, inspired composer and conductor, brilliant, innovative arranger and songwriter, crowned by a voice made of velvet and a stage presence that captivated audiences in a way that no other Bahamian entertainer before or since has been able to do.

Carolyn Bartlette recalls that her father, businessman and entertainer Franklyn Samuel Williams, who had formed the Rudy Williams Band, discovered Freddie Munnings when he attended music lessons at Mr. Bain's studio on Market and Lewis Streets. He performed at the Silver Slippers night club in the mid to late 40's. He eventually took over the Rudy Williams Band.[25]

Freddie Munnings' career in show business began in earnest at the Zanzibar nightclub, then on to the Silver Slippers, where he and the Freddie Munnings Orchestra played to adoring crowds. Despite his early successes, Freddie harboured a yearning to consolidate his mastery of music through formal study. In the early 1950's, he went on a sabbatical to Boston where he immersed himself in the study of Musical Theory and Composition at the famed New England Conservatory of Music.

Not long after his return to Nassau, his genius now in full flower, Freddie would lay the cornerstone for his place in history at a spot on Nassau Street called the "Cat N' Fiddle".

In an interview, Duke Errol Strachan traced the success of Freddie Munnings in drawing crowds and in ensuring the success (or failure) of a nightspot. "While at the Silver Slippers, Felix Johnson made him an offer to perform at the Zanzibar in 1952. When Freddie left the Silver Slippers, that club died. He stayed at the Zanzibar for a year and a half and then went back to the Silver Slippers in 1953/54. Then the Zanzibar died in 1956. He made a deal with the owner of the Cat N' Fiddle and then both the Zanzibar and Silver Slippers died."[26]

In 1955, Freddie Munnings purchased the Cat N' Fiddle nightclub from Stanley Toogood. The visionary Freddie Munnings then "took entertainment to a higher level by expanding into the promotional business".[27] In addition to the fabulous local shows at the Club, Munnings, as a promoter, brought top-name entertainers from all over the world to Nassau. Some of the stars which performed included Nat King Cole, Roy Hamilton, Dinah Washington, Sammy Davis, Jr., Sam Cooke, Harry Belafonte, Aretha Franklin, Brook Benton, The Ice Follies et cetera. As had been done by Paul Meeres a decade earlier, Freddie used the Cat N' Fiddle to expose young Bahamians and to launch careers of upcoming talent. Sweet Richard, world famous dancer, Fireball Freddie, local magician, and crooners, like Cy Roberts and Dudley Capron, received their start at the Cat N' Fiddle. The Cat N' Fiddle remained popular until 1969.

Freddie Munnings and his band gained widespread popularity, locally and internationally. A "ladies man", he was adored by all. Indeed, he was welcomed as a guest even at the establishments which refused to admit black people. His son, Ray Munnings related the story of his father being invited to dine at the Grand Central in the early 1950's, but was told that his black companion could not accompany him. Munnings emphatically refused the offer and exclaimed that if his friends were not welcomed he would not grace the doors of the establishment. One of the newspapers carried the story. This was no surprise, since Freddie had a passionate concern for social justice, an abiding sense of ethnic pride and had played a pioneering role in the civil rights movement in the late 1940's.[28]

Freddie's involvement in the life of his country was reflected in many diverse ways. He was a founding father of the Bahamas Musicians and Entertainers Union and a charter member of the Kiwanis club. He was also, at the height of his fame, a successful entrepreneur who used his wealth generously to help others get their start in business or to further their education through scholarships he donated anonymously. Ray Munnings also recalled that his father would bring a band to Junkanoo on Bay

Street and set up by Prince George Hotel to give free entertainment to the huge crowds between groups.

Sir Stafford Sands valued Freddie Munnings as an entertainer and promoter. He would often ask Freddie to coordinate a team of entertainers to travel overseas to promote The Bahamas.

In 1969, when native nightclubs began to struggle for survival against competition from casino shows, "FM", as he was often called, was retained for a short period by the Ministry of Tourism as Director of Bahamian Entertainment. He fought vigorously to save the local nightspots. During this period, when his professional career had come to a close, he continued to encourage up-and-coming musicians in search of help with music composition or any musician in need of his assistance.

Freddie made many recordings including "Sloop John B", "Come to the Caribbean", "Little Nassau", "Bahama Lullaby", and "Nassau Nassau".

His immense and varied contribution to the social and cultural development of The Bahamas was officially recognized in 1977 when he was awarded the Most Excellent Order of the British Empire (OBE), personally invested by Her Majesty Queen Elizabeth II, during her visit to Nassau that year. He died on 3rd June, 1995, leaving behind an unmatched legacy in music and Bahamian entertainment.

Joseph Spence
Legendary Folk Musician
1910-84

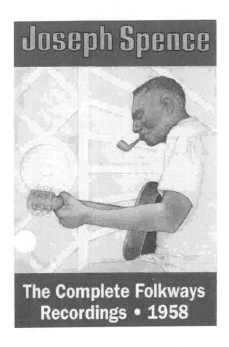

Joseph Spence was born on Andros on 3rd August, 1910. He had been playing the guitar for social events since he was 14. He moved to Nassau to work as a stone mason and, in the 1940's, he spent two years in the United States on the "Project" as a migrant farm worker, returning to Nassau in 1946. It was while he was visiting friends in, Andros, that his unique style was "discovered" and given international publicity.

In 1958, Samuel Charters, an American, along with a companion, travelled to The Bahamas in search of folk music. Charters was disappointed in the music of Nassau and the other islands, which he felt had been influenced by tourism and by the popular calypso music of Trinidad. Charters reports that while he was walking in Fresh Creek, he encountered men working on the foundation of a new house. As he came closer, he could hear guitar music. "It was one of the most exuberant, spontaneous, and uninhibited guitar playing we had ever heard. But all we could see

441

was a man in a faded shirt and rumpled khaki trousers sitting on a pile of bricks", wrote Charters. "He had a large acoustic guitar in his lap. I was so sure two guitars were playing that I went along the path to look on the other side of the wall to see where the other musician was sitting." They had just met Joseph Spence. Further describing his experience, Charters wrote, "I had never heard anything like Spence. His playing was stunning. He was playing simple popular melodies, and using them as the basis for extended rhythmic and melodic variations. He often seemed to be improvising in the bass, the middle strings and the treble at the same time."[29]

Later that evening, Joseph Spence, then in his late 40's, went to the house that Charters was renting and agreed to perform some of his songs. "He did a version of a popular island folk song to warm up and tune the guitar, then, without stopping to do much more than laugh and joke with the women between the pieces, he recorded the instrumental solos that became the first Smithsonian Folkways LP, and then one side of a subsequent Folklife release.

When Charters returned to New York with the tapes, he was so excited about Spence's music that he put together a separate LP on this unknown folk artist and presented it to the Smithsonian Folklife department. Other albums featuring Joseph Spence were released over the next thirty years, and Spence continued to be idolized by guitar players. After the Folkways release, Spence was visited by a number of other musicians, including Taj Mahal. Many Europeans were among his admirers, including Guy Droussart, a Belgian, who was a constant visitor at his home.

Spence enjoyed music and would share his talent with anyone who would listen, from the fruit vendors and fishermen at the dock to the more formal audiences, or the young children in the school yard. In his later years, Spence worked as a caretaker at Oakes Field Primary School. The then principal of Oakes Field Primary, Mrs. Eva Hilton, recalls that Spence would ride to school on his bicycle with guitar across his shoulder and pipe clenched in his teeth. She noted that, apart from carrying out his job impeccably well, he often entertained students during assembly, and was an important feature of the many productions which the school staged throughout the year. He would thrill young children with his amusing stories of his adventures as a "sponger man" and on the Project. [30] The children who were fortunate enough to have met this warm-hearted genuine entertainer had a good introduction to rich, but simple, Bahamian culture.

Although he toured the United States in 1964, and on other occasions, at the invitation of promoters, he never felt comfortable on the big scene.

Spence was respected because of his unique style. Many learned and adapted from him; but nobody could play like him. His music was intense and mostly religious, very happy and strong, and his character was the same. His music remains at the Smithsonian Institution as a permanent record of this legendary Bahamian.

Spence died in Nassau in March 1984, at the age of 73. Many of his American and European admirers travelled to Nassau for the funeral of this unique and talented guitarist.

George Symonette
King of Goombay

Born in 1915, George Symonette was a pharmacist by profession, and worked at the Bahamas General Hospital, the now Princess Margaret Hospital, for a time before opening his own drug store in the Kemp Road area of Nassau. Symonette was a talented pianist. His beginnings in music were no doubt influenced by the music of the church. His father was the late Reverend Alfred Carrington Symonette of Acklins, Bahamas. George became the organist at the St. James Baptist Church, off Kemp Road. While the guitar and assorted percussion instruments were the instruments of choice for most calypsonians, George entertained from behind the piano.

According to The Nassau Magazine, George Symonette, along with Berkeley "Peanuts" Taylor, entertained guests at The Waterside Club on the site of the old Spider Web premises in the late 1950's. This was only one of the many jobs that George Symonette held as a leading musician of that era. He also played at The Imperial Hotel Garden from 10 p.m. to 2 a.m. in between his shows at The Waterside Club.

Alexander Maillis of The Imperial Hotel recalls that after the hotel lost the popular entertainer Blind Blake to The Royal Victoria Hotel, George made quite an impact as Blind Blake's replacement. Always accompanying his own singing, he mastered and transferred the rhythmic riffs usually played on the guitar to the piano. His unique style no doubt helped earn him the title "King of Goombay". His music took him to the United States, where he performed at various hotels and clubs. He performed at every leading club on the island of New Providence. George also played with The Chocolate Dandies, a popular orchestra in the late 1930's and early 1940's.

George recorded many Goombay albums. Although the reputation of this tall, nearly six and a half feet giant spread in the sporting and medical field, his greatest contribution is said to have been in the area of music.

His recordings include other fine musicians such as Jack Roker (guitar), Harold McNair (flute), Leonard Dillet (drums), Dennis Donaldson (bass), and Peanuts Taylor and himself, to form a sextet. Together they made memorable music. Although the unique Goombay sound of George Symonette has since been duplicated by others, he has influenced some of the country's finest piano players including Theophilus Coakley of T-Connection, the internationally popular group.

(adapted from Web site of Christian Justilien, with his permission)

TOURISM STALWARTS
OF THE 1960's, 1970's AND
1980's

Paul Aranha

Longest-Serving Pilot and Airline Entrepreneur

Paul Aranha (left), longest serving Pilot and Airline Entrepreneur

Paul Aranha learned to fly in 1953, while attending boarding school in England. He obtained his Bahamas Private Pilots flying license in 1955, after returning home. For many years, he flew with the Nassau Flying Club and was a flying instructor. At the end of 1961, he started his own air charter business—O.B. Air Freight Charters—along with partners Maurice and Roy Cole. After the charter company ran out of money he took a job with brothers Neville and Dawson Roberts, as their Executive Pilot, for one year.

In 1963, Aranha joined Bahamas Airways Limited and remained with this company until it was put into voluntary liquidation, in 1970. In 1963, he was co-Pilot on the DC-3 but by the end of 1964 he was upgraded to Captain on the DC-3. When the airline ordered jets, he started flying jets. He was later promoted to Senior Routes Manuals Officer, with responsibility for collating all information needed by pilots for new routes and putting this information into a Manual.

As one of the senior Pilots at Bahama Airways, Paul Aranha vividly recalls the devastation he, other pilots and staff experienced when they heard the shocking news on 9th October, 1970 of the liquidation of Bahamas Airways Limited (BAL). He recalled that he had recently arranged for free Bahamas Airways tickets to two LACSA pilots, who had helped him with planning BAL's planned new route between Miami and Grand Cayman. By the time they would have received them, the tickets were worthless. Paul also recalled that BAL had ordered another jet, and on the same day that BAL when into liquidation, the new plane had made its test flight at the factory.

From 1970-73, Paul Aranha worked with his good friend, Frank Treco, at Trans Island Airways (TIA). After the demise of BAL, when Government had divided the airline's routes between Flamingo and Out Island Airways, Paul flew for Flamingo on two occasions for a total of two months, and then left for England.

In 1973, while stationed in West Berlin, he flew for an American company called Modern Air Transport, taking German tourists to vacation in Italy, Spain, North Africa, the Canary Islands, and Istanbul, Turkey. A call from Capt. Henry Pyfrom told him that Bahamasair had been created on 26th June, 1973, and invited him to return home as captain, flying the BAC 1-11. He worked with Bahamasair from 1st October, 1973 until 1st April, 1974.

From 1974 to 1992, Paul operated Trans Island Airways. He bought the company in 1977. The company did very well except during the last years—the late 1980's and early 1990's—when illegal businesses, operated by hackers and drug smuggling, were prevalent.

Captain Aranha served on the Board of Bahamasair from 1992-94.

In an interview with Paul Aranha, he paid tribute to other experienced aviation professionals like Harold Woodman, Colin Rees, Philip Farrington (who served in World War II and whom he described as a living legend), Henry Pyfrom, Al Hall, Leonard Thompson and Tommy Bethel of Abaco, and Harcourt Fernander.

Hats off to one of our most-experienced, dedicated and knowledgeable aviation professionals, who has trained and mentored many young pilots.

Mr. Basil Albury

One of the Bahamian pioneers in the Ministry of Tourism

Mr. Basil Albury, born on San Salvador, was educated in Nassau, Canada and the United States Mr. Albury joined the Public Service in 1965 as a Teacher at the Government High School. He served as Assistant to the Deputy Director of Education, Ministry of Education and Assistant Secretary, Cabinet Office, before joining Tourism.

In 1971, he was appointed Assistant Director of Tourism. Shortly after his appointment, he underwent training/orientation at three National Tourist Organizations—the Irish Tourist Board, British Tourist Authority, and Swiss Tourist Board (Geneva and Zurich), as well as at IUOTO (now the World Tourism Organization).

During Mr. Albury's tenure in the Ministry of Tourism he has made tremendous contributions in product development, sales, marketing and administration. While heading product development, he was responsible for industry training, including the Bahamahost programme, People-to-People programme; and modernization of tourist attractions. In 1972, he pioneered the development of domestic tourism and organized the first campaign which succeeded in promoting the Family Islands to local residents, with special rebates making the Islands affordable to Bahamians.

He developed new onshore campaigns including Poinciana June. For several years, he coordinated the annual Goombay Summer Festival succeeding his colleague, E. John Deleveaux, in this responsibility.

At various times in his professional tourism career, Mr. Albury was the Ministry of Tourism's representative for the Caribbean Tourism Association; Caribbean Tourism Research & Development Centre; Bahamas Hotel Training Council; Steering Committee, Centre for Hotel and Tourism Management. University of the West Indies; and the Bahamas National Trust as Council Member and Executive Member. He worked closely with these organizations in developing policy and carrying out their mandate.

Mr. Albury also served as Chairman of the Masquerade Committee (now National Junkanoo Committee) for ten years (1973-83) and was a Member of the first Board of the Hotel Corporation of The Bahamas from 1976-78.

In 1974, Mr. Albury was promoted to Deputy Director General with responsibility for Europe, and supervised the tourism expansion into Germany, France and Italy. In 1978 he served as Acting Regional Manager, Bahamas Tourist Office, Miami.

From 1987 to 1995, Mr. Albury served as Secretary of the Gaming Board. In January 2003, he was appointed Director of Investments in the Ministry of Financial Services and Investments, after serving as Executive Director of the Bahamas Investment Authority in the Office of the Prime Minister.

Mr. Albury holds a B.Sc. degree (St. Meinrad's Seminary College), a Master's degree in Educational Administration (University of Toronto) and a M.B.E. (University of Miami). He also holds a Diploma in Tourism from the International Centre for Advanced Tourism Studies, Italy, and a Certificate in Travel and Tourism Management from New York University.

Active in civic and church affairs, Mr. Albury serves as a member of St. Martin's Convent Advisory Development Council; Chairman, Board of Directors, Nazareth Centre; Member, the Catholic Archdiocesan Communications Commission; Chairman, Board of Directors of Abilities Unlimited; and Board Member, Bahamas Telecommunications Company (BTC); a member of the Tenders Commission on the privatization of BTC; a Catholic Christian Doctrine teacher and Eucharistic Minister at St. Anselm's parish. He is a member of the SKAL Club, the Rotary Club of East Nassau (Paul Harris Fellow) as well as a member (Chevalier), Confrerie de la Chaîne Des Rôtisseurs.

Mr. Albury is married to Cheryl A. P. Albury, Acting Justice of the Supreme Court of The Bahamas. They have two adult daughters.

Joan Albury

First Woman President of a Major Marketing Company

With more than three decades in research, advertising and public relations, Joan Albury is a seasoned communications professional and president of The Counsellors Ltd, the largest full-service marketing agency in The Bahamas, with offices on New Providence and Grand Bahama. Joan has led The Counsellors since 1985 when she left her position as General Manager of Advertising at the Ministry of Tourism to carve out her own destiny.

Beginning in 1973, two years after earning a Bachelor's Degree from the University of Toronto and a brief stint at the Ministry of Labour, Joan embarked on what would be a twelve-year tenure and lifelong association with the Ministry of Tourism. First as Sr Research Officer, and then as head of the Ministry's research department, Joan developed and oversaw a number of projects significant to the development of tourism in The Bahamas. Perhaps the most enduring was the redesign and evolution of the exit survey, in conjunction with the Ministry of Immigration, which would garner more relevant and useful information.

In 1982, Joan earned an MBA from the University of Miami. Now in addition to her focus in research, Joan was also working extensively in marketing, marrying the two disciplines to concentrate the country's advertising efforts. Her consumer studies, activities surveys, work in the travel trade, and data analysis allowed the Ministry to direct its financial and human resources to target specific markets. She was also intricately involved in a landmark study conducted in the mid-1980's to study the 'multiplier effect' of the tourism dollar. She also made important contributions to one of the first drafts of the national tourism development plan.

In 1985, while serving as General Manager of Advertising, Joan joined a consortium of Bahamian professionals who had the opportunity to purchase The Counsellors, which housed the former Bahamas News Bureau and coordinated public relations for entities in the financial services industry. Since assuming the role of president, Joan has expanded the company's service catalogue to include market research, advertising, graphic design and video production.

She is an innovator and has been at the heart of many 'firsts' in the Bahamian business communications industry including, for the past 15 years, the annual *Bahamas Business Outlook* conference, which brings together the top businesspeople in the country and marks the official start of the new business year. She is also the architect of ZNS TV local classics such as *Tourism Today, You and Your Money*, and *Electric Air*, as well as the innovative *bahamas@sunrise*—The Bahamas' only live TV morning show.

At The Counsellors, she strongly feels she has found her true niche and declares, "This is what I want to do for the rest of my life."

Joan is married to Frederick Albury, an architect, and the couple has two sons.

Donald Michael Archer

Seasoned Freeport Hotelier

Donald Archer was born in Nassau, New Providence where he completed his primary and secondary education. A graduate of Queen's College, he continued his education abroad, graduating from the Ray Vogue School of Arts, Chicago, Illinois and the Drake Business School, New York. He also studied at Cornell University.

Mr. Archer originally travelled to Freeport to work at the then International Hotel, as an interior decorator when he met Chuck Shlackman, the managing director of Kings Inn & Golf Club, and quickly moved up the ranks to Group Sales Representative and Director of Convention Services. He was later employed with the Lucayan Country Clubs ("Club 54"), with responsibility for three golf courses, restaurants and bar services. He was promoted to a variety of positions at the Bahamas Princess Resort and Casino including Director of Convention Services, Director of Sales and Golf Operations and Manager of Administration. In 1982, he was promoted to the position of General Manager at the Princess Tower, and held this position until May 2000, when he was promoted to Vice President of Administration. He was appointed to the position of Senior Vice President at the Resort at Bahamia in 2001, and which subsequently closed in 2004 as a result of Hurricanes Frances and Jeanne.

Mr. Archer has participated in a variety of organizations in the Hospitality Industry to enhance the tourism product and the tourist experience in The Bahamas, particularly on Grand Bahama. He is a Director of the Bahamas Hotel Association, an Executive Member of the Grand Bahama Island Tourism Board, Chairman of the Freeport Hotel & Employers' Association and Director of the Bahamas Hotel & Allied Industries Pension Fund.

Mr. Archer is respected throughout the industry as a veteran hotelier who has made a tremendous impact in developing the tourism industry on Grand Bahama. When asked to reflect on his career, Mr. Archer said, "In shaping a career for myself to eventually benefit my family, I sought to make a difference in the Hospitality Industry, so that those persons who spend their money to enjoy themselves in our country would be able to receive value for their money. I trust that I have been able to make their experiences, particularly at our resort, more enjoyable for them," he concluded.

He is married to the former Deborah Miller. They have a son, d'Von.

Dr. Thomas Bastian, OBE, JP

Trade Union Leader

Thomas Bastian was born on 14th June, 1939, in Sugar Loaf, San Salvador. He was educated at the San Salvador Public School, and later came to Nassau.

While still a young man, he worked at City Lumber Yard for 16 years as an engineer, an experience which served him to greater advantage in later years.

After working for many years and becoming increasingly aware of the need for workers' rights and justice for all, Thomas Bastian made a conscientious decision to become actively involved in the Bahamas Hotel Catering & Allied Workers Union (BHC&AWU). This involvement began in the early 1960's, and by 1969 he was appointed an organizer, and later elected to the position of Trustee and Vice President of the Union.

As the years progressed, the BHC&AWU saw the need for a more organized and effective organization, and Thomas Bastian was selected to attend the University of the West Indies, Mona Campus, Jamaica, where he successfully pursued a course in Trade Unionism. He later continued his studies at the Royal Institute in Virginia, the George Meany School of Labor Studies, Silver Springs, Maryland, and the Afro-Asian Institute, Tel-Aviv, Israel.

In 1978, Mr. Bastian was assigned to Freeport in the capacity of Vice President of the BHC&AWU, where he headed the office for several years. In 1982, he was elected President of the Union. During his tenure, the Union made great strides in Nassau, Grand Bahama and the Family Islands. In 1979-80, Workers House, Freeport, was constructed along with a housing complex with 58 two-bedroom, one-bath units. In Nassau, in 1985, Workers House and Harold Road Laundromat & Eatery were built. The Nassau facilities were further expanded in the 1990's with the construction of the Day Care/Night Care Centre in 1995, and Workers Bank in 1995-97. Expansion to the Family Islands took place when Workers House, with state-of-the-art meeting facilities and 96 bedrooms, was built on Eleuthera. In 2000, groundbreaking took place for Workers House on San Salvador.

Mr. Bastian worked closely with the International Labour Organization (ILO), headquartered in Geneva, Switzerland, which is one of the specialized agencies of the United Nations. Over the years, Mr. Bastian participated in many seminars and conferences at the international level. Noteworthy, he represented workers in The Bahamas at the ILO seminars in 1974, 1986 and 1998. Mr. Bastian is also an on-going participant at the International Monetary Fund's seminars and board meetings.

He has made an important contribution to the benefits, rights and empowerment of workers as President of the Union and in many other capacities. He served as Chairman of the National Workers' Cooperative Credit Union and of Workers Bank, Trustee of the Bahamas Hotel & Allied Industries Pension Fund, Ex-Officio Chairman of Workers Child Care Centre, Director/Board Member of the Hotel Corporation of The Bahamas and the Bahamas Hotel Training College, Member of the Labour Advisory Committee and of the National Insurance Board, Treasurer of the National Congress of Trade Unions, Justice of Peace and President of the National Trade Union Council.

He was awarded an Honorary Doctorate Degree from Virginia Seminary and College and was the 1998 recipient of the Queen's OBE medal.

Rev. Dr. Baltron B. Bethel, CMG, Kt

First Bahamian Director General of Tourism

Baltron B. Bethel was born in Palmetto Point, Eleuthera, on 13th October, 1933. He was educated at Palmetto Point Public School, the Government High School, Nassau, and University of Manchester. He has also pursued numerous professional programmes including management, marketing, planning, economics, tourism development, and theological studies.

Before joining Tourism, he had an illustrious career in the public service, reaching the level of Permanent Secretary in key Ministries including the Cabinet Office, the Ministries of Education, Finance and Home Affairs. He became the first Bahamian Director General of Tourism in May 1978, and served in this post until 1992. He also served as Chief Executive Officer of the Hotel Corporation of The Bahamas from 1988 to 1992. He has been credited with steering The Bahamas to an annual billion-dollar tourism industry. During his tenure, The Bahamas became the Number One tourism destination in the Caribbean through accelerated growth from 1,381,400 arrivals in 1977 to 3,622,218 in 1991. Annual tourist expenditure or income rose from $460 million in 1977 to $1.2 billion in 1991.

During his tenure, the Ministry of Tourism continued as the leader in the Caribbean in tourism statistics, research and planning, marketing and product development, despite several recessions, oil/energy crises, stock market crash, the Gulf War and intense competition.

Bethel fostered a strong and close working relationship between the Ministry of Tourism and private sector organizations like the Bahamas Hotel Association, the three Promotion Boards, the Bahamas Hotel Catering & Allied Workers Union, Taxi Cab Union, Tour Operators Association, Straw Vendors Association, Bahamas Chamber of Commerce, et cetera.

He implemented top and award winning advertising, public relations and promotional campaigns. The Bahamas Tourist Offices (BTOs) in the United States, Canada and Europe became known as being among the most efficient and effective sales/promotion public sector units in the marketplace worldwide. He opened additional tourist offices in Philadelphia, Atlanta, Houston, San Francisco, Paris and Milan. In addition to expanding the traditional markets of United States, Canada, and Europe, he opened up the Latin American, Japanese and Far East markets.

Recognizing that success in tourism is directly related to accessibility, he negotiated with carriers and vigorously pursued new routes within the United States, Canada, Europe, the Far East and Latin America. He pioneered 3-4 day vacations in the US and Canadian markets and two-centre European/Caribbean market.

Very close alliances were formed with the world's most influential travel associations like the American Society of Travel Agents, Canadian Association of Travel Agents, British Association of Travel Agents, the Society of American Travel Writers. He brought national and regional meetings of these associations to The Bahamas.

The Family Islands were promoted as separate destinations and were made accessible from Florida, Canada and Italy, through direct air routes by well-known carriers like USAir, Comair, Air Canada, Air Europe and American Eagle. Also during his tenure, hundreds of millions of dollars were invested in infrastructural developments in the Family Islands.

He rebuilt the yachting/boating market from Florida/Bahamas and charter boating. Numerous new ships were attracted to Nassau and to new ports in The Bahamas—Eleuthera, the Berry Islands, Bimini, and Abaco. Cruise ship ports were greatly expanded or new ones opened in Nassau, Freeport, Abaco, Eleuthera, the Berry Islands, et cetera.

International airports were built or expanded at Treasure Cay, Governor's Harbour, Andros Town, Congo Town, Paradise Island, and Moss Town. Nassau International Airport and Prince George Dock were expanded and redeveloped among the largest and best facilities in the Caribbean. He also influenced the construction of new hotels and tourist attractions on New Providence and Grand Bahama and numerous small hotels and marinas on the Family Islands.

A number of foreign organizations have studied the successful tourism development programmes of The Bahamas during his tenure in office, and his expertise has been utilized in the preparation of tourism development plans in other countries.

Beyond his influence on Bahamian tourism, Mr. Bethel gained international attention as he led regional tourism bodies. He served as president of the Caribbean Tourism Association (CTA) in the late 1980's and was instrumental in negotiations to merge CTA with the Caribbean Tourism Research & Development Centre to form the Caribbean Tourism Organization (CTO). He was elected as CTO's first Chairman. In this position, the entire Caribbean region benefitted from his innovative ideas and philosophies. It was also Mr. Bethel's pioneering efforts that brought expanded training and marketing opportunities to the Caribbean. He also helped foster stronger links with the Caribbean Hotel Association, travel agents and international tourism organizations.

He has been a member of the American Society of Travel Agents (ASTA) and was the only Bahamian to serve as a member of the executive Committee of ASTA. He has earned countless awards and special recognition for his unwavering leadership and commitment to tourism. In terms of regional awards, in 1982, he won the Caribbean Man of the Year in the World Travel Awards programme, was the recipient of CTO's esteemed Hall of Fame award in 1991, and was honoured by CTO in New York on the occasion of the organization's 50th Anniversary in May 2002. He was also the recipient of international awards. He was named "Man of the Year of the Tourist Industry" in December 1985 by the Grand Prix Mondial Du Voyage Committee, France, and, in 1987, he received the Inter-American Gold Key Award from the Avenue of the Americas Association of New York for his contribution to economic growth and development through tourism. He has been honoured by the Queen, the Bahamas Government and numerous organizations in The Bahamas. In 1988, he received the Bahamas Chamber of Commerce Distinguished Citizens Award in the area of Government. In 1990, he was awarded the Companion of the Order of St. Michael and St. George (CMG) by the Queen. During the 25th Independence Anniversary celebrations in 1998, he received from the Bahamas Government the Gold Silver Jubilee Award for his contributions to national development in the field of tourism. In 2001, he was named by Jones Communications as being among the 100 most outstanding Bahamians of the 20th century.

In June 2002, Mr. Bethel was re-appointed as Managing Director and Deputy Chairman of the Hotel Corporation of the Bahamas. He is an ordained Minister and serves as an Associate Minister at Salem Union Baptist Church. He and his wife, Helen, are parents of five children, all of whom have distinguished careers. He was knighted in the Queen's Honours of 2007.

Baltron Bethel honoured at special luncheon in 2005. From left Hon. Paul Adderley (Chairman of Hotel Corp in 1980's), George Smith (Hotel Corp. Chairman from 2002), Philip Bethel (former Cabinet Minister and brother of Baltron Bethel), Perry Christie (Prime Minister), Baltron Bethel (Managing Director and Deputy Chairman of the Hotel Corp.), Hon. Arthur D. Hanna (Governor General), Sir Clement Maynard (former Minister of Tourism)

Ronnie Butler, MBE

Veteran Entertainer

Born on 17th August, 1937, Ronnie Butler loved music from his early childhood. He started out playing the maracas at the age of 16 with a neighbour from Trinidad, who played the Hawaiian guitar, and Nattie, one of the premier conga drummers in The Bahamas. At the age of 17, while working as a construction worker, he took his first job playing music at the Carlton House Hotel on East Street. A year and a half later, he was a part of "Alexander's Trio". From here on, The Bahamas witnessed how a young man who grew up in the Montrose/Mt. Royal Avenues in Nassau became one of the premier entertainers of The Bahamas. It was not long before Alexander's Trio was performing every evening at Carlton House, which, at the time, was located on East Street, between Shirley and Bay Streets.

Ronnie further developed his musical talents when he joined "King Eric & His Knights" in 1958. According to King Eric Gibson, Ronnie became one of his most outstanding sidemen, "always on time, always properly dressed, just a good man to work with". They would work in clubs like *The Skylark, Captain Kidd*, and *The BAMA*.

In 1962, it seemed inevitable that Ronnie was destined to lead his own band, and so he formed *Ronnie and The Ramblers*, consisting of Charlie Dean—drums, Sidney Darling—bass and Carl "Flash" Rodgers—guitar. They became a household name for some 17 years thereafter. Their first job was at *The Big Bamboo* club, and subsequently they performed at the British Colonial, and at the *Rum Keg* at the Nassau Beach Hotel.

For over 50 years, his voice has thrilled locals and visitors with sweet down-home Bahamian music in his own inimitable style. A veteran entertainer, Ronnie Butler is timeless and synonymous with ballads, dancing ditties, and songs for every age.

Mr. Butler has classics under his belt like, "Goin' Down Burma Road" and "Age Ain't Nothing But A Number". From the early 1950's, he has performed in other hot night spots such as the *Trade Winds,* and *Ronnie's Rebel Room*. He was also one of the first of many artists who appeared at the Nassau Beach Hotel's *Out Island Bar.*

Mr. Butler's Colours of Life album reflected all the aspects of Bahamian life and inspiration over his 50 years of recording. Included was "Dance With Me" a duet done with Sonovia Pierre of Visage, "Sweet Music Man", and "What We Ga Do". What's most amazing about this musical genius is that he never made a conscious decision to be a musician or entertainer. He just sort of drifted into it, decided he liked it and did not want to do anything else.

Ronnie took some time off and spent about one year in Washington D.C., where he performed at *Alfio's*. This also was an important time in history, as Martin Luther King, Jr., civil rights leader, was shot while he was in Washington. Ronnie witnessed first hand the looting and rioting which resulted. Additionally, Ronnie recalls the attitude towards blacks all over the South during his travels. The amazing thing to him was the change of attitudes displayed by whites once they found out he was from The Bahamas.

Ronnie returned home in 1971 to begin a stint at the *Out Island Bar* in the Nassau Beach Hotel. It was during this time that he recorded some of his greatest Bahamian hits, classics like "Burma Road", "Bahama Rock", and "Crow Calypso". In the latter part of 1973, Ronnie recalls beginning a ten-year run at *Ronnie's Rebel Room* at the Anchorage Hotel. Locals and tourists alike flocked to the club to be entertained by Ronnie and his Ramblers. These years would strongly impact the music of The Bahamas forever.

The rhythms that Ronnie developed during these years were based on Latin rhythms that he had heard on the radio during that time. The fusing with Goombay rhythms has become a style that has further defined the Bahamian sound. The stress points in Goombay music were played predominantly on the strong beats, much like the walking bass line in Jazz. Ronnie then adopted the salsa and samba style of bass which emphasized the weak beats and fused it with the Goombay rhythms, in turn creating a new style of playing Bahamian music.

Eddie Minnis, composer, formed an alliance with Ronnie & The Ramblers and recorded most of his songs about island life. The Ronnie Butler sounds, mixed with the humour and story telling songs composed by Minnis, were a great and successful combination.

Another contributing factor in Ronnie's sound was the introduction of electric instruments. The bands before played acoustically. The softer, more mellow, sound was very different from the sound created by the use of the electric bass, electric guitar, and the introduction of microphones for vocalists. The volume of the music drastically increased and was quite attractive to the younger generation of Bahamians.

Following his years at the *Rebel Room*, Ronnie & The Ramblers would disband. His new group Ronnie Butler & Fire came about in the late 1980's and would perform at the *Tradewinds Lounge* on Paradise Island for eight years before the industry took a downward turn in 1990.

For three years following that, Ronnie had difficulty finding work in Nassau. These were challenging times. Ever since that time, the industry has continued to deteriorate, according to Ronnie. The blame for the downward spiral, according to Ronnie, must be equally shared between the artists themselves, and management of hotels and entertainment venues. When the disco era rolled in, if musicians were more disciplined and responsible, management would have had no reason to displace them with the DJ's that accompanied the disco craze. The related problems, like tardiness, drinking on the job, and other irresponsible behaviour, are said to have greatly diminished the appeal for management to deal with live entertainment all over The Bahamas.

Looking back at Ronnie's career, although filled with many challenges, his contribution has left an indelible mark on the Bahamian music industry. He has recorded over 15 albums. Millions all over the world have enjoyed his music over the years.

At the turn of the new millennium, Ronnie continues to re-invent himself. His alliance with producer/musician/composer Fred Ferguson re-introduced Ronnie to the new generation of Bahamians. Songs like "Look What You Do" (sung with Sweet Emily), and "Age Ain't Nothing But A Number" (with Count Bernadino) brought to the fore, once again, the talent of this Bahamian giant.

Ronnie Butler has been honoured on numerous occasions for his contribution to the growth and development of his community. He was awarded the "Member of the Most Excellent Order of The British Empire" (MBE) for his contribution to the music industry and, at the prestigious Cacique Awards of the Ministry of Tourism, Butler received the 2003 Lifetime Achievement Award for his outstanding contribution to the development of tourism. When asked about his awards, he simply replies, "these are the people's awards, if it weren't for the everyday people who supported me over the years, there would be no Ronnie".

John "Chippie" Chipman, MBE
Renowned Drummaker and Entertainer

John "Chippie" Chipman, MBE, was born on 5th October, 1928. As a boy, he learned to play the saxophone, and continues to do so with various marching bands, although he is best known for his achievements with the traditional Goombay drum.

Chippie has made and played drums for over 60 years, and has been an integral part of the evolution and design changes in these uniquely Bahamian instruments, from the traditional manufacturing technique of salt beef and nail barrels with goat and sheep skins to tin barrels. He still prefers the wooden conga or goombay drum although, over the past two decades, most drummers in The Bahamas have switched to metal drums. When salt beef no longer was packaged in the barrels, but rather in plastic containers, his raw materials became scarce. "We had to find new ideas and we tried the skins on tin barrels, small paint tins and the like." He supplies drums for the whole island—the schools, Junkanoo groups, the various bands—making eight to ten a day, and approximately 4,000 drums a year.

Chippie's studio at his home off East Street is a musical recycling plant. Explaining the drum-making process, Chippie noted that he also makes use of detergent and cleaning fluid containers from the cruise ships for his drums. The maracas are fashioned from plastic orange juice bottles with pigeon peas inside. Most of the goat and sheep skins come from Long Island, although he occasionally uses donkey skins from Inagua. One large skin will cover three big drums, with enough small pieces left over for a few small paint cans. The cow skin gives you the bass, while goat and sheep skins give the high notes, he explains. "Wet weather flattens the skin. Sun and cold bring it up taut. In between, that's when we put the fire to it," he says. Bahamian musicians soak the skins in lime water for one or two days to get the hair off, explains Chipman, but every country has its own method. In Jamaica, for example, they rub hot sand on the skin and scrape the hair off with a board or stick. In other countries they shave it off with a piece of broken bottle or a razor, he says. "We don't have to go to the music shops," says Chipman.

Chipman notes, with pride, that these drums have taken him around the world and that he enjoys playing. He has travelled all over the world, creating his magical and enchanting rhythms. Reminiscing of his many experiences, Chippie recalled a visit to the Netherlands when he was bestowed the honour of "King of the Drums" by a traditional Indian Hill Tribe. He is indeed the master of the Goombay Drums and is well respected in his homeland, being called upon by schools, charities, churches and organizations to share the deep Bahamian cultural heritage of which he is an integral living symbol. A local folk hero, he has taken hundreds of young Bahamians under his wings, teaching them how to make and play the Goombay drums, thus extending his influence over several decades.

Chippie has been a cultural icon in The Bahamas for over half a century. His group, Chippie and the Boys, welcomes cruise ship passengers at Festival Place on Prince George Dock with their brand of traditional Bahamian music.

His wife, Becky, also boasted an illustrious career in entertainment. Asked how he met Becky, Chippie said he danced a Rhumba with Becky when she was only 16 which prompted everyone on the dance floor to leave the floor and applaud. It was then that Chippie knew that Becky was "born to dance". Becky became Chippie's dance partner on stage until "she gained weight and he could no longer lift her". Becky then moved into fire dancer and, according to Chippie, "invented" the fire dance as it is performed in The Bahamas. She performed in every leading hotel in The Bahamas and all over the world. Many of his children are entertainers, thus keeping the unique Chipman entertainment tradition and style alive.

Chippie has appeared in international movies including *Island Woman* and *Banana Boat Beat*. He has received countless community awards such as the Dundas,

Hugh Campbell, Conch Shell and Grant's Town Community Awards as well as the Junkanoo Gold Award and a special award from his church family, St. Agnes Anglican Church. He has been honoured by Government on numerous occasions and was the recipient of the National Tourism Achievement Award by the Ministry of Tourism in 1985 and the Cacique award in 1997. He was awarded the "Member of the Most Excellent Order of The British Empire" (MBE) for his contribution to the entertainment industry as well as the Bahamas Merit Award.

Maureen DuValier, MBE

"Bahama Mama"

Maureen DuValier is the original Bahama Mama. This outstanding lady has been entertaining and leading the way as one of the premier female icons in The Bahamas.

Born on 14th May, 1926 in Nassau, Maureen is the daughter of Eustace Edward DuValier, born in Inagua, who was the second brother of Francois "Papa Doc" DuValier, past president of Haiti. Maureen recalls visiting Haiti as a child during the summers. She got to know her family quite well during these visits. Later on in life, while performing on a cruise ship, Maureen received the royal treatment with full private escorts, at the invitation of her uncle, Papa Doc DuValier.

Maureen grew up mainly with her godparents, Bert and Doris Cambridge. Cambridge, a prominent musician, who was a member of the Chocolate Dandies group and headed his own orchestra for a time, helped to mold her talents as a young vocalist. Maureen's early childhood education began at the Sands School, on Shirley Street. There her contralto voice was oftentimes utilized by her teacher for reciting poems to her classmates. The church also played an important part in her development and appreciation of music. Regular rehearsals held at Cambridge's home provided Maureen the opportunity to learn songs from lead sheets lying around the practice area. On occasion, she was invited to rehearse with the band. Her time of worship was shared between Salem Baptist Church, where her godmother was a member, and St. Agnes Anglican Church, where her godfather was a member.

When Maureen was about eleven, Bert Cambridge took her to the Jungle Club where he was performing at the time. Although Maureen was young, she had already developed a repertoire that her godfather couldn't resist exposing to the public. Peanuts Taylor (propped up on a chair) and a lady by the name of Big Biner (Ms. Lewis) were among the entertainers featured at the Jungle Club at that time.

She entered the entertainment industry professionally as a vocalist at 17 with the world famous Freddie Munnings Orchestra at the Silver Slippers. Inspired by a Betty Gables musical she saw at the Palace Theatre, later named the Cinema, she and Freddie introduced 'floor show' to the Silver Slippers. She became a versatile singer. One of her favourite songs, which she copied, adapted and made popular was 'I Put the Peas in The Pot to Cook.' 'Ask Me Why I Run' is the hit on the only album she recorded in 1955.

Maureen attended New York University where she majored in drama from 1952-54 but could not complete her education because she was forced to return to Nassau to care for her ill mother.

One who loves Bahamian culture, Maureen was a pace-setter for women in Junkanoo. She started rushing on Bay Street as a little girl with her uncle, Freddie Bowleg. Most persons thought she was a boy. When she unmasked, other women soon followed her lead. She spent much time researching the origin of Junkanoo so that she could be better equipped to explain Junkanoo to the world.

In 2006, when she turned 80, Maureen DuValier boasted that she still has her voice and would continue to perform when asked. A multi-talented, multi-faceted entertainer, she noted the importance of choosing a career that you love and having pride in whatever one does.

She has been honoured by many organizations and has been named a Member of the Most Excellent Order of the British Empire (MBE) by Her Majesty Queen Elizabeth II.

(adapted from Web site of Christian Justilien—*http://mail.vandercook.edu/~cjustilien/ index.html*—as well as personal interview with Maureen DuValier)

E. John Deleveaux

First Bahamian Deputy Director of Tourism—"Mr. Goombay"

Mr. John Deleveaux began his tourism career in 1969 as Assistant Regional Manager of the Bahamas Tourist Office (BTO) in New York. Previously, he had risen to a management position at First National City Bank, New York, after completing bachelor's and post graduate training in business administration at Baruch College and Manhattan College, New York.

On transferring to the Ministry of Tourism's head office in 1970, as Assistant Director of Tourism, Mr. Deleveaux was granted a four-month study tour of official tourism organizations, chambers of commerce, hotel associations, hotel schools and training institutions in the United Kingdom and Western Europe so that he could gain a thorough indoctrination into tourism management. He became the first Bahamian appointed to the post of Deputy Director General and has held key management positions with responsibility for public relations, product development, sales and promotions.

Mr. Deleveaux is credited with the coordination and promotion of the successful Goombay Summer programme, starting in 1981. Through this programme he was responsible for introducing many aspects of Bahamian culture into the tourism industry. He was dubbed "Mr. Goombay" by his peers and the trade because of his enthusiastic and innovative approach in spearheading this promotion.

He has always had a passion for empowering Bahamians and encouraging Bahamianization of the hospitality industry. He initiated sales training programmes for Bahamians in BTOs and coordinated the Cornell Summer School programme for the training of Bahamians in hotel management. Deleveaux was the Ministry of Tourism's representative, along with Hugh Sands of the Ministry of Education, and George Myers and Trevelyn Cooper of the hotel sector, that created the Bahamas Hotel Training College.

In 1974, he was posted to New York for four years as General Manager of the BTO and marketing worldwide, except Europe. He worked closely with each of his BTO managers and introduced Strategic Planning throughout the system. He was responsible for marketing, sales and promotions when the "It's Better in The Bahamas" campaign was conceived and launched. He organized the initial formal joint marketing concept between the Ministry of Tourism and the Bahamas Hotel Association, chaired the committee for many years, and led many large impactful delegations into the travel marketplace in North America and also spearheaded The Bahamas' initiative in the Far East, Mexico and South America.

He was also instrumental in the establishment of the Bahamas Film Commission and became the first Film Commissioner for The Bahamas.

He was the senior Bahamian official who participated in the conferences which led to the transformation of IUOTO into the World Tourism Organization as an agency of the United Nations. He was the recipient of the Golden Helmsman International Award in 1981 for contributions to tourism.

In 1987, he took up the post of Executive Vice President of the Bahamas Hotel Association (BHA). He transformed the BHA into a vibrant body, which not only met the needs of its members, but also promoted tourism awareness, industry training and education within the entire industry. A notable achievement was the introduction of tourism education into the national curriculum and the development of the "Adopt-A-School" programme, which introduced students to exciting opportunities in the tourism industry. He played a key role in the creation of the Cacique Awards, an outgrowth of the BHA Awards programme which was unveiled in 1987, when he first joined the BHA. He served as President of the Caribbean Society of Hotel Association Executives from 1990-94. He was recognized by the Caribbean Hotel Association for outstanding leadership and contribution to the professional development of Hotel Association Executives in the Caribbean.

He and his wife, Carolyn, have two daughters, Jennifer and Chrissy.

J. Barrie Farrington, CBE

Pioneer Hotel Employers' Association President

J. Barrie Farrington's relationship with the hotel industry began with Nassau Marine Services Limited, the owner and operator of the Nassau Yacht Haven and Pilot House Hotel. Starting as an Account Clerk in 1954, he progressed to President of the company in 1967. In December 1971, he joined Paradise Island Limited, the owner of the Paradise Island Casino, and, in March 1973, he was made Vice President and Treasurer. With the formation of Resorts International (Bahamas) Limited in 1980, he was promoted to Senior Vice President in charge of Administration. During the years 1991 through 1993, he served in the office of the President of Resorts International Bahamas Ltd. Mr. Farrington presently holds the position of Senior Vice President—Administration with Sun International Bahamas Ltd., the company which acquired Resorts International in May 1994.

Mr. Farrington has actively participated in the administration of the Bahamas Hotel Employers' Association for more than 25 years, serving over 20 terms as President of the Association. He has had the honour of representing the Bahamas

Hotel Employers' Association in negotiations with the Bahamas Hotel Catering and Allied Workers' Union, and has gained the respect of all parties concerned. His involvement with the union has brought about a new era of informed and responsible partnership between employers and the employees in the industry.

There are many associated areas where his involvement has and continues to foster improvement in the tourism product. He was appointed a Trustee of both the Bahamas Hotel & Allied Industries and the Bahamas Hotel Industry Management Pension Funds in 1970. He serves as Director of the Bahamas Hotel Association and the Bahamas Hotel Training College, a member of the Apprenticeship Board, a former Director of the National Insurance Board, former Director of the Workers Bank Limited, Director of Commonwealth Bank and Executive Chairman of the Bahamas Electricity Corporation.

In 1997, Mr. Farrington received recognition from Her Majesty Queen Elizabeth II for his service to the business and community, when she bestowed on him the honour of Commander of the British Empire (CBE).

An avid sportsman, Mr. Farrington was Commissioner of Baseball for several years and is a two-time Past President of the Bahamas Lawn Tennis Association. He and his administration initiated the Bahamas Lawn Tennis Association Youth Development Programme. He was instrumental in the staging of International Tennis events for 25 years. Mr. Farrington is the top ranked player in The Bahamas in the 55 and over division.

Mr. Farrington is a highly respected Bahamian businessman who demonstrates honesty in his dealings. He can best be described as a man who, in his time, touched the lives of many for good. We have all benefitted and prospered by his vision and involvement.

Leviticus Romeo Farrington

Taxi and Executive Limousine Service Entrepreneur Extraordinaire

Leviticus Romeo Farrington (right)—exemplary Taxi and Executive Limousine Service

Mr. Romeo Farrington entered the transportation industry in 1967 after realizing his deep affection for people. He completed the first Bahamahost training programme in 1978, when he graduated as the plaque winner for the most outstanding student. In 1979, he won the National Tourism Achievement Award. By this time he had started his own limousine company under the name "Romeo's Executive Limousine Services".

In 1993, his company won the 18th International Award for Tourist and Hotel Industry in Madrid, Spain. In 1996, he won the Cacique Award for Transportation. He also holds many certificates of merit for development of the tourism industry.

A man of many talents, which include singing and acting, Mr. Farrington has had small parts in television shows such as "Roy Clarke's T.V. Special" as well as in movies "Never Say Never Again", "Jaws the Revenge", and "The Love Boat Valentine Special". He was chosen as one of the persons to pose for the Pride and Joy posters that were displayed throughout the country in the 1980's.

Mr. Farrington constantly receives accolades from persons with whom he comes into contact—Prime Ministers, actors, dignitaries and ordinary people. He treats everyone with respect and renders outstanding service to all patrons as well as to his fellow Bahamians. In 2003, Mr. Farrington received the highest recognition in the tourism industry when he was awarded the coveted Lifetime Achievement prize at the Cacique Awards by Minister of Tourism, the Honourable Obie Wilchcombe.

A lecturer for the Bahamahost programme for over 16 years, he often reminds participants in the classes that tourism is like a relay race, with the Immigration officer passing the baton (visitor) to the Customs Office, taxi driver, hotel bellman and so on, and that if anyone drops the baton the entire experience for the visitor is destroyed. He emphasizes the importance of professionalism, courtesy and exceeding visitor expectations. He has always held the highest respect for time and will never be late for an appointment. He strives to make his company the best limousine service in the world.

Mr. Farrington is married to Curlene Farrington (nee Barr), and has been blessed with eight children, all of whom, at one time, have worked with their father in the transportation business.

"King" Eric Gibson

Veteran Entertainer

"King" Eric Gibson—King Eric and His Knights

Eric Gibson was born on the island of Acklins. From a musical family, his mother would play the organ in the little church on Acklins and his father was the choir director. All his siblings learned to play an instrument, except for Eric, who would stick to singing. His favourite pastime was sailing and fishing.

In 1948, he moved to Nassau to live with his brothers. He had several jobs in Nassau, including yard boy at the estate of Sir George Roberts, a clerk at City Lumber

Yard, where he learned all about wood, a short order cook in a candy kitchen, and was later recruited as a farm worker in the United States. He was mentored by his brother, John, who was adept on the saxophone. After his friends cajoled him into picking up a guitar, he practised continuously. All the musical education he had as a boy, that had been dormant, came to the surface. He discovered that music gave him a certain freedom of mind no other work could. The house in which he lived on Kemp Road soon became the "Music House" where young people gathered to jam. He played in church and lodge halls in a quintet comprised of Eric, "Duke" Hanna, "Flash" Carl Rogers, "Lord" Cody and Charley Smith.

At the invitation of Gene Toote, he performed as a musician at the *Conch Shell Club* on Baillou Hill Road, followed by *Flowers Night Club*, with Eric on guitar. He later moved to play at the *Capt. Kid* on West Bay Street, owned by Hubert Pinder. Eric was joined by Everett Henfield and Ronnie Butler and the band became known as the *Capt. Kid Trio*. King Eric groomed his band members and insisted on versatility, with each member learning to play several instruments, to enhance the sound and give the security that the band could perform even if a member is missing. When Ronnie branched out to form his own band, it was no surprise to Eric, who gave him his blessing like a proud father.

Capt. Kid developed into a great hang-out for teenagers. When Hubert Pinder left the island, Eric moved almost next door to the *BAMA* Club and became **King Eric and His Knights**. The *BAMA* became a favourite spot for tourists and locals alike in the 1960's. By 1965, the band consisted of King Eric (guitar, steel drum and vocalist), his brother Arthel (bass), Frankie Adams (bass, drum and vocalist), Paul Hanna (drums and vocalist), who had replaced Ronnie Butler.

The band was never into drinking or smoking. During breaks, they would chat with guests. Eric would drink a glass of milk. It was the audience that gave them a high and the knowledge that they were all genuine crowd pleasers.

Eric went to New York to music school. This enabled him to be a good teacher and also to make his own arrangements. By 1966, he had his own recording studio, ELITE, on Baillou Hill Road. He became his own sound engineer and recorded many records for local artists like Al Collie and the VIPs, Washie Collie, Duke Errol and the Lords, "Duke" Hanna, Little Joe and the Calypsonians, Ronnie and the Ramblers, Wendell Stuart, Ezra Hepburn, Cecil Dorsett, Rupert and the Rolling Coins, Kenny and the Beach Boys, et cetera.

King Eric and His Knights moved to the *Big Bamboo* and from there to the *Nassau Harbour Club* as popularity increased. When Arthel left, brother John Gibson, famous for his saxophone, stepped in. Jim Duncombe replaced Paul Hanna when he decided to make it on his own. Later, Stuart Halbert, formerly with the *Nassauvians*, joined King Eric, and the group was complete.

King Eric was an excellent leader, teacher and mentor. He instilled life-long principles in his band members, who became a close-knit family. He laid several ground rules, like not borrowing money from one another for longer than a week and settling disputes before the show to ensure harmony. He created a free atmosphere where an entertainer could perform unencumbered and unfold his or her talents. Talent, he said, is important, but just as important are principles of discipline, attitude, desire to learn and ambition.

Fans were enthused and some went to the extent of taking steps to share this Bahamian musical experience with their hometown audience. An American, June Lothrop, sponsored the band to play in New York. A trip to Las Vegas proved to be a learning experience and they returned full of ideas and enthusiasm. In 1970, the band went to Australia. The Australians liked them so much that they offered them citizenship. On their return they took up a contract to play at the Sheraton British Colonial Hotel. The band was well on its way to changing from a dance band to a show band.

The band continued to perform throughout the United States and Canada—in Detroit, Montreal, Vancouver, Toronto, Cleveland, Miami, Atlanta, New Orleans and Chicago—as musical ambassadors on many promotional trips organized by the Ministry of Tourism. An all-time favourite was Toronto. They played in Ontario Place in front of 12,000 people. The two dailies gave them top marks and headlines two days in a row, describing the band as lively, their interactions harmonious, and the music unique in style with an exceptional repertory of songs, not just the expected "Island in the Sun". Many repeat visits were staged in that metropolis.

In the early 1970's, the Bahamas Musicians and Entertainers Union negotiated a contract for Bahamian musicians to be allowed to play in the lounges of the big brand new hotels. King Eric and His Knights became the first Bahamian band to play in the Trade Winds Lounge. Despite their success, King Eric knew that unless they would find a home for themselves they could not be really happy.

When Cedric Saunders' *Doubloon Club* on West Bay Street became available in 1973, they had found their home, **The King and Knights Club**, which quickly became Nassau's foremost and favourite night spot for people from all walks of life, tourists and Bahamians. King Eric's revue featured King Eric and His Knights, the King and Knights Dancers, a fire dancer (Princess Asheba and, later on, Trixie), a limbo act (Lord Ching, then Jerry and Buttercup), and a stand-up comedian (The Big "H"). Fate struck a heavy blow when the King and Knights Club burned down in January 1985. The band had lost its home and Nassau its favourite nightspot.

King Eric continued to make an impact as trainer and motivator of young musicians, and as a negotiator and counsellor on the governing board of the Bahamas Musicians and Entertainers Union. His advice to young people is: "Condition your mind so you will be able to cope. Face facts, and set yourself attainable goals towards which you walk a step at a time. Develop good habits while you are young. Join people from whom you can learn". A musical legend, you can also find King Eric on the water, sailing the A-Class sloop "Thunderbird" and the B-Class Sloop "Queen Drucilla", or on the golf course.

Hats off to a man of incredible talent and high principles, who has made a tremendous contribution to the growth of Bahamian entertainment in the country!

Frederick Asa Hazlewood

Entrepreneur Extraordinaire

Frederick Hazlewood, President of John Bull Group of Companies and Coffee Cay Ltd. (Starbucks Bahamas), is the son of Frank and Macushla Hazlewood and grandson of Sir Asa Pritchard, who, in 1929, opened John Bull. He was educated at St. Andrew's High School and Staunton Military Academy, where he was the recipient of the highest leadership award.

He has had a distinguished career, spanning 37 years of retail excellence. As President of the John Bull Group of Companies, he has been responsible for much of the innovations and growth experienced by that company in the last four decades. Other members of his family are active in the business—his uncle Emmet Pritchard, Vice president, Asa H. Pritchard Holdings, Ltd., and John Bull Ltd., and mother Macushla Hazlewood, Vice President of John Bull, and other family members, Hugh and Robert Pritchard, treasurer and secretary.

John Bull in downtown Nassau has an interesting history. The name is derived from a character in British satire, "Law Is a Bottomless Pit", written in 1712. John Bull represented a stout Englishman wearing a top hat, waistcoat, knickers and high boots. At that time, England was known for its famous Woodbine cigarettes and Briar pipes. The year 1929 was a time of depression when the Stock Market fell and The Bahamas experienced its worst hurricane ever, certainly not a time to start a business. Nevertheless, it was during this time that Fred Hazlewood's grandfather, Sir Asa Pritchard, opened an Old English Tobacco House, "*John Bull*", on Bay Street north, just east of East Street. John Bull Tobacconist prospered, catering to local residents and tourists until World War II when the tourism industry diminished and the armed forces became Nassau's guests.

John Bull continued as a tobacco shop until the 1950's when Sir Asa's children and their families, in particular his daughter, Macushla, and her husband, Frank Hazlewood, and later their son Frederick, injected new ideas and capital into the business. A stationery department evolved into the foremost business centre in The Bahamas. In 1955, watches, toys and gifts were added, with John Bull becoming the exclusive representative for the Rolex Agency. In the 1960's, jewellery and cameras became an important part of John Bull's business, with the tobacco and toy departments slowly phased out. The 1970's through 1980's brought further expansion in the company with the addition of other major watch and jewellery designers. Designer Boutiques and a La Parfumerie Division were also added. During the 1980's, Forbes magazine placed John Bull in the category with top stores in Hong Kong for best buys; and Knight Rider newspapers recommended them as a "must" in tourist shopping in The Bahamas.

Throughout his tenure as President of John Bull, Fred Hazlewood has been at the forefront of positive change not only for John Bull but for the entire tourism industry. He has assisted in the upgrading of the Ministry of Tourism's Bahamahost programme, by contributing funds to digitalize the lectures so that this service improvement programme could be extended throughout New Providence and to the Family Islands. He continuously contributes to projects designed to improve the downtown area and has always been a Director and active participant in the Nassau Tourism Development Board.

In keeping with Government's revitalization of Bay Street in the 1990's, John Bull led the way in expanding its operation. With the closure of the Nassau Shop, the Hazlewood family acquired the prime location, 284 Bay Street, in 1996 and completed major refurbishment before re-opening its flagship store with six departments including Leather, Perfume & Cosmetics, Tobacco, Jewellery, Watches and Cameras, and world-renowned designer products. By 2002, John Bull, described as the "Shopping Paradise of the Islands", boasted six branches in The Bahamas (4 in Nassau and one each on Paradise Island, and Abaco).

The John Bull Group of Companies, under the able and creative direction of Frederick Asa Hazlewood, remains committed to excellence in all facets of the organization. During this relentless pursuit of excellence, he insists that John Bull exceed the expectations of clients and industry partners, while affirming its position as the shopping mecca of the Caribbean.

Hazlewood has been honoured by many organizations and groups in the United States and The Bahamas. In October 1973, he was recognized by Governor Wendell H. Ford of Kentucky. He received a letter of commendation from the White House (President Richard Nixon). In April 1988, he was recognized by the Bahamas Ministry of Tourism on the 10th Anniversary of Bahamahost, for his invaluable contribution to the success of the programme. On 15th November, 1991, he was recognized by the Giddron Secret Society (University of Georgia) and in 1993 was named Businessman of the Year by the Bahamas Chamber of Commerce. In 1996, John Bull was the recipient of the Ministry of Tourism's prestigious Cacique award for retail excellence, and, in October 1997, Hazlewood was recognized by the Bahamas Ministry of Tourism & the Nassau Tourism Development Board during the Florida Caribbean Cruise Association Conference. In September 2001, he was the recipient of the CEO Network's Business Award.

Mr. Hazlewood has always supported local community activities, youth groups and various charities. He is a former Member of the Young Presidents Organization (YPO), and is a member of the World Presidents Association (WPO). He is a supporter of the Teen Challenge drug rehabilitation programme, the Cancer Society and numerous youth development programmes. He is also a member of the Royal Nassau Sailing Club and Honorary Member of the University of Georgia Athletic Association.

David L. Johnson
Sales and Airline Professional

A veteran of 35 years in the tourism and aviation industry, David Johnson was born on 23rd November, 1951 in Nassau, Bahamas to parents, Vernon Montague Johnson [deceased] and mother Maria Theresa Johnson.

After graduating from Queen's College High School, he joined the Ministry of Tourism as a young recruit in August 1970 to be enrolled in a pilot sales training programme for Bahamian executives in the Bahamas Tourist Offices in North America. He is also the holder of an MBA from University of Miami.

After successfully completing the initial training programme in Detroit, Michigan, Johnson received his first assignment as Sales Representative in January 1971, with a posting in Toronto, Canada. This was followed by a subsequent promotion to Senior Sales Representative assigned to the Miami Office. Subsequent promotions were to the posts of Regional Manager, Boston, Senior Regional Manager, New York, Area Manager for the Northeastern USA, followed, in 1982, by the top overseas post of Director for The Americas & Far East, based in New York.

In 1986 Johnson entered the aviation industry as Director, Sales & Marketing at the national flag carrier, Bahamasair, and subsequently as General Manager of the airline in 1987, where he remained until his return to the Ministry of Tourism as Deputy Director General in 1991.

He joined the Grand Bahama Island Tourism Board as Executive Vice President in 1994 and President from 2004 to 2005, while retaining the post of Deputy Director General of the Ministry of Tourism. In 2006, he took over responsibility for Planning and Investments in the Ministry of Tourism.

He and his wife, Sabrina, have two sons, Shane and David, Jr.

His hobbies include the sports of golf and fishing as well as reading.

George Myers
Veteran Hotelier

Few individuals in the hotel industry can match the achievements of George Myers, Chairman and CEO of the Myers Group Ltd., which was formed in 1992.

With an illustrious career spanning more than 40 years, Mr. Myers has played an essential role in the success of the Bahamian tourism industry. Mr. Myers was virtually born into the hotel business. His family owned a hotel—the Miranda Lodge—in his native Jamaica, and, as a youngster, he worked at the hotel. In his early 20's, Mr. Myers tried his hand at a career in banking, a field he ultimately left, finding it too staid for his affable personality. Returning to his first love, the hospitality industry, George Myers apprenticed for two and a half years at London's famed Westbury Hotel, starting as a trainee in the kitchen, and rapidly worked his way up through the various hotel departments, which helped to round out his experience.

In January 1963, Mr. Myers came to The Bahamas as Bar Manager at the Nassau Beach Hotel, where he was subsequently promoted to Convention Sales Manager. From 1965 to 1967, he served as General Manager of the Lucayan Harbour Inn & Marina in Freeport and as Director of Sales for both the Lucayan Beach Hotel and Lucayan Harbour Inn. Quickly moving through the ranks of management,

Mr. Myers returned to the Nassau Beach Hotel in 1967 as Resident Manager and Director of Sales, and, in 1968, he was promoted to Vice President and General Manager of the property. In 1978, Mr. Myers was given further recognition by being promoted to Vice President for Trust House Forte Hotels in The Bahamas, Venezuela and Jamaica.

In 1977, Myers accepted the post of Executive Vice President of Paradise Island Limited, then a subsidiary of Resorts International, Inc, and, in January 1980, was promoted to President of Paradise Island Limited. One year later, he was named President and Chief Operating Officer of Resorts International (Bahamas) Ltd., where he guided the company's growth and development, as it quadrupled in size on Paradise Island.

Along with his well-rounded executive skills running a major resort hotel and vacation complex, Myers demonstrates an instinctive flair for salesmanship and enjoys an excellent relationship with tour operators, travel agents and airline owners and operators.

Myers is recognized not just for his business acumen, but also for his dedication to enriching his community and improving his industry. He has served as president of the Caribbean Hotel Association, the Bahamas Hotel Association, and the Bahamas Hotel Employers' Association. He was founding chairman of the Nassau/Paradise Island Promotion Board, and founding chairman of the Paradise Island Tourism Development Association. He also served on the Bahamas Tourism Advisory Committee, the Prices Control Commission, the Bahamas Hotel Training Council, the Bahamas Airport Advisory Committee and the Board of Bahamasair, the national airline. He is Director for Life of both the Caribbean Hotel Association and the Bahamas Hotel Association.

Both the Caribbean Hotel Association and the Bahamas Hotel Association have honoured Mr. Myers with the "Hotelier of the Year" Award. He is also the recipient of a Golden Helmsman Award. On the occasion of the Silver Jubilee Celebrations of the Bahamas' Independence, the Bahamas Government presented George Myers with the Silver Jubilee Award in recognition of his outstanding contribution to national development in the field of tourism. He was honoured by the Caribbean Tourism Organization on 31st May, 2002, in New York, on the occasion of CTO's 50th Anniversary Regional Awards. He received the 2005 Lifetime Achievement Award at the Cacique ceremony in January 2006.

Rev. Oswald Nixon

Long Serving President of the Bahamas Taxicab Union

Oswald Nixon was born in Steventon, Exuma to the late Mr. & Mrs. James Nixon, on 26th September, 1940. He was educated at the Roberts Point All-Age School, Rokers Point, Exuma. He later moved to Nassau and attended the Southern Senior School and was employed with Cavalier Construction Company as a carpenter for about ten years.

Being an adventurous person, Mr. Nixon entered the hospitality industry as a taxicab driver in the late 1960's. As a taxicab driver, he often went beyond the call of duty to ensure his guests had an enjoyable stay while in The Bahamas. Numerous complimentary letters about his performance were sent to the Ministry of Tourism by visitors whom he chauffeured. He became one of the first graduates of the Ministry of Tourism's Bahamahost training programme for taxi and tour operators, and actively worked to assist other drivers to upgrade their knowledge and performance.

Mr. Nixon was elected as President of the Bahamas Taxicab Union on New Providence in the 1970's. He served in that capacity for over 13 years, becoming the longest serving president of that union. During this period, he travelled with the

Bahamas Ministry of Tourism on many promotional trips to the United States and Canada, and also visited the Family Islands on product development ventures.

Nixon served on the Tourism Advisory Board and also became an active member of the Bahamahost Association.

On 28th November, 1977, he received the Ministry of Tourism's National Tourism Achievement Award for meritorious contribution to the growth and development of tourism in The Bahamas. On 29th October, 1984, he became the recipient of the Golden Helm Award, an international award for tourism, for his competence and dedication to the development of Tourism.

He is a founding member of the New Lively Hope Baptist Church on Jerome Avenue and Chesapeake Road, New Providence. He served faithfully as a deacon for 16 years, Sunday School Superintendent, chairman of the church audit board, president of the Men's Fellowship and choir member. He was ordained a Minister of the Gospel on 4th June, 1989, under the pastorage of the late Rev. Roger Gladstone Adderley.

Rev. Nixon returned to his birthplace, Exuma, in August 2001 where he is actively involved in the George Town community as well as the People-to-People Programme. He is also a marriage officer and a Justice of the Peace for the Commonwealth of The Bahamas.

Married to the former Betty Maurice Campbell, the couple has seven children.

Robert D. L. "Sandy" Sands

First Bahamian Hotel General Manager

Robert Delano Lascelles Sands is a veteran in the hotel industry in The Bahamas.
Born in Nassau on 31st May, 1954, Mr. Sands attended St. Anne's Primary and High Schools, Nassau, St. Augustine's College, Nassau, Scarisbrick Hall School, Ormskirk, Lancashire, England, Ryerson Polytechnic Institute, Toronto, Canada, where he won the Carling O'Keefe Award for Consistently High Academic Achievement. After completing his Bachelor's degree in Hospitality and Tourism Management at Ryerson Polytechnical Institute, Toronto, he started his career in 1974 at the Nassau Beach Hotel, a Trusthouse Forte Hotel, where he had interned the previous three years. He had the opportunity to work in virtually all aspects of the hotel business, as Accounts Clerk, Head Cashier, Sales Clerk, Assistant Sales Manager, Group & Convention Manager, Front Desk Manager, Senior Assistant Manager—Operations, Housekeeping, Bell Service, Switchboard, Gardens and Pool. In 1979, he was seconded to the Trusthouse Forte Hotel properties in London as a participant in the company's management development programmes. He gained valuable experience in management positions at renowned hotels such as Grosvenor House and the Hyde Park Hotels in London.

In 1982, Mr. Sands was posted to Guyana as General Manager of Trust House Forte's Pegasus Hotel, becoming one of the first qualified Bahamians to hold such a senior post in the industry. From 1984 to 1988, he was named General Manager of the Jamaica Pegasus Hotel. The innovations he introduced to these two Caribbean properties are a testimony to his sound training.

On returning to The Bahamas in 1988, he was appointed General Manager of the Nassau Beach Hotel. A year later, he moved up to Senior Vice President of Hotel Operations at the Carnival Crystal Palace Resort and Casino (which later became the Nassau Marriott Resort and Crystal Palace Casino, then the Wyndham Nassau Resort). In 1992, he was made Senior Vice President. He presently serves as Senior Vice President, BahaMa/Cable Beach Resorts, Ltd.

Mr. Sands has always been an active and innovative industry leader. He is a Director and Past President of the Bahamas Hotel Association, Trustee of the Bahamas Hotel Association Scholarship Fund, Trustee of the Bahamas Hotel Association Management Pension Fund, Senior Vice President of the Bahamas Hotel Employers' Association, Director of the Nassau/Paradise Island Promotion Board, Trustee of the Bahamas Hotel Industry Management Pension Fund, Chairman of the College of the Bahamas School Of Hospitality & Tourism Studies, Director of the Caribbean Hotel Association, Director of the Steering Committee for the University of the West Indies Centre for Hotel and Tourism Management and Member of the National Insurance Board Appeal Tribunal. He has made a tremendous contribution in upgrading the hospitality curriculum, raising standards within the industry, and introducing students to the hotel industry. He initiated many innovative programmes to improve the image of the hospitality sector throughout the country and has always been willing to share his knowledge and experience with youngsters interested in tourism career.

Mr. Sands is also active in charitable, community and church organizations and has always been willing to lend a helping hand to those in need. He is a member of the Advisory Board of the Salvation Army, member of the Vestry of Epiphany Anglican Church, Director of the Elizabeth Estates Children's Home, Director of Bahamas Abaco Markets, BISX, Member of the National Insurance Board Appeal Tribunal, Member of the Royal Eagle Lodge 33° Mason and Past Sire Archon, Delta Lamdba Boule.

He is married to the former Michelle Pindling and is the father of five children.

Vernal Sands

Goodwill Ambassador

Vernal Sands (right)—Goodwill Ambassador

When a visitor or Bahamian hears the line "Top of the morning to you", he/she knows that the venerable Vernal Sands is in the room.

Recognized around the world for his flamboyant coats and extensive bow-tie collection, Vernal Sands is The Bahamas' Goodwill Ambassador whose number one goal is to make guests happy. Mr. Sands is a second-generation hospitality worker who learned well the lessons of giving good service from his mother.

As a young boy, he accompanied his mother to work, which allowed him to interact with the winter tourists who stayed at the Emerald Beach Hotel. At the age of 12, he was given a job as a towel boy—picking up towels off the beach at Paradise Island. From the beach, Sands worked his way up to the dining room, first as a busboy, later an apprentice waiter, captain and eventually becoming the first Bahamian maitre' d at Villa d'Este on Paradise Island.

In 1983, when the Cable Beach Hotel opened, Sands was appointed Assistant Director of Food and Beverage. His magnetic personality caused many of his visitor friends to follow him from Paradise Island to Cable Beach. Over the years, he has exchanged birthday cards, anniversary notes, golf victories, and birthday celebrations with thousands of visitors.

Sands' career spans 40 years, with the last 17 at the Crystal Palace under different owners. The man with the beaming smile and booming voice is the human personification of a word we all use too liberally, "hospitality". His smile, his warmth, his joy at making people feel at home in a foreign place, making them want to come back time and time again, are what hospitality is all about.

Hospitality has garnered Vernal many awards including the National Tourism Achievement Award, precursor to the Cacique Awards, and letters of commendation from the former Prime Minister, Sir Lynden Pindling and Governor-General, Sir Orville Turnquest.

Along with Vernal's awards, he has been successful in attracting a myriad of fans, including Robert Ludlum, author, Regis Phelbin, talk show host, Huey Lewis of Huey Lewis and the News, Muhammad Ali, the legendary boxer and John Travolta, actor.

In recognition of his significant achievements spanning four decades, he received the 2000 Lifetime Achievement Award at the Ministry of Tourism's prestigious Cacique Awards Ceremony.

William "Bill" Saunders

Outstanding Tour Operator

William Saunders was born on 29th March, 1929. His maternal ancestors, the Roberts family, came to Abaco in 1788 from Carolina as loyalists. His father, Arnold Saunders, was employed for many years with the Water and Sewage Corporation.

Bill Saunders received his early education in the public school system in Nassau. At the age of 14, he left school to seek employment, in order to help his mother. He married Iris Isabel Lowe and in 1947, after the war, he emigrated to Canada, where he lived for five years working for an insurance company. When he returned to Nassau in 1952, he began his illustrious career in the tour business. He was employed with Howard Johnson Tours for four years, then in 1956 joined Nassau Tours, where he learned the business and made valuable contacts. His goal was to open his own business; however the two banks operating at the time in The Bahamas, Royal and Barclays, refused to give him a loan.

On 1st May, 1958, Bill Saunders opened Majestic Tours with a £100 loan that his wife, Iris, had secured from Norman Solomon, with whom she worked as Stockroom Manageress. He bought the first car for the business and, since they could not afford to hire the staff needed to run the business effectively, his wife left Norman

Solomon to help him grow the business. They worked around the clock carrying out all of the business functions—driving the vehicle, as well as sales, marketing and office management. Gradually, Majestic gained the confidence of North American wholesalers and he was able to expand, purchase more vehicles and hire staff. One of the American producers to whom Bill attributes much of his initial success is Mr. Haroche of LibGo, who gave him full support.

Despite the company's initial success, Majestic was still unable to get a loan during the first four years of operation, since, according to Bill, the two banks were greatly influenced by his competitors. It was not until the Bank of London and Montreal opened in The Bahamas that he was able to secure finance, enabling the company to expand significantly. Soon afterwards, Majestic was appointed a wholesaler for The Bahamas, increasing the commission from 10% to 20% on business booked.

Bill Saunders was among the founding members of the Bahamas Tour Operators Association. The other original members of the association were Playtours, Howard Johnson Tours, Michael Maura Tours, Philip Brown Tours and Nassau Tours. Bill Saunders travelled throughout North America, Europe and the Far East promoting The Bahamas and played an active role in the growth of tourism during the last four decades.

Over the years, Majestic Tours has become the most respected and productive tour company in The Bahamas. In describing the road to his success, Bill Saunders explained that he had only one thing to sell, and that was service. "Good service", he said, "comes from a hands-on operation". He worked Saturdays and Sundays because "that is the nature of the tour business". He carefully selected his team and can boast of extremely hard-working and dedicated staff, many of whom are from Long Island. He rewards his staff by giving them good benefits, including automatic participation in a Pension Plan after ten years of service.

Bill Saunders also invested in the entertainment industry. He, along with Howard Johnson and Peanuts Taylor, owned the Goombay Club which was popular in the 1960s.

William Saunders is a sterling example of a self-made Bahamian—one who, through hard-work, perseverance and dedication to a vision, has achieved success in a competitive environment.

Stephen Sawyer

Exemplary Hotelier

A native of The Bahamas, born in 1954, Stephen Sawyer has had an illustrious career in tourism and moved up the ranks at an early age. He started his career in 1973 at the Nassau Beach Hotel after attending Westminster's Hotel School in London. He was ultimately responsible for all front office operations.

From 1977 to 1979 he was General Manager of the 120-room South Ocean Hotel and Golf Club. In 1979 he joined the all-inclusive resort, Zemi Hotel, in the capacity of Assistant General Manager. In1980, he was appointed General Manager and held that post until 1982. He was responsible for initiating the operational changes to convert the all-inclusive resort to traditional hotel operation, and it became the Bahamas Beach Hotel.

In 1982, he was appointed General Manager of the prestigious Ocean Club, a 70-room deluxe hotel on Paradise Island, and remained there through 1989. Shortly after his appointment, the Paradise Island golf course was placed under his responsibility.

In 1989, he left the Ocean Club, Paradise Island to join the Carnival Crystal Palace Casino & Golf Resort in its developmental stages and was responsible for the opening of 612 new rooms in four towers. As Vice President of Hotel Operations, he was responsible for all the budgeting, new hiring, pre-opening, and operational responsibilities. Shortly thereafter, in 1989, he joined the Wyndam Hotel Group as the General Manager of the 400-room Wyndham Ambassador Beach Hotel and later returned to Paradise Island to take up the post of Senior Vice President of Hotel Operations, Atlantis Beach and Coral Towers.

Stephen Sawyer has been very active in Bahamian Tourism, and was past President of the Bahamas Hotel Association, Treasurer of the Nassau-Cable Beach-Paradise Island Promotion Board and Chairman of the joint industry and the Ministry of Tourism Product Improvement Task Force. He was Chairman of the Cable Beach Resort Association, which undertook the major development and beautification of the Cable Beach median. He is a Director of the Bahamas Hotel Employers' Association and of the Bahamas Hotel Industry Management Pension Fund.

The Caribbean region has also benefitted from his experience and organizational ability. He was the 3rd Vice President of the Caribbean Hotel Association, and is past Chairman of the Caribbean Hotel Association's Insurance Company, a member of the Government Affairs Committee of the Caribbean Hotel Association, and Director of the Caribbean Hotel Training Institute of the Caribbean Hotel Association.

Stephen Sawyer's contribution to the industry is well-recognized and appreciated. He has a won several prestigious awards, including the Bahamas Hotel Association's Hotelier of the Year Award in 1989, and in 1981, during his tenure at Wyndham Hotels and Resorts, he was the recipient of the General Manager of the Year Award. He was named Caribbean Hotel Association's *Hotelier of the Year* for 1997. Presently, he is Sr. Vice President of Hotel Operations/General manager, Atlantis Royal Towers.

Norman Solomon

Outstanding Bay Street merchant and tourism leader

A politician, a businessman, a social activist and a leader are only some of the attributes of Mr. Norman Solomon, who has played a significant role in the development of tourism for the past thirty years.

Mademoiselle, "The House that Fashion Built", is one of the success stories for Bahamian tourism and a credit to Mr. Solomon. This retail outlet has catered to tourists and Bahamians alike and has popularized the Androsia batik fabric by selling it at its stores on Paradise Island, Cable Beach and Bay Street.

Another of his significant contributions is the Ardastra Gardens Conservation Centre and Zoo, located in Chippingham. He turned this failing business into a success story after acquiring it in the 1980's, and making improvements to the property. Today, Ardastra Gardens has seen the addition of exotic animals, birds and rare plants, and has become a fixture in Bahamian tourism.

Ardastra Gardens has been visited and enjoyed by millions of visitors from around the world, highlighted in many magazines and books and featured on international travel shows.

Ardastra Gardens is a teaching tool for Bahamian students learning about different species of animals, including the national bird, the West Indian Flamingo. Students are also taught the importance of conservation on visits to the Gardens.

Mr. Solomon is credited for his efforts to rebuild tourism in the country after the setback of the 1980's. He was a member of the Bahamas Duty-free Board, which evolved into the Nassau Tourism Development Board. He has served tirelessly and quietly as the wit and brains behind these organizations, working closely with the Ministry of Tourism to provide cultural and other activities for visitors in the downtown area.

This man is described as an individual who believes in doing the great things and the small things to make visitors feel welcome. From consoling visitors who have been injured or attacked, to sending people to the doctor and paying the bill, and putting toilet paper in the public restrooms at Rawson Square . . . he has done it.

Norman Solomon continues to educate Bahamians about the importance of tourism, reminding that "you never get a second chance to make a first impression".

He received the prestigious 1998 Lifetime Achievement Award at the Ministry of Tourism's Cacique Awards ceremony in recognition of his continuous contribution to the growth of tourism.

"Duke" Errol Strachan

Businessman and Developer of Young Musicians

"Duke" Errol Strachan, born in Acklins, has dedicated his life to music. In the early 1950's, Strachan began singing with Freddie Munnings Sr. In 1954, he and his cousin, Eric Gibson, formed a band. He moonlighted as a taxi driver from 1957 to 1963, while performing at night at numerous venues including the Emerald Beach Hotel. In the 1960's, the band was given a permanent job at the British Colonial Hilton and continued there for seven years, one of the longest periods that any single band has performed at that hotel. Over the years, Duke Errol has played at most of the major hotels on the island and toured numerous cities in North America and Europe.

In an article which appeared in the February 1978 edition of *Bahamas TV Guide*, a Canadian artist, Hal Hennesey, wrote an article about his encounter with Duke Errol. Wrote Hennessey "I escorted a friend into the club at the British Colonial Hilton. A muscular man dashed into the place, ran down the centre aisle and up onto the stage". Hennesey's first thought was that the club was being raided. Continued Hennessey: "No—the intruder seized a mike and began singing into it. And the whole place came alive! For this was Duke Errol, the show's leader and headliner.

His eyes, luminescent in the dark face, seemed to contain an inner fire that lit up the room."

Duke Errol has always had a head for business. He opened his first music store on Nassau Street—The Edem Music Store. He branched out into a separate Sports Centre. Although a talented musician and businessman, his greatest legacy is the contribution of his time and expertise to the development of young musicians throughout the country.

In 1973, Duke Errol began teaching music to any youngster who wanted to learn. When he operated his music store, word spread that the Duke would give a youngster an instrument and teach him to play. He taught the sax, flute, trumpet, piano and vocals.

In 1978, Duke Errol Strachan formed the "Young Soul Orchestra". In 1992, the Bahamas Youth Orchestra was formed, led by Duke Errol. The orchestra has made numerous performances both in The Bahamas and abroad.

Netica "Nettie" Symonette
Outstanding Woman Hotelier and Entrepreneur

Netica Symonette was born in Rock Sound, Eleuthera and educated at the Rock Sound Elementary School, the Government High School and the Hotel Training College. Her career in tourism started on Andros, in 1954, as secretary to the Financial Controller at the Lighthouse Club, Andros, owned by Alex Wenner-Gren. Although her education was limited, management was so impressed by her work ethic and pride in the job that she was promoted to work in the office of the General Manager. During her four years at the Lighthouse Club, she interacted with many celebrities who were guests of the hotel, including Benny Goodman, and Dag Hammershold, and points out that she saw a $1,000 bill for the first time during this period.

From 1958 to 1962, she worked at the Carlton House Hotel on East Street, Nassau, as Assistant Controller. In 1962, she moved to the Beach Inn on Paradise Island in the dual role of Assistant Controller and Chief Liaison Officer between the Hotel and Government. During her tenure at Beach Inn, she was given her first opportunity to promote the resort by blitzing travel agents in the United States, and has continued to promote The Bahamas throughout the world. She also attended summer programmes three years in a row at Cornell University. Because of her outstanding performance, she was recommended for promotion to General Manager of Beach Inn, Nassau. Because of the racist policies of the period, the promotion was not approved. In 1971, she moved on to the 500-room Holiday Inn, Paradise Island, as Assistant Innkeeper. She was in complete charge of the Front of the House (rooms, transportation, communications, pool and beach, training and Government Relations). During her tenure, the Holiday Inn attained occupancy of over 90% in three consecutive years. She also served at Holiday Inn, Freeport, for six months. Nettie did not like the big hotel scene, and in 1973 she moved to Eleuthera as General Manager of the new Cape Eleuthera Hotel and Golf Club. This posting, she said, was difficult and challenging.

In May 1975, she was invited by Prime Minister Lynden Pindling to manage the government-owned Balmoral Beach Hotel, Cable Beach. While at the Balmoral, she acquired property on West Bay Street and, in 1977, constructed her own hotel, *Casuarinas of Cable Beach*, which opened as 3 units and expanded to 91 units. Her entrepreneurial spirit led her to branch out into Abaco. After acquiring 635 acres of Crown land, mostly swamp and waste land, she created a unique ecotourism resort which she opened in 1992 and aptly named *Different of Abaco*. The environmentally sensitive property includes a bonefishing lodge, living museum depicting the culture and heritage of The Bahamas, Lucayan Village and 20-suite Sea Shell Beach Club, in a natural setting of beaches, wetlands, native trees, home to endemic plants and wildlife.

Netica achieved outstanding success while raising seven children as a single parent, with the help of her devoted mother. She instilled in her children, all of whom have achieved success, principles of hard work and discipline. She has passed on to them the real-life lessons which kept her in good stead, reminding them to "keep their feet on the ground and their head in the air", never to give in to peer pressure, and to be prepared to offer service beyond the call of duty.

When reminiscing about her exciting career, she noted that, through the hospitality industry, many doors were opened to her that would not have been possible under ordinary circumstances. She speaks fondly of invitations to luncheons in Beverly Hills from the President of Loramar Studios, touring the facility, sitting at J.R. Ewing's desk and on Miss Ellie's bed. She has been interviewed by television stations throughout the United States.

Nettie is the winner of numerous awards and citations. In 1976, she was named the Most Outstanding Woman in Business by the Broadcasting Corporation of The Bahamas. In 1980, she received the National Tourism Achievement Award from the Ministry of Tourism; in 1981—the Golden Helmsman International Award; in 1985—the Bahamas Chamber of Commerce Distinguished Citizen Award for

Business; 1987—BHA's Hotelier of the Year award; 1987—Dollars and Sense International Award for Top Women in Business; 1988—Most Outstanding Woman in Business from the Business & Professional Women's Association; 1990—Bahamas Who's Who Society Hospitality Hall of Fame Award; 1996—Cacique Award for Ecotourism; 1996—Order of Merit (Bahamas Government); Zonta's Woman of the Year; 1988—Silver Jubilee Award (Bahamas Government), among others.

Nettie is actively involved in the community, serving on boards and participating in civic activities. She has served as President of the Bahama Out Islands Promotion Board, Chairperson of the Small Hotels of The Bahamas, Director of the Bahamas Development Bank and Bahamasair, Treasurer of the Nassau, Paradise Island Promotion Board. Nettie was invited to lecture by the NAACP and is constantly giving of herself to uplift, challenge and motivate others.

Here's to a lady who has made a great contribution to the tourism industry and has dared to be different!

John Berkeley "Peanuts" Taylor, MBE
Legendary Drummer and Entertainer

John Berkeley "Peanuts" Taylor was born on 20th June, 1935. After his mother, Eunice Higgs, died at an early age, he was reared by his grandmother, Ethel Stubbs. In an interview, Taylor discussed his career as an entertainer. He fondly recalled that as a young child, he would pass the Paul Meeres Theatre on the way home from Our Lady's Catholic Primary School and hear music coming from the club. He slipped into the club one day and watched with eager eyes as Paul rehearsed. Taylor mischievously shouted, "I can sing and dance better than you!" Meeres retorted, "A little 'peanut' like you?" Amused by the challenge, Meeres jokingly said he would like to see the young boy dance one day. Shortly after, Berkeley got the opportunity to audition for Meeres, who was so impressed that he allowed the 4-year-old lad to perform with him, to the amazement and enjoyment of his audience. Thus began a lifetime relationship between the veteran, Paul Meeres, and the aspiring young performer. The nickname "Peanuts" which Meeres had invented, stuck with him.

In 1939, Paul Meeres created a popular "odd-couple" dance team featuring little Peanuts and the 450-lb "Princess Augusta". Peanuts was loved by all for his unusual talent and personality. A year later, Peanuts performed for the Duke and Duchess of Windsor, while the royal couple served in The Bahamas. In that decade, he performed in the Matinee Talent Contests at both the Savoy and Cinema Theatres.

Peanuts recalled that George Symonette, the renowned calypsonian, was a strong influence in his life. It was George Symonette who discovered Peanuts' talent as a drummer, when he asked him to fill in for a drummer who was sick. From that day, his great calling as a powerful drummer was fully exploited. He and George Symonette filled engagements at all the major hotels in Nassau and made several popular recordings. In 1952, Peanuts began representing the Development Board on tourism missions as an entertainer and goodwill ambassador, travelling all over Canada.

In 1955, while Peanuts was studying to be a schoolteacher at the Bahamas Teachers College, he was offered a job to work in Bermuda as a drummer, performing with Paul Meeres, Jr. and his partner, LaRaine. While in Bermuda, actresses Ann Miller, Linda Darrell and Hermes Pans invited him to California. While in California in December 1955, Peanuts worked with Nat King Cole. Peanuts' role was to play drums while Nat King Cole and his band were setting up their instruments to perform; hence Peanuts' drumming solo became the "Opening Act" for Nat King Cole. After returning to Nassau, he leased the old Paul Meeres Club, which he ran successfully, in partnership with Rene Yogh, from 1958 to 1961, when the club went up in flames.

Throughout his career, Peanuts Taylor maintained a series of his own nightclubs. He opened his first club, *Tropicana*, at the age of 22, *Goombay* came next in 1960, followed by his most popular club which he built on the site of the world famous Paul Meeres Theatre. On Sunday, 29th March, 1964, he officially opened the *Drumbeat Club*, on Market and Fleming Street, which attracted capacity crowds for each of its three nightly shows. Regular headliners with Peanuts Taylor were Eloise Edwards, one of the world's few female calypso singers, Pat Rolle, whose smooth singing was reminiscent of the late great Nat King Cole, Becky Chipman, a fire dancer on broken glass, and Deacon Whylly, the limbo king, along with numerous guest artists. The Drumbeat Club opened in the Nassau Beach Hotel in February 1975, and later moved to the Western Esplanade.

During his illustrious career, Peanuts shared his mesmerizing beat with celebrities and media personalities abroad. In addition to performing with Nat King Cole, he made guest appearances on The *Steve Allen Show, Jack Parr Show*, Ed *Sullivan Show, Johnny Carson Show, Bill Cosby Show*, and *I've Got a Secret*. He performed with numerous other international stars like Arlene Francis and Dave Garraway. In 1967, Peanuts, Eloise and the Deacon performed on a European tour organised by the

Ministry of Tourism, the Bahamas Hotel Association, the Bahamas Sightseeing and Tour Operators Association and British Overseas Airways Corporation (BOAC). The two-week tour included visits to Great Britain, Sweden, Germany and Switzerland. The trip was so successful, generating tremendous publicity in European media, that the European tour became an annual event. He has been featured in media worldwide: CBS, BBC, and on German and Swedish television. Publications such as The Telegram (Toronto), Newsweek, St. Petersburg Times, The Automobilist (Manchester, New Hampshire), the Jewish Chronicle (London), Harper's Bazaar, and The New Yorker all carried stories on this legend. Taylor and four other entertainers were selected to perform nightly on Norwegian Caribbean Line's 2,400-passenger cruise ship SS Norway.

Taylor provided many benefit performances, the most noteworthy of which was the annual Drumbeat for Heart concert to aid the Victor Sassoon Memorial Heart Fund. Started in 1967, Peanuts served as chairman of the fundraising event, donating Drumbeat as the venue.

His spellbinding talent as a performer was eloquently captured by writer, Melissa K. Sweeting:

> Sitting in the audience during Peanuts' performance, one is almost out of breath just watching, trying to imagine what lies in that soul and rushes out—uninhibited—into such unspeakable energy. There are five or six drums behind which this little man sits perched on his stool. His face is glowing from his smile. Shrewd, glistening eyes scan his audience, pulling even the unwitting under his spell of pure, unadulterated pleasure. And when he starts playing, the effect is so subtle, so unpretentious, so simple, really that you wonder, 'what was all the hullabaloo about?' Until you notice the way that hand flicks one place, then the next, and that elbow is brought in to strike a precise tone and then the speed is beginning and, all of a sudden, out of nowhere, it's already too much. The rhythm of the simplest, childhood song is being deconstructed and re-created, at a speed and with an energy the ear is unable to interpret to the brain fast enough. At some point, your brain convinces you there's no point in trying to learn this language on an intellectual level, since you could never express it. You feel, finally, relaxed enough to simply listen with your soul to what Peanuts' soul is attempting to convey. In the final analysis, you see that his beat will go on, with or without the world, with or without someone to listen. But, if you want to listen, he'll beat that drum for you as though you're the only one on earth. That's the remarkable thing about Peanuts: the unconditional, infinite capacity of his soul to give and give and give. No matter what language you speak, the rhythm is gonna get you!

In recognition of his tremendous contribution in the promotion of tourism, his unrelenting energy, community involvement, and outstanding success as a bongo drummer who spread peace and love throughout the world, he received numerous awards: the Timothy Award for Top Entertainer and Best Night Club Show from 1975 to 1978, the Ministry of Tourism's National Tourism Achievement Award in 1982, the Distinguished Citizen's Award in the Field of Creative and Performing Arts from the Chamber of Commerce in 1990, Tourism's Cacique Award in 1995, the Legend Award in 1996, the 1998 Merit of Honour Award and 25th Jubilee of Bahamian Independence Award. In 1993, he was named a Member of the Most Excellent Order of the British Empire (MBE) by Her Majesty Queen Elizabeth II. In 1998, he became the first person outside of Cuba to receive the prestigious "Laurete Seal of Honour" for entertainment from the Cuban government.

TOURISM STALWARTS

OF THE 1990'S

Etienne Dupuch, Jr. and Sylvia Perfetti Dupuch

Veteran Publishers of Tourist and Business Magazines

Etienne Dupuch, Jr. and Sylvia Perfetti Dupuch—Veteran Publishers of Tourist and Business Magazines

The publishing empire launched by Etienne Dupuch, Jr. in the late 1950s has played, and continues to play, a key role in growing two industries that now account for 75 per cent of the Bahamian economy: tourism and the financial industry.

In particular, the 650-page *Bahamas Handbook and Businessman's Annual* has been used since its inception in 1960 not only to entertain and inform, but also to promote The Bahamas as an exciting vacation spot and a premier place to live, work and do business.

Wallace Groves, the visionary founder of Freeport, bought thousands of *Handbooks* every year in the early 1960s, which he distributed to captains of industry all over the world, including the CEOs of large corporations, bankers, trust company presidents, real estate developers and leaders in tourism. One year alone, he did a blitz mailing of 10,000 books. In a letter to their licencees in 1964, Freeport co-founder Sir Jack Hayward wrote, "The *Handbook* has made a great many people in many parts of the world very much aware of this new area of Freeport." In fact, Freeport "relied on the *Handbook* more than any other publication to bring big money into Freeport and ultimately into the pockets of every licencee." Additional accolades came from Bahamian premier, Sir Roland Symonette, Sir Stafford Sands, the father of modern tourism in The Bahamas, newspaper baron Lord Beaverbrook, Canadian tycoon E. P. Taylor, founder of Lyford Cay, Arthur Godfrey, the immensely popular American radio broadcaster, and many prominent American politicians, including President Lyndon B Johnson.

Then, as now, the *Handbook* attracted top writers who contributed greatly to the book's reputation. It has been lauded by leading publications, including *The Miami Herald, The New York Times*, the old *New York Herald Tribune*, the *Financial Post* of Canada, *Holiday, The Saturday Evening Post, Look, The Christian Science Monitor, the New Haven Register* and a host of others. Beatrice Washburn of *The Miami Herald* wrote in 1960: "Virtually every Bahama topic from yachting and fish catching to the art of setting up a multi-million dollar tax-free corporation is packed into the new Bahamas Handbook . . . While the world is well-papered with publications touting the pleasures and climate of these nearby islands, this is the first full-scale and authoritative treatment of its financial climate . . ."

Etienne Dupuch Jr comes from a long line of journalists. His grandfather, Leon, founded *The Tribune* in 1903. His father, Sir Etienne, took over in 1919 and served as editor until 1972, and as a contributing editor until 1991. Etienne Jr began his publishing career while still a young man, working at *The Nassau Daily Tribune* as a reporter, photographer and cartoonist. While a few foreign publications were promoting tourism to The Bahamas at that time, theirs was not a consistent, full-time effort. There was no local publication that pointed out the attractions of the destination, from museums, galleries and historic sites to the excursions, restaurants and nightclubs that flourished in The Bahamas.

Seeing this as an opportunity, young Etienne's first publication was the *What-to-do* magazine, launched in 1951 and still published twice yearly. He produced those first books almost single-handedly. He wrote the copy and the headlines, laid out the pages, sold the advertising, supervised the printing and saw to the distribution. Eight years later, Etienne and his wife, Sylvia Perfetti Dupuch, founded Etienne Dupuch Jr Publications. He was 28 and she was 25. The multi-talented Sylvia was a rising star in journalism at the time, a *Phi Beta Kappa* graduate from Bates College and a journalism graduate from Columbia University in New York. She took over as editor and was involved in every aspect of the business, located on Hawthorn Road in Oakes Field. The two made a powerful team.

From Oakes Field, the company published the first *Bahamas Handbook and Businessman's Annual* in 1960. Today, the 670-page *Handbook* is published with full-colour photography and stories on the people, history and islands of the archipelago, including carefully researched articles in the business section. Much of the book's reputation rests on the encyclopaedic Blue Pages, a 200-page compendium of the most up-to-date information available on The Bahamas today. There is also a separate section on Freeport.

The Dupuches began publishing the Nassau Trailblazer Maps in 1973, followed five years later by the Freeport *What-to-do*. Next came *Welcome Bahamas* (Nassau) in 1985, a hardback book placed in hotel rooms throughout The Bahamas. The popular *Dining & Entertainment Guide* made its appearance in 1987, followed by *Welcome Bahamas* (Freeport) in 1988 and the first Freeport *Trailblazer Maps* in 1994. The latest venture is *The Bahamas Investor*, which made its debut in 2006. A semi-annual magazine, the *Investor* covers business and economic developments in The Bahamas, especially in the country's burgeoning financial services industry, along with the ongoing development of Freeport, with its busy container port, ship repair facilities, airport and modern tourism facilities.

Over the years, Dupuch has always invested in the best publishing equipment available—from the days when copy was set on linotype machines and held in place with hot lead, to the most modern, high-speed offset technology offered by printers today. Partly because of the equipment, but mostly because of the high standards demanded by Etienne and Sylvia, Etienne Dupuch Jr Publications has always enjoyed a reputation for excellence, not only for the quality of the writing and photography, but also for the physical appearance of the books. Today, Dupuch publications reach millions every year, including visitors to The Bahamas, investors, residents, academics, sportsmen and businessmen.

Etienne and Sylvia were assisted in all these endeavours by their sons Etienne III and Graham. The latter was the winner of the 1996 Cacique award for photography. Etienne Dupuch, Jr. received the National Tourism Achievement Award in 1990, as well as the Cacique Lifetime Achievement Award in 1996, in recognition of his outstanding contribution to Bahamian tourism. In giving the award it was said that "it was a combination of strong management, consistent high quality, service and dedication that made his products the leading publications today."

Michael Symonette

Successful Entrepreneur

Michael Symonette's experience as an entrepreneur started shortly after his university training. His first job as a public relations officer with a marketing communications firm was exciting and fulfilling. The challenges served as learning experiences that he was to retain and would prove beneficial later in his personal and business development. He suddenly lost his job less than a year later as the two principals of the company left The Bahamas and the company closed. He was devastated and vowed that he would never let this happen again.

Michael took his two weeks' pay in lieu of notice and rented office space in the Norfolk House to start his own business. Shortly thereafter, he won several clients of his former firm, with whom he had developed a close business relationship. He never looked for alternate employment, as most college graduates are content to do in order to earn a steady salary to pay off college loans and other expenses. Instead, he decided to build his career as an entrepreneur. This move led him to provide consultancy in varied fields in the business community, such as finance and banking, tourism, retail and manufacturing. It was this exposure that encouraged him to continue on the path of entrepreneurship.

In 1973, on the eve of Independence, a client of his firm encouraged him to produce a newsletter that would provide business and investment information. After careful research and planning, he founded the Bahamas Financial Digest, which, in 2004, celebrated its 31st year of publishing a full-colour slick gloss business and investment journal. He contributed to his country and authored a book entitled "Discovery of a Nation"—an illustrated history of The Bahamas.

Michael's next excursion in entrepreneurship came when a client who had lived in The Bahamas returned to Canada and invited his company to purchase his elegant sailing yacht. Again after careful research and development of a business plan, he accepted the offer and started a business which provided day sailing to Rose Island and also pioneered the Sunset dinner cruises excursion. He later diversified into the ground tour business and made a great success of that investment.

The principals of his company would never invest in a business simply because they wanted to or had some special preference for having a particular business in its group. Their goal was always to find a business that could provide a return on investment. They constantly search for windows of opportunity but only proceed after extensive and exhaustive marketing research. Some of the questions they ask themselves include:

- Can they provide these goods or services better than the present providers?
- How will the products or services affect the consumer marketplace?
- Should they seek out companies that are service providers to the tourism sector with its significant share of the GNP?
- Can they provide computer services to the financial and business houses?
- Can they provide Internet services for business houses, schools and homes or can they produce Web pages for the same?

In reflecting on lessons learned that can benefit other prospective entrepreneurs, Michael points out that first, one must develop and produce a business plan. This business plan should include research into the area in which one is thinking of investing. Included in that plan would be a strategic marketing plan, estimates of income over three to five years, identification of a potential customer base, one's experience and/or background in the respective field, among others. The successful entrepreneur is prepared to take risks. This person should also be prepared to believe in his or her project even when no one else does and to show enthusiasm when others share doubts. One must be prepared to manage for a slowdown in the economy. Therefore, unless one has a bread and butter product line, it might be prudent to diversify the line of goods and/or services offered.

Good advice from a very successful entrepreneur!

Vincent Vanderpool Wallace
Innovative Director General of Tourism

Born in Nassau, Bahamas, Mr. Vanderpool-Wallace attended the Government High School, where he won the Princeps Prize for scholarship and later graduated with a Bachelor's Degree *cum laude* from Harvard University in May 1975.

Mr. Vanderpool-Wallace began his full-time employment at the Bahamas Ministry of Education and Culture and later joined the Ministry of Tourism. While at the Ministry of Tourism from 1978-1982, he took a 13-month leave of absence to obtain his MBA degree from the University of Miami in 1981 where he finished at the top of his class.

In 1982, Mr. Vanderpool-Wallace joined the staff at Resorts International Bahamas where he remained for 11 years. He held various managerial positions throughout the company rising ultimately to the position of Senior Vice President as part of the three-man Office of the President.

He was appointed Director General of the Ministry of Tourism in 1993, months after the Free National Movement had seized power from the Progressive Liberal Party. He is credited with helping to revitalize the Bahamian travel product. During his tenure, the Ministry of Tourism developed a closer working relationship with the private sector and together they executed an innovative and multi-faceted marketing strategy that increased annual tourism revenue by over half a billion dollars. The Ministry reached out to travel agents with a special Bahamas training and promotional programme that detailed the assets, attributes and diversity of the nation of 700 islands. Additionally, the Ministry promoted infrastructure and service standards improvements that increased the value of The Bahamas' vacation experience and, in turn, the financial benefits for business and employment opportunities for residents. He personally put forward the idea for many innovative programmes such as Cacique Awards.

Vanderpool-Wallace was named Person of The Year for the Caribbean by Travel Agent Magazine in 1998 and served for many years as Chairman of The Marketing Committee of the Caribbean Tourism Organization (CTO).

In January 2001, he received the Albert E Koehl Award for Lifetime Achievement in Advertising by Hospitality Sales & Marketing Association International (HSMAI). In May 2001, he received the Atlas Award for Lifetime Achievement from the Association of Travel Marketing Executives International. In March 2002, he was recognized by Fast Company magazine as one of the 50 global champions of innovation from among 1,650 entries. At the 50th Anniversary Celebrations of the Caribbean Tourism Organization, he was recognized as one of 50 people who contributed most to Caribbean Tourism in the past 50 years.

Vanderpool-Wallace has served as Chairman of the Management Committee of the Bahamas Tourism Training Centre, Director of the Central Bank of The Bahamas, Director of the Bank of The Bahamas and Deputy Chairman and Chairman of the Hotel Corporation of The Bahamas where he participated in the privatization of eight government owned hotels.

He also served as Deputy Chairman of the Caribbean Hotel Association Charitable Trust (CHACT) the private public sector organization created to market the Caribbean after 11th September, 2001.

In June 2005, Vincent Vanderpool Wallace was appointed to the position of Secretary General of the Caribbean Tourism Organization and relocated to Barbados, after serving as Director General of the Bahamas Ministry of Tourism for 12 years.

He has four children, Aleksandr, Arianna, Kilian and Cydnay and is married to the former Tietchka Knowles of Nassau.

Vernice Walkine

First female Director General of Tourism

Vernice J. Walkine has led an exemplary professional and civic life. She has been in the public service for more than two decades and has had a tremendous impact on Bahamian tourism. She is the highest-ranking woman in the history of Bahamian tourism, presently holding the position of Director General of Tourism.

Ms. Walkine headed to the College of The Bahamas after earning five General Certificate of Education (GCE) 'O' levels at Government High School. At COB, she received two GCE 'A' levels and an Associate's Degree in French and Spanish. Her Bachelor's Degree in French and Spanish came from Elmira State College, New York in 1979. Later, she earned a Master's Degree in Business Administration from the University of Miami.

Upon obtaining her Bachelor's Degree in New York, Ms. Walkine returned home to face a pivotal decision that would define her professional life. She originally studied with the intention to teach foreign languages in The Bahamas, but she considered how she could best serve Bahamians while having a rewarding career. She considered a position in the Ministry of Foreign Affairs, but she finally settled on joining the Ministry of Tourism because she was more interested in the travel and tourism industries.

Ms. Walkine joined the Ministry of Tourism as a Bi-lingual Tourist Information Assistant. In her 26 years at the Ministry, she has coordinated sales conferences, strategic planning sessions, local and overseas travel agent events, media plans, major publicity events and the Bay Street redevelopment plan. She has conducted public speaking engagements and media interviews, and developed workshops, media plans and draft legislation governing vendor publics.

Initially, she was charged with translating collateral materials, such as posters and brochures, into French and Spanish. However, her abilities soon earned her more responsibilities. In 1983, she interned in the Marketing Department as a Junior Marketing Executive, training in advertising production, media evaluation and buying, collaterals production and the development of marketing plans.

Three years later, Ms. Walkine became Deputy General Manager/Marketing, taking responsibility for Tourism's worldwide advertising programmes for which she had to supervise a multi-million-dollar budget. She assumed responsibility for the Product Development Department of the Ministry of Tourism in 1993. Her duties included implementing and managing marketing programmes for the Nassau/Paradise Island destination. She also had to develop programmes aimed at the tourism and travel trade markets and restructure the Bahamas Tourist Offices in North and South America.

In June 2005, Ms. Walkine was appointed Director General of the Ministry of Tourism, becoming the first woman to hold the post.

Ms. Walkine is a member of several community and social organizations that work for the betterment of the Bahamian society. Some of these organizations also have considerable impact abroad. Ms. Walkine holds membership in The National Art Gallery of The Bahamas Committee, the Tourism Committee of the Bahamas Chamber of Commerce, and Strathmore's Who's Who Society. She is a past international board member of Hospitality Sales and Marketing Association International (HSMAI), and a past board member of the Nassau Tourism and Development Board.

Ms. Walkine is a member of the Zonta Club of New Providence, which has honoured her as a "Living Legend" for her substantial contributions to the advancement of Bahamian women and the society as a whole.

National Tourism Achievement Awardees 1976-91

1ˢᵗ Presentation—12ᵗʰ October, 1976 **Awards presented by Governor General,**
Sir Gerald Cash

Mrs. Sylvia Cole — Senior Nurse at Drs. Esfakis, Lorenz & Hall,
Outstanding People-to-People volunteer (later hired as
People-to-People Coordinator, Ministry of Tourism)

Mrs. Chena Gibson — Manageress at Solomon's Mines, Freeport
Mr. Peter Johnson — Customer Services Manager, Nassau Beach Hotel
Mr. William Miller — Maitre d', Romora Bay Club, Harbour Island
Mr. John Morley — Happy Tours
Rev. I. W. Rodgers — Concierge, Balmoral Beach Hotel
Mrs. Mamie Worrell — Proprietress of Laurelhurst-by-the-Sea guest house

2ⁿᵈ Presentation—4ᵗʰ March, 1977 **Awards presented by Governor General,**
Sir Gerald Cash

Mr. Alphonso "Blind Blake" Higgs — Musician
Mrs. Kenris Carey — Ticket Agent, Eastern Airlines
Mrs. Mildred Sands — Social Hostess, Holiday Inn, Paradise Island
Dennis Morgan — Royal Bahamas Police Force Band
Mr. Joseph Cartwright — Asst. Manager, Grand Bahama Hotel, West End

3rd Presentation—28ᵗʰ November, 1977 **Awards presented by Governor General,**
Sir Gerald Cash

Mrs. Flo Major — Guest House Operator
Mr. Charles Poitier — Tour Guide
Mr. Oswald Nixon — President, Bahamas Taxicab Union

4th Presentation—12ᵗʰ July, 1978 **Awards presented by Governor General, Sir Gerald Cash**

Kirk Brown — Doorman, Nassau Beach Hotel

Mrs. Lerlene Saunders	—	Pantry Cook, Balmoral Beach Hotel
Alonzo Taylor	—	Captain, Nassau Beach Hotel
Ms. Elvera Grant	—	Training Supervisor, Dundas Civic Centre
Rudolph Turnquest	—	Tour Director, Grand Bahama
Mrs. Ivy Simms	—	Straw business person, Long Island
Louis Adams	—	Entertainer
Mrs. Telator Strachan	—	President, one of the Straw Vendors' Associations

At the November presentation a plaque was presented to Ardastra Gardens (Mr. Headley Edwards), in recognition of the contribution of this attraction to tourism satisfaction

5th Presentation—20ᵗʰ November, 1978   **Awards presented by Governor General, Sir Gerald Cash**

Ms. Beverly Brice	—	Advertising Executive and Publisher of "Best Buys"
Mr. George Nathaniel Brown	—	Immigration Officer
Mr. Vernon Bullard	—	Veteran taxi driver
Mr. Simpson Penn, MBE	—	Founder of the Boys' Brigade movement in The Bahamas
Mr. Jerald Deveaux	—	Employee, Ocean Club, Paradise Island
Mrs. Diana Thompson	—	President—one of the Straw Vendors Associations
Mrs. Leta Ferguson	—	Maid, Café Martinique
Mr. Alexander Davis	—	Food & Beverage Manager, Pink Sands Hotel, Harbour Island

6ᵗʰ Presentation—20ᵗʰ April, 1979   **Awards presented by Governor General, Sir Gerald Cash**

D'Yanza "King Conch" Burrows	—	Exponent of Bahamian cuisine
Rudolph Cleare	—	Maitre d', Loew's Paradise Island Hotel
Allan Ingraham	—	Tour Director and Driver
Tony McKay	—	Bahamian entertainer based in USA

7ᵗʰ Presentation—19ᵗʰ November, 1979   **Awards presented by Governor General, Sir Gerald Cash**

Kermit Rolle	—	Businessman and civic worker, Rolleville, Exuma
Eddie Minnis	—	Song writer and artist
Mrs. Leslie Higgs	—	Author and local authority on gardening and bush medicine
Romeo Farrington	—	Taxi driver
Mr. Bruce Huyler	—	Taxi driver
Mrs. Mildred Hepburn	—	Employee, Flagler Inn Hotel

8th Presentation—16th June, 1980 **Awards presented by Governor General,**
                   Sir Gerald Cash

Mrs. Gloria Patience	— Deep Sea Charter Boat Captain, the Ferry, Exuma
Mr. Simpson McKinney	— Asst Manager, Treasure Cay Hotel, Abaco
Mr. Emmerson Roberts	— Manager, Underwater Tours
Mr. Richard Moss	— President of Royal Palm Tours and former President of The Bahamas Taxicab Union)
Ms. Netica Symonette	— Owner Manager, Casuarina Hotel
Mr. "King" Eric Gibson	— Nightclub owner & entertainer

9th Presentation—9th November, 1981 **Awards presented by Governor General,**
                    Sir Gerald Cash

Mr. George Audley Basden	— A retired Bartender
Mrs. Iva Bowe	— Owner/Operator, Central Highway Inn Restaurant, George Town, Exuma
Ms. Emily Cooper	— Owner/Manager, "The Blue Bee Bar", Green Turtle Cay, Abaco
Mr. Roy Davis	— Sales Manager, Eastern Airlines
Mrs. Evelyn Gordon	— President, Straw Vendors Association, Freeport
Mrs. Doris Toote,	— Vice President, Bahamas Taxicab Union
Mr. Frank Penn	— Composer
Mr. George "God Bless" Moxey	— Band Leader

10th Presentation—22nd November, 1982 **Awards Presented by Governor General,**
                     Sir Gerald Cash

Mr. Felix "Sonny" Johnson	— Musician/Entertainer, Freeport
Mr. Dan Knowles	— Taxi driver
Mr. A.B. Malcolm	— Businessman
Mr. Freddie Munnings Sr.	— Entertainer
Mr. Clarence "Uncle Bill" Saunders	— Porter
Mr. John Berkley "Peanuts" Taylor	— Musician/Nightclub Owner
Mrs. Myrtis I. Thompson	— Straw business person
Mrs. Ella Muriel Della Wilson	— Straw business person

11th Presentation—28th November, 1983 **Awards Presented by Governor General,**
                     Sir Gerald Cash

Ben Astarita	— Owner/Operator, Astarita Associates, Founding Member, BASRA, Nassau

Mrs. Theaziel Rolle	—	Assistant Manager, Happy People Marina, Staniel Cay, Exuma
Franklyn "Count Bernardino" Ellis	—	Musician/Entertainer
Mr. Eric Minns	—	Songwriter/Entertainer
Mr. Clement Bethel	—	Director, Cultural Affairs, Ministry of Youth, Sports & Community Affairs
Mrs. Rhonda Johnson	—	Owner/Operator, Johnson Seafood, Freeport, Grand Bahama
Mr. Leonard "Bowetie" Bowe	—	Tour Driver/Owner, Operator B & B Tours

12ᵗʰ Presentation—26ᵗʰ November, 1984 **Awards Presented by Governor General, Sir Gerald Cash**

Mr. Frederic Maura	—	Sr. Photographer, Bahamas News Bureau
Mrs. Pearl Cox	—	Owner/Operator, Pearl's Guest House
Mr. Garth Green	—	Superintendent, HM Customs
Mrs. Naomi Bastian	—	Hostess/Maitre d' Captain Nemo's Restaurant
Mr. Curtis Johnson	—	Owner/Operator, Seafloor Aquarium, Owner, Johnson Brothers
Mr. Joseph Finlayson	—	Retired Taxi driver
Mr. Lermon Rolle	—	Bartender, Peace & Plenty Hotel, George Town, Exuma
Mr. Vernal Sands	—	Assistant Director, Food & Beverage Dept., Cable Beach Hotel
Mr. Naaman Rollins	—	Fishing Guide & Chef, Bimini, Bahamas

13ᵗʰ Presentation—25ᵗʰ November, 1985 **Awards presented by Governor General, Sir Gerald Cash**

Mrs. Maureen DuValier	—	Entertainer
Mr. Charles G. Rolle	—	Manager, Buena Vista Restaurant
Mrs. Roberta "Bobby" Sands	—	Reservations Manager, Bahamasair
Mr. John "Chippie" Chipman	—	Entertainer
Mr. Vernon Curtis	—	President, Exuma Kiwanis/People-To-People host
Mr. Vernon Wilkinson	—	Manager, Café Martinique Restaurant, Paradise Island

10ᵗʰ Anniversary Awards— 10ᵗʰ November, 1986 **Awards presented by Governor General, Sir Gerald Cash**

Mrs. Phyllis Mercedes Harris	—	Retired Manager, British Airways/People-to-People Volunteer
Mr. Rudolph Henry Ferguson	—	Food and Beverage Director, Holiday Inn, Paradise Island
Mr. Nathaniel "Jack" Roker	—	Guitarist, Café Martinique
Mr. Errol Beckford	—	Self-employed Taxi driver
Mr. Bertie John Panza	—	Woodwork Teacher, R.M. Bailey High School

Mr. Israel Rolle "Bonefish Foley"	—	Boat Captain/Fisherman, West End, Grand Bahama
Mrs. Erma Grant Smith	—	President & Managing Director, Sun Island Tours, Freeport, Grand Bahama
Mr. Donald Smith	—	Dock master, Bimini Big Game Fishing Club, Bimini
Mr. Ronnie Butler	—	Musician/Entertainer
Mr. Samuel George Pratt	—	Bus driver/Valet, Paradise Island, Resort & Casino, Paradise Island

15th Presentation—9th November, 1987   **Awards presented by Governor General, Sir Gerald Cash**

Mrs. Sylvia Watkins	—	Veteran employee of Nassau Beach Hotel
Mr. Pedro A. McFall	—	Taxi driver
Mrs. Mable Colton	—	Activities Director, Jack Tar hotel and Country Club, West End, Grand Bahama
Mr. Fred Adderley	—	Porter, former Pan Am seaplane, Oakes Field and Nassau International Airports
Mrs. Elmena Stubbs-Forbes	—	Goodwill ambassador, Cat Island
Mr. Alton Lowe	—	Artist and founder of Alton Lowe Museum, Green Turtle Cay, Abaco

16th Presentation—November 1988   **Awards presented by Governor General, Sir Henry Taylor**

Mrs. Rebecca Chipman	—	Dancer/Entertainer
Mr. Rudy Gardiner	—	Food & Beverage Manager, Crystal Palace Hotel
Mrs. Dolly Cox	—	Housekeeper—Buena Vista Hotel
Mrs. Sylvia Cambridge	—	Owner Operator, Cambridge Villas, Gregory Town, Eleuthera
Mr. Osbourne King	—	Doorman—Paradise Towers
Mrs. Pearl McMillan	—	Straw business person, Market Plaza
Mr. Jay Mitchell	—	Musician/Entertainer
Mr. Joseph Delancy	—	Glass Bottom Boat/Taxi driver
Mr. Alpheus Miller	—	Taxi driver
Mr. Samuel Brown	—	Public Bus driver/Bartender, Bimini
Mr. Joey Johnson	—	Hotelier

17th Presentation 23rd November, 1989   —   **Awards presented by Governor General, Sir Henry Taylor**

Mr. Leonard Rolle	—	Island Cruises
Mr. Addison Culmer	—	Taxi Driver, Freeport, Grand Bahama
Mrs. Stephanie Garvey	—	Station Manager, Bahamasair. Freeport

Mr. Cyril Ferguson	—	Entertainer/Musician, Freeport
Mr. Wilfred "Willie Love" Knowles	—	Supervisor—Executive Tours
Mr. Stephen Burrows	—	Sculptor Artist/Bahamas Electricity Corp.
Mrs. Naomi Taylor	—	Dancer/Entertainer
Mr. Charles Francis Lowe	—	Taxi Driver, Treasure Cay, Abaco
Mr. Eric Russell	—	Musician
Mr. Leonora Roker	—	Straw business person, Market Plaza
Mrs. Irene Bantouvanis	—	Owner Operator, Mitchell's Guest House
Captain Donald Rolle	—	Glass Bottom Boat Owner/Operator

18th Presentation—November 1990   **Awards Presented by Governor General,**
                                       Sir Henry Taylor

Mrs. Deborah Forbes	—	Straw business person, Market Plaza
Mr. Nehemiah Francis	—	Superintendent, H.M. Customs
Mr. Edward Knowles	—	Chief Immigration Officer, Bahamas Immigration
Mrs. Isabella Bootle	—	Manager, Private Villa, Treasure Cay, Abaco
Mr. Lloyd Delancy	—	Taxi Driver
Rev. Harriet McDonald	—	Straw Vendor, Minister of Religion
Mr. David Kemp	—	Retired Entertainer
Mr. Samuel Culmer	—	Maitre D', Rock Sound Club, Rock Sound, Eleuthera
Mr. Charles Daniel Cooper	—	Retired Entertainer, Rock Sound, Eleuthera
Mr. Cedric Lewis	—	Resident Manager, Bahamas Princess Towers, Freeport, Grand Bahama
Mr. Frederick George Taylor	—	Entertainer/Director of Entertainment, Holiday Inn, Freeport, Grand Bahama
Mr. Etienne Dupuch, Jr.	—	Publisher, Publisher, tourist and business publications
Mrs. Doris Burrows	—	Self-employed caterer
Mr. Percy "Vola" Francis	—	Junkanoo Art/Front Desk Supervisor.

19th Presentation—1991   **Awards presented by Governor General,**
                                    Sir Henry Taylor

Mrs. Winnifred E. Bannister	—	Salesperson, John Bull
Ms. Valderine Barnett	—	People-to-People Volunteer
Mr. Leroy Bowe	—	Bowe's Scooter Rental, Freeport, Grand Bahama
Mr. Alfred Brown	—	Taxi driver
Mrs. Edwina G. Burrows	—	Edwina's Place, Rock Sound, Eleuthera
Mr. Gladstone Christie	—	Taxi driver
Mr. Randolph Clare	—	Taxi driver
Ms. Delores Colebrook	—	Pirate's Cove, Holiday Inn
Ms. Ena Mae Davis	—	Straw business person

Mr. Wendal "Chalker" Evans	—	Taxi driver
Mr. Lincoln Jones	—	Sports fishing guide, Other Shore Club, Green Turtle Club, Abaco
Mrs. Ruby Percentie	—	Owner/Operator, Tingum Village Resort, Harbour Is.
Mrs. Sheila Iris Rolle		People-to-People Volunteer
Mr. William "Bill" Saunders	—	Ground tour operator, owner, Majestic Tours
Ms. Doris Strachan	—	Straw business person
Mr. James Sweeting	—	Doorman, Wyndham Ambassador Beach Hotel
Ms. Mabel Strachan	—	Proprietor, Mabel's Gift Shop
Mr. James "Biggie" Taylor	—	Taxi driver
Mr. Cleophas Tucker (deceased)	—	Taxi driver
Mrs. Norma Wilkinson	—	Bimini Big Game Club, Bimini
Mrs. Genevieve "Abby LeFleur" Sherman-Ware	—	Professional dancer
Mr. Sydney Woods	—	Musician

Cacique Award Winners 1995-2005

Lifetime Achievement Award/Sir Clement Maynard Lifetime Achievement Award

1995 Fred Maura	2001 Denis Donaldson
1996 Etienne Dupuch, Jr.	2002 Genevieve Sherman Ware
1997 Jimmy Nixon	2003 Romeo Farrington
1998 Norman Solomon	2004 Ronnie Butler
1999 Telator Strachan	2005 Sir Albert Miller—*Winner of the first Sir Clement T. Maynard Lifetime achievement Award*
2000 Vernal Sands	2006 George Myers

Minister of Tourism's Award

1995 Sheila Rolle	2000 Diana Thompson
1996 Mildred Sands	2002 Anthony "Zips" Hanna
1997 Rev. Newton Hamilton, Andros	2003 Ansil Saunders
1998 Margo Wring	2004 Margarita Clarke
1999 Louise Grant	2005 Israel "Bonefish Foley" Rolle, Grand Bahama

Retail

1995 Shelly Kelly	1998 Norma Griffin Johnson, Eleuthera
1996 John Bull	1999 Lois Albury, Abaco
1997 Claire Sands	2000 Dwight Caleb Thurston

Arts & Craft

1995 Wendy Kelly	2000 Harl Taylor
1996 Eddie Minnis	2001 Antonius Roberts (The Arts)
1997 Anastacia Charlow	2002 Helen Astarita and Berta Sands
1998 Omealia Marshall, Andros	2003 Vertrum Lowe
1999 Henry Wallace, Andros	2004 Joseph Albury, Boatbuilder, Abaco
1999 Alton Lowe (The Arts)	2005 Miralee Rose, craft

Human Resources/Education

1995 John Burrows	2000 Karen Carey
1996 Mary Nabb, Freeport	2002 Donald McCartney, Freeport
1997 Vernal Culmer-Butler, Freeport	2003 Barbara Barnes
1998 John Rosevear	2004 Felice Renee McKinney, Freeport
1999 Olivia Mortimer	2005 Dr. Sophia Rolle

Transportation

1995 Clifford Fernander, San Salvador	2000 Hadley Forbes, Freeport
1996 Romeo Farrington	2002 Bahamas Ferries
1997 William Saunders	2003 Chalk's Ocean Airways
1998 Steven O. Symmonett	2004 Michael Thompson, Grand Bahama
1999 Richard Moss	2005 Floyd Lowe, Abaco

Sports, Leisure & Events

1995 Rev. Samuel Ellis	2000 Joseph Cleare, Eleuthera
1996 Messrs. Samuel and Wilmore Rolle, Exuma	2002 Albert Richard "Bert" Bell
1997 Charles "Charlie" Smith	2003 Prescott Smith
1998 Captain Michael Brown	2004 David & Kathleen Ralph, *Regatta Time in Abaco*
1999 Captain Rupert Leadon, Andros	2005 Simon Bain, Bonefish guide

Nature Tourism/Ecotourism/Sustainable Tourism

1995 Netica Symonette, Abaco	2000 Erika Moultrie-Gates, Freeport
1996 Pericles Maillis	2002 Sir Nicholas Nuttall
1997 Small Hope Bay Lodge, Andros	2004 Ben Rose, Grand Bahama
1998 Kenneth and Diane Balcomb, Abaco	2005 Brendal Stevens
1999 Basil Minns, Exuma	

Writer

1995 Patricia Glinton-Meicholas	1998 Deborah Nash
1996 Dr. Gail Saunders	1999 Ashley Saunders, Bimini
1997 Lyn Sweeting	

Motion and/or Still Photography

1995 Roland Rose	1998 Sean Johnson
1996 Graham Dupuch	1999 Andrew Aitken
1997 Gavin McKinney	2000

Music & Entertainment/Creative Arts

1995 John Berkeley "Peanuts" Taylor	2000 "Duke" Errol Strachan
1996 Royal Bahamas Police Force Band	2002 Franklyn "Count Bernadino" Ellis
1997 John "Chippie" Chipman	2003 Eric Minns
1998 Edwin "Apple" Elliott, Freeport	2004 Elyse Wasile (Creative Arts)
1999 "King" Eric Gibson	2005 Jay Mitchell

Company or Group

1995 Sun International's Atlantis, Paradise Island	1998 Club Peace and Plenty, Exuma
1996 SuperClubs Breezes	1999 Bahamas National Trust
1997 Café Johnny Canoe	2000 Small Hope Bay Lodge

Special Award

1995 Ronald Kelly	2004 Kamalame Cay, Andros (Brian & Jennifer Hew)
2003 Dolphin Encounters/Project Beach	

Hotel Industry and International Awards

	Supervisor of the Year	Manager of the Year	Sales Executive of the Year
1995	Valderine Major	Jeffrey Hepburn, Freeport	Francis "Ted" Adderley
1996	Stacy Cox	Sandle Major	Hiltrud Augustine
1997	Anthony Adderley	Don Lionel Ingraham	Merrit Storr
1998	Anville Brown	Derek Smith	Joy Smith
1999	William King	Andrea Sweeting	Charmaine Burrows
2000	Pedro Davis	Jacklyn Gurrier	Hedda Smith
2002	Anthony Pinder	Ivan Evans	Karen Elizabeth Cargill
2003		Juanita Greene	Andre Newbold, Sandals

2004	Stephen Moncur, Radisson	Lynn Johnson, Green Turtle Cay, Abaco	Andre Newbold, Sandals
2005	Raymond Lowe, Green Turtle Club, Abaco	Avis Miller, Treasure Cay Club, Abaco	Marva Munroe, Pelican Bay Resort, Grand Bahama
	Employee of the Year	**Chef of the Year**	**Casino Executive of the Year**
1995	Sheldon Saunders, Freeport		Gerald Simons
1996	Hartman Carey	Edwin Johnson	Kendal Munro
1997	Betty Lloyd	Charles Smith	Salvatore Cuccurullo
1998	Pyvonne Rolle-Schmidt	Christopher Chea	Barbara Foreman
1999	Judeen Pennerman	Kerry Robinson	Carl Haven
2000	Rondell Dames, Freeport		Lincoln Hercules
2002	Carnetha Carew		
2003	Tiffany Knowles	Tracey Sweeting	
2004	Dellarese Frazier, Radisson	Jasmin Young, Atlantis, P.I.	
2005	Wilbert Knowles, Atlantis	Jason McBride, Radisson	
	Hotelier of the Year	***International Writer***	**International Tour Operator**
1995	J. Barrie Farrington	Chelle Walton	Apple Vacations
1996	Brendon Foulkes	Rich Rubin	Apple Vacations
1997	Jeremy MacVean	Martin Elder (Travel Trade) Cheryl Blackerby (Consumer)	Nassau/Paradise Island Express
1998	Dion Strachan	Sue Juliano (Travel Trade) Gully Wells (Consumer)	GoGo Worldwide Vacations
1999	Barbara Hanna-Cox	Laura Dennis (Travel Trade) Florence Williams (Consumer)	Travel Impressions
2000	Iris Dillet-Knowles	Felicity Long (Travel Trade) Charles Greenfield (Consumer)	Grand Bahama Vacations
2001	Alfred Gorlick		

2003	Michael Hooper		
2004	Paul D. Thompson		Paradise Island Vacations
2005	Paul O'Neil, Atlantis	Sara Macefield, U.K.	
	International Airline	**International Travel Agent**	**International Photographer**
1995	Delta Airlines		Bob Krist
1996	American Airlines	John Papas	Catherine Karnow
1997	American Airlines	Vicki Borenstein	Forest Johnson
1998	American Eagle	Christina Vadala	Jordon Klein
1999	US Airways	Greg Welpe	Brent Spector
2000		Gayle Naugler	Al Roker Productions
2004	Air Tran Airways	Neil Henderson (Banana Travel, UK)	
2005	Spirit Airlines	Thomas Cook, Canada	
	International Cruise Lines/Cruise Ferry		
1995	Carnival Cruise Lines & Discovery Cruise Lines		
1996	Florida Caribbean Cruise Association (Cruise Stay)		
1997	Royal Caribbean International		
1998	Disney Cruise Lines		
1999			
2000	Royal Caribbean Cruise Lines Discovery Cruise Lines (Cruise Stay)		
2004	Discovery Cruise Lines		
2005	Carnival Cruise Lines		

People's Choice Bahamian Song Competition (Award category established in 2003)

Year	Best Secular Song (Artist)	Best Gospel Song/Artist
2003	*"Drunk Again"*, Eugene Davis "Geno D"	*"Junka Praise"*, Tamika Smith
2004	*"Mr. Gofa"*, Phil Stubbs, Freeport	*"Hold on to Jesus"*, Da Fam
2005	*"Civil Servant,"* Kirkland "KB" Bodie	*"I'm a Soldier"*, Jawanza "Spike" Munroe

Selected Cacique Winners

Joseph Albury—Boatbuilder, Abaco, 2004 Cacique winner

Andrew Aitkin—Photographer, 1999 Cacique winner

Barbara Hanna Cox, 1999 Hotelier of the Year

Edwin "Apple" Elliott—Band leader, 1998 Cacique Winner, Category: Music & Entertainment

Rev. Newton Hamilton, Andros, taxi driver & goodwill ambassador, 1997 Minister of Tourism's Award

Mary Nabb, Grand Bahama educator—1996 Cacique Winner, Category—Human Resources:

Jeremy McVean—1997 Hotelier of the Year

Eddie Minnis, Artist, Songwriter—1996 Cacique Winner, Category: Arts

Basil Minns, Environmentalist—1999 Cacique Winner, Category: Sustainable Tourism

Sir Albert Miller, Grand Bahama Port Authority, Winner of first Sir Clement Maynard Lifetime Achievement Award

Richard Moss, ground tour operator—1999 Cacique Winner, Category: Transportation

Jimmy Nixon, Game Warden, Inagua—1997 Lifetime Achievement Award

Royal Bahamas Police Band—Winner of 1996 Cacique, Category: Music and Entertainment

Israel "Bonefish Foley" Rolle, bonefish guide, Grand Bahama, 2005 Minister of Tourism's award

Mildred Sands, Bush Medicine expert, 1996 Minister of Tourism's Award

2003 Cacique winner, Ansil Saunders, Bonefish guide and boatbuildter, Bimini, pose with visitors after arranging a marine wedding for the couple

Dr. Gail Saunders—1996 Cacique winner: Category—Writing

Dion Strachan, 1998 Hotelier of the Year

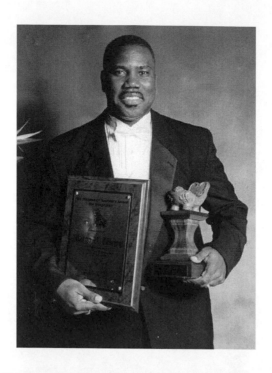

Margo Wring, Airline executive, 1998 Minister of Tourism's Award

Francis "Ted" Adderley, 1995 Sales Executive of the Year

Clifford Fernander, San Salvador, 1995 Cacique Winner
in the *Transportation* category

Blue Ribbon Cacique Panel 2005. Seated: Dr. Keva Bethel (left) and Dr. Patricia Rodgers (right), who served as Chair for the Cacique Awards from 1995-2003. Kneeling: Dr. Davidson Hepburn, Chair of the Blue Ribbon Panel. Standing from left: Colin Higgs, Jackson Burnside, Hugh Sands and Terrence Roberts

APPENDICES 1A-1D

GLOBAL TRAVEL STATISTICS

Appendix 1A. International Tourist Arrivals and Receipts (1950-2005)

Year	International Arrivals	International Tourism receipts (excluding transport)
1950	25.3 million	$2.1 billion
1960	69.3 million	$6.8 billion
1961	75.3 million	$7.3 billion
1962	81.3 million	$8.0 billion
1963	90.0 million	$8.9 billion
1964	104.5 million	$10.1 billion
1965	112.9 million	$11.6 billion
1966	119.8 million	$13.3 billion
1967	129.5 million	$14.4 billion
1968	130.9 million	$15.0 billion
1969	143.1 million	$16.8 billion
1970	159.7 million	$17.9 billion
1971	172.2 million	$20.8 billion
1972	181.8 million	$24.6 billion
1973	190.6 million	$31.0 billion
1974	197.1 million	$33.8 billion
1975	214.3 million	$40.7 billion
1976	220.7 million	$44.4 billion
1977	239.1 million	$55.6 billion
1978	257.4 million	$68.8 billion
1979	274.0 million	$83.3 billion
1980	285.9 million	$105.3 billion
1981	287.1 million	$107.4 billion
1982	286.0 million	$100.9 billion
1983	289.5 million	$102.5 billion
1984	316.3 million	$112.7 billion
1985	327.1 million	$118.1 billion
1986	338.8 million	$143.4 billion
1987	363.6 million	$176.8 billion
1988	394.7 million	$204.5 billion
1989	426.3 million	$221.4 billion

1990	457.2 million	$263.4 billion
1991	462.7 million	$276.9 billion
1992	500.9 million	$315.4 billion
1993	516.0 million	$321.9 billion
1994	550.3 million	$354.9 billion
1995	571.2 million	$406.2 billion
1996	584.3 million	$436.5 billion
1997	608.6 million	$439.7 billion
1998	628.9 million	$442.5 billion
1999	652.2 million	$455.4 billion
2000	696.7 million	$475.8 billion
2001	692.7 million	$463.6 billion
2002	714.6 million	$474.0 billion
2003	694.0 million	$514.0 billion
2004	766.0 million	$633.0 billion
2005	800 million (est.)	$682.0 billion

Source: *World Tourism Organization*

Appendix 1B. Leading Generators of International Tourism

COUNTRY	AMOUNTS SPENT ON TRAVEL ABROAD 1995		POPULATION 1994	AVERAGE SPENDING PER CAPITA—1995	
	Mn US$	Rank	(Thousand)	US$	Rank
EUROPE					
Germany	48,101	1	81,410	591	9
U.K.	24,625	4	58,090	424	13
France	16,315	5	57,750	283	16
Italy	12,411	6	57,190	217	18
Austria	11,699	7	8,030	1,457	2
Netherlands	11,455	8	15,380	745	7
Belgium	7,995	11	10,080	793	6
Switzerland	6,543	12	6,990	936	4
Sweden	5,422	14	8,790	617	8
Spain	4,421	17	39,190	113	21
Denmark	4,282	18	5,210	822	5
Norway	4,221	20	4,330	975	3
Finland	2,383	24	5,090	468	11
AMERICAS					
USA	45,350	2	260,650	174	19
Canada	9,661	9	29,250	330	14
Brazil	4,245	19	153,730	28	24
Mexico	3,153	22	93,010	34	23
EAST ASIA & PACIFIC					
Japan	36,737	3	124,960	294	15
Taiwan	8,457	10	19,300	438	12
Korea, Rep.	5,919	13	44,450	133	20
Singapore	5,134	15	2,930	1,752	1
Australia	4,574	16	17,930	255	17
Thailand	3,403	21	59,400	57	223,150
REST OF WORLD					
Israel	3,150	23	5,460	577	10

Source: UNWTO's 1995 International Tourism Overview,
World Tourism Organization, Madrid, Jan. 1996

Appendix 1C. Tourism In The Economy of Caribbean Countries

1994

COUNTRIES	RECEIPTS PER CAPITA US$	RECEIPTS PER VISITOR US$	TOURISM RECEIPTS AS % OF GNP
Anguilla	5,100	1,159	91.07
Antigua and Barbuda	5,629	1,545	86.98
Aruba	6,443	775	35.91
Bahamas	4,937	879	43.59
Barbados	2,300	1,404	36.91
Bermuda	8,733	1,260	30.39
Bonaire	3,200	571	
British Virgin Islands	9,400	787	31.47
Cayman Islands	10,933	962	
Cuba	78	1,378	4.47
Curacao	1,220	769	8.71
Dominica	443	544	15.58
Dominican Republic	148	669	11.36
Grenada	667	550	23.26
Guadeloupe	1,167	881	40.83
Haiti	7	657	2.63
Jamaica	368	941	25.87
Martinique	1,024	905	27.07
Montserrat	1,900	905	37.25
Puerto Rico	470	568	6.48
St. Kitts and Nevis	1,875	798	41.44
St. Lucia	1,600	1,023	46.67
St. Maarten	13,600	696	-
St. Vincent/Grenadines	464	927	21.79
Trinidad and Tobago	63	301	1.65
Turks and Caicos	5,700	792	
U.S. Virgin Islands	9,190	1,702	68.38
CARIBBEAN AVERAGE	325	851	14.17

Source: Caribbean Tourism Organization

Appendix 1D. Stopover Tourist Arrivals in the Caribbean: 1990 vs. 1980 and 2005

Country	2005	1990	%	1980	%	% Change	% p.a. Chg
Anguilla	62,084	30,600	0.3%	5,700	0.1%	437%	18% p.a.
Antigua	245,384	205,700	1.7%	86,600	1.3%	137%	9% p.a.
Aruba	732,514	432,800	3.7%	188,900	2.8%	129%	9% p.a.
Bahamas	1,608,153	1,561,100	13.2%	1,181,300	17.8%	32%	3% p.a.
Barbados	547,534	432,100	3.6%	369,900	5.6%	17%	2% p.a.
Belize	236,573	221,800	1.9%	63,700	1.0%	248%	13% p.a.
Bermuda	269,576	432,700	3.7%	491,600	7.4%	-12%	-1% p.a.
Bonaire	62,550	41,300	0.3%	25,200	0.4%	64%	5% p.a.
British Virgin Islands	337,135	160,600	1.4%	97,000	1.5%	66%	5 % p.a.
Cayman Is.	167,801	253,200	2.1%	120,200	1.8%	111%	8% p.a.
Cuba	2,319,334	320,000	2.7%	na	na	na	na
Curacao	222,070	207,700	1.8%	184,700	2.8%	12%	1% p.a.
Dominica	79,257	45,100	0.4%	14,400	0.2%	213%	12% p.a.
Dominican Rep.	3,690,692	1,533,200	13%	301,100	4.5%	409%	18% p.a.
Grenada	98,244	82,000	0.7%	29,400	0.4%	179%	11% p.a.
Guadeloupe		271,600	2.3%	156,500	2.4%	73%	6% p.a.
Guyana	116,596	67,000	0.6%	na	na	na	na
Haiti	112,267	120,000	1.0%	138,000	2.1%	-13%	-1% p.a.
Jamaica	1,465,292	840,800	7.1%	395,300	5.9%	113%	8% p.a.
Martinique	484,127	281,500	2.4%	158,500	2.4%	78%	6% p.a.
Montserrat	9,690	17,000	0.1%	15,500	0.2%	10%	1 % p.a.
Puerto Rico	1,465,292	2,645,400	22%	1,627,400	24%	63%	5% p.a.
Saba	11,462	11,700	0.1%	6,000	0.1%	95%	7% p.a.
St. Eustatius	10,355	6,600	0.1%	10,000	0.2%	-34%	-4% p.a.
St. Kitts & Nevis		75,700	0.6%	32,800	0.5%	131%	9% p.a.
St. Lucia	317,939	138,400	1.2%	79,700	1.2%	74%	6% p.a.
St. Maarten	467,861	564,700	4.8%	179,000	2.7%	215%	12% p.a.
St. Vincent & Gren.	95,505	53,900	0.5%	50,400	0.8%	7%	0.7% p.a.
Suriname	159,852	28,500	0.2%	48,400	0.7%	-41%	-5% p.a.
Trinidad & Tobago	460,195	194,000	1.6%	199,200	3.0%	-3%	-0.3% p.a.
Turks & Caicos		41,900	0.4%	11,900	0.2%	252%	13% p.a.
US Virgin Islands	697,033	522,900	4.4%	380,000	5.7%	38%	3% p.a.
CARIBBEAN		11,841,500	100%	6,648,300	100%	78%	6% p.a.

Source: *Caribbean Tourism Research Centre Annual Reports (Various)* and
Caribbean Tourism Organization

Appendix 1E
Cruise Visitors to the Caribbean

		2003	2004	2005
	ALL BAHAMAS	**2,970,174**	**3,360,012**	**3,078,709**
1	NASSAU/P.I. (BAH.)	1,687,851	1,981,883	1,880,696
	GRAND BAHAMA. BAH.)	203,312	327,933	321,582
	FAMILY ISLANDS (BAH.)	1,079,011	1,050,196	876,431
2	COZUMEL (MEXICO)	2,708,913	1,862,036	2,519,179
3	CAYMAN ISLANDS	1,818,979	1,352,556	1,798,999
4	U.S VIRGIN ISLANDS	1,773,948	1,964,689	1,912,539
5	PUERTO RICO	1,234,992	1,381,411	1,315,079
6	St. MAARTEN	1,171,734	1,348,450	1,488,461
7	JAMAICA	1,132,596	1,099,773	1,135,843
8	BELIZE	575,196	851,436	800,331
9	BARBADOS	559,122	737,626	563,588
10	ARUBA	542,327	576,320	552,819
11	DOMINICAN REPUBLIC	398,263	456,321	289,805
12	ST. LUCIA*	393,240	481,279	394,364
13	ANTIGUA & BARBUDA	385,686	522,753	466,851
14	CURACAO	279,378	219,385	276,217
15	MARTINIQUE	268,542	59,416	93,064
16	BERMUDA	226,097	206,133	247,259
17	BRITISH VIRGIN ISL.	304,338	466,601	449,152
18	DOMINICA	177,044	80,608	301,294
19	GRENADA	146,925	163,521	275,082
20	ST. VINCENT & GREN.	64,965	74,657	69,391
21	TRINIDAD & TOBAGO	55,532	4,254	67,193
22	BONAIRE	44,601	53,343	40,077
	HAITI			368,018
	TOTAL	**17,232,592**	**18,772,580**	

Source: CTO and Ministry of Tourism, Research & Statistics Department
(Data supplied by CTO member countries Feb.2006

APPENDIX 2

MEMBERS OF THE BAHAMAS DEVELOPMENT BOARD
1914-1931

1914/1915 1915/16 1916/17	1917/1918 1918/19	1921/1922 1922/23 1923	1926/27	1930/1931
Hon. **F.C. Wells Durant,** MA, KC—Chair	**Charles E. Albury**—Chair	**G.H. Gamblin**—Chair (1921); **A.K. Solomon**, MEC—Chair (1921-1925)	**R.H. Curry**—Chair	**Dr. G.H. Johnson**, MEC MHA—Chair
W.P. Adderley	George W. Armbrister	Geo. W.Armbrister	R.T. Symonette	Mary Moseley
L.G.Brice	E.L. Brown	T.A. Toote	S.C. McPherson	L.C. Brice
H.W. Lightbourn	Frank Holmes	Frank Holmes	Frank Holmes	S.C. Farrington
W.C.B. Johnson	W. Hilton	R.H. Curry	W.C.B. Johnson	H.P. Sands
G.H. Gamblin	C. Tucker Sands			
H.H. Brown	Hon. H.P. Lofthouse	H.P. Lofthouse		

APPENDICES 3A-3F

VISITOR STATISTICS
for selected years
1949-1964

Extracted from

"A Resume´ of Tourist Travel to the Bahamas"
Annexed to Annual Reports of the Development Board

Prepared by the News Bureau of
The Bahamas Development Board

Under the direction of Mr. Stafford L. Sands, M.H.A., Chairman
Courtesy: Department of Archives

Appendix 3A. Visitor Breakdown
1949-1964

YEAR	VISITORS TO NASSAU/ PAR.IS.	VISITORS TO GRAND BAHAMA	VISITORS TO FAMILY ISLANDS	TOTAL VISITORS*	TOURISM BUDGET
1949	32,018			32,018	£94,031
1950	45,371			45,371	£156,150
1951	68,502			68,502	£199,474
1952	84,718			84,718	£292,247
1953	90,485			90,485	£311,490
1954	109,605			109,605	£340,386
1955	132,434			132,434	£413,326
1956	155,003			155,003	£475,242
1957	194,618	15,095**		209,713	£556,813
1958	177,867	18,791**		196,658	£658,482
1959	244,258	20,500**		264,758	£730,250
1960	305,553	36,424**		341,977	£807,696
1961	314,126	54,085**		368,211	£902,864
1962	335,993	13,269	95,608	444,870	£1,004,130
1963	398,676	26,894	120,834	546,404	£1,136,186
1964	399,907	109,295	95,969	605,171	£1,233,656
1965	494,552	147,032	78,836	720,420	£1,464,580
1966	531,167	191,244	99,906	822,317	+B.$4,992,968

*   Excludes yachtsmen   rate: £ = $2.80

**   **These 1957-1961 figures represent visitors to both Grand Bahama and Family Islands**

+   **The Bahamas converted to decimal currency in 1966. The budgets for 1966 and beyond are shown in Bahamian dollars**

Appendix 3B. Nassau Tourist Arrivals By Month
1951-1959

	1951	1952	1953	1954	1955	1956	1957	1958	1959
Jan.	9,334	8,344	9,968	10,777	12,309	15,024	13,771	8,515	23,601
Feb.	10,549	12,597	13,092	13,749	16,892	18,833	22,491	16,594	27,552
Mar.	11,886	12,617	13,079	12,603	16,483	18,411	22,112	20,974	29,704
Apr.	5,163	6,003	7,726	8,587	11,794	14,264	18,496	16,821	23,404
May	3,705	5,652	3,967	7,150	8,936	12,919	15,988	12,775	16,162
June	3,571	5,726	5,939	7,322	9,146	11,103	13,866	13,407	18,454
July	4,991	7,863	7,443	10,372	12,562	14,905	16,331	16,447	22,247
Aug.	4,090	7,185	8,345	10,687	11,613	11,453	17,077	17,202	21,752
Sept.	2,066	2,032	4,385	4,672	4,985	6,643	10,300	8,256	11,652
Oct.	3,565	3,520	4,968	6,442	6,333	8,280	12,844	12,025	13,977
Nov.	3,613	5,264	4,402	6,352	8,932	10,068	13,528	16,721	16,380
Dec.	5,969	7,915	7,171	10,892	12,449	13,100	17,814	18,130	19,374
Total	68,502	84,718	90,485	109,605	132,434	155,003	194,618	177,867	244,258

Appendix 3C. Visitor Arrivals—Nassau
Stopovers vs. Transients—By Month, By Biennium

	1953			1955			1957		
	Stop-overs	Tran-sients	Total	Stop-overs	Tran-sients	Total	Stop-overs	Tran-sients	Total
Jan.	4,410	5,558	9,968	6,472	5,837	12,769	7,275	6,496	13,771
Feb.	6,737	6,355	13,092	8,712	8,180	17,273	10,381	12,110	22,491
Mar.	6,792	6,287	13,079	8,049	8,434	16,881	12,220	9,892	22,112
Apr.	3,917	3,809	7,726	5,827	5,967	12,359	9,130	9,366	18,496
May	2,699	1,268	3,967	3,877	5,059	9,559	7,741	8,247	15,988
June	3,168	2,771	5,939	4,440	4,706	9,686	7,994	5,872	13,866
July	3,748	3,695	7,443	5,792	6,770	1,353	9,011	7,320	16,331
Aug.	3,863	4,482	8,345	5,526	6,088	12,466	9,196	7,881	17,077
Sept.	1,815	2,570	4,385	2,334	2,651	5,980	5,947	4,353	10,300
Oct.	2,107	2,861	4,968	3,501	2,832	7.196	8,234	4,610	12,844
Nov.	2,678	1,724	4,402	4,977	3,955	9,655	8,488	5,040	13,528
Dec.	4,236	2,935	7,171	5.088	6,361	13,363	9,138	8,676	17,814
Total	46,170	44,315	90,485	65,594	66,840	140,750	104,755	89,863	194,618

Appendix 3D. Total Visitors to Nassau
By Air and Sea &
Stopovers vs. Transients
1949-1957

	Air	Sea	Total	Stopovers	Transients	Total
1949	21,722	10,296	**32,018**	14,865	17,153	32,018
1950	33,426	11,945	**45,371**	21,093	24,278	45,371
1951	50,802	17,700	**68,502**	38,998	29,504	68,502
1952	50,581	34,137	**84,718**	43,186	41,532	84,718
1953	55,535	34,950	**90,485**	46,170	44,315	90,485
1954	67,122	42,483	**109,605**	54,066	55,539	109,605
1955	75,298	57,136	**132,434**	65,594	66,840	132,434
1956	92,655	62,148	**155,003**	79,169	75,834	155,003
1957	125,721	68,897	**194,618**	104,755	89,863	194,618

Appendix 3E. Origin of Visitors
1955-1957

Area	1955	1956	1957
Area 1 —Florida		21,763	29,038
Area 2 —Alabama, Georgia, Kentucky, Mississippi, Carolinas, Tennessee, Virginia		7,546	9,110
Area 2B —Arkansas, Louisiana, Oklahoma, Texas		4,243	4,585
Area 3 —Connecticut, Delaware, Washington, Maryland, New York, New Jersey, Pennsylvania, Rhode Island.		30,862	40,557
Area 3B —Maine, Massachusetts, New Hampshire, Vermont		3,694	4,270
Area 4 —Illinois, Indiana, Iowa, Kansas, Michigan, Minnesota, Missouri, Nebraska, N. & S. Dakota, Ohio, Wisconsin		20,073	23,480
Total—U.S.A.	**75,076** **(91.9%)**	**91,481** **(91.7%)**	**114,979** **(91.4%)**
Total Canada	**3,591** **(4.4%)**	**4,805** **(4.8%)**	**6,108** **(4.8%)**
Total—United Kingdom	**1,368** **(1.7%)**	**1,600** **(1.6%)**	**1,864** **(1.5%)**
Other Countries	1,618	1,791	2,897
Grand Total	**81,653**	**99,677**	**125,848**

Appendix 3F. Breakdown of International Air and Sea Visitors— By Carrier—The 1950's

AIR	1953	1956	1957
Pan American, Miami	30,188	48,634	114,917
Pan American, N.Y.			10,626
Pan American, Charter			5,960
BOAC, Miami	14,370	7,445	20,780
BOAC, New York		8,840	8,007
BOAC, London/Bermuda		1,948	2,495
BOAC, Montreal			97
Trans Canada Air Lines	1,239	1,644	2,451
Mackey Air lines	7,307	21,740	26,073
Resort Air Lines	1,669		
Cubana Air Lines			1,124
Miscellaneous	762	1,512	1,840
Total—Air	**55,535**	**92,855**	**125,721**
SEA			
SS Nassau	13,980	15,646	15,461
Florida			18,183
Evangeline			5,041
Yarmouth Castle			5,041
Nuevo Dominicano	4,690		
Reina del Pacifico	861	599	
Caronia	1,172	138	780
Queen of Bermuda	4,080	3,967	4,253
Silver Star	3,867	1,962	
Ocean Monarch	3,291	2,154	4,682
Mauretania	1,427	4,066	2,506
Ryndam			588
Olympia			1,810
Homeric			1,296
Arosa Star			1,691
Berlin			419
Andes			399
Kungsholm			782

AIR	1953	1956	1957
Matspmoa			700
Neptunia	430		
Patricia	28		
New Amsterdam	741		659
Queen of Nassau		200	
Stockholm		358	778
Maasdon		587	1,498
Bergensfjord		472	
Reina del Mar		124	1,183
Reina del Pacifico			482
Arosa Sun		490	
Oslofjord		375	387
Andes		396	
New York		565	
Miscellaneous	383	23,190	278
Total—Sea	34,950	62,148	68,897
Grand Total—Air and Sea	90,485	155,003	194,618

Note: Family Island Visitors in 1953: Bimini 2006; Green Turtle Cay—3; Fresh Creek—16; Family Island Visitors in 1956—7,324 (incomplete returns)

APPENDIX 4

DEVELOPMENT BOARD AND MINISTRY OF TOURISM BUDGETS
1949-2006

YEAR	BUDGET	YEAR	BUDGET
1949	£94,031	1978	$11,717,600
1950	£156,150	1979	$14,916,090
1951	£199,474	1980	$18,368,230
1952	£292,247	1981	$24,100.000
1953	£311,490	1982	$19,900,000
1954	£340,386	1983	$28,400,000
1955	£413,326	1984	$26,200,000
1956	£475,242	1985	$27,200,000
1957	£556,813	1986	$29,800,000
1958	£658,482	1987	$32,800,000
1959	£730,256	1988	$37,600,000
1960	£807,696	1989	$41,000,000
1961	£902,864	1990	$39,500,000
1962	£1,004,130	1991	$41,700,000
1963	£1,136,186	1992	$43,600,000
1964	£1,233,656	1993	$34,200,000
1965	£1,464,580	1994/95	$35,500,000
1966	*B.$4,992,968	1995/96	$41,600,000
1967	$5,499,405	1996/97	$50,400,000
1968	$6,160,050	1997/98	$53,300,000
1969	$6,499,400	1998/99	$57,200,000
1970	$6,696,636	1999/2000	$57,000,000
1971	$6,879,713	2000/2001	$61,000,000
1972	$8,132,810	2001/2002	$61,214,915
1973	$8,100,000	2002/2003	$69,408,691
1974	$8,500,000	2003/2004	$69,500,000
1975	$8,831,800	2004/2005	$76,000,000
1976	$9,900,798	2005/2006	$78,000,000
1977	$10,500,000	2006/2007	$80,200,000

* The Bahamas converted to decimal currency in 1966. Exchange rate £ = $2.80

Source: *Development Board and Ministry of Tourism Annual Reports*

APPENDICES 5A AND 5B

FOREIGN ARRIVALS TO THE BAHAMAS

These statistics are based on ship manifests and the count of the Immigration cards collected from all arriving foreigners, except military and diplomatic personnel entering on official duty, foreign residents in the Bahamas and ship and airline crew who do not stay overnight in The Bahamas. The statistics reflect the First Port of Entry where visitors enter The Bahamas and do not necessarily reflect where the visitor actually stayed.

Appendix 5A   Foreign Arrivals by First Port of Entry in The Bahamas
1962-2005

Appendix 5B   Distribution of Visitor Arrivals to The Family Islands
1975-2005

Source: Research Department, Ministry of Tourism

Appendix 5A. Foreign Arrivals by First Port of Entry in The Bahamas 1962-2005

YEAR	NASSAU/ P.I.	% of Total	GRAND BAHAMA	% of Total	FAMILY ISLANDS	% of Total	TOTAL BAHAMAS
1962	335,993	75.5	13,269	3.0	95,608	21.5	**444,870**
1963	398,676	73.0	26,894	4.9	120,834	22.1	**546,404**
1964	399,907	66.1	109,295	18.1	95,969	15.9	**605,171**
1965	494,552	64.6	147,032	25.3	78,836	10.8	**720,420**
1966	531,167	64.6	191,244	23.3	99,906	12.1	**822,317**
1967	576,846	63.0	231,382	25.3	107,045	11.7	**915,273**
1968	664,755	62.0	308,737	28.8	98,721	9.2	**1,072,213**
1969	725,572	54.5	497,644	37.3	109,180	8.2	**1,332,396**
1970	730,611	56.3	496,040	38.2	71,700	5.5	**1,298,351**
1971	838,186	57.3	543,070	37.1	82,330	5.6	**1,463,586**
1972	941,533	62.3	472,560	31.3	97,770	6.5	**1,511,863**
1973	987,219	64.9	428,680	28.2	104,110	6.8	**1,520,009**
1974	925,888	66.7	350,080	25.2	112,070	8.1	**1,388,038**
1975	911,970	66.0	349,880	25.3	119,010	8.6	**1,380,860**
1976	884,900	63.0	382,180	27.2	136,570	9.7	**1,403,650**
1977	867,000	62.8	354,330	25.7	160,070	11.6	**1,381,400**
1978	1,024,760	50.0	469,180	27.5	212,990	12.5	**1,706,930**
1979	1,060,550	59.3	508,170	28.4	220,700	12.3	**1,789,420**
1980	1,090,900	57.3	540,040	28.4	273,620	14.4	**1,904,560**
1981	989,800	56.1	484,380	27.5	289,140	16.4	**1,763,320**
1982	983,320	50.5	670,620	34.4	293,800	15.1	**1,947,740**
1983	1,284,060	57.7	667,080	30.0	272,950	12.3	**2,224,090**
1984	1,407,720	60.5	626,770	27.0	290,760	12.5	**2,325,250**
1985	1,588,510	60.4	749,060	28.5	294,400	11.2	**2,631,970**
1986	1,732,750	57.6	890,950	29.6	383,600	12.8	**3,007,300**
1987	1,658,580	53.8	1,072,715	34.8	350,075	11.4	**3,081,370**
1988	1,617,034	51.2	1,169,913	37.0	371,144	11.8	**3,158,091**
1989	1,745,835	51.4	1,149,583	33.8	502,893	14.8	**3,398,311**
1990	1,957,913	54.0	1,175,537	32.4	495,069	13.6	**3,628,519**
1991	2,022,570	55.8	1,086,097	30.0	513,551	14.2	**3,622,218**

YEAR	NASSAU/ P.I.	% of Total	GRAND BAHAMA	% of Total	FAMILY ISLANDS	% of Total	TOTAL BAHAMAS
1992	1,875,968	50.8	1,062,466	28.8	751,109	20.4	3,689,543
1993	1,749,315	47.5	1,165,440	31.7	767,505	20.8	3,682,260
1994	1,882,527	54.6	899,574	26.1	664,275	19.3	3,446,376
1995	1,754,249	54.2	918,443	28.4	566,463	17.5	3,239,155
1996	1,858,410	54.4	953,174	27.9	604,274	17.7	3,415,858
1997	1,933,955	56.0	860,580	24.9	659,232	19.1	3,453,767
1998	1,889,742	56.4	809,860	24.2	648,063	19.4	3,347,665
1999	2,288,899	62.6	668,957	18.3	697,983	19.1	3,655,839
2000	2,685,819	63.9	676,098	16.1	841,917	20.0	4,203,834
2001	2,711,851	64.8	633,632	15.1	837,273	20.0	4,182,756
2002	2,583,811	58.6	635,639	14.4	1,186,521	26.9	4,405,971
2003	2,635,112	57.4	630,871	13.7	1,328,059	28.9	4,594,042
2004	2,957,746	59.1	729,632	14.6	1,316,589	26.3	5,003,967
2005	2,971,481	62.2	651,802	13.6	1,156,134	24.2	4,779,417

Appendix 5B. Distribution of Visitor Arrivals to The Family Islands 1975-2005

Port of Entry	1975		1980		1985		1995		2000		2005	
	Air	Total	Air	Total	Air	Total	Air	Total	Air	Total	Air	Total
Abaco	32,660	32,870	56,990	58,990	70,010	77,400	78,329	87,641	89,354	145,215	94,715	202,939
Andros	6,970	6,070	8,180	8,270	6,680	6,710	6,671	7,046	8,749	9,480	8,799	9,965
Berry Islands	8,020	8,610	9,180	19,610	8,190	89,420	6,959	224,426	10,009	247,584	9,790	319,262
Bimini	21,530	44,840	24,210	51,410	19,420	48,240	15,235	46,919	12,894	48,270	14,512	45,804
Cat Cay	*		2,890	10,920	2,200	16,110	2,349	9,988	2,985	10,087	4,444	12,899
Cat Island	*	*			*		385	390	1,446	1,455	3,975	3,975
Eleuthera	18,400	18,540	40,990	41,200	42,770	42,990	42,262	165,017	34,511	164,717	34,511	300,318
Exuma	5,280	5,440	5,870	6,210	10,200	10,740	9,323	10,316	11,256	11,851	35,712	36,284
Inagua	470	470	1,590	2,220	1,320	2,200	276	2,076	188	1,549	182	2,118
Long Is.	**	**	**	**	**		1,902	2,039	977	977	1,417	1,427
Little San Sal	*	*	*	70,360	*			781	0	185,828	0	208,072
San Salvador	2,160	2,160	3,910	4,440	600	600	9,394	9,824	13,603	14,904	14,875	15,071
Total Family Islands	95,490	119,000	153,810	273,630	160,780	294,410	173,085	566,463	185,972	841,917	222,932	1,156,134

*   Not a Port of Entry in given year

APPENDIX 6

PROMOTION OF TOURISM ACT

The Promotion of Tourism Act authorizes the Minister of Tourism to:

a) Make all such enquiries and to collect such information as may be deemed necessary for the purpose of promoting and thoroughly advertising the Colony as a tourist resort and for the purpose of materially facilitating and increasing the tourist traffic to the Colony;

b) Adopt all such measures as, in the opinion of the Minister, may be necessary for promoting and thoroughly advertising the Colony as a tourist resort, and for the purpose of materially facilitating and increasing the tourist traffic to the Colony;

c) Appoint any person or agent, for all or any of such purposes, as the Minister may deem necessary and to arrange for the remuneration of the same either by salary, commission or otherwise as the Minister may think proper;

d) Accept from any hotel, development or transportation company any contribution for all or any of the purposes of this Act and to administer the same either solely or by joint arrangement with any such hotel, development or transportation company;

e) Enter into and make such contract or contracts as the Minister may deem necessary for all or any of the purposes of this Act;

f) Make any contract, for the special purposes of this Act, for the provision of air or steamship communication between the Colony and any other place and to pay for or contribute towards the same or towards advertising or promoting the same by way of annual or periodical subsidy, a guarantee of debenture interest, commission on the number of passengers brought to the Colony or by any other method of payment sanctioned by the Minister

g) Take all such measures, generally, as the Minister may deem likely to carry out most effectively the objects of this Act.

   (Bahama Islands Statute Law, Revised Edition 1965, Chapter 13, Promotion of Tourism Act.)

APPENDICES 7A-7C

HOTEL ROOMS

Appendix 7A Hotel Rooms in The Bahamas: 1960-2005

Appendix 7B Hotel Rooms in The Islands of The Bahamas for selected years: 1957-2005

Appendix 7C Hotel Occupancy: 1975, 1985, 1995 and 2005

Appendix 7A. Hotel Rooms in The Bahamas
1960-2005

Year	Nassau/Paradise Is. Rooms	Grand Bahama Rooms	Family Islands Rooms	Total Bahamas Rooms
1960	1,900	325	345	**2,570**
1961	2,032	305	522	**2,859**
1962	2,153	397	805	**3,355**
1963	2,099	536	820	**3,455**
1964	2,159	1,444	852	**4,455**
1965	2,142	2,180	1,038	**5,360**
1966	2,684	2,159	1,164	**6,007**
1967	3,867	2,849	1,442	**8,158**
1968	3,867	2,849	1,570	**8,286**
1969	4,370	3,620	1,513	**9,503**
1970	3,909	3,905	1,773	**9,587**
1971	5,097	3,884	1,866	**10,847**
1972	5,005	4,136	2,086	**11,227**
1973	4,835	4,648	2,078	**11,561**
1974	5,092	4,394	2,216	**11,612**
1975	5,016	4,340	2,039	**11,395**
1976	4,733	4,310	2,064	**11,107**
1977	5,307	3,856	2,279	**11,442**
1978	5,223	3,808	2,144	**11,175**
1979	5,170	3,880	2,361	**11,411**
1980	5,333	3,880	2,214	**11,427**
1981	5,433	4,168	2,302	**11,903**
1982	6,212	4,001	2,193	**12,406**
1983	7,107	3,855	2,271	**13,233**
1984	7,427	3,527	2,166	**13,120**
1985	6,963	3,889	2,314	**13,166**
1986	6,970	3,672	2,245	**12,887**
1987	7,006	3,816	2,362	**13,184**
1988	6,897	3,324	2,259	**12,480**
1989	7,914	3,628	2,319	**13,861**
1990	7,797	3,574	2,104	**13,475**

Year	Nassau/Paradise Is. Rooms	Grand Bahama Rooms	Family Islands Rooms	Total Bahamas Rooms
1991	7,780	3,211	2,174	**13,165**
1992	7,886	3,333	2,322	**13,541**
1993	7,849	3,290	2,382	**13,521**
1994	7,618	3,253	2,527	**13,398**
1995	7,574	3,262	2,585	**13,421**
1996	7,471	3,366	2,451	**13,288**
1997	7,421	3,422	2,528	**13,368**
1998	8,355	3,296	2,592	**14,243**
1999	8,319	3,596	2,678	**14,593**
2000	8,329	2,670	3,596	**14,595**
2001	8,605	2,564	3,576	**14,745**
2002	8,703	2,885	3,889	**15,396**
2003	8,738	2,839	3,816	**15,393**
2004	8,523	3,829	3,156	**15,508**
2005	8,662	2,994	3,144	**14,800**

Source: Hotel Licensing Department, Ministry of Tourism

Appendix 7B. Hotel Rooms in The Islands of The Bahamas for selected years 1957-2005

Island	1957	1962	1967	1972	1977	1982	1987	1992	1997	2005
New Providence /Paradise Island	1,795	2,233	3,867	5005	5284	6,212	7,006	7,886	7,421	8,662 (4,037 PI)
Abaco	52	187	243	336	448	436	613	569	626	720
Acklins					4	4		15	5	35
Andros	43	99	188	263	188	160	210	207	200	397
Berry Islands	16	16	56	151	254	55	55	71	43	17
Bimini	114	146	189	240	214	128	150	175	193	323
Cat Cay	36	36								
Cat Island				36	48	54	59	66	113	323
Crooked Is.				25	25	29	26	23	18	41
Eleuthera	95	163	345	543	529	752	672	631	595	247
Exuma		28	237	196	183	221	213	126	147	438
Grand Bahama	135	397	2,849	4136	3844	4,001	3,816	3,333	3,422	2,994
Harbour Island	78	99	151	147	173	190	178	175	163	219
Inagua			4	16	11	13	13	13	23	21
Long Island			45	35	49	56	6828	72	41	147
Mayaguana								4	5	21
Rum Cay			2			7	16			
San Salvador		19	24	24	44	44		135	328	328
Spanish Wells	10	10	59	74	45	44	61	40	25	19
Total	**2,374**	**3,433**	**8,158**	**11,227**	**13558**	**12,406**	**13,184**	**13,541**	**13,368**	**14,800**

Source: Bahamas Ministry of Tourism Annual Reports and Hotel Licensing Department Reports (licensed hotels only)

Appendix 7C. Hotel Occupancy

	Nassau/Paradise Island				Grand Bahama				Family Islands			
	1975	1985	1995	2005	1975	1985	1995	2005	1975	1985	1995	2005
Month	%	%	%	%	%	%	%	%	%	%	%	%
January	64.1	70.0	63.2	60.4	49.1	58.0	57.5	53.4	31.7	31.2	31.0	33.0
February	81.0	80.4	68.1	82.2	76.7	73.0	74.5	66.9	48.9	45.9	43.3	44.1
March	82.8	89.3	79.8	91.3	78.1	88.1	87.9	84.0	65.1	65.3	49.4	54.4
April	67.8	83.4	73.4	82.7	64.8	81.4	82.9	71.7	45.6	57.7	52.3	48.0
May	57.1	74.0	62.4	75.2	55.4	68.2	74.9	60.1	29.9	47.6	44.4	46.8
June	48.5	67.9	67.7	85.3	44.8	66.7	78.4	73.9	26.0	51.8	43.9	56.9
July	60.4	69.3	77.0	91.3	47.5	71.6	77.3	72.2	30.9	49.2	45.5	45.4
August	65.7	70.5	77.4	81.4	54.5	71.2	72.9	58.4	36.7	55.3	35.6	31.9
September	35.2	47.2	59.5	49.2	31.2	47.4	53.8	45.4	11.3	25.8	25.1	17.3
October	42.9	58.1	59.4	56.9	39.3	46.0	63.6	56.9	18.7	27.4	24.1	19.5
November	60.3	63.9	70.1	73.6	59.4	64.3	72.7	67.7	30.9	35.5	27.3	33.2
December	59.6	61.4	56.0	67.0	57.7	47.2	65.3	54.4	36.8	41.3	27.9	34.5
Average Occupancy	60.4	69.6	67.7	75.4	56.1	65.2	72.1	63.7	35.4	45.7	38.0	39.8

Source: Ministry of Tourism Annual Reports

APPENDIX 8A

SUMMARY BREAKDOWN OF TOTAL VISITORS
STOPOVERS vs. CRUISE and AIR vs. SEA
1964-2005

YEAR	STOP-OVERS (% of Tot)	CRUISE (% of Total)	DAY & TRANSIT (% of Total)	TOTAL. FOREIGN ARRIVALS	% INC.	AIR (% of Total)	SEA (% of Total)
1964	N/A	N/A	N/A	**605,171**	10.8	364,611 60%	240,560 40%
1965	N/A	N/A	N/A	**720,420**	19.0	440,338 61%	280,082 39%
1966	N/A	N/A	N/A	**822,317**	14.1	549,423 67%	272,894 33%
1967	N/A	N/A	N/A	**915,273**	11.3	649,388 71%	265,885 29%
1968	N/A	N/A	N/A	**1,072,213**	17.1	818,994 76%	253,219 24%
1969	N/A	N/A	N/A	**1,332,396**	24	970,325 73%	362,071 27%
1970	891,480 68.7%	351,865 27.1%	N/A	**1,298,344**	-2.6	916,479 71%	381,865 29%
1971	960,820 65.6%	435,825 29.8%	N/A	**1,463,591**	12.7	970,965 66%	492,626 34%
1972	1,015,320 65.6%	420,860 27.8%	67,060 4.4%	**1,511,860**	3.3	1,044,970 69%	466,890 31%
1973	976,760 64.3%	462,390 30.4%	71,200 4.7%	**1,520,010**	0.5	1,021,840 67%	498,170 33%
1974	876,080 64%	386,680 28%	116,072 8%	**1,378,310**	-8.7	966,560 70%	421,480 30%
1975	827,760 60%	421,280 31%	127,030 9.2%	**1,376,070**	-0.5	917,670 66.5%	463,190 33.5%

YEAR	STOP-OVERS (% of Tot)	CRUISE (% of Total)	DAY & TRANSIT (% of Total)	TOTAL FOREIGN ARRIVALS	% INC.	AIR (% of Total)	SEA (% of Total)
1976	818,720 58.5%	404,620 29%	176,270 12.6%	1,399,610	1.6	953,930 68%	449,710 32%
1977	891,270 65%	352,945 26%	135,550 9.8%	1,379,755	-1.6	982,220 71%	399,190 29%
1978	1,083,180 64%	449,625 26.5%	160,940 9.5%	1,693,745	23.6	1,181,580 69%	525,360 31%
1979	1,129,430 64%	476,159 27%	160,200 9.1%	1,765,789	4.8	1,252,270 70%	537,150 30%
1980	1,181,260 62%	577,631 30%	145,960 7.7%	1,904,560	6.4	1,262,330 66%	642,230 34%
1981	1,030,640 59%	596,870 34%	128,270 7.3%	1,763,320	-7.4	1,105,560 63%	657,760 37%
1982	1,101,130 57%	719,586 37%	126,360 6.5%	1,947,740	10.5	1,121,070 58%	826,680 42%
1983	1,239,750 56%	854,112 38.5%	124,050 5.6%	2,224,090	14.2	1,220,480 55%	1,003,620 45%
1984	1,278,500 55%	907,760 39%	133,870 5.8%	2,325,250	4.5	1,321,330 57%	1,003,920 43%
1985	1,368,300 52%	1,136,454 43%	124,050 4.7%	2,631,970	13.2	1,385,260 53%	1,246,700 47%
1986	1,375,220 46%	1,495,562 50%	132,060 4.4%	3,002,842	14.1	1,378,600 46%	1,628,700 54%
1987	1,479,855 48%	1,434,245 47%	165,285 5%	3,079,385	2.5	1,455,921 47%	1,625,449 53%
1988	1,474,980 47%	1,505,143 48%	177,905 5%	3,158,028	2.6	1,448,679 46%	1,709,412 54%
1989	1,575,070 46%	1,644,583 48%	178,605 5%	3,398,258	7.6	1,490,006 44%	1,908,305 56%
1990	1,561,665 43%	1,853,897 51%	212,885 6%	3,628,447	6.8	1,516,396 42%	2,112,123 58%
1991	1,427,035 39%	2,019,964 56%	174,890 5%	3,621,889	-0.2	1,303,318 36%	2,318,900 64%
1992	1,398,895 38%	2,139,383 58%	150,360 4%	3,689,543	1.9	1,227,703 33%	2,461,840 67%
1993	1,488,680 40%	2,047,030 56%	146,170 4%	3,682,260	-0.2	1,327,319 36%	2,354,941 64%

YEAR	STOP-OVERS (% of Tot)	CRUISE (% of Total)	DAY & TRANSIT (% of Total)	TOTAL. FOREIGN ARRIVALS	% INC.	AIR (% of Total)	SEA (% of Total)
1994	1,516,035 44%	1,805,607 52%	122,135 4%	3,446,376	-6.4	1,332,280 39%	2,114,096 61%
1995	1,598,135 49%	1,543,495 48%	96,625 3%	3,239,155	-6.0	1,317,078 41%	1,922,077 59%
1996	1,633,105 48%	1,685,668 49%	96,050 3%	3,415,858	5.5	1,368,038 40%	2,047,820 60%
1997	1,617,595 47%	1,743,736 51%	78,135 2%	3,446,363	0.9	1,368,107 40%	2,078,256 60%
1998	1,527,707 46%	1,729,894 52%	n/a	3,347,665	-2.9	1,304,851 39%	2,042,814 61%
1999	1,577,066 43%	1,981,471 54%	n/a	3,648,291	9.0	1,438,887 39%	2,209,404 61%
2000	1,543,959 37%	2,512,626 60%	144,456 3%	4,203,834	15.2	1,481,492 35%	2,722,342 65%
2001	1,537,780 37%	2,551,673 61%	116,149 2%	4,182,756	-0.5	1,428,209 34%	2,754,547 66%
2002	1,513,151 34%	2,802,112 64%	n/a	4,405,971	5.3	1,402,894 32%	3,003,077 68%
2003	1,510,169 33%	2,970,174 67%	n/a	4,594,042	4.3	1,428,973 31%	3,165,069 69%
2004	1,561,312 31%	3,360,012 67%	n/a	5,003,967	8.9	1,450,313 29%	3,553,654 71%
2005	1,608,153 34%	3,078,709 64%	n/a	4,779,417		1,514,532 32%	3,264,885 68%

Source: Research Department, Ministry of Tourism

APPENDIX 8B CRUISE VISITORS BY FIRST PORT OF CALL 1978-2005

	New Providence	%	Grand Bahama	%	Family Islands	%	Total Bahamas
1978	372,280	82.8	33,920	7.5	43,410	9.7	449,620
1979	389,630	81.8	59,720	12.5	26,810	5.6	476,160
1980	433,830	75.1	68,040	11.8	75,760	12.1	577,630
1981	434,810	72.8	56,110	9.4	105,950	17.8	596,870
1982	401,710	55.8	217,580	30.2	100,290	13.9	719,590
1983	570,930	66.8	218,730	25.6	64,450	7.5	854,110
1984	621,940	68.5	213,860	23.6	71,970	7.9	907,760
1985	766,310	67.4	292,750	25.8	77,400	6.8	1,136,450
1986	940,829	62.9	394,890	26.4	159,860	10.7	1,495,560
1987	807,630	56.3	492,495	34.3	134,120	9.4	1,434,245
1988	805,837	53.5	544,492	36.2	154,814	10.3	1,505,143
1989	837,123	50.9	521,103	31.7	286,357	17.4	1,644,583
1990	1,006,394	54.3	581,976	31.4	265,627	14.3	1,853,897
1991	1,179,458	58.4	547,420	27.1	293,086	14.5	2,019,964
1992	1,114,565	52.1	494,651	23.1	530,167	24.8	2,139,383
1993	948,440	46.3	565,016	27.6	533,574	26.1	2,047,030
1994	1,072,642	59.4	308,195	17.1	424,770	23.5	1,805,607
1995	918,838	59.5	287,337	18.6	337,320	21.9	1,543,495
1996	960,170	57.0	359,523	21.3	365,975	21.7	1,685,668
1997	1,033,118	59.0	313,942	17.9	404,080	23.1	1,751,140
1998	1,031,535	59.6	304,626	17.6	393,733	22.8	1,729,894
1999	1,276,803	64.4	266,396	13.4	438,272	22.1	1,981,471
2000	1,667,903	66.4	248,164	9.9	596,559	23.7	2,512,626
2001	1,746,540	68.4	210,709	8.3	594,424	23.3	2,551,673
2002	1,645,904	58.7	196,923	7.0	959,285	34.2	2,802,112
2003	1,687,851	56.8	203,312	6.8	1,079,011	36.3	2,970,174
2004	1,981,883	59.0	327,933	9.8	1,050,196	31.3	3,360,012
2005	1,880,695	61.1	321,582	10.4	876,431	33.7	3,079,709

APPENDICES 9A AND 9B

STOPOVER VISITORS

Appendix 9A Stopover Visitors by Country of Residence: 1977-2005
Appendix 9B Stopover Visitors by Destination in The Bahamas: 1977-2005

Appendix 9A. Stopover Visitors by Country of Residence 1977-2005

Year	U.S.A.	%	Canada	%	Europe	%	Rest of World	%	Total
1977	658,690	74	141,880	16	64,290	7	26,410	3	891,260
1978	819,960	76	143,250	13	86,740	8	23,230	3	1,083,190
1979	851,590	75	134,710	12	101,880	9	41,240	4	1,129,430
1980	884,030	75	129,780	11	114,070	10	53,390	4	1,181,260
1981	791,540	77	109,210	11	77,750	7	52,130	5	1,030,640
1982	910,770	83	82,730	7	57,280	5	50,350	5	1,101,130
1983	1,051,560	85	86,680	7	43,910	3	57,610	5	1,239,750
1984	1,083,240	85	85,350	7	40,700	3	69,210	5	1,278,500
1985	1,205,275	88	91,700	7	36,890	3	34,435	2	1,368,300
1986	1,223,620	89	72,190	5	46,450	3	32,980	2	1,375,220
1987	1,299,215	88	80,525	5	67.950	5	32,165	2	1,479,855
1988	1,274,365	86	84,330	6	85,135	6	31,150	2	1,474,980
1989	1,351,750	86	94,300	6	91,320	6	37,700	2	1,575,070
1990	1,321,930	85	96,755	6	96,625	6	46,355	3	1,561,665
1991	1,176,690	82	90,120	6	112,045	8	48,180	3	1,427,035
1992	1,128,025	81	97,640	7	122,140	9	51,090	4	1,398,895
1993	1,209,550	81	96,570	6	133,085	9	49,475	3	1,488,680
1994	1,254,210	83	99,025	6	109,730	7	53,070	3	1,516,036
1995	1,328,925	83	85,600	5	114,950	7	68,660	4	1,598,135
1996	1,341,300	82	85,760	5	127,620	8	78,425	5	1,633,105
1997	1,310,420	81	91,330	6	130,365	8	86,480	5	1,617,596
1998	1,250,026	82	83,086	5	117,954	8	76,641	5	1,527,707
1999	1,283,235	82	87,973	6	125,485	8	70,373	4	1,577,066
2000	1,294,295	84	82,840	5	104,610	7	62,214	4	1,543,959
2001	1,308,163	85	79,715	5	94,047	6	55,855	4	1,537,780
2002	1,310,140	87	68,592	4	79,564	5	54,855	4	1,513,151
2003	1,305,335	86	63,148	4	93,170	6	48,516	3	1,510,169
2004	1,360,912	87	68,462	4	83,590	5	48,348	3	1,561,312
2005	1,379,995	86	75,633	5	85,276	5	67,148	4	1,608,052

Source: Research Department, Ministry of Tourism

Appendix 9B. Stopover Visitors by Destination in The Bahamas 1977-2005

Year	Nassau/ Paradise Is.	%	Grand Bahama	%	Family. Islands	%	Total
1977	440,620	49.4%	286,280	32.1%	164,360	18.4%	891,260
1978	545,590	50.4%	352,330	32.5%	185,260	17.1%	1,083,180
1979	571,540	50.6%	351,120	31.1%	206,770	18.3%	1,129,430
1980	582,850	49.3%	381,980	32.3%	216,430	18.3%	1,181,260
1981	507,450	49.2%	328,250	31.8%	194,940	18.9%	1,030,640
1982	542,950	49.3%	351,680	31.9%	206,520	18.8%	1,101,150
1983	676,680	54.6%	347,080	28.0%	216,000	17.4%	1,239,760
1984	733,690	57.4%	321,570	25.2%	223,240	17.5%	1,278,500
1985	769,690	56.3%	382,545	28.0%	216,065	15.8%	1,368,300
1986	745,320	54.2%	399,010	29.0%	230,890	16.8%	1,375,220
1987	775,975	52.4%	475,650	32.1%	228,230	15.4%	1,479,855
1988	749,795	50.8%	500,100	33.9%	225,085	15.3%	1,474,980
1989	826,985	52.5%	520,730	33.1%	227,355	14.4%	1,575,070
1990	842,885	54.0%	484,880	31.0%	233,900	15.0%	1,561,665
1991	758,230	53.1%	452,655	31.7%	216,150	15.1%	1,427,035
1992	694,205	49.6%	482,885	34.5%	221,805	15.9%	1,398,895
1993	737,480	49.5%	514,435	34.6%	236,765	15.9%	1,488,680
1994	749,850	49.5%	525,065	34.6%	241,120	15.9%	1,516,035
1995	774,005	48.4%	587,250	36.7%	236,880	14.8%	1,598,135
1996	831,485	50.9%	552,385	33.8%	249,235	15.3%	1,633,105
1997	840,515	52.0%	512,710	31.7%	264,370	16.3%	1,617,595
1998	812,319	53.2%	474,784	31.1%	240,604	15.7%	1,527,707
1999	941,838	59.7%	360,687	22.9%	274,541	17.4%	1,577,066
2000	899,503	58.3%	378,101	24.5%	266,355	17.3%	1,543,959
2001	900,625	58.6%	406,766	26.5%	230,389	15.0%	1,537,780
2002	880,855	58.2%	410,687	27.1%	221,609	14.6%	1,513,151
2003	895,612	59.3%	376,425	24.9%	238,132	15.8%	1,510,169
2004	921,932	59.0%	374,433	24.0%	264,947	17.0%	1,561,312
2005	1,019,015	63.4%	316,265	19.7%	272,772	17.0%	1,608,052

APPENDICES 10A AND 10B

VISITOR NIGHTS IN THE BAHAMAS

Appendix 10A   Visitor Nights by Country of Residence: 1977-2005

Appendix 10B   Visitor Nights by Destination in the Bahamas: 1977-2005

Appendix 10A. Visitor Nights by Country of Residence
1977-2005

	U.S.A.	%	Canada	%	Europe	%	Other	Total
1977	3,766,070	65.4%	1,144,760	19.9%	593,610	10.3%	249,980	5,754,420
1978	4,645,870	66.7%	1,176,310	16.9%	837,710	12.0%	300,300	6,960,190
1979	5,241,170	66.2%	1,193,800	15.1%	1,110,500	14.0%	375,480	7,920,950
1980	5,527,390	65.5%	1,213,010	14.4%	1,216,760	14.4%	478,980	8,436,140
1981	5,016,070	67.1%	1,065,080	14.3%	915,680	12.3%	473,790	7,470,610
1982	5,481,490	73.2%	849,280	11.3%	703,250	9.4%	456,290	7,490,310
1983	6,165,550	75.7%	882,980	10.8%	587,910	7.2%	504,180	8,140,620
1984	6,239,160	76.2%	845,150	10.3%	533,770	6.5%	567,210	8,185,280
1985	6,746,295	80.6%	859,685	10.3%	474,745	5.7%	287,630	8,368,355
1986	6,870,260	82.0%	698,730	8.3%	546,850	6.5%	259,080	8,374,920
1987	7,032,800	81.0%	708,540	8.2%	691,825	8.0%	252,140	8,685,305
1988	6,905,830	79.3%	739,230	8.5%	813,875	9.3%	248,695	8,707,630
1989	7,069,340	78.7%	787,880	8.8%	847,280	9.4%	273,125	8,977,625
1990	6,939,085	77.4%	795,830	8.9%	920,830	10.3%	307,110	8,962,855
1991	6,304,555	75.0%	742,720	8.8%	1,035,540	12.3%	319,110	8,401,925
1992	5,979,955	73.6%	736,505	9.1%	1,095,770	13.5%	311,745	8,123,975
1993	6,293,840	73.3%	746,940	8.7%	1,239,335	14.4%	304,915	8,585,030
1994	6,633,250	75.0%	777,375	8.8%	1,091,540	12.3%	344,365	8,846,530
1995	6,787,890	75.2%	697,135	7.7%	1,106,835	12.3%	439,595	9,031,455
1996	7,037,780	74.4%	707,805	7.5%	1,221,055	12.9%	498,745	9,465,385
1997	7,058,185	73.2%	752,025	7.8%	1,252,630	13.0%	574,465	9,637,305
1998*	n/a	n/a	n/a	n/a	n/a	n/a	n/a	n/a
1999*	n/a	n/a	n/a	n/a	n/a	n/a	n/a	n/a
2000	7,005,453	77.4%	640,575	7.1%	973,979	10.8%	428,354	9,048,361
2001	7,082,835	78.9%	607,192	6.8%	898,023	10.0%	384,732	8,972,782
2002	7,045,452	80.9%	502,101	5.8%	762,517	8.8%	393,735	8,703,805
2003	7,172,831	80.1%	518,460	5.8%	883,192	9.9%	382,260	8,956,743
2004	8,012,064	80.9%	618,772	6.3%	659,719	8.7%	407,626	9,898,181
2005	8,176,385	79.4%	667,310	6.5%	900,251	8.7%	553,381	10,297,327

Source: Research Department, Ministry of Tourism

*Research documents for these years were destroyed in Ministry of Tourism's fire of 2001

Appendix 10B. Visitor Nights by Destination in the Bahamas 1977-2005

	Nassau/ Paradise Island		Grand Bahama		Family Islands		Total Visitor Nights
	No.	%	No.	%	No.	%	
1977	2,558,070	44.5	1,822,030	31.7	1,374,330	23.9	5,754,430
1978	3,276,210	47.1	2,114,100	30.4	1,569,880	22.6	6,960,190
1979	3,751,550	47.4	2,321,760	29.3	1,847,640	23.3	7,920,950
1980	3,849,190	45.6	2,613,630	31.0	1,973,320	23.4	8,436,140
1981	3,353,800	44.9	2,286,900	30.6	1,829,930	24.5	7,470,610
1982	3,372,920	45.0	2,134,080	28.5	1,983,310	26.5	7,490,310
1983	3,963,350	48.7	2,067,200	25.4	2,110,080	25.9	8,140,620
1984	4,074,100	49.8	1,964,730	24.0	2,146,450	26.2	8,185,280
1985	4,251,420	50.8	2,132,370	25.5	1,984,565	23.7	8,368,355
1986	4,113,610	49.1	2,135,300	25.5	2,126,010	25.4	8,374,920
1987	4,192,850	48.3	2,334,645	26.9	2,157,810	24.8	8,685,305
1988	4,122,370	47.3	2,459,640	28.2	2,125,620	24.4	8,707,630
1989	4,395,605	49.0	2,451,040	27.3	2,130,980	23.7	8,977,625
1990	4,454,070	49.7	2,252,920	25.1	2,255,865	25.2	8,962,855
1991	4,197,680	50.0	2,094,160	24.9	2,110,085	25.1	8,401,925
1992	3,819,375	47.0	2,125,405	26.2	2,179,195	26.8	8,123,975
1993	4,040,620	47.1	2,266,080	26.4	2,278,330	26.5	8,585,030
1994	4,134,885	46.7	2,381,250	26.9	2,330,395	26.3	8,846,530
1995	4,268,675	47.3	2,453,380	27.2	2,309,400	25.6	9,031,455
1996	4,650,095	49.1	2,322,445	24.5	2,492,845	26.3	9,465,385
1997	4,946,245	51.3	2,142,400	22.2	2,548,730	26.4	9,637,375
1998	n/a	n/a	n/a	n/a	n/a	n/a	n/a
1999	n/a	n/a	n/a	n/a	n/a	n/a	n/a
2000	4,615,786	51.0	1,922,195	21.2	2,510,380	27.7	9,048,361
2001	4,595,156	51.2	2,181,921	24.3	2,195,705	24.5	8,972,782
2002	4,692,646	53.9	2,091,616	24.0	1,919,543	22.1	8,703,805
2003	4,693,467	52.4	2,038,336	22.8	2,224,940	24.8	8,956,743
2004	5,260,830	53.1	2,055,766	20.9	2,571,586	26.0	9,898,181
2005	5,744,901	55.9	1,950,513	19.1	2,588,913	25.1	10,297,327

Source: Research Department, Ministry of Tourism

APPENDICES 11A-11C

VISITOR EXPENDITURE IN THE BAHAMAS

Appendix 11A Visitor Expenditure—Stopovers vs. Cruise
Appendix 11B Expenditure by Destination in The Bahamas
Appendix 11C Average Expenditure in The Bahamas

Expenditure information is derived through the Ministry of Tourism's Exit Surveys. Interviews are conducted of departing visitors, randomly selected, on a year-round basis at major airports and marinas throughout the country.

Source: Research Department, Ministry of Tourism

Appendix 11A. Visitor Expenditure—Stopovers vs. Cruise

Expenditure by

	Stopover Visitors	Cruise Passengers	Day Visitors	All Visitors
1968	$ 168,726,000	$ 11,668,000	N/A	$ 180,392,926
1969	$ 218,682,000	$ 16,769,000	N/A	$ 235,149,203
1970	$ 215,809,000	$ 17,030,000	N/A	$ 220,750,000
1971	$ 255,895,000	$ 21,791,000	N/A	$ 277,686,000
1972	$ 261,983,000	$ 18,939,000	N/A	$ 280,922,000
1973	$ 281,219,000	$ 20,808,000	N/A	$ 302,027,000
1974	$ 310,558,000	$ 17,401,000	N/A	$ 327,959,000
1975	$ 298,548,330	$ 18,957,600	N/A	$ 317,505,930
1976	$ 351,413,930	$ 16,540,990	N/A	$ 367,954,920
1977	$ 394,760,240	$ 17,647,000	N/A	$ 412,407,240
1978	$ 472,263,230	$ 22,481,000	N/A	$ 494,744,230
1979	$ 536,907,510	$ 24,760,760	N/A	$ 561,667,830
1980	$ 558,000,000	$ 31,000,000	$ 5,000,000	$ 595,453,490
1981	$ 602,000,000	$ 31,000,000	$ 5,000,000	$ 639,116,638
1982	$ 609,000,000	$ 39,000,000	$ 6,000,000	$ 654,513,326
1983	$ 715,000,000	$ 49,000,000	$ 6,000,000	$ 770,224,262
1984	$ 740,000,000	$ 54,000,000	$ 6,000,000	$ 801,503,210
1985	$ 920,000,000	$ 70,000,000	$ 5,000,000	$ 995,000,000
1986	$ 1,017,000,000	$ 81,000,000	$ 6,000,000	$ 1,105,000,000
1987	$ 1,063,000,000	$ 74,000,000	$ 8,000,000	$ 1,145,000,000
1988	$ 1,057,000,000	$ 83,000,000	$ 8,000,000	$ 1,149,000,000
1989	$ 1,205,924,150	$ 93,031,023	$ 10,573,200	$ 1,309,528,373
1990	$ 1,209,933,374	$ 110,547,285	$ 12,469,200	$ 1,332,949,859
1991	$ 1,082,047,732	$ 129,969,135	$ 10,377,000	$ 1,222,393,867
1992	$ 1,132,040,949	$ 102,577,088	$ 8,934,300	$ 1,243,552,337
1993	$ 1,199,189,895	$ 96,360,481	$ 8,662,500.	$ 1,304,212,876
1994	$ 1,231,077,220	$ 96,034,881	$ 6,985,800	$ 1,334,097,901
1995	$ 1,245,387,464	$ 95,714,096	$ 5,049,900	$ 1,346,151,460
1996	$ 1,291,514,273	$ 101,744,033	$ 4,235,100	$ 1,397,493,407
1997	$ 1,307,443,107	$ 105,203,398	$ 3,452,100	$ 1,416,098,605
1998	$ 1,244,433,081	$ 105,530,179	$ 4,093,680	$ 1,354,056,940
1999	$ 1,463,576,962	$ 114,909,132	$ 4,439,760	$ 1,582,925,855
2000	$ 1,582,023,959	$ 147,979,692	$ 6,751,620	$ 1,736,755,272
2001	$ 1,496,814,452	$ 147,579,684	$ 5,294,460	$ 1,649,688,597
2002	$ 1,605,405,547	$ 151,232,382	$ 6,022,980	$ 1,762,660,910
2003	$ 1,596,869,957	$ 157,006,162	$ 5,035,260	$ 1,758,911,379
2004	$ 1,693,486,565	$ 185,817,482	$ 5,177,460	$ 1,884,481,507
2005	$ 1,883,862,550	$ 179,979,078	$ 5,017,140	$ 2,068,858,768

Appendix 11B. Expenditure by Destination in The Bahamas

	Nassau/Paradise Is.	Grand Bahama	Family Islands	Total Bahamas
1989	$ 791,866,459	$ 341,505,264	$ 176,156,650	$1,309,528,373
1990	$ 802,410,959	$ 355,838,172	$ 174,700,728	$1,332,949,859
1991	$ 769,886,542	$ 304,902,183	$ 147,605,142	$1,222,393,867
1992	$ 738,283,225	$ 331,970,768	$ 173,298,344	$1,243,552,337
1993	$ 749,693,672	$ 350,479,959	$ 204,039,245	$1,304,212,876
1994	$ 738,366,455	$ 373,184,592	$ 222,546,854	$1,334,097,901
1995	$ 751,339,930	$ 416,410,060	$ 178,401,470	$1,346,151,460
1996	$ 860,151,125	$ 335,236,792	$ 202,105,490	$1,397,493,407
1997	$ 906,813,798	$ 280,724,254	$ 228,560,553	$1,416,098,605
1998	$ 877,250,320	$ 276,388,727	$ 200,417,893	$1,354,056,940
1999	$ 1,127,905,549	$ 214,058,676	$ 240,961,630	$1,582,925,855
2000	$ 1,255,499,511	$ 236,605,650	$ 242,373,225	$1,734,478,386
2001	$ 1,168,980,783	$ 256,418,671	$ 222,281,173	$1,647,680,627
2002	$ 1,234,826,111	$ 283,303,307	$ 236,650,873	$1,753,780,290
2003	$ 1,243,768,934	$ 261,054,827	$ 252,553,426	$1,757,377,187
2004	$ 1,303,535,288	$ 261,783,418	$ 319,162,800	$1,884,481,507
2005	$ 1,480,826,834	$ 249,966,687	$ 338,065,247	$2,068,858,768

Appendix 11C. Average Expenditure in The Bahamas—Stopover Visitors

	NASSAU/ PARADISE IS.	GRAND BAHAMA	FAMILY ISLANDS	**ALL BAHAMAS**
1996	$ 946	$ 558	$ 788	$ 791
1997	$ 982	$506	$ 840	$ 808
1998	$ 977	$538	$ 812	$ 815
1999	$1,093	$556	$ 848	$1,093
2000	$1,253	$590	$ 862	$1,253
2001	$1,155	$599	$ 915	$ 973
2002	$1,256	$664	$1,007	$1,061
2003	$1,237	$662	$1,000	$1,056
2004	$1,240	$653	$1,153	$1,084
2005	$1,299	$742	$1,191	$1,171

APPENDIX 12

LEADERS OF THE BAHAMAS

A. Royal Governors and Governors General

CROWN COLONY	1869—Sir James Walker	INTERNAL SELF GOVT
1717—Woodes Rogers	1873—Sir John Pope Hennessy	1964—Sir Ralph Grey
1721—George Phenney	1874—Sir William Robinson	1968—Sir Francis Cumming-Bruce
1729—Woodes Rogers	1880—Thomas Callaghan	1972—Sir John Warburton Paul
1733—Richard Fitzwilliams	1882—Sir Charles Cameron Lees	INDEPENDENCE
1740—John Tinker	1884—Sir Henry Blake	1973—Sir John Warburton Paul, (appointed July 10; Retired July 31, 1973)
1760—Major Gen. William Shirley	1887—Sir Ambrose Shea	
1768—Sir Thomas Shirley Bt.	1895—Sir William Haynes-Smith	1973—Sir Milo Butler (Aug 1 1973)
1774—Montfort Browne	1898—Sir Gilbert Thomas Carter	1976—Sir Gerald Cash
1783—John Maxwell	1904—Sir William Grey-Wilson	1988—Sir Henry Milton Taylor
1787—John Murray, Earl of Dunmore	1912—Sir George Haddon-Smith	1992—Sir Clifford Darling
1797—William Dowdeswell	1914—Sir William Allardyce	1995—Sir Orville A. Turnquest
1801—John Halkett	1920—Sir Harry Cordeaux	2001—Dame Ivy Dumont
1804—Charles Cameron	1927—Sir Charles.W.J. Orr	2005—Hon Paul Adderley (Acting)
1820—Sir Lewis Grant	1933—Sir Bede Clifford	2006—Hon. Arthur D. Hanna
1829—Sir James Carmichael Smythe	1936—Sir Charles. Dundas.	
1835—Col. William Colebrooke	1940—H.R.H. The Duke of Windsor	
1837—Sir Francis Cockburn	1945—Sir William Murphy	
1844—George Matthew	1950—Sir George Sandford	

1849—John Gregory	1951—Major Gen. Sir Robert Neville	
1854—Sir Alexander Bannerman	1953—Rt. Hon. Earl of Ranfurly	
1857—Charles Bayley, C.B.	1957—Sir Raynor Arthur	
1864—Sir Rawson W. Rawson, C.B.	1960—Sir Robert Stapeldon	

B. Premiers and Prime Ministers

1964-1967—Sir Roland Symonette	2002-2007—Perry Christie
1967-1992—Sir Lynden Pindling	2007- —Hubert Ingraham
1992-2002—Hubert Ingraham	

C. Ministers of Tourism

Sir Stafford L. Sands	1964-Jan.1967	Sen. Hon. Brent Symonette	Aug 1992-Dec.1994
Sir Lynden O. Pindling	Jan. 1967-Jan.1969	Hon. Frank Watson	Jan. 1995-1997
Sir Arthur A. Foulkes	Jan-Sept. 1969	Hon. Cornelius A. Smith	1997-2001
Sir Clement T. Maynard	Sept.1969-1979	Hon. Orville A.T. Turnquest	2001-2002
Hon. Livingston N. Coakley	1979-June1982	Hon. Obediah H. Wilchcombe	2002-2007
Hon. Perry G. Christie	Jun. 1982-Oct. 1984	Hon. Neko Grant (Tourism & Aviation) 2007-	
Sir Clement T. Maynard	Oct. 1984-Sept.1990	Hon. Branville McCartney (Minister of State)	2007-
Sir Lynden O. Pindling	Oct.1990-1992		

D. Directors and Directors General of Tourism

Som Chib	Sept.1967-April 1974	Baltron Bethel	May 1978-Dec.1992
Basil Atkinson	April 1974-June, 1976	Vincent Vanderpool Wallace	Jan. 1993-July 2005
Dan Wallace	June 1976-April 1978	Vernice Walkine	July 2005-

GLOSSARY OF TRAVEL TERMS

(Expressions, abbreviations and travel jargon)

Agency. Broadly, one who acts or has the power to act, as the representative of another. In travel, a specific kind of agent, as (1) a retail travel agent; (2) a carrier employee who sells tickets, a counter or ticket agent

All Inclusive. A packaging marketing concept in which visitors pay one price before departure from point of origin for everything they expect to enjoy during their vacation, without restriction as to extent of usage.

Amenities. Supplementary features eg recreation. **Guest Amenities.** Term used for a range of disposable items provided in guest room bathrooms and include items such as shampoos, conditioners, soaps, lotion, shower gel, shower caps, coffee/tea supplies, the cost of which is built into the room rates.

American Plan (AP). A hotel room rate which includes accommodations, with three meals included in the price of the room.

Apartment Hotel. Accommodation in apartment style units with in-suite cooking facilities. The complex may provide meals and alcoholic beverages in an on site restaurant/bar separate from the accommodation building(s), through in-house staff or outside food and beverage contractor.

Bed and Breakfast (B & B). A sleeping room rate, often in a guest house, which includes price of the room and breakfast.

Bond (bonding). A type of insurance or guarantee which is either mandatory or voluntary to protect a third party. In the travel industry, certain bonding programmes are mandatory e.g. travel agents may be bonded to protect the airlines against defaults.

Bulk fare. A net fare contract for a certain number of seats. Similar to blocked space except that the tour operator, wholesaler, or travel agent usually contracts for airline seats at a net price without the option of releasing space back to the airline. Thus, the operator/wholesaler/agent requires inventory.

Carrier. Any company that deals in transporting passengers or goods.

Central Reservations System (CRS). The ability of guests to make a reservation for one of a number of hotels by contacting one agency contracted by hotels acting as a group to operate this "central" reservations service.

Certified Travel Counselor (CTC). A professional certification, usually abbreviated CTC, awarded by the Institute of Certified Travel Agents to travel agents or other travel professionals with five years or more industry experience who have completed a two-year, graduate-level travel management programme.

Charter. v. To hire the exclusive use of any aircraft, vessel, bus, or other vehicle. n. A non-scheduled service on a plane, ship, bus, etc. A charter flight is usually booked for the exclusive use of a specific group or groups of visitors. A charter flight is normally less expensive than scheduled air services, operates under legislation, and is carried out by airlines (often scheduled airlines) which specialize in this service.

Collateral material. Term used to describe promotional and marketing type publications and materials such as brochures, tourism maps, information booklets, and logo items (T-shirts, pens, etc.)

Commission. The amount, which may vary, which a travel agent receives from the supplier for selling transportation, accommodations, or other services.

Configuration. The interior arrangement of seats, bathrooms, galleys, etc. inside a vehicle, e.g. aircraft or motor coach. The same aircraft, for example, might be configured for 190 Coach passengers, or for 12 First Class passengers and 170 coach passengers.

Confirmation. A confirmed reservation exists when a supplier, either orally or in writing, acknowledges that a booking has been accepted. Often a confirmation number is issued. Most confirmations are subject to certain conditions (e.g. a confirmation made without a credit card or payment may be subject to cancellation after 6 p.m. unless late arrival is specified).

Continental breakfast. A light breakfast, usually a beverage (coffee, tea or milk) and rolls or toast with butter or jam. Sometimes includes fruit juice.

Continental Plan. A hotel rate that includes room and continental breakfast.

Corporate Rate. A special rate negotiated between a supplier and a company.

Cruise. A sea voyage for pleasure (as opposed to one for transportation) which usually—but not always—returns to its departure point.

Customs. The federal or government agency charged with collecting duty (taxes) on specific items imported into the country and restricting the entry of forbidden items.

Day visitor/ Excursionist. A visitor who stays in the country visited for less than 24 hours without overnight stay.

Departure Tax. A fee collected from a passenger at point of departure from a city or country.

Deluxe. In travel usage, presumably "of the highest standard", although the term is often misused.

Domestic tourism. Residents of a country visiting their own country.

Direct Flight. A journey on which the passenger does not have to change planes. Not necessarily non-stop.

Double Occupancy Rate. The price per person for a room to be shared by two persons. The rate most frequently quoted in tour brochures.

Double Room Rate. The full price of a room for two people (Note: some people say double when they mean double occupancy).

Duty Free Shop. A store where departing international passengers may purchase items free of the import duty (tax) which that country normally assesses. Stores at certain destinations, called duty-free ports, sell items to departing non-residents duty free.

Efficiency. A hotel room or condominium with housekeeping facilities, usually including a stove, refrigerator, and sink.

European Plan (EP). A hotel rate that includes price of the room only (any meals are extra).

Excursion. A journey, usually short, made with the intention of returning to the starting point.

Familiarization Trip (Fam Trip). An educational trip to a destination or resort property for inspection of facilities, amenities and services. Usually targeted to the travel trade and sponsored by community tourism boards, promotion boards, hotel associations or by a particular resort or airline.

International Tourism. Travel to a foreign country either inbound tourism (visits to a country by non residents) or Outbound tourism (residents of a country visiting other countries).

Flag carrier. A carrier designated by its government to operate international services.

Foreign Independent travel (FIT). Travel arrangements for an individual who arrives on his own as opposed to being a part of an organised group. It can involve a custom designed, international, prepaid tour composed of many individualized arrangements.

Ground Operator (or Receiving Agent). A tour operator or travel agency which specializes in providing services to incoming passengers.

High (peak) Season. That period of consecutive months during which optimum room revenues, room occupancy and average room rates are generated. In the Caribbean, this is generally December through April.

Incentive Travel. A trip offered as a prize or bonus for superior performance. Often used by companies to motivate or reward employees.

Incidentals. Personal items, such as telephone calls, bar charges, movie rental, porterage, dry cleaning, which are usually excluded from the price of a tour, hotel room, cruise, etc.

Inclusive Tour Charter (ITC). The chartering of an entire aircraft by a tour operator or travel agent for visitors travelling on "inclusive" tours.

Infrastructure. The network of public utilities, roads, airports, etc. needed to support a tourism plant.

Internet. A system of computer networks joining many government, university and private computers together and providing an infrastructure for the use of E-mail, bulletin boards, file archives, hypertext documents, databases and other computational resources. The objective of the 1973 research programme of the U.S. Defense Advanced Research Projects Agency (DARPA) which created the Internet was to develop communication protocols which would allow networked computers to communicate transparently across multiple, linked packet networks.

Land (or Ground) Operator. A company that provides local travel services, transfers, sightseeing, guides, etc.

Load Factor. The ratio, expressed as a percentage of carrier capacity sold to total capacity offered for sale. If a 100 seat aircraft carries 75 paying passengers, that flight is operated at a 75% load. factor.

Low (Off Peak) Season. That time of the year at any given destination when tourist traffic and revenues (and often rates) are lowest.

Modified American Plan (MAP). A hotel room rate which includes price of the room along with breakfast and *either* lunch or dinner (usually includes breakfast and dinner).

Motel. A facility with overnight accommodations, originally targeted to automobile travellers, and therefore situated at roadside. A more contemporary definition would be the provision of accommodation only, with limited services and amenities provided.

MS. (in a ship's name). Motor Ship

MV. (in a ship's name). Motor Vessel.

National Tourism Office (NTO). An agency of a government dedicated to promoting tourism and shaping tourism policy.

Net Rate. A confidential rate given by a wholesaler, which is marked up by the retailer, with costs of services added, before it is resold to the consumer.

No-Show. (1) A passenger or guest who fails either to use or to cancel his reservation (2) A reservation neither cancelled nor fulfilled.

Occupancy Rate. The ratio, expressed as a percentage, of available rooms occupied. It is calculated by dividing the number of rooms occupied for a period by the number of rooms available for the same period, expressed as a percentage. See also **Load Factor**

Overbooking. (1) The practice by a supplier of confirming reservations beyond capacity in expectation of cancellations or no shows. (2) The same occurrence due to error. (3) Any reservation so dishonoured due to lack of space.

Override (or Overriding commission). An additional commission paid as a bonus for productivity and/or volume, or as an incentive to book particular arrangements. Airlines pay overrides on ticket sales made in conjunction with tour sales. Wholesalers pay them as bonuses for volume business. Suppliers pay them to provide a profit margin for wholesalers (who must themselves pay commissions). Hotel groups or governments pay them as a volume incentive to wholesalers.

Package (Package Tour). A number of arrangements bundled together and sold at a single all-inclusive price. Typically, the core package price would include: return transportation, ground transfers, baggage handling, accommodation, one or more meals per day, applicable taxes. Car rentals, recreation/entertainment and gratuities may also be included, but are more often supplementary to the core package price.

Promotional Fare. Any tariff below regular levels established to stimulate traffic, particularly at times when the carrier is not busy. Promotional fares are almost always roundtrips and are always restricted in one way or another. They may be good only at certain hours, on certain days, in certain seasons, or within certain time limits. Generally, the cheaper the fare, the more numerous the restrictions.

Proof of Citizenship. Any document that establishes the nationality of a traveller to the satisfaction of a government or carrier. If travellers are told to provide proof of citizenship, the implication is that some document of lesser stature than a passport will suffice.

Rack Rate. The full, undiscounted room rate (price). For a hotel, it is the official posted rate for each sleeping room. (This is not the rate used by tour operators).

Registry. A ship's certificate indicating ownership and the national flag under which it sails. Ships are registered in particular countries for tax purposes. The country of registry is not necessarily the same as the nationality of the owners or crew.

Resort Hotel. A hotel that caters mainly to vacationers, usually offering more recreational amenities and services in a more aesthetically pleasing setting than other hotels.

Scheduled Airline. An air carrier that offers service in accordance with a published timetable.

Service Charge. A fee added to a bill, usually in a hotel or restaurant, to cover the cost of certain services as a substitute for tipping.

Shoulder Season. A season between high (peak) and low (off peak)—usually the months of May, June, September, October, and November.

Single. Any facility or reservation to be used by one person.

SS. Steamship.

Supplier. The actual producer of a unit of travel merchandise—a carrier, hotel, sightseeing operator, etc.

Surcharge. An additional payment imposed by a supplier, either at certain times of the year, or to meet exceptional circumstances (e.g. rapidly rising fuel prices), or to provide special arrangements for a client.

Stopovers (Stopover Visitors). Persons who visit a country on an overnight stay.

Tariff. 1) An individual fare or rate quoted by any supplier; 2) Any class of fares or rates, e.g. a youth tariff; 3) Any published list of fares or rates established by a supplier; 4) a published compendium of listed fares or rates for any category of supplier; 5) An official publication containing all fares or rates, conditions of service, etc

Tender. A boat used when docking is not possible to transport passengers from ship to shore and back.

Time Sharing. A marketing and equity financing concept which permits participants to enjoy annual vacation accommodation for a fixed, one-time amount for life, or shorter contracted period. Time share properties are normally condominium-type apartment hotels.

Tourist. A person who travels outside his or her usual environment for more than one night but less than a year and whose purpose of travel is other than employment remunerated from within the place visited . . . . *World Tourism Organization definition*

Tour Operator. An organization (or individual) which actively manages and escorts tours and tour packages to FIT and group visitors. The tour operator often organizes components into packaged, inclusive arrangements and sells them through travel agents and sometimes directly to clients. Often used interchangeably with **Tour Wholesaler.**

Tour Wholesaler. An organization (or individual) which creates tours and tour packages for sale to tour operators or through retail travel agents. Often used interchangeably with Tour Operator. But generally the differences are: 1) A wholesaler normally sells nothing at retail; a tour operator often does both; 2) a wholesaler is less inclined than a tour operator to perform local services. Many travel companies perform all of the functions of wholesaler, tour operator and travel agent.

Transfer. Local transportation of visitors between point of arrival and selected hotel; and back again on departure day.

Travel Agent. A retail representative and sales arm of a particular producer/supplier, or a group of such producers/suppliers. The agent forms part of a distribution channel, matching goods or services with prospective buyers.

Upgrade. To move to a better accommodation or class of service.

Visa. An official authorization appended to a passport permitting travel to and within a particular country or region.

Walk In. A guest who checks in without an advance reservation.

Wholesaler. See **Tour Wholesaler**.

Sources: Institute of Certified Travel Agents, WTTC, and UNWTO

WORLD TOURISM ORGANIZATIONS, SELECTED TRAVEL TRADE ASSOCIATIONS AND ORGANIZATIONS WHICH REGULATE AND SUPPORT THE TRAVEL INDUSTRY IN THE AMERICAS

American Society of Travel Agents (ASTA). The leading trade association of United States and Canadian travel agents and tour operators, along with allied industry services. It was founded in 1931 as the American Steamship and Tourist Agents Association, with more than 60 agents that promised to protect and promote the mutual interests of its members, maintain a dignified code of ethics, combat unfair competition, stimulate the public's desire to travel and promote the use of ASTA members' services. ASTA has a worldwide membership of over 20,000 members which include travel agents and the companies whose products they sell such as tours, cruises, hotels, and car rentals. Through ASTA, these travel professionals all work together for mutual profit. ASTA's current mission is to enhance the professionalism and profitability of member agents through effective representation in industry and government affairs, education and training, and by identifying and meeting the needs of the travelling public. Web site: ***www.astanet.com***

Caribbean Hotel Association (CHA). A regional hotel trade association representing the entire spectrum of the Caribbean hospitality industry's private sector, comprising about 500 hotels, and encompassing about 30 Caribbean islands. Some 849 member hotels in 36 national hotel associations represent approximately 125,476 rooms in the Caribbean, from the small guest houses to the mega-resorts. The allied members: airlines, tour wholesalers and travel agents, trade and consumer press, advertising and public relations agencies, and hotel and restaurants suppliers, among many, account for more than 536 members. CHA is chartered as a not-for-profit limited liability corporation registered in the Cayman Islands, with offices in San Juan, Puerto Rico, and Miami, Florida. Web site: **www.caribbeanhotels.org**

Caribbean Tourism Organization (CTO). A cooperative promotional agency supported by Caribbean national governments. Its main objective is the development of sustainable tourism for the economic and social benefit of the Caribbean people. The CTO provides to and through its public and private sector members, the services and information to accomplish this goal. With headquarters in Barbados and marketing operations in New York, London and Toronto, CTO comprises membership of over 30 member governments and a myriad of private sector entities. The organization provides specialized support and technical assistance to member countries in the areas of marketing, human resource development, research and statistics, information technology and sustainable tourism development. Web site: **ww.onecaribbean.org**

Cruise Lines International Association (CLIA). Created in 1975, CLIA is the official trade organization of the cruise industry. Comprising 95% of the cruise capacity marketed from North America, it functions to promote the cruise product generically to both the selling agent and buying public through the broad activities of travel agent training, public relations and advertising. It also provides a forum for discussion among ship lines. CLIA's end objective is to raise awareness about the cruise experience. Web site: *www.cruising.org*

Federal Aviation Administration (FAA). An agency of the US Department of Transportation responsible for the safety of civil aviation. The FAA concentrates on passenger safety, aircraft certification, pilot licensing, and air traffic control. The Federal Aviation Act of 1958 created the agency under the name Federal Aviation Agency and its present name was adopted in 1967. The major roles of the FAA include: Regulating civil aviation to promote safety; Encouraging and developing civil aeronautics, including new aviation technology; Developing and operating a system of air traffic control and navigation for aircraft; Researching and developing the National Airspace System and civil aeronautics; Developing and carrying out programs to control aircraft noise and other environmental effects of civil aviation; and Regulating U.S. commercial space transportation. Predecessor organizations were the Civil Aeronautics Administration (CAA) and the Civil Aeronautics Board (CAB). The approaching introduction of jet airliners and a series of midair collisions spurred enactment of the 1958 Federal Aviation Act of 1958 which transferred CAA's functions for combating aviation hazards and the CAB's responsibility for safety rulemaking to this new independent body, the FAA. Web site: **www.faa.gov**

Hotel Sales Management Association (HSMA)—An international organization of marketing-oriented hotel/motel executives, with headquarters in New York City, that maintain liaison with all segments of the travel industry to discuss and implement areas of mutual interest.

Institute of Certified Travel Agents (ICTA), An organization which develops and administers educational programs designed to improve the standard of industry knowledge and excellence. Their training programmes are offered through The Travel Institute, established in 1964, which offers certification programmes such as the Certified Travel Associate (CTA), the Certified Travel Counselor (CTC) certification program and the Certified Travel Industry Executive (CTIE).

The National Transportation Safety Board (NTSB) is the world's premier independent accident investigation agency. Their responsibility is to make transportation safer, to determine the probable cause of accidents, and to develop safety recommendations aimed at preventing similar accidents. The reports contain, in a narrative form, the Board's actual findings and analysis leading to a probable cause. Web site: **www.ntsb.gov**

World Tourism Organization (UNWTO)—the intergovernmental body that serves as a global forum for tourism policy and issues. UNWTO formally came into existence on January 2, 1975; however its forerunner, the International Union of Official Organizations (IUOTO) was created in 1925. UNWTO brings together governments of over 100 member countries and technical knowledge of more than 150 affiliate members from the public and private sector. Its mission is to promote and develop tourism as a significant means of fostering international peace and understanding, economic development and international trade. Its general programme of work covers six broad areas: cooperation for development; education and training; environment and planning; statistics and market research; quality of business services; and communication and documentation. Since May 1976 UNWTO has been the executing agency of the United Nations Development Programme (UNDP) and assists countries in carrying out UNDP-financed tourism projects. Its headquarters is in Madrid, Spain. Web site: **www.world-tourism.org**

World Travel & Tourism Council (WTTC)—WTTC is the forum for global business leaders comprising the presidents, chairs and CEOs of 100 of the world's foremost companies. This body representing the private sector in all parts of the Travel & Tourism industry worldwide. With headquarters in London England, WTTC's mission is to raise awareness of the full economic impact of the world's largest generator of wealth and jobs—Travel & Tourism. Web site: **www.wttc.org.**

BIBLIOGRAPHY

ALBURY, Paul, *The Story of the Bahamas*, Macmillan Education Ltd., London, 1975. ISBN 0-333-17132-2

AUGIER, F.R. AND SHIRLEY C. GORDON, *Sources of West Indian History*, Longman Caribbean Lid, Trinidad and Jamaica, 1962, Longman Group Limited, London, Fifth Impression, 1970 SBN 76303 7

BARRATT, Peter, *Grand Bahama: A Rich and Colourful History*, David and Charles (Pub), Great Britain, 1972, IM Publishing, 2002

BERGER, Fred, "*An Analysis of the Infrastructure of The Bahamas as it relates to tourism and its potential for future development*" prepared by Fred Berger, a consultant to Hill and Knowlton, Inc

BURKART, A.J. AND MEDLIK S., *Tourism: Past, Present and Future*, Heinemann, London, second edition, 1981

CARIBBEAN INVESTMENT PROFILES: THE BAHAMAS SPECIAL REPORT, Caribbean Investment Profiles Limited, Cholmeley College, London, 2000

CLEARE, Angela, **The Organisation of the Tourist Industry in the Commonwealth Caribbean, June, 1971,** Paper presented as a requirement for the university programme in Management—UWI library, Kingston

CRATON, Michael, *A History of The Bahamas*, Collins Clear-Type Press, St. James's Place, London, Revised edition, 1968

CRATON, Michael, *Pindling: The Life and Times of Lynden Oscar Pindling, First Prime Minister of The Bahamas, 1930-2000*, Macmillan Education, Oxford, 2002

CRUISE LINES INTERNATIONAL ASSOCIATION, *The Cruise Industry—an Overview*—Marketing Edition, September, 2001, CLIA, 500 Fifth Avenue, New York, N.Y. 10110

DEMARIGNY, Alfred, *A Conspiracy of Crowns: The True Story of the Duke of Windsor and the Murder of Sir Harry Oakes,* Crown Publishers, Inc., New York, 1990

DAVIDOFF, Philip G and Doris S., *Sales and Marketing for Travel and Tourism*, National Publishers of the Black Hills, Inc., 1983

DUPUCH, Etienne, *Bahamas Handbook and Businessman's Annual*, 1960-2002 editions

FAWKES, Sir Randol, *The Faith That Moved The Mountain*, A Memoir of a Life and The Times, 1979

FNM MANIFESTO, 1992

GERMAN FEDERAL AGENCY FOR NATURE CONSERVATION, *Biodiversity and Tourism: Conflicts on the World's Seacoasts and Strategies for Their Solution*; Springer 1997 ISBN 3-540-62395-7

JONES, Wendall K., *The 100 Most Outstanding Bahamians of the 20ᵗʰ Century*, Jones Communications International Ltd., Media House, East Street North, 2000

JONES, Wendall K., (editor and publisher; Co-Editor—Dr. D. Gail Saunders), *Bahamas Independence and beyond* (articles, essays and photographs by various authors on the first thirty years of nationhood of the Commonwealth of The Bahamas), Jones Publications, in association with Jones Communications Intl Ltd., 2003

LEWIS, Gordon K., *Growth of the Modern West Indies*, Monthly Review Press, New York, 1968

LIGHTBOURN, Ronald G., *Reminiscing II: Photographs of Old Nassau*, published by Ronald G. Lightbourn, P.O. Box N-236, Nassau, Bahamas, 2005

LUNDBERG, Donald E., *The Tourist Business*, Van Nostrand Reinhold Company Inc., New York, Fifth Edition

MACKEY, George, *Millennium Perspectives*: A Selective Compilation of Viewpoints, published by George Mackey, 2001, ISBN 976-8108-48-7

PINDLING, Sir Lynden, **The Vision of Sir Lynden Pindling: In His Own Words**, Compiled and Edited By Patricia Beardsley Roker, The Estate of Sir Lynden, Pindling, September 2000, ISBN 976-8108-42-8

MOSELEY MOSS, Valerie, *Reminiscing: Memories of Old Nassau*, Edited by Ronald G. Lightbourne, Media Publishing, Nassau, 2001

NASSAU MAGAZINE, December 1941, Volume Nine, 1950s, 1960s and 1970s

PATTERSON, Dr. Sandra, *A Longitudinal Study of Changes in Bahamian Drinking*, 1969-1977, A Dissertation presented to the Florence Heller Graduate School for Advanced Studies in Social Welfare, Brandeis University, in partial fulfillment of the requirements of the Degree of Doctor of Philosophy, July 1978

POON, Dr. Auliana, Caribbean Futures, *The Bahamas Tourism Sector Study: Focus on the Family Islands*, Main Report & Plan of Operations, An IDB/Ministry of Tourism Project, May 1992

POWLES, Louis Diston, *Land of the Pink Pearl*, London, 1888

SAUNDERS, Gail, *Bahamian Society After Emancipation,* revised edition, 2003, Ian Randle Publishers, Kingston, ISBN 976-637-084-2

SAUNDERS, Ashley B, *History of Bimini*, Volume 1, New World Press, Post Office Box 652, Alice Town, Bimini, Bahamas, 1990, ISBN: 0-80-829-219 (S)

SAUNDERS, Gail, *The Bahamas: A Family of Islands*, Macmillan Publishers Ltd., 1988

SAUNDERS, GAIL, *Slavery in The Bahamas 1648-1838*, Nassau, 1985, ISBN 976-8012-50-1

SAUNDERS, Gail, *The Changing Face of Nassau: The Impact of Tourism on Bahamian Society in the 1920's and 1930's*, New West Indian Guide/Nieuwe West-Indische Gids Vol. 71. No. 1 & 2 (1997)

STARK, J.H., *Stark's History of and Guide to the Bahama Islands,* Boston, 1891

STARR, Nona, CTC, *Marketing for the Travel Industry*, ICTA CTC Certification Text Series, 1984

THE TRIBUNE HANDBOOK: *The Standard Guide to Nassau and the Bahama Islands.* First edition 1924, Published by the Tribune, Nassau, N.P., Bahamas

TOURISM, Ministry of, *Annual Reports*, 1967 to 1988

TOURISM, Ministry of, Annual **Statistical Reports**, 1967 to 2004

Tourism in The Bahamas: The Impact of the Tourism Dollar, A report prepared for the Bahamas Ministry of Tourism, under the auspices of the Commonwealth Fund for Technical Cooperation, by Brian Archer, Institute of Economic Research, University College of North Wales, Bangor, Gwynedd, United Kingdom, 30th April, 1976

VILLARD, Henry S., *Royal Victoria Hotel*, Nassau, N.P., 1976

WHARTON ECONOMETRIC FORECASTING ASSOCIATES (THE WEFA GROUP), *The impact of Tourism on The Economy of The Bahamas*, Prepared for The Ministry of Tourism, Nassau, Bahamas, by William Belchers, November 1988

WHIPPLE, A.B.C., *Pirates: Rascals of the Spanish Main*, Victor Gollanz pub., reprinted in Nassau Magazine, Fall 1957

WORLD TOURISM ORGANIZATION, *Tourism in 1992: Highlights, (WTO),* Madrid, Spain, Jan. 1993

WORLD TOURISM ORGANIZATION, *Tourism in 1993: Highlights, (WTO),* Madrid, Spain, Jan. 1994

WORLD TOURISM ORGANIZATION, *International Tourism Overview*, World Tourism Organization, Madrid, January 1996 and 2000

WORLD TOURISM ORGANIZATION, *1995 International Tourism Overview: A Special Report*, WTO, Madrid, Spain, January 1996

WORLD TOURISM ORGANIZATION, *Report on the International Conference on Travel and Tourism Statistics, Ottawa (Canada), 24-28 June, 1991*, published by WTO Madrid, July 1991

WORLD TOURISM ORGANIZATION, *WTO News*, July-August 1991, No. 6, March 1997, WTO, Madrid Spain

Internet Sites:
World Tourism Organization—*www.world-tourism.org*
Airline history—*www.airlinehistory.com*
www.chalksoceanairways.com
History of the Lodging Industry—*informationcenter@ahla.com*; *www.ahma.com*
Travel Wire News—*http://www.travelwirenews.com*
Marketing & Tourism Trends, Ferri & Partners LLC—*www.ferriandpartners.com*
Caribbean Tourism Organization—*www.onecaribbean.org*
Bahamas Ministry of Tourism—*www.bahamas.com* and *www.tourismbahamas.org*

ENDNOTES

Chapter 1

1   World Tourism Organization, *International Conference on Travel and Tourism Statistics,* Ottawa (Canada), 24-28 June, 1991, Conference Resolutions, Madrid Spain, July 1991

2   Burkart and Medlik, *Tourism: Past, Present and Future*, William Heinemann Ltd., London, 1974

3   The history of lodging, Overview. Retrieved from *http://schonwalder.org/Hotels/hotel_c.htm, Oct. 8, 2004*

4   Epperson, Arlin, "*Why People Travel*", Leisure Today, April 1983, p. 54

5   Institute of Certified Travel Agents, *Marketing for the Travel Industry*, Nona Starr, CTC, editor, ICTA, CTC Certification Text Series, 1984

6   *Biodiversity and Tourism: Conflicts on the World's Seacoasts and Strategies for Their Solution,* German Federal Agency for Nature Conservation (Ed.), Springer 1997

Chapter 2

1   Craton, Michael, *A History of The Bahamas*, Collins, London, p. 34

2   Albury, Paul, *The Story of The Bahamas*, Macmillan Education Limited, London, 1975

3   Whipple, A.B.C., *Pirates: Rascals of the Spanish Main*, Victor Gollanz, pub., reprinted in Nassau Magazine, Fall 1957

4   *Ibid*

5   *Ibid*

6   *Ibid*

7   *Ibid*

8   Craton, Michael, *A History of The Bahamas*, *op. cit.*, p. 121

9   Saunders, Gail, *Slavery in The Bahamas, 1648-1838*, Nassau, p. 3

10 Bruce, P.H., Memoirs, *Memoirs*, London, 1782; see also Saunders, *Slavery in The Bahamas*, p. 8, 11

11 Albury, Paul, **The Story of The Bahamas**, *op. cit.*

12 Saunders, Gail, *Slavery in The Bahamas, 1648-1838, op. cit.*, p. 11

13 Albury, Paul, *The Story of The Bahamas, op. cit.*, p. 115

Chapter 3

1   Encyclopedia: *The New Book of Knowledge*, Volumes 16 and 17, Grolier Incorporated, Danbury, Conn

2   McCourt, Edward G, CTC, *A History of Travel*, printed in Leisure Travel and Tourism, Institute of Certified Travel Agents, Wellesley, Massachusetts, 1989

3   Craton, Michael, *A History of The Bahamas, op. cit.*, p. 226

4   *Ibid*, p. 228

5   *Ibid*, p. 236

6   Stark, J.H., *History of and Guide to the Bahama Islands*, New York, 1891

7   Saunders, Gail, *Slavery in The Bahamas 1648-1838*, Nassau, p. 11

8   *Ibid*

9   Craton, Michael, *A History of The Bahamas, op. cit.*, p. 305

0   *Highlights in the History of Communication in The Bahamas—1784-1965*, A booklet of the Department of Archives Exhibition held 9-27 February, 1998, p. 3

11 *Nassau Guardian and Colonial Advertiser*, Wednesday, November 28, 1849

12 Albury, Paul, *The Story of The Bahamas, op. cit.*, p. 221

13 Craton, Michael, *A History of The Bahamas, op. cit.*, p. 224

14 Villard, Henry S., *Royal Victoria Hotel*, Nassau, N.P., 1976, p.12

15 *Ibid*, p. 5

16 *Ibid*, p. 14

17 *Ibid*, p. 14

18 *Ibid*, p. 16

19 *Ibid*, p. 16

20 "Highlights in the History of Communication in The Bahamas 1784-1956: A Booklet of The Bahamas Archives Exhibition, p. 28-29

21 Craton, Michael, *A History of The Bahamas, op. cit.*, p. 255

22 Albury, Paul, *The Story of The Bahamas, op. cit.*, p 53, 79

23 *Ibid*, p. 198

24 *Ibid*, p. 79

25 Craton, Michael, *A History of The Bahamas, op. cit.*, p. 247

26 deMarigney, *op. cit.*, P. 147

27 Craton, Michael, *A History of The Bahamas, op. cit.*, p. 259

28 Statute laws of The Bahamas, 1929, Volume 2; Archdeacon Caulfield to Rogers, 11th July, 1861 C023/16/502

29 Albury, *The Story of The Bahamas, op. cit.*, p. 124

30 Saunders, Gail, *Slavery in The Bahamas, op. cit.*, p. 194

31 *Ibid*, p. 109, 112

32 *Ibid*, p. 114

33 *Ibid*, p. 144

34 *Ibid*, p. 160

35 *Ibid*, p. 185-6

36   Powles, Louis Diston, *Land of the Pink Pearl,* (London: 1888). Cited in: John W Nunley and Judith Betteleim, Caribbean Festival Arts: Each and Every bit of Difference (Seattle: The St. Louis Art Museum in association with the University of Washington Press, 1988), p. 72

Chapter 4

1   Retrieved from http://www.geocities.com/CapeCanaveral/4294/history/1920_1935. html#airlinegrowth

2   Retrieved from www.airlinehistory.com

3   Retrieved from www.chalksoceanairways.com

4   Retrieved from http://www.geocities.com/CapeCanaveral/4294/history/1920_1935. html#airlinegrowth

5   *Ibid*

6   Retrieved from http//www.airlinehistory.com

7   Retrieved from http://www.cmgww.com/football/rockne/krbio.html

8   History of the Lodging Industry, American Hotel & Lodging Association—Information Center, Washington DC. informationcenter@ahla.com)

9   Albury, Paul, *The Story of The Bahamas, op. cit.*; also, Craton. Michael, *A History of the Bahamas, op. cit.*

10   Villard, Henry S., *Royal Victoria Hotel, op. cit.,* p. 5

11   Nassau Magazine (NM), Spring 1954, p. 29

12   Saunders, Ashley, *History of Bimini,* Volume 1, 1990

13   *Ibid,* p. 94-5; see also South Florida History Magazine: article "The Bimini Bay Rod and Gun Club" by Jane S. Day, pages 10-15

14   "Montagu Beach Hotel Named for Fort Built 213 Years Ago" by Mary Moseley, Nassau Magazine, Spring 1955

15   Moseley Moss, Valeria, *Reminiscing,* Media Publishing, Nassau, 2001, p. 24

16   *The Tribune Handbook:* The Standard Guide to Nassau and the Bahama Islands. First edition 1924 published by the Tribune, Nassau, N.P., Bahamas, p 173-81

17   Dupuch Publications, *Bahamas Handbook and Businessman's Annual* (*Bahamas Handbook*), 1999, p, 108

18   Annual Reports of Development Board, Department of Archives

19   *Ibid*

20   The Development Board, Annual Report, 1916

21   The Development Board, Annual Report,

22   *Ibid*

23   Stark, J. H., *History of and Guide to the Bahama Islands, op. cit.,* p. 542A

24   Mackey, George, *Millennium Perspectives: A Selective Compilation of Viewpoints,* p.70, 72

25   "A stroll through Old Nassau", *Reminiscing,* Moseley Moss, *op. cit.,* p.22

26   The Bahamas During the Early Twentieth Century 1900-1914, Dept. of Archives

27 "Highlights in the History of Communication in The Bahamas 1784-1956": A booklet of the Department of Archives Exhibition, 27th February, 1998, p.32

28 *Ibid*

29 Documents supplied by the Royal Bank and the *Tribune Handbook*

30 deMarigney, Alfred, *A Conspiracy of Crowns*, Crown Publishers, Inc., New York, 1990, p. 148

31 Nassau Magazine, Midseason, 1954, p 25, 27; See also National Film Preservation Board Home Page, *http://www.loc.gov/film/taves6.html*; *www.amnh.oceans.jewilliamson*. Some information was also obtained in conversations with Paul Aranha and Mrs. Sylvia Munroe, Mr. Williamson's daughter on May 12, 2006.

32 Moseley Moss, Valeria, *Reminiscing*, *op. cit*, p. 24, 25

33 *Ibid*, p. 46, 50

34 The Nassau Magazine (NM), Mid-season 1960

35 Dupuch Publications, *Bahamas Handbook*, 1988, "Sir Bede and His Lady: A Bahamian Camelot", p. 15-33

36 Highlights in the History of Communication in The Bahamas 1784-1956: *op. cit.*, p. 38

37 *Nassau Guardian*, 17th December, 1932, p. 1

38 Highlights in the History of Communication in The Bahamas 1784-1956, *op. cit.*, p. 40, 43
aasdasdas

39 "*Civic Centre: H.E. the Administrator Performs Opening Ceremony, Ideals of Institution outlined in interesting Speeches*", *Nassau Guardian*, Sat., June 13, page 1

40 "*The Wider Field for the Civic Centre: The Honourable Mrs. Dundas Reviews Growth to Date*", *Nassau Guardian*, May 11, 1938

41 *Ibid*

42 *Ibid*

43 "The Dundas Civic Centre Story", *Nassau Guardian*, March 2,1965

44 *Aviation in the Bahamas:* An Address to the Bahamas Historical Society by Capt. Paul Aranha, F.R.G.S., Life Member of the B.H.S., 19th February, 2004; see also "*Black Flight*" published in 2001 by Roger Albert Forsyth, M.D.—ISBN 0-9715414-1-8

45 *Ibid*

46 *Ibid*

47 Dupuch Publications, **Bahamas Handbook**, 1979, p. 18

48 deMarigney, Alfred, *A Conspiracy of Crowns*, *op. cit.*, p. 152

49 *Ibid*, p. 153, 158, 160

50 "Crown to build Aerodrome in Bahamas", *Nassau Guardian*, April 22, 1939

51 "Land Plane from Miami", *Nassau Guardian*, December 14, 1939

52 *Ibid*

53 Saunders, Ashley, *History of Bimini*, *op. cit.*, p. 18

54 *Ibid*, p. 119-126

55 Nassau Magazine, Winter, 1955-56, p. 44

56 "The first band of Musicians" by Bert Cambridge, *The Tribune*, Thursday 9th July, 1981

57 Interviews with Duke Errol and Peanuts Taylor, 23rd July, and 2nd September, 2002

58 Saunders, Ashley, *History of Bimini*, *op. cit.*, p. 18

59 Albury, Paul, *The Story of the Bahamas*, *op. cit.*, p. 141

60 Dupuch Publications, *Bahamas Handbook*, 1988, "Sir Bede and His Lady", *op. cit.*, p. 17, 19

61 *Ibid*, p. 22

62 deMarigney, *A Conspiracy of Crowns*, *op. cit.*, p. 149

Chapter 5

1 History of the Lodging Industry, American Hotel & Lodging Association—Information Center, Washington DC. informationcenter@ahla.com

2 *Aviation in the Bahamas:* An Address to the Bahamas Historical Society by Capt. Paul Aranha, F.R.G.S., Life Member of the B.H.S., 19th February, 2004: also Interviews with Paul Aranha at his home in Lyford Cay

3 *Ibid*

4 *Ibid*

5 *Ibid*

6 *Ibid*

7 *Ibid*

8 *Ibid*

9 *Ibid*

10 *Ibid*

11 *Ibid*

12 *Ibid*

13 *Ibid*

14 *Ibid*

15 Albury, Paul, *The Story of The Bahamas,* *op. cit.*, p. 207-8.

16 Fawkes, Randol, *op. cit.*, p 22-26

17 *Ibid*, p 27, 33

18 Dupuch Publications, *Bahamas Handbook*, 1991, "Rocky Road of A Royal Administration And the Memorable Events of a Rather Turbulent Era", p. 15-33

19 *Ibid*

20 Saunders, Ashley, *History of Bimini*, *op. cit.*, p. 87

21 Nassau Magazine, March 1941, and Feb-March, 1942 editions

22 *Ibid*

24 *Ibid*

25 *Ibid*

26 Interview with Urban Bostwick at his home on Young Street, west of East Street, 27th July, 2005

27 Saunders, Ashley, *History of Bimini*, *op. cit.*

28 Nassau Magazine

29   Interview with Dr. Juliette Barnwell, daughter of Dr. Claudius Walker, Jan 15, 2002

30   Interviews with Sir Clement Maynard, 15th October, 2005 and Mrs. Vernice Cooper, 10th October, 2005

31   Documentation supplied by Commissioner's office, Royal Bahamas Police Force

Chapter 6

1   American Hotel and Lodging Association. **History of Lodging**, Retrieved 20th August, 2003, from http://www.ahma.com/products_lodging_history.asp

2   *Ibid*

3   *Nassau Guardian*, editorial, 5th January, 1952

4   Nassau Magazine, Summer, 1956

5   NM Winter 56-57 p. 29

6   NM winter 57-58, p. 29 NM 58-59 p. 39-40; also see ad NM midseason 1959, p 38

7   NM 1959 mid-season p. 25-27

8   NM Summer 56, p 17

9   Nassau Magazine, Summer 1956 and Spring, 1957

10 Barratt, Peter, *Grand Bahama: A Rich and Colourful History*, Third Edition, IM Publishing, 2002

11 *Ibid*, p. 68

12 *Ibid*, p. 60-64

13 *Ibid*, p. 73-78

14 Speech by Mr. Albert Sands on November 17, 2004, on the occasion of the signing of the Heads of Agreement at 4 Points Restaurant, Rock Sound Eleuthera.

15 *National Parks, National Treasures*, Bahamas National Trust, Nov. 2003

16 *Ibid*

17 Development Board annual reports, 1958 and 1959; see also article in Dupuch Publications *Bahamas Handbook, 1960,* "The Tide That Washes in Prosperity", by Stafford L. Sands

18 *Ibid*

19 *Ibid*; see also Nassau Magazine, Summer 1956

20 Dupuch Publications, *Bahamas Handbook,* 1966-67 "Tourism and the Master Plan", p. 436-446; also Interview with Etienne Jr. and Sylvia Perfetti Dupuch, 25th May, 1998

21 Interviews with Juanita Gonzales and Frank Ramey, former employees of the Development Board and Ministry of Tourism, 2nd February, 1970

22 Brief history of the 48th National Family Island Regatta, commemorative booklet

23 *Ibid*

24 "On the Pry—Workboat racing at the Family Islands Regatta in George Town, Bahamas", 48th National Family Island Regatta, p. 33

25 Interviews with Bill Saunders, 21st January, 2003 and Don Delahey, 10th April, 2003

26 NM, Summer 1956, p. 11-15

27 NM, Summer 1956, p. 15
28 Development Board Annual Report; see also Dupuch Publications *Bahamas Handbook*, 1961-62, "Island Playground for Major Conventions by V.E. Chenea
29 "Aerial Influx Sets Foreign Record for Bahamas", *Nassau Guardian*, October 8, 1954
30 NM, Fall 1957
31 NM Winter 56-7
32 NM Winter 57-8 p. 41
33 NM Summer 57, p.24
34 NM Summer 57. P. 29
35 Interviews with Duke Errol
36 Interview with Sir Clifford Darling, 9th August, 2002
37 Highlights in the History of Communication in The Bahamas 1784-1956, p 14
38 Interview with Sir Clifford Darling, 9th August, 2002
39 Insert footnote
40 Dupuch Publications, *Bahamas Handbook*, 1960, p. 194.

Chapter 7

1 Saunders, Ashley, *History of Bimini, op. cit.,* p, 23-4, 34, 35
2 Fawkes, Sir Randol, *The Faith That Moved The Mountain*, 1979, p. 204
3 Dupuch Publications, *Bahamas Handbook*, 1973, p. 179
4 Dupuch Publications, *Bahamas Handbook,* 1961-62, "Tourism Builds A Prosperous Empire" by Stafford L. Sands
5 Dupuch Publications, *Bahamas Handbook,* 1965-66, p. 144
6 *Ibid*, p.146
7 Dupuch Publications, *Bahamas Handbook*, 1965-66, "Conventions Fly In for Foreign Fun" by V.E. Chenea, p. 449-451
8 Dupuch Publications, *Bahamas Handbook,* 1966-67, p. 262
9 Interview with Berkeley "Peanuts" Taylor; also, see article by P. Anthony White, "It's Better in The Bahamas with Peanuts", The Punch, May 10, 1991
10 Interview with Duke Errol at his home on Soldier Road, 10th August, 2003
11 *Ibid*, September 2003
12 Interview with Sabu, October 2, 2003
13 Interview with Berkeley "Peanuts" Taylor, 13th January, 2002

Chapter 8

1 The Vision of Sir Lynden Pindling: In His Own Words: Letters and Speeches 1948-1997, compiled and edited by Patricia Beardsley Roker, 2002, p. 25
2 Checchi and Company, Washington, D.C., A Plan for Managing the Growth of Tourism in the Commonwealth of The Bahamas, August 1969

3   *Aviation in the Bahamas:* An Address to the Bahamas Historical Society by Capt. Paul Aranha, F.R.G.S., Life Member of the B.H.S., 19th February, 2004: also Interviews with Paul Aranha at his home in Lyford Cay

4   "Bahamas Airways Goes Out of Business", *The Tribune*, Oct. 10, 1970, p.3

5   "PM's Statement on Closure of BAL", *The Tribune*, Oct. 13, 1970

6   *Ibid*

7   *Ibid*

8   "Bahamas Airways Goes out of business" *The Tribune*, Oct 10, 1970

9   *The Tribune* Editorial—Tuesday, October 13, 1970, p. 3 "A Bad Decision"

10   *The Tribune*, October 13, 1970, p.1 & 3: also *The Tribune,* October 14, October 15, 1970; Interview with Paul Aranha, May 2004

11   Interview with Paul Aranha, May 2004; see also Craton, *Pindling, op. cit.*, p. 232

12   Villard, Henry S., *Royal Victoria Hotel, op. cit.*

13   Craton, Michael, *Pindling: The Life and Times of the First Prime Minister of The Bahamas*, Macmillan Education, 2002

14   Interviews with Police Band and History of the Police Band submitted by office of Police Commissioner

15   Lewis, Gordon K., *Growth of the Modern West Indies*, Monthly Review Press, New York, 1968

Chapter 9

1   For further background reading on deregulation, see "Airline Deregulation by Alfred Kahn http://www.econlib.org/library/Enc/AirlineDeregulation.html

2   Retrieved from *http://avstop.com/History/HistoryOfAirlines/Eastern.htm*, also Eastern Airlines Retirees Association Web site, http://www.eara.org/history.html, December 15, 2004

3   American Hotel and Lodging Association: History of the Lodging Industry, retrieved from http://www.ahla.com/products_lodging_history.asp, 10th February, 2003.

4   *The Cruise Industry: An Overview*, Cruise Lines International Association, New York, Marketing Edition, September 2001

5   *A Survey of the US Vacation Market*, A Study produced by the Inter-American Development Bank on behalf of the Bahamas Ministry of Tourism, August 1986

6   *Ibid*

7   *Survey of US Travel Agents*, produced for the Bahamas Ministry of Tourism by N.W. Air Advertising Agency, New York, November, 1984

8   Villard, Henry S., *Royal Victoria Hotel, op. cit.*, 1978, p.20

9   *Pindling: The Life and Times of the first Prime Minister of The Bahamas, op. cit.*, p.354

10   *Ibid*

Chapter 10

1 Agenda 21 for the Travel & Tourism Industry: Towards Environmentally Sustainable Development, Progress Report No. 1, WTTC, London, 1996
2 Retrieved from New York Times on the Web, *http://www.nytimes.com/indexes/2001/09/11/* and This History Channel, This Day in History, www.history channel.com/tdih
3 Retrieved from tourism-newswire@sidsnet.org
4 *Ibid*
5 The history of Timeshare: ***Timeshare Today and in the Future***. Retrieved from *www.vacationclub.com*, and oaistimeshare.com//history,htm.www.rci.com/Guide/factsFigs
6 The history of Timeshare: *www.vacation* club.com oasistimeshares.com/history,htm, *www.rci.com/Guide/factsFigs* Timeshare today and in the Future
7 Timeshare in The Bahamas, information document produced by Diana Lightbourne, Undersecretary, Ministry of Tourism, 2005
8 ***Travel Weekly*** 2002 US Travel Industry Survey
9 "***An Analysis of the Infrastructure of The Bahamas as it relates to tourism and its potential for future development***" prepared for The Bahamas Ministry of Tourism by Fred Berger, a consultant to Hill and Knowlton, Inc., New York, August 2002
10 Foodways, printed in ***Cultural Perspectives 2003***, on the occasion of The Bahamas Heritage Festival, 4-8 March 2003, edited by Gail Saunders, p46-8
11 History of John Bull, supplied by Inga Bullard, John Bull, January 2005; see also an expanded history of John Bull in the Biography of Frederick Hazlewood, in the back of this document.
12 Downtown Nassau Harbour Renaissance Plan: *Recapturing the Romance and the Bahamian Spirit*, EDAW

Chapter 11

1 Dupuch Publications, ***Bahamas Handbook***, 1961-62, "Tourism Builds A Prosperous Empire", by Stafford L. Sands, CBE, MHA, Chairman, Bahamas Development Board
2 Checchi and Company, Washington, DC, ***A Plan for Managing the Growth of Tourism in the Commonwealth of The Bahamas***, *op. cit.*
3 ***Tourism in The Bahamas: The Impact of the Tourism Dollar***, A report prepared for the Ministry of Tourism, Commonwealth of The Bahamas under the auspices of the Commonwealth Fund for Technical Cooperation, by Brian Archer, Institute of Economic Research, University College of North Wales, Bangor, Gwynedd, United Kingdom, 30th April, 1976
4 *Ibid*

[5]   *The Impact of Tourism on the Economy of The Bahamas,* Prepared for the Ministry of Tourism, Nassau, Bahamas by the Wharton Econometric Forecasting Associates (WEFA), Pennsylvania, November 1988

[6]   *The Impact of Visitor Expenditure on the Economy of The Bahamas 1997*, Funded by the European under the Caribbean Regional Tourism Sector Programme, Caribbean Tourism Organization, March 2001

[7]   *Tourism in The Bahamas: Employment and Tourism in the Bahamas.* A report prepared for the Ministry of Tourism, Commonwealth of The Bahamas under the auspices of the Commonwealth Fund for Technical Cooperation, by Brian Archer, Institute of Economic Research, University College of North Wales, Bangor, Gwynedd, United Kingdom, 30th April, 1976

[8]   *The Impact of Visitor Expenditure on the Economy of The Bahamas 1997, op. cit.*

[9]   Mackey, George, *Millennium Perspectives, op. cit.,*. p. 70, 72

[10] The Impact of the Tourism Dollar, Brian Archer, *op. cit.*

[11] Stark, J.H., *History of and Guide to the Bahama Islands, op. cit.*

[12] *The Tribune,* March 12, 1930, cited in Gail Saunders, *op. cit.*, p30

[13] *The Tribune,* October 4, 1933, cited in Gail Saunders, *op. cit.*, p. 31

[14] Saunders, Gail, *The Changing Face of Nassau: The Impact of Tourism on Bahamian Society in the 1920's and 1930's*, New West Indian Guide/Nieuwe West-Indische Gids vol. 71. No. 1 & 2 (1997): 21-42)

[15] **A Longitudinal Study of Changes in Bahamian Drinking,** 1969-1977, A Dissertation presented to the Florence Heller Graduate School for Advanced Studies in Social Welfare, Brandeis University, in partial fulfillment of the requirements of the Degree of Doctor of Philosophy, by Sandra Dean Patterson, July 1978

[16] *The Tribune,* 6th January, 1938, also cited in Cash, Gordon & Saunders 1991:285 and *The Tribune,* 6th January, 1938

[17] Gail Saunders, *op. cit.*, p.34 Interview with Maxwell Thompson

[18] **A Longitudinal Study of Changes in Bahamian Drinking,** 1969-1977, Patterson, *op. cit.*

[19] World Tourism Forum for Peace and Sustainable Development Lauded by UN Chief", Washington D.C, December 12, 2003, Contact: Val Orekhov—*cval@counterpart.org*

[20] *Ibid*

[21] Macaulay, Thomas Babington, *The History of England, 5th ed. Vol. 1, chapter 3, p. 370 (1849)*

Chapter 12

[1]   Ferri & Partners Marketing & Tourism Trends April 15, 2004, newsletter@ferriandpartners.com

[2]   World Tourism Organization, Facts & Figures, Information, Analysis and Know-how, "World Market Trends", http://www.world-tourism.org/facts/tmt.html, retrieved on June 25, 2004

[3]   *Ibid*

4   ETurbo Travel Wire News, Feature Story, "International tourism up by 5.5 to 808 Million Arrivals in 2005", http//www.travelwirenews.com/news/25JAN2006.htm, retrieved 26th January, 2006

5   World Tourism Organization: Facts and Figures, Information, Analysis and Know-how, "Tourism 2020 Vision", http://www.world-tourism.org/facts/2020.html

6   http://www.travelwirenews.com/09NOV2004.htm

7   *Ibid*

8   PhoCusWright Report: Online Travel Booking Continuing To Grow; More Booking All Travel Online, www.phocuswright.com

9   Ferri & Partners Marketing & Tourism Trends April 15, 2004, *op. cit.*

10   Ibid

11   http://www.mediaexchange.info/tmp/SimonSuarezCMEx.jpg.

12   Speech by Jean Holder, Secretary General of the Caribbean Tourism Organization at CTO Conference

13   Speech by Vincent Vanderpool Wallace, Secretary General of the Caribbean Tourism Association at International Downtown Association Caribbean Leadership Forum, Willemstad, Curacao, 24-28 February, 2006

14   *Ibid*

15   *Ibid*

16   *Ibid*

17   Caribbean Community and Common Market (CARICOM) Single Market and Economy, http://www.mfaft.gov.jm/Intl_Community/Caricom.htm

18   BBC News, International version, "Airbus unveils 'superjumbo' jet", 18th January, 2005, http://news.bbc.co.uk/2/hi/business/4183201.stm

19   *Ibid*; See also "Further A380 delays in Asia, Pacific" by Y. Sulaiman, Global Travel Industry News—eTurboNews 20 June 2006", retrieved from *news@eturbonews.com* on June 22, 2006

Biographies of Tourism Giants and Stalwarts

1   Dupuch Publications, **Bahamas Handbook and Businessman's Annual**, 1978-79

2   *Ibid*, 1978-79, pp. 28, 30

3   *Ibid*, p. 29

4   *Ibid*, p.30

5   NM, Summer 1956, p. 15

6   Dupuch Publications, **Bahamas Handbook,** 1978-79, p. 34

7   *Ibid*

8   *Ibid*, p. 34.

9   Interviews with Frank Ramey et al, 1981

10   Interviews with staff—Frank Ramey, Juanita Gonzales—who worked with Sir Stafford

11   Guest Commentary, *Sir Stafford was the architect of Bahamian Prosperity*, by Rev. Dr. J. Emmette Weir, **Nassau Guardian**, April 10, 2000, page 10A.

[12]   ***Nassau Guardian***, Editorial: *Who are our heroes? Oswald Brown Writes,* October 10, 2003, p.4

[13]   Data and documents supplied by Ding Cambridge, 20th July, 2003

[14]   de Marigny, *op. cit.*, p. 150

[15]   Dupuch Publications, ***Bahamas Handbook*** 1979, p. 18

[16]   ***The Tribune***, November 21, 1985 p,1

[17]   ***The Tribune,*** November 21, 1985 p,1

[18]   ***Nassau Magazine***, Mid Season 1960, p. 19

[19]   Interview with Sir Clifford Darling, November 11, 2004

[20]   *Ibid*

[21]   *Ibid*

[22]   Interview with Mr. Delahey at his home, 30th July, 2003

[23]   Retrieved from http://www.livelucaya.com/history.asp

[24]   Barratt, *op. cit.*, p. 60

[25]   Telephone interview with Carolyn Bartlette, 10th February, 2003

[26]   Interview with Duke Errol Strachan, Jan 30, 2003

[27]   The 100 Most Outstanding Bahamians of the 20th Century, Jones Communications, International Limited, 2000.

[28]   Interview with Ray Munnings, 20th August, 2003

[29]   "Joseph Spence—An Introduction", by Samuel Charters, Joseph Spence: The Complete Folkways Recordings, 1958, Smithsonian Folkways, Washington, DC

[30]   Interview with Eva Hilton, former Principal of Oakes Field Primary School, 10th December, 2003

INDEX